Centennial Address
by Josiah Quincy.
page 312. —

Centennial Ode
by Charles Sprague
page 358. —

Presented to President Angell
for the Library of
The University of Michigan,
by Eliza Susan Quincy.

5 Park St.
Boston. Massachusetts.
February 11. 1872.

H. Billings del. C. F. Wagstaff & J. Andrews Sculp.

View of the Market House erected in 1826, and of Faneuil Hall from the East.

A

MUNICIPAL HISTORY

OF THE

TOWN AND CITY OF BOSTON,

DURING

TWO CENTURIES.

FROM

SEPTEMBER 17, 1630, TO SEPTEMBER 17, 1830.

BY

JOSIAH QUINCY.

BOSTON:
CHARLES C. LITTLE AND JAMES BROWN.
1852.

CAMBRIDGE:
STEREOTYPED AND PRINTED BY
HOUGHTON AND HAYWOOD.

PREFACE

THE municipal affairs of the inhabitants of Boston were conducted under the form of town government, established by the early settlers of New England, from 1630 to 1822, when, on their petition, they were incorporated into a city by the Legislature of Massachusetts. Through eight succeeding years, three successive administrations presided over the new form of government thus established. The author of this history held the office of Mayor during almost six of these years, at a period when the principles, by which legislative and executive measures ought to be guided, were diligently sought and carefully applied, according to the powers conferred by the city charter. The people of Boston had surrendered, with reluctance, the management of their municipal concerns, which they had maintained in popular assemblies for nearly two centuries; and the jealousy with which they watched the measures of the new authorities, rendered a frequent and full development of motives and consequences expedient and important.

At the close of his administration, it therefore appeared to the author, that a municipal history of the town, and an accurate account of the transactions in the first years of the city government, would be useful and interesting to the public in future times, and was due to the wisdom, fidelity, and disinterested services of his associates.

These views were intimated in an address to the Board of Aldermen, on taking final leave of the office of Mayor, on the third of January, 1829; and on the sixth, on his petition, the succeeding City Council having granted liberty of access to the City Records, this History was commenced. The completion of it was unavoidably postponed by the acceptance of the Presidency of Harvard University, an appointment made and confirmed by the Corporation and Overseers of that Seminary, on the fifteenth and twenty-ninth of the same month, and by the official duties assumed and discharged until August, 1845.

After the lapse of twenty years, at the urgency of friends who had a right to influence, the work was resumed; and, being finished, is now, at the close of the author's eightieth year, offered to his fellow-citizens, with his best wishes for their long enjoyment of an efficient municipal government, and for the uninterrupted prosperity of the city of Boston.

JOSIAH QUINCY.

BOSTON, February 4, 1852.

CONTENTS.

CHAPTER I.

TOWN GOVERNMENT. 1630-1783.

CHAPTER II.

TOWN GOVERNMENT. 1783-1821.

CHAPTER III.

TOWN GOVERNMENT. 1821-1822.

CHAPTER IV.

CITY GOVERNMENT. 1822-1823.

JOHN PHILLIPS, *Mayor.*

A*

CHAPTER IX.

CITY GOVERNMENT. 1824-1825.

JOSIAH QUINCY, *Mayor.*

CHAPTER X.

CITY GOVERNMENT. 1824-1825.

JOSIAH QUINCY, *Mayor.*

CHAPTER XI.

CITY GOVERNMENT. 1824-25.

JOSIAH QUINCY, *Mayor.*

CHAPTER XII.

CITY GOVERNMENT. 1825.

JOSIAH QUINCY, *Mayor.*

CHAPTER XVI.

CITY GOVERNMENT. 1828.

JOSIAH QUINCY, *Mayor.*

CHAPTER XVII.

CITY GOVERNMENT. 1828.

JOSIAH QUINCY, *Mayor.*

CHAPTER XVIII.

CITY GOVERNMENT. 1828.

JOSIAH QUINCY, *Mayor.*

CHAPTER XIX.

CITY GOVERNMENT. 1829.

HARRISON GRAY OTIS, *Mayor.*

APPENDIX.

MUNICIPAL HISTORY.

CHAPTER I.

TOWN GOVERNMENT. 1630-1783.

Constitution of Towns — Settlement and Organization of Boston — General Proceedings — Instructions to Selectmen and the Watch — Establishment of an Almshouse — Of Schools — Erection of Faneuil Hall — Manifestations of the Spirit of Liberty by the Inhabitants of Boston — Attempt to change the Form of Town Government — Population under the Colonial Government.

THE settlements made in 1630 around the Bay of Massachusetts, by John Winthrop and his associates, early received the name of "towns," under the sanction of the colonial legislature, denominated, in conformity with the language of the first charter, "The General Court."

After declaring "that particular towns had many things which concerned only themselves, and the ordering their own affairs, and disposing of business in their own town," the General Court, in 1630, ordered that "the freemen of every town, or a major part of them, should have power to dispose of their own lands and woods, to grant lots, and choose their own particular officers, as constables, surveyors of highways and the like, annually, or otherwise, if need required; also to make such laws and constitutions as concern the welfare of their town. Provided they are not of a criminal, but of a prudential nature, and that their penalties exceed not twenty shillings for one offence, and that they be not repugnant to the public laws and orders of the country." In case of the refusal of any inhabitant to obey the laws of the town, the appointed penalty was authorized to be levied by "distress." If any person behaved offensively in *town meeting*, those present had power to sentence him for the offence to pay any sum, not exceeding the above-prescribed penalty. To every town was also granted the power to choose yearly, or for less time, "a convenient number of fit men, to order the prudential affairs of the town, according to instructions given them in writing, they doing nothing contrary to the laws and orders of the country; and the number of selectmen to be not above nine." The local limits of each town, within which its jurisdiction extended, were established, enlarged, or diminished by the General Court, who subsequently authorized new officers to be chosen and granted new powers to each town, as new wants arose, or as local interests or state policy suggested.

Such was the first and simple outline of that constitution of towns, which, originating in the convenience and practical spirit of those early emigrants, and being thus gradually modified, by occurring exigencies and policy, formed that assemblage of republics, with qualified powers, which constitutes some of the peculiar characteristics of Massachusetts and the other New England States, and had an effective, indeed, a controlling influence upon their principles and destinies.

One of the earliest of these settlements was established on the peninsula formed at the mouth of Charles River, by its waters and those of the Bay of Massachusetts. From the Indian natives it received the name of "Shawmut;" from the inhabitants of Charlestown, that of "Trimountain;" and from the General Court, by an order passed on the seventh of September, (old style,) 1630, that of "Boston." In 1632, the same colonial legislature declared it to be "the fittest place for public meetings of any place in the Bay," and thenceforth it was, and ever since has continued the capital of Massachusetts.

The peninsula of Shawmut, being only about four miles in circumference, did not offer sufficient accommodation for pasturage and cultivation of the land. The General Court, therefore, during the four or five first years after the settlement, included within the boundaries of Boston the islands in the harbor, Muddy River, (now Brookline,) Winnisimet, (now Chelsea,) Mount Wollaston, and the land east of Neponset River, afterwards incorporated into a town by the name of Braintree, and now constituting the towns of Braintree, Randolph, and Quincy. The assignment of house lots within the peninsula, and the allotting farms to succeeding emigrants, formed the chief business of the town authorities for nearly half a century.

Boston being the place of the residence of John Winthrop, the first Governor of Massachusetts, and of some of the principal assistants, they took the lead in the early conduct of its affairs. The first order on the town records is dated 1634, March 7th day, 1st month, and purports to be passed by John Winthrop and nine others, but they take not the name of "selectmen," or any other indicative of authority. The order related only to laying stones and logs near landing places, so as not to be seen at high water, without some beacon to give notice thereof, "under pain of paying recompense, by way of damage, for any vessel injured thereby." The persons passing this order, however, seem to have been under some apprehension lest their authority might be questioned, for the order adds, "it being only a declaration of the common law herein."

The name of "selectmen" does not appear on the records of the town until November, 1643, and then only incidentally. The persons chosen to do the business of the town are often without any designation of their office. Sometimes they are called "the overseers of the town concerns;" at others, are designated as persons "chosen for the occasions of the town," and for the first time on the town records, on the 29th of November, 1645, John Winthrop and nine others are formally stated to be chosen "selectmen." The duties of the persons thus chosen, as expressed in one of the votes of the inhabitants, were "to oversee and take order for all the allotments within us, and for all comers into us, and also for all other the occasions and business of this town."

The allotments of land assigned within the peninsula were very limited in extent. Those out of it, and within the jurisdiction of the town, were large, and granted with great liberality. In the 9th of the 12th month, (February, 1635,) the rule established by the town for these allotments was, "two acres to plant on, and for every able youth, one acre within the Neck and Noddle's Island." As to those at Mount Wollaston and Muddy River, the allotters were authorized to "take a view and bound out what may be sufficient there" for the particular farms of the allottees, and four hundred acres were often given to a single individual. The year 1635, however, did not elapse before, in conformity with the settled policy of the emigrants at that period, the town "agreed that no further allotments should be granted unto any new-comer, but such as may be likely to be received members of the congregation."

During the political ascendency of Henry Vane, the name of Winthrop does not appear on the town records. As governor of the colony, in 1636, Vane probably assumed the superintendence of the concerns of the town. But in November, 1639, the name of John Winthrop, Governor, appears, with the names of nine others, chosen, as formerly, for the town's affairs; and he held this relation until 1648, the year before his death.

At this early period, the limits between the powers of the colonial legislature and those of the town seem not to have been well defined or carefully observed. Besides the local authority incident to municipal jurisdiction, such as "taking care of the common fences," "regulating the going at large of cattle, goats, and swine;" "the cutting wood upon the Neck;" and reserving that "near Roxbury for the poor," — the town, in 1635, undertook to exercise a more extensive power, and one somewhat dubious, both in point of principle and expediency. Thus, it then appointed a committee "to set prices upon all cattle, commodities, victuals, and laborers' and workmen's wages, and that no other prices or rates be given or taken." They also voted that "none of the members of this congregation, or inhabitants among us, shall sue one another at the law, before that Mr. Henry Vane, and the two elders, Mr. Thomas Oliver and Thomas Leverett, have had the hearing and deciding of the cause, if they can." In the same year it was voted, "that whosoever, at any public meeting, shall fall into private conference, to the hindering of public business, shall forfeit for every such offence *twelve pence*, to be paid into the constable's hands for public use." In this year the town first assumed the care of the schools, by voting that "our brother Philemon Pormont be entreated to become schoolmaster, for the teaching of the children among us."

The General Court having rejected the persons they had chosen as their deputies to that body, the spirit of the inhabitants was manifested by the following proceedings:—

"The 9th of ye 3d Mo. 1637. At a general meeting, upon private or particular warning, from house to house, and by reason of the Court's refusal of the former choice, Mr. Henry Vane, Esq., Mr. William Coddington, Mr. Atherton Hough, are *now again chosen* deputies, or committees, for the service of the present General Court, and that upon warrant to us from the Court for a new choice." Notwithstanding the obnoxiousness, at that time, of these deputies to the predominating party in the Court, they were in consequence admitted to their seats.

The records of the town, though voluminous, contain little of permanent importance or interest. A few of them, indicative of the opinions and views of the inhabitants in those early times, will be here recapitulated: —

1638. Allotments were granted on condition of "inoffensive carriage."

1652. No strangers were permitted to live in the town, without giving bonds to save the town harmless from all damage and charge for entertaining them. It was ordered, that persons whose houses were pulled down by the authorities, in case of fire, should "not be entitled to damages therefor."

1653. Leave was given to a citizen "to sink a twelve-feet cistern, at the pump which stands in the highway, to hold water to be helpful against fire, he making it safe from danger of children." Ladders were placed at the meeting-houses, with penalty against their use, except in case of fire. At the same place were also hung strong crooks and chains, poles and ropes, for the same purpose. Every householder was required to have a ladder which should reach to the roof of his house.

1655. "For galloping through the streets, except upon days of military exercise, or any extraordinary case require," a fine of two shillings was imposed. Football was prohibited from being played in the streets. Butchers were ordered to cast all their offal into the mill creek, and not elsewhere; and all rubbish to be removed before every house.

1657. None but admitted inhabitants could keep shop or set up a manufacture within the town, except those who were twenty-one years of age, and had served seven years' apprenticeship, under penalty of ten shillings a month. An inhabitant was allowed "to set up a pump in the streets, and might deny any neighbor its use who did not contribute to the expense."

Licences were required for drawing beer, wine, brandy, strong water, cider; for keeping a public house, and for selling coffee and chocolate.

1658. The order passed in 1652 was revoked, and owners of

houses pulled down by the authorities in case of fire, were entitled to damages. No person was allowed to carry fire from one house to another, except in some safe vessel secure from wind. If a chimney took fire and flamed out, the owner was fined ten shillings. Persons were appointed to inspect the chimneys of the town, and cause defects in them to be remedied so as to be safe against fire.

1659. Inhabitants were fined "for entertaining foreigners," and ordered to discharge them from their houses. If they received "inmates, servants, or journeymen, coming for help in physic or surgery, without leave of the selectmen, and without giving bonds to save the town harmless, their fine was twenty shillings a week."

1662. Persons were appointed to prevent disorders by youth on the Lord's day; particularly in the meeting-house, in time of God's solemn worship; with authority to correct those who were disorderly with a small wand, and in case of contempt, to take their names and bring them before the magistrates.

1670. "There having been found a great want of water in case of fire, every inhabitant was ordered to have a hogshead well filled with water near his door, with the head open, under a penalty of five shillings."

1672. Under the authority of colonial laws, the selectmen ordered parents to put their children out to service, or to indent them out; and if they did not, the authority had power to take them from their parents for that purpose.

1678. Every family was ordered to be provided with "fire-buckets, swabs, and scoops, according to their state." In the same year an engine was imported from England, and persons appointed to take charge of it in case of fire.

1683. Those who had the care of the water engine, (now called fire engines,) were exempted from "train bands."

1702. Two water engines were ordered to be imported from England.

The inhabitants in general town meeting were accustomed, annually or semi-annually, to vote instructions to their selectmen, presenting the objects of attention, and their duties concerning them. Those issued in 1657 were full, and the following abstract will give an idea of their general tenor, and throw light on the character of the times: —

"Relying on your wisdom and care in seeking the good of the town, we recommend, that you cause to be executed all the orders of the town which you have on the records, according to the power given you by law, as found in the printed laws, under the titles of Townships, Ecclesiastics, Freemen, Highways, Small Causes, Indians, Corn Fields, Children, Masters, Servants, Pipe Staves, Stones, Weights and Measures, and any other orders in force; and where you find any defect, to issue thereon good orders, to be approved by the town and the General Court. Subjects most necessary to be understood are, (1.) About entertaining new inhabitants. 2. That none transplant themselves from the country to inhabit here without giving notice; concerning whom you may inquire their calling and employment, and whether they are about to live under other men's roofs as inmates, and deal with them according to law. If they are poor and impotent, deal with them as directed, under the title of Poor. If they buy houses and land, have a vigilant eye that they live not idly, but be diligently employed in some lawful calling. If, by reason of sickness, they cannot subsist their children, you are to take their children from them, and put them to apprenticeship. If any be debauched and live idly, you must provide a house of correction for them, at the charge of the town and the county. We commit unto you the disposal of the waste lands belonging to the town, for the benefit of the town, giving account from time to time.

"We require you to make some effectual order to prevent harm from swine. As to the law relative to particular highways, to each man's lot, if the General Court's order do not reach it, you must remind our deputies to procure some addition. You are to take constant precaution as to buildings, that they encroach not on the streets or town's lands. You are to appoint meet persons to keep the streets and flats near wharves and places of land clear of stones and other encumbrances. You must see that some life be put into the laws about casks, and that they be of due gauge to prevent fraud, and that deceitful packing of beef and pork be duly punished; that sworn men be appointed for measuring grain, cording wood and boards. We think it meet a jury should be chosen on weights and measures, to observe defects in chimneys, and in houses in danger of falling, and to present the same to the county courts; that orders be passed against regrators and forestallers, and our deputies get them confirmed by the General Court.

"That a meeting be held by you, at least monthly, seriously to consider these things, for the good of the town, the glory of God, and establishing truth and love among us.

"That every half year a town meeting be called, the orders passed submitted for its approbation; the accounts may be credited, and particularly of what has been spent for buckets, hooks and ladders, and for powder, and whether ladders have been provided for each house, according to law; also as to what has been spent as to the great guns and ammunition of the town, that provision may be made for them.

"These orders, with occasional variation, were apparently renewed every year in town meeting, until the year 1694."

The orders to the town watch also characterize the state of the times.

"The town watch to be set at nine and dismissed at five. It shall not be trusted to youth, but one half consist of householders; none to be employed of notorious evil life; nor those who would watch two nights together, not having sufficient sleep between; the number to be *eight*. The following charge to be given unto the watch every night:—

"1. To walk two by two together; a youth to be joined with an older and more sober person.

"2. If after ten o'clock they see lights, to inquire if there be warrantable cause; and if they hear any noise or disorder, wisely to demand the reason; if they are dancing and singing vainly, to admonish them to cease; if they do not discontinue after moderate admonition, then the constable to take their names and acquaint the authorities therewith.

"3. To watch the water side and about the shore, and prudently take account of such as go out or come in, not hindering lawful business, but preventing unlawful practice and disorders.

"4. To look at the guns and fortifications.

"5. If they find young men and maidens, not of known fidelity, walking after ten o'clock, modestly to demand the cause; and if they appear ill-minded, to watch them narrowly, command them to go to their lodgings, and if they refuse, then to secure them till morning.

"6. That the watch be exemplary themselves, using no corrupt language, and so conduct themselves, that any persons of quality who are abroad late may acknowledge that the watch does not neglect due examination nor misconduct."

In 1660, the first steps towards erecting an almshouse were taken, by authorizing the selectmen to use a piece of ground for that purpose. In 1662, the design was carried into effect, in consequence of the encouragement given by sundry legacies and subscriptions. The building thus erected having been burnt down, a vote was passed by the town, in 1682, for rebuilding it. In this vote the object of the institution is specified to be "for the relief of the poor, the aged, and those incapacitated for labor; of many persons who would work, but have not wherewithal to employ themselves; of many more persons and families, who spend their times in jolliness and tipling, and who suffer their children shamefully to spend their time in the streets, to assist, employ, and correct whom the proposed institution was provided."

It appears, however, by the records, that the original design of the house, for the accommodation of the respectable poor, was in a great measure defeated from the predominating character of its inmates; and in 1712, an attempt was made by the town "to restore the almshouse to its primitive and pious design, even for the relief of the necessitous, that they might lead a quiet, peaceable, and godly life there, where it is now made a bridewell and house of correction, which obstructs many honest poor people going there for the designed relief and support." As a remedy, the town proposed the building a house of correction, and a committee was raised for that purpose. That committee reported that "the poor honest people, who were sent as objects of charity, should be kept separate; and that the justices of the peace of the county should be petitioned to erect a house of correction, as the law directs." Nothing farther was done upon the subject until the year 1720, when a vote was passed in town meeting for the erection of a workhouse, independent of an almshouse. This design was not, however, carried into effect until 1735, when measures were adopted for the enlargement and erecting new buildings, in connection with the preëxisting almshouse, in virtue of the province law, passed in that year, on the special representation and petition of the town to that effect. The land now included, between Park and Beacon Streets, and the west line of the burying ground to the north line of the land now occupied by Park Street Church, was at that time the site appropriated for this establishment. The expenses incident to the erection of the buildings were originally defrayed from the funds of the town, aided by subscriptions of private individuals. It early received the name of the Boston Almshouse, probably to render a resort to it less obnoxious to the more respectable class of poor. But this appellation had no sanction in the province law authorizing its erection. "Workhouses for the idle and the indigent," "houses of correction for rogues and vagabonds," are the only designations given by that law, to institutions for either of those objects. The defects and inconveniences of the Boston Almshouse, which the comparative poverty of the times, and the embarrassments consequent on the revolutionary war, prevented from being remedied until after its close, will be noticed hereafter in this work.

The obedience of the town to the province law, which required that every town having fifty householders should be provided with a schoolmaster to teach children and youth to read and write, and having one hundred families, with a grammar school, with some discreet person well instructed in the tongues to keep such school, seems, from the earliest times, to have been constant and regular. Their proceedings are not very distinctly traced in the town records. In 1662, the rent of Deer Island was appropriated for the use of free schools. And, in 1679, two free schools were established "to teach children to write and to cipher," accompanied with a recommendation to "those who sent their children to school and were able, to pay something for the encouragement of the master." It was not until 1709, that the town, on the report of a committee, voted "annually to appoint a certain number of gentlemen of liberal education, together with some of the reverend ministers of the town, to be inspectors of the schools, and, under that name and title, to visit the schools when, and as often as they think fit, to inform themselves of the methods used in teaching of the schools, and to inquire of their proficiency, and to be present at the performance of some of their exercises, the master being before notified of their coming, and with him to consult and advise of further methods for the advancement of learning and the good government of the school; and, at their visitation, one of the ministers by turns to pray with the scholars, and entertain them with some instructions of piety specially adapted to their age and education." By the same vote, "the inspectors were authorized, with the master, to introduce an usher upon such salary as the town shall agree to grant for his services." Five inspectors of the schools were accordingly appointed, and the system was persevered in for several years; afterwards it was discontinued; and the practice prevailed for the selectmen annually to visit the schools, accompanied by as many gentlemen as they chose to invite, which were often not less than fifteen or twenty. This practice continued until after the American Revolution and the treaty of peace subsequent. The proceedings of the town in relation to these institutions will be related hereafter in connection with those of the city.[1]

For more than a century after the settlement of the town, it was destitute of an established public market. Provisions were brought in carts to the doors of the inhabitants, and an opinion generally prevailed that the tendency of a local market was to

[1] In 1739, the whole number in all the town schools was 593
1741, " " " " " 474
1743, " " " " " 585
1754, " " " " " 848
1763, " " " " " 832
1773, " " " " " 719

encourage forestalling and raise the price of provisions. In 1733, the question of establishing a public market was first decided in the affirmative; ayes 366, nays 339. But at an adjourned meeting, a few days after, the former vote was rescinded, and the question decided in the negative; 390 ayes, 415 nays.

In 1734, by way of compromise, three markets were established by vote of the inhabitants, — a south, centre, and north.

In April, 1737, the town voted that the south and north market should be appropriated to some other use; and to what use they should be put was referred to the selectmen. Before their decision was known, the centre market, near the town dock, was pulled down by a mob, and the selectmen reported that the south market should be leased for shops, and that the north market should be removed.

This report occasioned warm debates, and one of the inhabitants was reprimanded by the town, and ordered to be silent, for language implying that the selectmen had made their report in agreement with the mob. Their report was accepted, and the subject was not again revived until 1740, when Peter Faneuil offered, "on his own proper cost, to build a noble and complete structure to be improved for a market, for the sole use and benefit of the town, provided the town would accept the same, and make proper regulations," a meeting being called "to know the minds of the inhabitants, whether they would accept the same, *on condition that the market people should be at liberty to carry their marketing wheresoever they pleased about town.*" Notwithstanding this condition, and although a vote was passed thanking Mr. Faneuil for his generous offer, the question of accepting it was carried only by a majority of *seven;* 367 ayes and 360 nays.

In 1742, the market house was erected by Mr. Faneuil on the town's land, near the dock. The edifice was of brick, two stories in height, and one hundred feet in length by forty in breadth. "A noble structure," say the records, "far exceeding his first proposal, inasmuch as it contains not only a large and sufficient accommodation for a market-place, but has also superadded a spacious and most beautiful town-hall over it, and several other convenient rooms." Votes were immediately passed by the town, appointing the selectmen and the representatives, and twelve others of the most distinguished inhabitants, a committee to wait upon Mr. Faneuil, and "in the name of the town to render him their most hearty thanks for so bountiful a gift, with their prayers that this and other expressions of his bounty and charity may be abundantly recompensed by the Divine blessing. It was also voted that, "in testimony of the town's gratitude, and to perpetuate his memory, the hall over the market-place should be called Faneuil Hall, and that a picture of him, at full length, be drawn, and placed in said hall, at the expense of the town."

Mr. Faneuil died on the third of March, 1743, and, on the fourteenth, "being the first meeting in Faneuil Hall after his death," at the request of the selectmen, "John Lovell, master of the South Grammar School, delivered, in presence of the town, an oration on his death; the moderator's seat being hung in mourning cloth on the occasion." This oration was transcribed at length on the town's records, and celebrates with great pathos and power "the largeness of his heart, the unbounded nature of his private charities," and his "public spirit and munificence."[1] Afterwards the arms of his family were placed in Faneuil Hall by vote of the town. These proceedings did not extinguish the spirit of opposition to a market-house.

In 1746, a number of the inhabitants petitioned "that Faneuil Hall should be shut up, and the building appropriated to some other purpose." Although the attempt was not at this time successful, it was renewed the next year, (1747,) and the market shut up until September following, and then till March, 1748, when it was again opened, at first for three days, and afterwards for every day in the week. In 1752, the contest was again renewed, and the market was shut up until the farther order of the town. In August of that year, the question of opening the market was again raised, and, after violent debates, passed in the negative; only one hundred and two votes being in the affirmative, and one hundred and twenty-nine in the negative. In March, 1753, however, a vote for opening it was obtained, and the stalls were authorized to be leased; in which result the inhabitants finally acquiesced.

In February, 1761, Faneuil Hall was destroyed by fire, the

[1] Mr. Faneuil's mansion house was situated in Tremont Street, in the midst of extensive gardens, opposite the Chapel Burial Ground. His family fled from France with the Huguenots, in 1686. The grasshopper, on the vane of Faneuil Hall, was the crest of their arms.

Note ×

A distant view of the mansion & grounds, of Mr Faneuil, was accidentally given in the frontispiece of this volume over the roof of Faneuil Hall. — The sketch copied by the engraver was taken in 1827. At that time the house & gardens remained in perfect preservation & were the property and residence of William Phillips Esq; — Lt Gov'r of Massachusetts for many years, and the uncle of Mr Quincy. — The artist not aware of the coincidence merely sketched the scene before him. — The mansion of Mr Faneuil, & its surrounding resembled a French Chateau_ thus, marking the Huguenot origin of the family.— It was situated on the slope of Beacon hill, with a deep court yard filled with flowers & shrubs. The mansion of three stories, was of brick painted white, with busts carved in white marble over the windows. In the centre over the front door was a large window with a semicircular balcony.— The windows of the drawing rooms opened on a grass plot, divided by a broad walk paved with white marble, & bounded by a wrought-iron balustrade surmounted by gilt balls. From thence a broad flight of steps of iron stone, led to a continuation of the walk to Tremont St.— There was a spacious hall in the centre of the house, with an elegant staircase, & opening on each side into drawing & dining rooms which extend the width of the mansion having windows looking towards the garden in the rear. There was a court yard paved with small stones of different colors in a pattern from which flights of stone steps ascended the glaces above, supported by massy walls of hewn granite, & surmounted by a summer house commanding a fine view of the town, harbour & environs of Boston. The trees seen in the frontispiece were among the first objects descried by seamen, entering the harbour & were long an important land mark.

In 1836. these gardens & the adjoining estates were levelled & Pemberton Square & the adjoining streets now occupy their site.—

The Faneuil mansion & gardens were so peculiar and historical that some description of them may prove interesting to some of the readers of the History of Boston; & it is therefore inserted.—

Eliza Susan Quincy.

5 Park St. Boston.
February 11 1872.

walls only being left standing. The town resolved, in March following, that the edifice should be rebuilt, and that the lower part should "not be improved as a market until the farther order of the town." To defray the expense, the General Court granted a lottery. The first meeting in the hall, after it was repaired, was on the fourteenth of March, 1763. The original dimensions of the building, as erected by Mr. Faneuil, were not enlarged until the year 1805, when it was extended in breadth to eighty feet, and a third story was added to its height.

The spirit of liberty and jealousy of town and colonial rights breathe through the records of Boston from the earliest period of the settlement. By the early laws of the colony, every town having *ten* freemen might send *one* deputy to the General Court. Every town having *twenty* freemen might send *two*; but no town more than two. The town of Boston, as its population increased, became sensible of the inequality of their influence in the colonial legislature, compared with their numbers. "We have four churches," say the records; "our members are twenty times twenty; the number of our representatives should be proportionate." No relief was, however, granted in this respect, until after the charter of William and Mary, in 1692, by which the legislature of the province was allowed to fix the number of deputies each town might send; and Boston was immediately allowed four representatives.

The practice of instructing the representatives of the town in the General Court was early adopted, and occasionally, and often annually, continued through every period of colonial history. In these instructions, not only objects of temporary and local interest were pressed upon the attention of their representatives, by the town, but the views and feelings of the inhabitants of a general nature were indicated, and their sentiments concerning municipal and colonial rights unequivocally expressed. Thus, in 1751, they were instructed to obtain the passage of laws regulating "the accepting and entertaining new inhabitants;" against persons "transplanting themselves from one place to another, without notice to the selectmen;" and for "inquiring concerning the calling and employment of those who present themselves as inhabitants;" and, subsequently, in almost every successive year, the subjects most interesting at the period, such as measures for "preventing the poor from being chargeable to the town," and "providing workhouses for the idle and debauched," were urged upon the notice of their representatives. The vigilance of the inhabitants in regard to their charter rights and privileges, never failed to be shown, on these occasions, by their votes; thus, in 1677, when the claims of Mason and Gorges struck at the powers of the colonial government, "it is a time," say the inhabitants to their representatives, "to unite, and for peace and amity to be attended to," and they were warned, "in matters of judicature, not to assume any arbitrary power," and "to do nothing which should, in the least measure infringe our liberties, civil or ecclesiastical, granted us by our charter."

After the commencement of the eighteenth century, and in the incipient stages of those discontents, which ultimately resulted in the American Revolution, the votes of the inhabitants of the metropolis exhibited a spirit, which, in fact, constituted a leading influence in the policy of the colony. Thus, in 1721, their representatives were instructed "to maintain our just rights and privileges; to pass laws encouraging trade, husbandry, and manufactures; to vindicate the town against the aspersions which had been made against it of being inclined to mobs and tumults; in all elections to have regard to the preservation of the just and laudable usages and customs of reserving the allowances, gratuities, &c., until the acts and elections be fully completed." In 1723, the town addressed the king, repelling the charge "of being under no magistracy and of being of a mutinous disposition," which had been brought against it by Governor Shute.

In 1728, the town voted extra pay to their representatives for unusual hardships they had sustained, "for their steadfast adherence to the rights and privileges of the people." In the same year, the question was taken in town meeting, whether "the governor, (Burnett,) shall have a salary settled upon him for the time being, and the vote was unanimously in the negative; and the same was the result on the question whether "a salary might be settled upon him for a limited time." In the same spirit the town instructed their representatives, in 1729, "to pay due respect to the governor, but to use your utmost endeavors that the house of representatives may not, by any means, be prevailed upon, or brought into the fixing, a certain salary for any certain time to the governor. But that they improve their usual freedom, in granting their money from time to time, as they shall judge the province to be able, and in such a manner as they shall think most for the benefit and advantage thereof; and if your pay should be diverted, you may depend upon all the justice imaginable from this town whom you represent."

The same direct and jealous spirit, manifested in the votes of the town in successive causes of popular discontent, from this period to the declaration of independence, shows the leading influence of the town of Boston on all the measures which were the precursors of that event. But as these proceedings belong to the general history of Massachusetts, only some of the chief occasions seized upon to excite an interest and union in the principles of civil liberty will be enumerated. Thus, in 1732, resistance "to granting a certain salary to the governor," and "to compliance with his majesty's instructions, relative to supplying the treasury," was enjoined by the town on its representatives. In almost every subsequent year, until 1754, a similar spirit is evidenced in the votes of the town, accompanied sometimes, as in 1736 and the years ensuing, with complaints of the disproportion of taxation, misapplication of public moneys, against the excise upon spirits; and, in 1745, their representatives were instructed "to take care that excisemen and their assistants should be excluded from the house of representatives;" and, in 1754, to obtain "a law, whereby the seats of such gentlemen as shall accept posts of profit from the crown or the governor, shall be vacated agreeably to an act of the British Parliament, until their constituents may have an opportunity of reëlecting them, if they please." When the policy of the British government, to collect a revenue from the colonies, was manifested by the stamp act and its accompanying measures, the spirit of the town was evidenced by votes of the most decided character, expressed in instructions to their representatives, and in petitions and remonstrances to the king and the people of Great Britain.

In 1767, the town voted funds to procure the pictures of Colonel Barre and General Conway, and which, when received, they ordered to be hung in Faneuil Hall, as indications of their gratitude for their opposition to the projects of the ministry. From that period to the declaration of independence, the unanimity of the inhabitants, and the principles by which they were actuated, are inseparably identified with the chief causes and characters of the American Revolution, and are among the most prominent and effective influences of that momentous crisis.

During the seventeenth century, no indication of dissatisfaction with the form of town government is apparent on the records. As early as 1667, among the instructions given by the town to its representatives, there was inserted the endeavor to obtain a law "making the town a corporation, or making it a county by itself." But this desire had probably no connection with any discontent at that self-government which a town organization secured to its inhabitants; but exclusively with that of getting rid of the Court of Sessions, whose authority it was thought might more properly be vested in the selectmen, and give more efficiency and uniformity to the proceedings of the town. In that court was invested the power to establish a house of correction, which, in utter neglect of the injunctions of the colonial law, they had omitted to erect, choosing, from motives of economy, to use the common jail for that purpose; an omission of which the town had reason, and did not fail occasionally, to complain. The first proposal of change in the form of town government appears to have originated with the selectmen themselves, who, in 1708, offered to the inhabitants, at a meeting called for that purpose, the following proposition for their consideration, namely: —

"That the orders and by-laws of this town already made, for the directing, ordering, and managing of the prudential affairs thereof, have not answered the ends for which they were made; and the principal cause thereof is a general defect or neglect in the execution, without which the best laws will signify little; and one great reason why they are no better executed, is the want of a proper head, or town officer or officers, empowered for that purpose, the law having put the execution of town orders into the hands of the justices only, who are not town, but county officers, and it cannot be expected that they should take the trouble and care, or make it so much their business, as a town officer or officers, particularly appointed or chosen thereunto, must needs do. And, indeed, for any body or society of men, as a town is, to be vested with power to make rules and by-laws for their own good regulation, and not to have power to choose and appoint the head officer or officers, who shall have power to execute their own orders and by-laws, seems incongruous, and good order is not to be expected while it remains so; for as a town grows more populous, it will stand in need of more strict regulation. The said selectmen, therefore, propose that this town do now choose a committee of a considerable number of the freeholders and other inhabitants of the town to draw up a scheme or draft a charter of incorporation for encouragement and better government of this town, in the best manner they shall think suitable, and of the best and most suitable means for the obtaining thereof, and to present the said scheme or draft to the town, at their annual meeting in March next."

A vote to that effect was accordingly passed. Thirty-one inhabitants of chief influence were elected to constitute the committee. On the fourth of March, 1708 – 9, they reported the required draft or scheme. But the town not only refused to accept it, but also refused to refer the subject to any future meeting; at the same time passing votes of thanks to the committee for their labors. In May, 1744, the subject was again revived, in a form, as was probably supposed, less exceptionable. "The town," say the records, "having grown exceedingly populous, a proposition was made to apply to the General Court, that the selectmen, for the time being, might have power, with the consent of the Court of Sessions, to make by-laws, with a penalty not exceeding forty shillings; and that they might be constituted a court of record, to try and determine all offences against the by-laws, with an appeal from their judgment to the Court of Sessions." The proposition, however, after a long debate, received a decided negative from the inhabitants, and no similar attempt was made until after the peace of 1783. The few municipal relations, during this period of general and permanent interest and importance, will be found hereafter stated in this history, in connection with some of the principal institutions of the town and city.

The receipts and expenditures of the town, during its colonial period are obscurely traced on its records, and the glimpses they give of its wants and resources excite neither interest nor curiosity. The ratio of the increase of its population cannot at this day be ascertained. It was slow and gradual. During the seventeenth century, it never exceeded seven thousand. In 1730, at the close of the first century from its settlement, its population was only fifteen thousand; and, although in the middle of the eighteenth century its numbers rose to eighteen thousand, yet the effects of wars with France, Spain, and the Indians, and that of the American Revolution, reduced that amount, at the peace of 1783, to twelve thousand, according to the most exact estimates. The wants of the community were during this period of the first necessity, and its resources of the most limited and attainable kind. The government being popular, and in effect democratic, the study of those who managed its concerns was chiefly to avoid debt and taxation; and when exigencies requiring an enlargement of means occurred, even where the objects were both general and permanent, a resort was had to the liberality of the rich, to avoid the recurrence to a tax, which might excite the discontent of the less prosperous. Thus, the establishment of an almshouse, a workhouse, and even the provision for the absolute wants of the inmates of those institutions, were occasionally provided for by subscriptions, which were regarded and responded to as approved means in all such exigencies.

During the revolutionary war, the exertions of the inhabitants of the town were directed to providing for the urgent wants of the period.

In 1776, the town was occupied in measures encouraging the declaration of independence, and in pledging unanimously their lives and fortunes for its support; in forming committees of correspondence and of safety; offering bounties for volunteers for the army, and providing arms and ammunition for the inhabitants.

In 1777, the town negatived the proposition, to invest in the General Court the power of forming a constitution for the commonwealth; took measures to fortify the harbor; remonstrated against the return of the Tories; borrowed money for the town, and raised subscriptions for the poor, and recommended to the churches to make collections for the families of the non-commissioned officers and privates of the army.

In 1778, the articles of confederation were discussed and approved; monopolists and forestallers denounced; the inhabitants were desired, in consideration of the necessities of the time, not to have *more than two dishes of meat on their tables;* and committees were raised to provide shirts, stockings, and shoes for the army.

In 1779, measures were taken to relieve the town from the great scarcity of provisions and necessaries of life; to borrow money; to raise contributions for the poor; to form a convention; to frame a new constitution for the state; for protection against invasion; for regulating the prices of goods and provisions, and prosecuting those who violated the rules on this subject.

In 1780, the new constitution proposed for the state was considered by sections in town meeting; many days were occupied in the discussion, several amendments proposed, and the constitution partially accepted; measures were taken to enlist men for the army, and to raise contributions for the poor.

In 1781, heavy assessments were voted by the inhabitants for procuring men, and beef and clothing for the army, and for contributions for the support of the poor in the almshouse. Measures were also taken on the subject of the depreciation of paper money; and the subject of the fisheries was made a topic of earnest representation to the General Court. On occasion of a visit to the town by the Marquis Lafayette, he was formally addressed by the inhabitants, with expressions of "their cordial esteem and affection;" to which Lafayette responded, in terms manifesting his "lively sense of attachment and gratitude to the inhabitants."

In 1782, measures were taken, on the memorial of the overseers of the poor, who represented the inmates in the almshouse to be in want of the necessaries of life, and the master of it to be greatly in debt for his advances for their relief. Committees were raised on the subject of "the alarming combination of the bakers;" against "illicit trade;" and "the foolish predilection for British manufactures;" and for the purpose of forming associations to prevent smuggling; and for the memorializing the General Court on the unconstitutionality of the Lord's Day Act.

These measures, with others too numerous to be recapitulated, accompanied with reports, memorials, and instructions to representatives, which fill the town records, so engrossed the thoughts of the inhabitants with topics of general interest and vital importance, as to supersede all recurrence to subjects of a municipal character, until the peace of 1783.

CHAPTER II.

TOWN GOVERNMENT. 1783-1821.

State of the Public Schools — Measures in regard to them — Successive Attempts to change the Government of the Town — Plan of a City Government adopted.

For upwards of forty years after the adoption of the constitution of Massachusetts, in 1780, the municipal affairs of the town of Boston were conducted on the same simple and economical scale, which antecedent practice had sanctioned. During this interval, the management of the schools, the attempts to incorporate the town, and the arrangements for the support of the poor, constitute the chief topics of interest and excitement.

Our knowledge of the proceedings relative to the schools, from their first establishment under the colonial law, in 1635, until the American Revolution, is chiefly derived from the reports of the selectmen, or of committees annually appointed for their supervision. These state, in general, their good condition, and the number of scholars.

After the peace of 1783, a committee on the schools "lament that so many children should be found in the streets playing and gaming in school hours, owing either to the too fond indulgence of parents, or the too lax government of the schools. They deprecate the effect upon the rising generation; and recommend that the selectmen should be enjoined to take care that no person should open a private school without their recommendation, agreeably to the good and salutary laws of the commonwealth."

Occasional efforts were made for improvements of the schools; but no general system was adopted until October, 1789, when a large committee was appointed on the subject, who with much deliberation reported a system which, after some opposition, was sanctioned and carried into effect. The schools then constituted by this arrangement were, one for the instruction of boys in Greek and Latin, and for fitting them for the university, called the Latin School, in which duly qualified candidates might be admitted at *ten* years of age, and continue *four* years; three reading and three writing schools, one of each at the north, the centre, and the south part of the town, into which candidates were admitted at *seven* years of age, and might continue till *sixteen.* Boys might attend all the year round; girls, from the 20th of April to the 20th of October.

The selectmen, and twelve other persons, annually elected in town meeting by ballot, were authorized to superintend the schools; to appoint masters and ushers, and fix their salaries; to visit the schools once every quarter, by sub-committees, and exercise all the powers the selectmen had done under the colonial government. Votes were, subsequently, annually passed by the town, confirming the above authority, and occasionally enlarging and strengthening it.

The school committee was organized by this arrangement in 1790, and its records, which commence in 1792, have been regularly continued.[1]

At this period there were only seven town schools, denominated the Latin Grammar, the North Reading, the North Writing, the South Reading, the South Writing, the Centre Reading, and the Centre Writing Schools.

Their number was increased by the erection of the Mayhew School, at West Boston, in 1803; of the Hawes, at South Boston, in 1811; and of the Smith, for colored children, in 1812.

The inability of the poorer classes to qualify their children for admission to the common schools, led the town, in 1818, to sanction the establishment of primary schools, for the education of children between four and seven years of age.

For their management, the school committee were authorized, annually, to appoint three inhabitants in each ward, whose duty it was to provide instruction for children between the above-mentioned ages, and apportion the expenses among the several schools.

In 1818, the Boylston School was authorized, and a school-house erected in 1819.

In 1820, an English classical school was established, having

[1] The first elected members were, Hon. Thomas Dawes, Rev. Samuel West, Rev. Dr. Lathrop, Rev. James Freeman, Dr. Nathaniel Appleton, Dr. Aaron Dexter, Dr. Thomas Welsh, John C. Jones, Jonathan Mason, Jun., Christopher Gore, George Richards Minot, and William Tudor.

for its object to enable the mercantile and mechanical classes to obtain an education adapted for those children, whom their parents wished to qualify for active life, and thus relieve them from the necessity of incurring the expense incident to private academies. The candidates were to be admitted at twelve years of age, and continue three years; good acquaintance with reading, writing, English grammar in all its branches, and with arithmetic as far as Proportions, were requisite for admission.

At the time of the transfer of the schools from the town to the city, their number were as follows:

The Latin, established in 1635; the Eliot, in 1713; the Adams, in 1717; the Franklin, in 1785; the Mayhew, in 1803; the Hawes, in 1811; the Smith, in 1812; the Boylston, in 1819; and the English Classical, in 1820. The number of primary schools were thirty-five.

The annual expenses of the whole system, with sufficient accuracy, may be stated at forty thousand dollars. The salaries of the masters of the Latin and English Classical Schools were two thousand dollars each; of the sub-masters, twelve hundred; of their ushers, averaging at seven hundred. Those of the reading and writing masters being twelve hundred; of their ushers, six hundred, with some diminution of salary in respect of the master at South Boston, and of the master of the school for colored children; the former receiving only eight, and the latter only six hundred dollars annual salary.

The number of boys attending the Latin, English, classical, and reading schools being	1844	
Those attending the writing, ...	945	
		2789
The number of girls attending the reading schools, . .	883	
Those attending the writing schools, ...	864	
		1747
		4536

The above may be regarded, for all general purposes, a sufficiently near approximation to the number and expenses of the schools, and the number of those of both sexes instructed in them, when taken possession of by the city government.

The events of the American Revolution had strengthened the attachment of a great majority of the inhabitants of Boston to the form of town government. In town meetings their measures of opposition to the pretensions of Great Britain had been originated, been agitated and adopted, and the affection of the inhabitants to the forms, under which their efforts had been crowned with success, was increased. The name and character of "*town*," became identified with the idea of popular power and civil liberty. This sentiment, united with the natural reluctance with which every people part with authority they have long and successfully exercised, rendered all attempts at change, not so much unpopular, as hateful, to a majority of the inhabitants.

The inconveniences, resulting from the form of town government, became, however, every year more apparent to intelligent and influential citizens, and in May, 1784, on the petition of a large number of the inhabitants, a committee[1] of thirteen was appointed "to consider the expediency of applying to the General Court for an act to form the town of Boston into an incorporated city, and report a plan of alterations in the present government of the police, if such be deemed eligible." This committee was selected with great care from among the most influential and popular inhabitants, and on the fourth of June ensuing, they reported two plans[2] of a corporation, which, being read, were

[1] The committee were Samuel Adams, Joseph Barrell, Stephen Higginson, Charles Jarvis, William Tudor, Robert Treat Paine, Perez Morton, Samuel Breck, Edward Paine, James Sullivan, Thomas Dawes, Benjamin Hichborn, and Caleb Davis.

[2] The following condensed abstracts of these plans will give a sufficient general idea of their import: —

FIRST PLAN.

The town to be a body politic by the name and style of the Mayor, Aldermen, and Common Council of the City of Boston, with the following powers and privileges: —

1. To be invested with all the real and personal estate of the town, with power to dispose of the same under specified limitations.
2. To be capable to sue and of being sued.
3. Three meetings of the inhabitants to be held in the year, namely, — in March, to choose city officers; in April, to choose state officers; in May, to choose representatives. General meetings to be called by the mayor, at the request of fifty citizens.
4. In March, the qualified voters were to choose by ballot a mayor, a recorder, twelve overseers of the poor, sixteen firewards, seven assessors, a county treasurer and registrar; and, on the day following, the inhabitants of each ward to choose in its ward one alderman and two common councilmen.
5. The legality of the electors to be determined by the common council.
6. The city officers to take the oaths of allegiance and office.
7. The recorder to be a person discreet in the law.
8. The mayor, recorder, and common councilmen to constitute a common

ordered to be printed and distributed to each house, the town adjourning to the seventeenth of the same month to take them into consideration. At this meeting, it was voted that "the sense of the town be taken on the expediency of making any alterations in the present form of town government." On which question the records state, — "but the impatience of the inhabitants for the question being immediately put, prevented any debate thereon, and it passed in the negative by a great majority, and the meeting was immediately dissolved."

This result did not, however, deter the friends of a change from further effort; and in November, 1785, the attempt was renewed, on petition of a number of the inhabitants, and a committee was chosen "to state the defects of the present constitution of the town, and to report how far the same may be remedied without an act of incorporation." This committee, composed of men of great popularity and influence, reported, probably more from a sense of the impracticability of effecting any change arising from the existing state of prejudice, than from any want of perception of the inconveniences experienced, "that they do not report any defects in the constitution." After debate, this report was accepted, and leave given to the petitioners to withdraw their petition.

council, with power to make by-laws and ordinances not repugnant to the laws of the commonwealth, and not to be in force until published in two newspapers.

9. The common council to have power to raise money; of which the mayor and aldermen were to have the exclusive right of appropriating, laying an account of their expenditures before the people annually, in March.

10, 11, and 12, relate to the trial of breaches of the by-laws, the making a common seal, and to times of meeting of the common council.

13. No assembly was to be deemed a common council, unless either the mayor or recorder, at least seven aldermen and thirteen common councilmen were present.

The remaining articles relate to the choice of a town clerk, to the granting the freedom of the city, to the removal of city officers for misconduct, and to the filling vacancies in case of their death.

SECOND PLAN.

This coincides with the first, except that the style of the body politic was to be "The President and Selectmen of the City of Boston."

Art. 4. In March, the qualified voters were to choose by ballot a president and six selectmen, twelve overseers of the poor, sixteen firewards, seven assessors, a county treasurer and registrar; and the day following, each ward should choose one selectman for such ward.

Art. 7. The president and eighteen selectmen to constitute a city board. The president always to be present, with powers to make laws.

The other articles not materially different from those of the first plan.

The subject remained dormant until December, 1791, when it was again renewed, by a petition of a number of the inhabitants, "setting forth the want of an efficient police" on which was raised a large and respectable committee,[1] consisting of inhabitants of leading influence in both the political parties of the period. This committee, after long deliberation, reported a system,[2] which, after being read, discussed, amended in town meeting, and accepted by paragraphs, was ordered to be printed and distributed in handbills. The town then adjourned until the twenty-sixth of January ensuing, for its final consideration, when it was rejected; five hundred and seventeen voters being in the affirmative, and seven hundred and one in the negative.

In May following, the attempt to effect a change in the system of town police, and for the better execution of the laws, was revived, and met a similar fate.

No subsequent attempt of this kind was made until January, 1804, when, by the increase of its population, the inconvenience of conducting town affairs, in general meetings, became more apparent to the inhabitants. A large committee[3] was, in conse-

[1] The members of the committee were, — James Sullivan, Charles Jarvis, Thomas Dawes, Jr., Judge Paine, William Tudor, Caleb Davis, Benjamin Austin, Jr., Jonathan Mason, Jr., Stephen Higginson, William Eustis, Christopher Gore, William Little, John Q. Adams, Edward Edes, John Lucas, Thomas Tileston, James Prince, Thomas Edwards, Paul Revere, Edward Tyler, Charles Bulfinch.

[2] The following is a brief outline of the system reported: —

1. That the town be divided into nine wards, as equal as may be in point of the numbers of the inhabitants of each, which the selectmen might change, if they saw fit, once in three years.

2. Each ward to elect two men residing in the ward, who, with the selectmen, should constitute a town council, and possess the following powers: —

First, of making by-laws with limited penalties. No by-law to be enacted, until it shall have had three several readings on three several days, and shall have been published for the inspection of the inhabitants; nor be perpetual until reënacted by a subsequent town council, by the same formalities.

Second, to regulate all public carriages within the town, and to raise duties upon them.

Third, that the town council have power to appoint annually all the executive officers then appointed by the town, except selectmen, town clerk, overseers of the poor, assessors, town treasurer, school committees, auditors of accounts, firewards, collectors of taxes, and constables.

Fourth, to direct prosecutions for violations of the by-laws, and for this purpose to appoint an attorney.

Fifth, to apply to the General Court for the establishment of a tribunal with one judge, having exclusive jurisdiction of such prosecutions.

[3] The members of this committee were as follows: —

Josiah Snelling, Ozias Goodwin, Robert Gardner, Jacob Rhoades, Redford

quence, appointed, composed of persons very equally selected from the two political parties, which, at that time, divided the town and commonwealth, with instructions to consider and report any alteration in the town government they deemed expedient.

They had frequent meetings and long deliberations, and in March reported to the inhabitants a system [1] of municipal government, in which they had carefully endeavored to combine a strict regard to the efficiency of the new organization of authority, with as little offence as possible to the prejudices and habits of the inhabitants. Notwithstanding this endeavor, and, although the composition of the committee had effectually neutralized all political elements, the inherent attachment of the inhabitants to the form of town government was not diminished. A warm, and somewhat tumultuous debate ensued, resulting in a decided negative of the whole report.

No farther attempt to change the town organization occurred until 1815, when Charles Bulfinch, who had been chairman of the board of selectmen and superintendent of police ever since the year 1800, and two other efficient members of that board, were not reëlected. The circumstance was a subject of very general surprise and regret. Every elected member of the board of selectmen immediately resigned, and, on a second trial, Mr. Bulfinch [2]

Webster, Thomas Lewis, Jr., Amasa Stetson, Samuel Sturges, Thomas Edwards, Nathan Webb, Isaiah Doane, Joseph Hall, William Spooner, James Prince, William Smith, Edward Gray, Harrison G. Otis, Rufus Green Amory, James Sullivan, George Blake, John Davis, Charles Jarvis, William Brown, and Charles Paine.

[1] The following outline will give a sufficient general idea of this system: —

A town council to be constituted of the selectmen, chosen by the citizens in general meeting, and of two delegates from each ward, chosen in ward meetings. By this town council an intendant and all other town officers were to be chosen; except the town clerk, the overseers of the poor, board of health, firewards, school committee, and assessors, all of whom were to be chosen by the inhabitants in town meeting; the intendant to have the appointment of a police officer, and to be *ex officio* the presiding officer of the board of selectmen, and with them to have the superintendence of the police and execution of the laws.

[2] Few men deserve to be held by the citizens of Boston in more grateful remembrance than Charles Bulfinch. After being graduated at Harvard, his father, a physician of eminence and fortune, permitted him to travel in Europe and cultivate his taste for the fine arts. On his return, he turned his attention to the improvement of his native town, and induced other citizens of wealth and enterprise to unite with him in the purchase of a portion of waste and marsh land, in forming it into streets, and erecting a range of buildings, now known as Franklin Place. The cenotaph of Franklin and the open space around it were given by him and his associates to the public. This undertaking, which was too

and the other members of the board of the preceding year were reinstated by decided majorities.

These occurrences again directed public attention to the disadvantages of town government, and, on the petition of a large number of the inhabitants, a committee formed of two individuals, elected in each ward, was authorized to consider the expediency of a change of the government.

In October, 1815, this committee[1] presented a bill, accompanied by an explanatory report, which were printed for general distribution, and a town meeting was called on the thirteenth of November ensuing, to decide upon its acceptance. The system now proposed, was the nearest approximation to a city form of government any previous committee of the town had ventured to attempt,[2] and the result came nearest to success, it being rejected only by a majority of thirty-one; nine hundred and fifty-one being in the negative, and nine hundred and twenty in the affirmative.

expensive for the period, seriously affected his fortunes, and the art he had studied for amusement became his profession. As the principal architect of the town of Boston and its vicinity, the state house and many other public buildings were erected on his plans. During the many years he presided over the town government, he improved its finances, executed the laws with firmness, and was distinguished for gentleness and urbanity of manners, integrity and purity of character. Under his superintendence, Faneuil Hall was enlarged to double its ancient area, and the streets of the town greatly improved. In 1818, he was appointed by President Monroe architect of the Capitol at the city of Washington.

1 The members were, — John Phillips, John T. Apthorp, Ebenezer T. Andrews, Francis Welsh, John Mackay, Lynde Walter, Jonathan Whitney, William Homer, Jacob Rhoades, Thomas Badger, J. C. Rainsford, John Cotton, Redford Webster, A. Crocker, William Mackay, John Wood, Joseph Howe, James Robinson, Benjamin Smith, Josiah Quincy, George Blake, Benjamin West.

2 The following outline will give a sufficient general idea of this plan: —

The style or title for the municipal organization was proposed to be, — "The Intendant and Municipality of the Town and City of Boston." The municipality to consist of the selectmen chosen by all the citizens in town meeting, and of two delegates from each ward chosen by the inhabitants of the ward. This municipality to have power to elect annually all the officers now chosen by the town, except selectmen, overseers of the poor, school committee, town clerk, firewards, board of health, and assessors, who were to continue to be chosen by the inhabitants at large in town meeting. The "intendant" was to be chosen annually by the selectmen and delegates, together with the overseers of the poor and board of health. The powers to be exercised, according to this project, by the intendant and the other organic bodies it constituted, were marked out with sufficient general precision; and as all the then existing boards were continued, and to two of them a voice was given, in conjunction with the municipality, in the election of the intendant, it was hoped that a sufficient deference had been paid to popular habit and feelings, to insure its adoption.

In 1821, the impracticability of conducting the municipal interests of the place, under the form of town government, became apparent to the inhabitants. With a population upwards of *forty thousand*, and with *seven thousand qualified voters*, it was evidently impossible calmly to deliberate and act. When a town meeting was held on any exciting subject in Faneuil Hall, those only who obtained places near the moderator could even hear the discussion. A few busy or interested individuals easily obtained the management of the most important affairs, in an assembly in which the greater number could have neither voice or hearing.

When the subject was not generally exciting, town meetings were usually composed of the selectmen, the town officers, and thirty or forty inhabitants. Those who thus came were, for the most part, drawn to it from some official duty or private interest, which, when performed or attained, they generally troubled themselves but little, or not at all, about the other business of the meeting. In assemblies thus composed, by-laws were passed; taxes, to the amount of one hundred or one hundred and fifty thousand dollars, voted, on statements often general in their nature, and on reports, as it respects the majority of voters present, taken upon trust, and which no one had carefully considered except perhaps the chairman.

In the constitution of the town government there had resulted in the course of time, from exigency or necessity, a complexity, little adapted to produce harmony in action, and an irresponsibility irreconcilable with a wise and efficient conduct of its affairs. On the agents of the town there was no direct check or control; no pledge for fidelity, but their own honor and sense of character. The prosperity of the town of Boston, under such a form of government; the few defalcations which had occurred; the frequent, and often for years uninterrupted, reëlection of the same members to the officiating boards, are conclusive evidences of the prevailing high state of morals and intelligence among the inhabitants.

Besides the principal boards of selectmen, the overseers of the poor, and that of health, there were the board of firewards, of assessors, and of the committee of the schools. The executive power was, in effect, divided among the three first above-named. Each of these claimed independence of the other; each possessed a qualified control in respect of expenditures; while, at the same time, their respective authorities were often obscurely separated, and sometimes identical. It is evident that, among independent boards thus constituted, petty jealousies, rivalry, and collisions must occasionally take place; which accordingly happened.

The management of the finances of the town presented a curious and somewhat anomalous spectacle. The three boards, of selectmen, overseers of the poor, and board of health, being the exclusive expending agents of the town, were also constituted a committee of finance. They chose annually, in convention, the treasurer and collector of the town, settled his accounts, and every year, in the month of March, presented to the town a general statement of the expenditure of each board; and, after deducting the effective incomes, an estimate of the amount of tax necessary to be raised, to meet the anticipated expenditures of all the boards for the ensuing year. The tax thus proposed was often voted at a town meeting, in which the members of those boards themselves constituted a majority of the inhabitants present. When raised and collected, the proceeds of the tax were drawn for by each of these boards, according to their respective exigencies, of which each board was the sole judge for itself. Thus, while these boards were exclusively the expending power, they virtually exercised the whole power of taxation. For the annual town tax was almost ever, without exception, regulated by their estimates; and each board having, individually, or in conjunction with the other boards, the power of borrowing money and of making contracts, independent of any previous vote of the town, both the power of forming and declaring the requisite annual amount of tax was, in fact, in their hands. A conviction of the want of safety and of responsibility in a machine thus complicated and loosely combined, became at length so general, that the inherited and inveterate antipathy to a city organization began perceptibly to diminish. About this time, also, one of the most common and formal objections to a city organization was removed. The constitution of Massachusetts, which was passed in 1780, contained no express authority to establish a city organization; and, in every attempt to change that of the town, it never failed to be zealously contended, that the legislature of the commonwealth possessed no such power. But by the amendments to the constitution, made by the convention of 1820, and adopted by the people, this power was expressly recognized. The question, therefore, now stood on its own merits, and independent of constitutional objections. The debates, also, which occurred in this convention had a tendency to open the eyes of the inhabitants to their own interests, and to allay some of the long-cherished prejudices against a city organization.

The first step to the measures which finally led to this great change in the form of town government was rather incidental than preconcerted, and was the result of circumstances, which might be anticipated from the complicated and ill-arranged organization of the town system.

Early in the commencement of the civil year, 1821, votes had passed in town meeting, for uniting the office of county and town treasurer in one person. The three boards constituting the committee of finance had disregarded those votes, and different persons were chosen to these offices.

This proceeding was highly disapproved by the inhabitants. Votes were passed in town meeting censuring the committee of finance; and a committee was chosen to take measures for carrying into effect their views relative to the union of those offices in one person.

About the same time, great discontent arose in respect to the county expenditures; and a committee was chosen to devise measures that the town might become a county by itself. Very full reports were made by both these committees, and a very general desire became apparent, that a more economical and practical management of the town concerns should be effected. Accordingly, on the twenty-second of October, a committee of thirteen inhabitants[1] was selected, to whom the two former reports were referred, with instructions to report to the town "a complete system relating to the administration of the town and county, which shall remedy the present evils."

[1] The members of this committee were, — John Phillips, William Sullivan, Charles Jackson, Josiah Quincy, William Prescott, William Tudor, George Blake, Henry Orne, Daniel Webster, Isaac Winslow, Lemuel Shaw, Stephen Codman, Joseph Tilden.

On the tenth of December, 1821, this committee made their report;[1] but did not venture to go farther than to recommend some improvements in the government of the town; and directed their principal endeavors to the establishing of a police court, consisting of three justices paid by salaries, instead of a court of sessions, paid by fees; and to effect the transfer of the transaction of the financial and other business of the town from a general meeting of the inhabitants to a town council. The committee did not deem the inhabitants to be prepared to change the form of the executive of the town; they, therefore, left it in the hands of the selectmen, with such powers as the town council might from time to time confer on them.

After considerable debate, Benjamin Russell, an inhabitant at that period distinguished for his great activity and influence on all occasions of political excitement, popular with the party predominating at that time in the politics of the town, and a leader among the mechanics, openly declared that the committee "had not gone far enough in its alterations, and, in his opinion, a great change had been effected in the minds of the inhabitants on the subject of city government," and concluded his remarks, by moving "that the report should be recommitted to the same committee, with the addition of one person from each ward of the town, with instructions to report a system for the government of the town, with such powers, privileges, and immunities as are contemplated by the amendment of the constitution of the commonwealth, authorizing the General Court to constitute a city government." This motion was accordingly adopted, and twelve persons chosen and added to the former committee.[2]

On the thirty-first of December, 1821, this committee of twenty-

1 Of this system the following is a brief outline: —

The town government to be thus altered, — a body of assistants, to be chosen annually in the wards, in a ratio of one for each nine hundred inhabitants, which, according to the then last census, would constitute the number of forty-one. These assistants, with the selectmen, were to form a town council, and be charged with specified powers, and subject to specified restrictions.

The town to form a county by itself; and the treasurer of the town to be that of the county. The Court of Sessions to be abolished, and its duties transferred to other bodies.

A police court to be established, to have cognizance of all civil and criminal causes cognizable by justices of the peace.

2 This addition to the committee was constituted of George Darracott, Redford Webster, Thomas Badger, James Davis, Henry Farnham, Michael Roulstone, John Cotton, Lewis G. Pray, Benjamin Russell, William Sturgis, Daniel Messinger, and Gerry Fairbanks.

five reported a system of municipal government conformably to their instructions, recommending indeed a change of the name of "town" for that of "city," but not venturing to introduce the names usual in city organizations, lest the ancient jealousy, which now seemed to slumber, should be awakened. In their stead, the committee proposed that the executive should be called "Intendant," the executive board, consisting of seven persons, "Selectmen," and the more numerous branch "a Board of Assistants;" all of whom, in their aggregate capacity, should be called "the Common Council." The intendant to be elected by the selectmen; the selectmen by general ticket; the assistants, being forty-eight in number, four to be chosen for each ward; the overseers of the poor, firewards, and school committee, by the intendant, selectmen, and assistants; the state and United States officers by general ticket.

After a debate of three days, in which the report was amended, by denominating the executive board "Mayor and Aldermen," the latter to consist of eight persons, the name of the "Board of Assistants" being also changed into that of the "Common Council," and, in their aggregate capacity, "the City Council," the mayor, aldermen, overseers of the poor, firewards, state, and United States officers to be chosen by the citizens at large, voting in wards, the report was so far accepted as to be submitted to the inhabitants for their acceptance. On the points connected with these amendments, the debate in town meeting chiefly turned; but little opposition was made, or modifications proposed, to those features of the plan, which related to the distribution and limitations of powers among the several branches of the government, or to the organization of the police court.

During the debate of the three days, considerable warmth was manifested, and some confusion occurred; but the report, as amended, was finally submitted to the inhabitants for their sanction, in the form of five resolves, to be decided by ballot of yea and nay. Of which the tenor was as follows:—

1. That we approve of the alteration in the form of town government submitted by this report.

2. That the United States and commonwealth officers be chosen in ward meetings.

3. That the city council determine the number of representatives to the General Court.

4. That we approve that the town should be a county by itself, and that the town treasurer be county treasurer, that the court of sessions be abolished, and a police court substituted.

5. That the name of "Town of Boston" should be changed into that of "City of Boston."

On Monday, the seventh of January, 1822, the ballots of the inhabitants were taken on the above resolves, and all were passed in the affirmative as follows: —

	Yeas.	*Nays.*	*Majority.*
1.	2805	2006	799
2.	2611	2195	416
3.	2690	2128	462
4.	4557	257	4300
5.	2727	2087	640

The assent of the inhabitants being thus expressed in favor of this great change, measures were immediately taken to obtain the sanction of the legislature of the commonwealth.

CHAPTER III.

TOWN GOVERNMENT. 1821-1822.

The Almshouse removed from Beacon Street to Leverett Street — Overseers of the Poor remonstrate on its Condition — Proceedings of the Legislature of Massachusetts on the Subject of Pauperism — Erection of a House of Industry authorized by the Inhabitants of Boston — Noble Conduct of Samuel Brown — His Character — House of Industry erected — Act of Incorporation of the City obtained and accepted — John Phillips chosen Mayor.

The defects and insufficiency of the Boston Almshouse became a subject of earnest complaint soon after Massachusetts attained the rank of an independent state. By a report of a committee of the town in the year 1790, it appears that it was destitute of a separate hospital or infirmary; that persons of every age and character were lodged under the same roof; the sick disturbed by the noise of the healthy; and the aged and infirm endangered and annoyed by the diseased and profligate. All attempts to change the locality of the institution were unsuccessful until the year 1801, when an almshouse was erected in Leverett Street, and that in Beacon Street discontinued and the land sold.

The new building was of enlarged dimensions and accommodations, but its interior arrangements did not permit the separation of age and misfortune from vice and vagrancy. In 1802, one year after the removal of the almshouse to Leverett Street, the importance of erecting another building, for a house of correction, was forcibly urged on the town by a committee of the selectmen, of which Charles Bulfinch was chairman, accompanied by estimates of the probable cost. Its immediate erection was, however, postponed, on account of the pecuniary exigencies of the town. No further proceedings occurred until 1812, when the Overseers of the Poor themselves memorialized the town on the inconveniences of the Leverett Street Almshouse, and stated that among *four hundred* persons, then its inmates, *nearly three hundred* were aged, or invalids, or children; *fifty* were sick in the hospital, and *twenty* insane; that *fifty* were able to perform different kinds of work, some of whom were subjects of the House of Correction; and with much feeling and pathos urged upon the town the necessity of erecting a building for that purpose, in the yard of the Almshouse, and prayed for authority and an appropriation for the object. The report was unanimously accepted by the town, but nothing was effected in consequence; and the condition of the poor in the Almshouse continued without amelioration.

In 1820, the state of pauperism attracted the attention of the legislature of Massachusetts; and on the motion of one[1] of the representatives of the town of Boston, a special committee was raised on the pauper laws, of which the mover was appointed chairman.

On the recommendation of this committee, the legislature passed a resolve, requesting the towns in Massachusetts to transmit to the secretary of state such information as their experience had suggested, on the best mode of supporting the poor. In January, 1821, the returns of the towns were referred to the same committee, who made a report containing abstracts of the most important statements in those returns, and of their conclusions on the subject, which were printed by order of the legislature, and distributed throughout the Commonwealth.

In May following, the town of Boston, on the petition of Joseph May and others, raised a committee to consider the subject of "pauperism at large." Of this committee, the chairman of the legislative committee was also appointed chairman, and not having been present at the town meeting, he had no knowledge of the petition, until he was apprised by the petitioners that the cause of his selection, as the chairman of the committee, was the coincidence of their views with the principles of his legislative report. That committee, therefore, in general, guided their proceedings by those principles, and referred to them in their reports to the town, which, being successively sanctioned by the votes of the inhabitants, became the basis of the institution now called "the House of Industry," at South Boston.

The principles of that report to the legislature, being the results of the experience of both England and Massachusetts, were as follows: —

[1] Josiah Quincy.

"1. That of all modes of providing for the poor, the most wasteful, the most expensive, and most injurious to their morals, and destructive of their industrious habits, is that of supply in their own families.

"2. That the most economical mode is that of almshouses, having the character of workhouses or houses of industry, in which work is provided for every degree of ability in the pauper, and thus the able poor made to provide, partially, at least, for their own support; and also the support, or at least the comfort, of the impotent poor.

"3. That of all modes of employing the labor of the pauper, agriculture affords the best, the most healthy, and the most certainly profitable; the poor being thus enabled to raise always at least their own provisions.

"4. That the success of these establishments depends upon their being placed under the superintendence of a board of overseers, constituted of the most substantial and intelligent inhabitants of the vicinity.

"5. That of all causes of pauperism, intemperance in the use of spirituous liquors is the most powerful and universal."

Coinciding in the above views, the committee of the town of Boston[1] held frequent meetings and discussions; and examined particularly into the situation of the Boston Almshouse. Their views were corroborated and confirmed by a report made to them, at their request, by the Overseers of the Poor of the town, dated the twenty-ninth of March, 1821, which stated that only thirty-six rooms could be appropriated to lodging the inmates of the institution; that these rooms *ought not to have more than eight or ten persons each*, but that some of these rooms have been, in some winters, *crowded to nearly double that number* for a short time; that the overseers could not distinguish the cases of the deserving and undeserving by any certain rule, but that not more than one fourth part were absolutely of the former class; and that the others might be graduated from temporary to absolute dissoluteness, intemperance, &c.

The report further stated, that the old almshouse included

[1] This committee were, — Josiah Quincy, Joseph Lovering, James Savage, Henry J. Oliver, Francis Welsh, Joseph May, Thomas Howe, William Thurston, Abram Babcock, Samuel A. Welles, James T. Austin, Benjamin Rich, and Joseph Woodward.

three distinct establishments, — the almshouse, the workshop, and the bridewell. The first for the poor, who, from sickness, age, or infirmity, were unable to work at all; the second, for the poor who were able to work, more or less; the third, for persons committed on justices' warrants, for petty offences. That in December, 1800, the building in Leverett Street was erected and intended for an almshouse; but that "no building had been erected either for a workhouse or bridewell, and that, therefore, from necessity, the inhabitants of the three establishments were obliged to be all taken into the Almshouse, which had been thus occupied from the year 1800 to the date of that report, without the possibility of classing or separating them.

After receiving this report from the overseers, the committee visited Salem, Marblehead, and Cambridge, and minutely examined their respective almshouses; and in May, 1821, made a report embracing the same general views and arguments as those contained in the legislative report, and showing the success of similar institutions in other towns of the state, and urged on the inhabitants of Boston the duty of discriminating between the poor, by reason of misfortune, old age, and infancy, and the poor, by reason of vice; asserting the impossibility of making such a discrimination in the Boston Almshouse, and, after setting forth the advantages of having attached to the house erected for the poor a tract of land to give them the benefit of air, employment, and exercise, and the town that of their labor, concluded with recommending the establishment of a house of industry, with an extent of land not less than fifty acres, that twenty thousand dollars should be appropriated for its commencement, and authority given to purchase the land and erect such buildings as might be necessary.

This report was accepted by the inhabitants, the appropriation voted, and a committee appointed to carry it into effect.[1]

At the time this report was presented, the committee had selected as the most eligible locality for the proposed institution, that beautiful hill and site, commanding a view of Boston and its whole harbor, where the House of Industry, of Correction,

1 This committee was composed of the same individuals as the former, except that David W. Child, John Bellows, John French, and George Darracott were substituted for Messrs. Austin, Lovering, May, and Woodward, who declined longer service upon it.

and of Juvenile Offenders are now (1851) erected, being at that time an open country, with comparatively no inhabitants in its vicinity. The tract of land, including upwards of sixty acres, with an immense extent of flats annexed to them, was then the property of Samuel Brown, a merchant, distinguished on the Boston Exchange for his integrity and capacity; and it is due to the memory of this noble spirited individual, that a fact relative to this purchase should be here recorded.

As soon as the committee had agreed on the eligibility of this estate for the location of the House of Industry, the chairman waited on Mr. Brown, and fully explained their plans, and that if authorized by the town, they wished to purchase it for that purpose, if it could be obtained for a fair price. Mr. Brown replied, that he highly approved the object, thought the situation an eligible one, and that he had valued the land at *one hundred dollars* an acre, at which price the committee should have it, provided an authority should be obtained to purchase, and a selection made of it by the committee within three weeks. On being asked to make that promise in writing, he declined; saying only, "on the terms above expressed, you shall have the whole tract, being sixty- [illegible] three [illegible] acres for six thousand three hundred dollars." ×

A vote of the town was accordingly obtained, and the committee authorized the chairman, within the three weeks, to close the bargain with Mr. Brown on the terms specified. On stating the facts to that gentleman, he replied,—"Mr. Quincy, you know the agreement was verbal, and not binding in law; and since our interview I have been offered *five hundred dollars an acre* for my land, making a difference to me over your offer of upwards of *twenty-five thousand dollars*. However, sir, I like the object. I think the land uncommonly well adapted to it. You have my word, and I am not disposed to fall back from it. You shall have my deed." This was accordingly prepared immediately and executed. The value of the lands in that vicinity immediately rose to one thousand dollars an acre, and at no subsequent period could they have been purchased for less.

Samuel Brown had been the architect of his own fortunes, was active, judicious, and punctual, as a man of business; of a high sense of honor, distinguished for his readiness to assist his friends with his advice and his fortune; public spirited, without ostenta-

× In 1872, this estate is worth millions.—

tion or any selfish views in exhibiting it. Respect for his memory should ever be cherished by the citizens of Boston.

The estate thus obtained, was laid out by the committee, the House of Industry erected upon it, and on the twenty-second of October, they presented a detailed report, stating the peculiar adaptation of the situation to the wants of the contemplated institution to be altogether unequalled; the soil being excellent and various; the distance from the centre of the town, only two and a half miles by land and one and a half by water, with a certainty that the facility of communication must daily increase, and the natural growth of the town soon intimately connect the site with the ancient parts of it; that the building erected was two hundred and twenty feet in length, forty-three feet broad, twenty-nine feet high; that strength, durability, and adaptation to the wants of the inmates had been consulted without special regard to the gratification of taste or architectural effect.

The committee received the thanks of the town, and an additional appropriation of six thousand dollars was voted for the object.

On the twenty-eighth of March, 1822, the committee made their last report to the town. The inhabitants had, prior to this meeting, accepted the charter for a city, which the legislature had granted, and which was to be organized on the May ensuing. In this report the committee represent the progress of the work; recall the attention of the inhabitants to the original design of the institution; moral effect; separation of the idle and vicious poor from those of an opposite character, secluding them from any occasional intercourse with the populous parts of the town and their old haunts, affording to them moral and religious instruction; relieving the town from open drunkenness and street beggary, and the petty pilfering carried on by children of the idle and vicious poor, on the wharves, in the streets and the market-places, and thereby, if possible, diminish also the expenses of the town. The inhabitants accepted the report; placed the additional appropriation asked for at the disposal of the committee; authorized them to provide for the care of the house and land, to prepare a system for the general conduct and management of the institution, and to lay the same before the city authorities, who were requested to take the subject into their early consideration, and to carry the same into effective operation; the overseers being also requested to deliver over any of the able-bodied poor, on the application of the committee, to be employed at the House of Industry.

This was the last meeting, and one of the last acts, of the "town of Boston;" and in this position the subject of the House of Industry stood at the organization of the city government in May, 1822.

After the peace of 1783, the increase of the population of the town of Boston was slow and gradual, amounting in 1790 to about eighteen thousand; in 1800, to twenty-five thousand; in 1810, to thirty-three thousand; and in 1820, to forty-three thousand, which may be regarded, with sufficient accuracy, the number of inhabitants at the period of the change of Boston from a town to a city. During the latter years of the town government, the data for its financial history are very complete and satisfactory, and evidence the wisdom and fidelity with which its affairs had been conducted. The only debt transferred from the town to the city government but little exceeded *seventy-one thousand dollars*, which was wholly incurred by the cost of two prisons, then in the course of erection, and a new court house. If little had been done by the town government for the widening of streets and increasing the general comfort of the inhabitants, expenditures had been kept within its incomes, and the resources of the town were unembarrassed and unimpaired.

The property delivered over by the town to the city was large and valuable, but unproductive, consisting chiefly of lands on the Neck or the islands, and the market under Faneuil Hall. The entire annual income of this property did not exceed eighteen thousand dollars.

The measures taken to obtain from the legislature of Massachusetts a charter of incorporation were successful; and, on the twenty-third of February, 1822, an act passed that body, entitled "An Act Establishing the City of Boston," commonly called "The City Charter."

In conformity with its provisions, the inhabitants assembled in general meeting on the fourth of March ensuing, and accepted the act by vote, taken by ballot, by a majority of nine hundred and sixteen. The whole number being four thousand six hundred and seventy-eight, of which two thousand seven hundred and ninety-seven voted in the affirmative, and one thousand eight hundred and eighty-one in the negative.

On the eighth of April ensuing, a meeting of the citizens was held for the election of city officers. The whole number of votes for mayor was three thousand seven hundred and eight. They were chiefly divided between Harrison Gray Otis, and Josiah Quincy; but neither having a majority, no choice was effected.

Immediately on this result, Mr. Otis and Mr. Quincy each declined being a candidate for the office. On the sixteenth of April, John Phillips was elected mayor with great unanimity.[1]

[1] The following brief outline of the principal features of this charter will enable those who have not the means of being familiar with its details, to compare its general provisions with the former unsuccessful attempts to obtain an act of incorporation for the city: —

1. The title of the corporation to be, "The City of Boston."

2. The control of all its concerns are vested in a mayor; a board of aldermen, consisting of eight; and a common council, of forty-eight inhabitants; to be called, when conjoined, "The City Council."

3. The city to be divided into twelve wards. The mayor and aldermen, and the common council, to be chosen annually by ballot, by and from inhabitants; four of the common council from and by those of each of the wards.

4. The city clerk to be chosen by the city council.

5. The mayor to receive a salary. His duty — to be vigilant and active in causing the laws to be executed; to inspect the conduct of all subordinate officers; to cause carelessness, negligence, and positive violation of the laws, to be prosecuted and punished; to summon meetings of either and both boards; to communicate and recommend measures for the improvement of the finances, the police, health, security, cleanliness, comfort, and ornament of the city.

6. The mayor and aldermen are vested with the administration of the police, and executive power of the corporation generally, with specific enumerated powers.

7. All other powers belonging to the corporation are vested in the mayor, aldermen, and common council, to be exercised by concurrent vote.

CHAPTER IV.

CITY GOVERNMENT. 1822-1823.

JOHN PHILLIPS, *Mayor.*[1]

Inauguration — Address of the Selectmen, on surrendering the Government and Muniments of the Town of Boston — Reply of the Mayor — Measures adopted to carry into effect the City Charter — Donation of Mr. Sears — Proceedings relative to the House of Industry — Result of the First Year's Administration of the City Government — Tribute to Mr. Phillips.

THE city government was organized, for the first time, on Wednesday, the first of May, 1822, with a solemnity adapted to the general interest excited by the occasion, and the great advantages anticipated from the new powers conferred by the city charter.

A platform was raised at the west end of Faneuil Hall, with seats for the mayor, aldermen, and city council; the selectmen of the past year, with other town authorities, and the chief officers of the Commonwealth. The floor of the house and the galleries were filled with a crowded assembly. The city charter, inclosed in a silver case, was laid upon a table in front of the city council. After prayer, offered by the Rev. Thomas Baldwin, D.D., the oldest settled clergyman in Boston, the oaths of allegiance and of office were administered to John Phillips, the mayor elect, by Isaac Parker, Chief Justice of the Commonwealth; and afterwards, by the mayor, to the aldermen and common council.

The chairman of the last board of selectmen[2] then rose and addressed the convention, stating the grant of a city charter by the legislature of the State to the inhabitants of Boston; their

[1] The whole number of votes cast at this election for city officers were 2650; of which Mr. Phillips had 2500. The aldermen elected were: —

Samuel Billings,	Joseph Jenkins,
Ephraim Eliot,	Joseph Lovering,
Jacob Hall,	Nathaniel P. Russell,
Joseph Head,	Bryant P. Tilden.

[2] Eliphalet Williams.

acceptance of it; their election of the members of the respective executive and legislative boards; the presence of these boards, and their complete organization, according to the provisions of the city charter. In obedience, therefore, to the law, and in conformity with the will of the inhabitants of Boston, and in behalf of the selectmen of the ancient town, he delivered into the charge of the new authorities the town records and title deeds, and the act establishing the city of Boston. He then concluded with congratulating his fellow-citizens on the organization of their municipal affairs under a city charter, and on the wisdom with which they had selected those who were destined to give the first impulse and direction to the operations of the new government.

The Mayor, in reply, paid a just tribute to the wisdom of our ancestors, as displayed in the institutions for the government of the town of Boston, under which, for nearly two centuries, so great a degree of prosperity had been attained, and during which the great increase of the population of the place had alone made this change in the administration of its affairs essential. He then responded to the congratulations and civilities of the Chairman; acknowledged the obligations of the city government for the care the selectmen had taken in providing for the accommodation of their successors; and bore testimony to the full evidence, exhibited by the records, of the ability, diligence, and integrity of those who had been successively, and justly, denominated "The Fathers of the Town."

The Mayor then proceeded to remark, in respect of those "who encouraged hopes, which could never be realized, and of those who indulged unreasonable apprehensions, in regard to the city charter, that they would derive benefit from reflecting, how much social happiness depended on other causes than the provisions of a charter. Purity of manners; general diffusion of knowledge; strict attention to the education of the young; and, above all, a firm, practical belief in Divine revelation and its sanctions, will counteract the evils of any form of government; and, while love of order, benevolent dispositions, and Christian piety, distinguish, as they have done, the inhabitants of Boston, they may enjoy the highest blessings under a charter with so few imperfections as that which the wisdom of the legislature had sanctioned."[1]

[1] See Appendix A.

After retiring from Faneuil Hall, the members of the respective boards met in separate rooms, and the common council, having chosen their president[1] and clerk,[2] both boards assembled in convention and elected a city clerk.[3] They then, respectively, in their separate chambers, proceeded to the consideration of business requiring immediate attention; established rules and orders regulating the intercourse between the two boards; passed orders continuing in force the by-laws of the late town; establishing rules and regulations for the preservation of public health, and for the appointment of temporary health commissioners. And in due course of the ensuing and succeeding months, all the various measures, for the choice of city officers, and for the efficient organization of the different departments incident to city police, and required by law, were taken; and, as far as practicable, the customs and forms to which the citizens had been familiarized under the government of the town, were adopted. Three surveyors of highways were appointed, and also a committee of the board of aldermen for their advisement. The city engines were intrusted to the firewards. Salaries for the respective city officers voted. A board, consisting of a joint committee of the two boards, denominated "Auditors of City Accounts," was constituted, whose prescribed duty it was to audit them, to report cases of difficulty, with their opinion, to the city council, monthly. The amount of each account, when sanctioned by them, was drawn for, on the city treasurer, by the city clerk.

A city seal was adopted, its impression exhibiting a general view of the city of Boston, with the respective dates of the foundation of the city and of the grant of its charter, bearing the motto, "*Sicut Patribus sit Deus nobis.*" In December of this year a vote passed both boards, authorizing an application to the legislature for investing the mayor and aldermen with the power of surveyors of highways. No further steps were taken, however, to effect this change in the provisions of the city charter.

Early in 1823, a collision of opinion occurred between the mayor and aldermen and the common council, concerning the interest of the city, which brought before those authorities, for distinct consideration, the question, whether the mayor and aldermen had the power to receive a gift, upon condition, for the

[1] William Prescott. [2] Thomas Clarke.
[3] Samuel F. McCleary.

benefit of the city, without the concurrence of the common council. David Sears, a citizen distinguished for wealth, liberality, and public spirit, had transferred rights, consisting of *six hundred shares* in certain lands and buildings, near the public market of the city, called "Museum Hall," of the estimated value of sixty thousand dollars, to the mayor and aldermen of the city, on condition that the whole property should be vested and managed by them at their discretion; and one half of the income, forever, paid over to Mr. Sears or his heirs, and the other half be applied to improving or ornamenting the lands of the city, lighting the streets, and other specified objects. This donation was received unanimously by the mayor and aldermen. And, so much pleased were they with the gift, that, at their suggestion, Mr. Sears, at some labor and expense, possessed himself of the whole remaining rights in those lands and buildings, consisting of *two hundred* additional shares, of the estimated value of sixteen hundred dollars, and transferred them to the same board, on like conditions. The arrangement had proceeded thus far before it was communicated to the common council; and, when apprized of this transaction, that board took it into very serious consideration by a committee, and finally voted unanimously that it was not for the interest of the city to accept the donation. Whatever other motives may have mingled in producing the rejection of this gift, the principal reason stated was, that it would interfere with the profitable employment of the property which the city then held, and thus prove ultimately injurious to it.

The consequent embarrassment of the mayor and aldermen was of course excessive; which was increased by the declaration of the committee of the common council to the donor, that, although it might be a complete contract between him and the present mayor and aldermen, as individuals, it would not bind their successors, as the transaction had not the concurrence of the common council.

From the dilemma in which the mayor and aldermen were thus involved they were immediately relieved, in a highly honorable manner, by Mr. Sears; who, in writing, requested them to reinvest him with the property, preferring to bear the great loss to which he was thus subjected, rather than be the occasion of any embarrassment to that body, or any cause of controversy between the two boards. The reinvestment was accordingly made; and a vote passed by the mayor and aldermen, expressing their respectful sense of Mr. Sears's intentions and views, and their high approbation of his delicacy, in relieving the city government from the embarrassment in which it had been involved, by the different views taken by the common council and the board of aldermen of this donation.

During the first year of the city, its financial concerns were managed on a scale not materially varying, either in spirit or amount, from that of the town government. The committee on that subject expressed "their unqualified approbation of the manner in which the affairs of Boston have hitherto been conducted, throughout all the departments;" and their "hope, that changes, not absolutely necessary, will be made with caution and distrust, and with much consideration." These views had been carried into effect by the first administration, and this hope realized. No new debt had been created during the year. The expenses, both of the county and city, had been kept within their incomes; and the second administration received from the first all the property it had received from the town, unembarrassed and unimpaired.

Under the town government, the financial year had commenced on the first day of May. This year, its commencement was changed to the first day of June. The change was not found convenient; and in the year 1826, the first of May was again constituted its commencement.

In July, 1822, the sole existing debt of the city to be provided for, was stated to be $ 100,000.

The current expenses were estimated to amount, in round numbers, to		$ 249,000
And were provided for by loan of .	$ 28,000	
By specified ways and means . .	81,000	
And by a city tax	140,000	
		$ 249,000

The course pursued by the city government, in relation to the House of Industry, forms an important feature of its proceedings during this period. The first city council of Boston were organized on the first of May, 1822. On the third of that month, the committee on the House of Industry made a communication to the city council, recapitulating the authority given to them by the town, to prepare a system for the general conduct, management, and discipline of the institution; and informing that body that, by the laws of the Commonwealth, the power to devise such a system was specially invested in the Board of Overseers of the Poor, a fact which was not considered by the town when that vote was passed. The Committee, therefore, stated, that they had omitted the execution of that authority until they apprized the city government of that fact, and received their instructions. They also stated, that the House of Industry was far advanced towards its completion, and would be in a condition to receive tenants in five or six weeks; and suggested the expediency of an application to the legislature of the Commonwealth, or a reference of the subject to the Overseers of the Poor.

Several considerations induced the Committee to adopt this course. In the first place, doubts began to be entertained, whether the House of Industry would ever be put into operation. The Overseers made no concealment of their hostility to the plan of removing the poor to South Boston. It was known that there was a powerful influence at work in that body in favor of selling the House of Industry, and enlarging the accommodations in Leverett Street. It therefore could not be expected the Committee should assume the labor and responsibility of preparing the details of a system for an establishment which might never be carried into effect; and, if it were, might be placed in hands hostile or indifferent to the principle on which they might recommend it should be conducted. They were also apprehensive that, if they assumed, even under the vote of the town, the authority which the laws of the Commonwealth invested in the Overseers of the Poor, it might create an increased repugnance in them to the institution at South Boston.

The animosity of that board to this establishment will appear hereafter. It is here alluded to, as explaining why the House of Industry remained unoccupied the whole of the first year of the city government, and indicating the cause of the general course of proceeding during that year, in relation to it.

The communication of the Committee was referred by the City Council to the Overseers of the Poor, and to the Committee of the House of Industry; and they were requested, in conjunction, to take the subject into consideration, and to devise a plan for the superintendence and government of said house, such as they should deem useful, and report it to the City Council.

Those two bodies had, accordingly, several meetings on the subject, in which the Overseers made no concealment of their want of sympathy with the institution at South Boston; refused to be in any way concerned in its superintendence; and declined entering upon the consideration of a system for its discipline and management. The result of their deliberations was reported to the City Council by the Committee of the House of Industry: that the Board of Overseers and that Committee, after joint consideration, were unanimous in the opinion that, in the present increased and rapidly increasing state of this metropolis, and the necessarily extensive character of the contemplated institution, it would be impracticable for the Overseers of the Poor to undertake the management and discipline of said house; and recommended that an application should be made to the legislature of Massachusetts for the establishment of a new board, for these purposes, with powers similar to those now possessed by the Overseers of the Poor; reserving to the latter a concurrent power, of committing persons liable to be sent to that house. A bill was also prepared by the Committee, which, if approved by the City Council, they recommended as the basis of an act to be applied for to the State legislature. The City Council accepted the report, adopted the bill, and requested the representatives of the city to endeavor to obtain an act from the legislature in conformity with its provisions. Objections to the bill were raised, and nothing effectual done by the legislature during the spring session of that body.

In June, 1822, Mr. Brooks, chairman of the Committee of Finance, addressed a note to the chairman of the Committee of the House of Industry, inquiring concerning "the time and manner in which it was proposed to put that establishment into operation; and whether any further sums would be wanting from the city treasury?" To which it was replied, that, "in all essential and important particulars, the building had been erected within the appropriations; that furniture, fences, workshops, and subsidiary buildings were still to be provided. That the Committee of the House of Industry considered themselves only as agents, to carry into effect the wise and humane intentions of the inhabitants; that they wanted no additional appropriation; and that they were preparing to deliver up the house to the care of the city authorities, as soon as certain minor details were effected." This they accordingly did, on the sixteenth of September following, in a report stating the degree of completeness it had attained; and that, excepting fences and outbuildings, the establishment was ready for occupation. After recapitulating the several successive authorities under which the land had been purchased, the house built, and the amount expended, (forty thousand and one hundred dollars,) they expressed a hope, that the great and interesting objects the inhabitants of the town had in view in its foundation, might be attained under the wise management of the City Council; and that it might result, "as they cannot doubt it will, in much moral reformation among the poor, and in a considerable annual reduction in one of the heaviest branches of city expenditure."

The City Council referred this report to a joint committee; but before any proceedings occurred under that reference, a vote passed both branches of that body, on the twenty-third of the same month, implying a neglect of duty in the Committee of the House of Industry, in the following words: "Whereas, the Committee raised to erect a House of Industry were instructed in the month of March, 1821, '*to form a system for the conduct of that institution;*' and that Committee having reported that the house is nearly completed, *but that Committee not having reported any such system,* — voted, that the Mayor of the city be requested to call on that Committee to favor the city government with their opinion on the most expedient mode of putting the said institution to the uses intended by the establishment thereof."

The object of this vote was too apparent not to be perceived by the Committee of the House of Industry. They held an immediate meeting; and, on the thirty-first of October, their chairman, under their sanction, made a report, stating, in vindication of the Committee, "that, so far from neglecting the duty imposed upon them by the town, as the vote of the City Council indicated, that Committee did, on the third of May, two days after the organization of the city government, make a communication to the City Council, informing them that, by the laws of the Commonwealth, the power to devise such a system for the poor, as the vote of the town indicated, was vested alone in the

Overseers of the Poor; that the City Council had thereupon referred that subject to the Overseers of the Poor and the Committee of the House of Industry; that, on the seventeenth of May, those two bodies met in convention, agreed upon the provisions of a bill for the discipline and management of said house, which, having been subsequently modified in both branches of the City Council, had been referred to the representatives of the city, for the purpose of obtaining the sanction of the legislature; and that thus, the Committee of the House of Industry, so far from not having fulfilled the instructions of the town, as the vote of the City Council intimated, they had specifically performed it, as far as the nature of their powers authorized, and this, not only with the acquiescence, but under the sanction and with the assistance of the City Council which had passed this vote of implied censure.

Touching the most expedient mode of putting the institution to the uses proposed by those who established it, they intimated that the first step was to obtain the sanction of the legislature to the bill which the City Council had recommended; that, whenever such a bill should pass, and the superintending board of directors be elected, it would be easy to adopt a system for its discipline and management, by selecting and collating the wise rules which the experience of other towns in the Commonwealth had shown to be effectual for the attainment of the object the inhabitants of the town proposed to themselves by its establishment, namely, — 1st. To occupy the able-bodied poor on the land, thereby giving them a healthful exercise, and enabling them to contribute somewhat to their own support. 2d. By giving the sick and infirm poor a freer air, and enabling them to have a freer range for exercise, in a farm of fifty or sixty acres, than it was possible in thickly settled parts of the town to obtain. 3d. By removing them from the city, within which the necessity of allowing the inmates of the Almshouse an opportunity to take air and exercise, led to a practice of turning them weekly upon the inhabitants, subjecting families to a weekly visitation of vice and beggary; a practice not less annoying to the citizens, than it was incompatible with good order and discipline.

The Committee proceeded to state, that the want of an institution of this kind had long been felt, and had been urged on the town, by one of its committees, in the year 1802. Again, in 1812, the Overseers of the Poor themselves had memorialized the town on the subject of the inadequacy of the Boston Almshouse to the necessities of the town. In 1821, it had been taken up by the inhabitants, on their own voluntary motion; and that the House of Industry had been built, and the land on which it was located purchased, at an expense of nearly fifty thousand dollars. The Committee then proceeded to illustrate the views entertained by the friends of the institution, and to show how it was expected both to promote the comfort of the poor and diminish the expenditures of the town. They then illustrated the extraordinary convenience and adaptation of the location for such an institution; recommended its being put into immediate operation in the spirit and on the principles in which it originated, as soon as the ensuing season will permit; and tendered to the City Council their collective and individual communication of whatever knowledge or opinion they may possess on the subject of the government and discipline of the house, whenever the City Council should honor them with such a request.

This report was committed to a joint committee of the City Council, of which the Mayor, (John Phillips,) was chairman; who, on the twelfth of December following, reported to the City Council that they had examined the House of Industry and its buildings; that great credit was due to the Committee which had superintended it; that the Committee of the City Council were surprised to find so spacious and convenient a structure, with a wharf, barn, and house for a superintendent, completed for forty thousand dollars; *that whatever doubt the Committee might have felt in recommending the erection of such an establishment*, they declare their opinion that it ought now to be completed; and they recommend a further appropriation of five thousand dollars, to be placed at the disposal of the same Committee, who had so generously and faithfully superintended the erection of the building, to lay out the grounds and purchase implements of agriculture, and for the erection of additional outhouses.

As to the occupation of the house, the Committee of the City Council expressed great difficulty. They recommend, however, that such of the poor as were capable of labor should be removed to it, as soon as the contemplated improvements were completed, they being of opinion that the poor of the city would be more comfortably situated at South Boston than in the Boston Almshouse, the air being more pure, the buildings more commodious, the yard more spacious and comfortable; and they declared themselves not aware of any inconvenience which would attend their removal.

This report was accepted in the Board of Aldermen, and was the only step taken during the first year of the city government indicative of even an intent to carry the project of a transfer of the poor to South Boston into execution.

The measures proposed by the aldermen were, however, checked in the Common Council, by a vote recommitting the whole subject, and "instructing the Committee to report to what use the House of Industry may be put; and what difficulties present themselves, if any, in using the said house conformably to the original objects in creating said establishment; and that said Committee be requested to report in writing their opinion, in conformity to this vote; and that if said Committee should be of opinion that any legislative act be necessary, that they report any bill, in conformity with that opinion."

Under this vote, on the recommendation of that Committee, the bill originally submitted by the Committee of the House of Industry was revived by vote of the City Council; and, on the third of February, 1823, an act was obtained from the legislature of Massachusetts, vesting in the Directors of the House of Industry like powers, relative to governing that house, as were before had and exercised by Overseers of the Poor, with other provisions the above Committee had recommended.

On the thirteenth of January, 1823, the subject had assumed a different attitude. Another Committee of the City Council had reported that a house of correction was wanted in the County of Suffolk; that the Almshouse in Boston was now the only place of restraint; *that it had only thirty-two rooms for the accommodation of more than three hundred and eighty inmates; that some contain fourteen persons, and none less than five, of all ages and colors, and in every stage of poverty and disease, produced by misfortune and vice; in rooms miserably adapted to the numbers crowded into them; that few places exhibit a more incongruous and unfit mixture of the departments of a hospital, — an almshouse and house of correction; that those who would contribute to their own maintenance cannot in such a place, and that many could do so cannot be doubted.*

They, therefore, recommend that the Boston Almshouse and the House of Industry should both be maintained; the former to be a receptacle of the aged, infirm, and sick poor, and little children, under the care of the Overseers of the Poor, the latter to be a house for the employment of those poor who are subjects of commitment to a house of correction, and under the care of the Directors of the House of Industry.

This report was accepted in both branches of the City Council. And in concurrence with its recommendations, the act authorizing the City Council to choose nine directors of the House of Industry contained a section, giving to the Overseers of the Poor and Justices of the Police Court concurrent jurisdiction and the same powers, in relation to commitments to the House of Industry as previously existed in the laws of the Commonwealth in relation to commitments to houses of correction.

This attempt to turn the House of Industry into a house of correction, was not only wholly incompatible with the original design of the town, in authorizing its erection, but would have defeated the whole project had it been carried into execution. The comfort, the health, the exercise, and the useful employment of the virtuous and respectable poor, was the fundamental principle of the design. The superior advantage for these purposes, in a situation removed from the throng of a city, and having space enough for the useful employment of the poor on the land, and the adaptation of this mode of employment for every age, sex, and state of capacity for labor, were among the declared inducements for the selection of the location and the appropriation for the building. The House of Industry was not constructed, nor had it any strong rooms and iron vaulted cells, for the restraint of sturdy rogues and vagabonds.

The picture drawn by this last Committee of the City Council, of the actual state of the Boston Almshouse, is sufficient to show not only the wisdom, but the necessity of a total change in that institution. It was not exaggerated; but, on the contrary, deficient in details, of a very gross and disgusting character, establishing still more strongly the necessity of a change in the local relations of the poor in the city of Boston.

Such was the state of the question, relative to the establishment of the House of Industry, at the termination of the first year of the city government. The decided animosity to the institution now began to assume an unquestionable shape, and it was very apparent to all who took an interest in the subject that its fate depended upon the character and dispositions of the next City Council.

The preceding outline embraces all the measures during this year of the city government, which were important or conclusive, except those which are incident annually to the organization of every municipal authority; — such as the organization of the several boards of firewards, health, and highways; appointing the various officers of police and finance, with the several classes of surveyors, sealers, and inspectors; superintending the public lands and public schools; establishing rules and regulations for the watch; repairing of the streets and public buildings; licensing theatrical and other exhibitions; establishing the salaries of city officers; and, in general, exercising all the duties naturally incident to the ordinary routine of municipal organization and to the exercise of municipal powers.

The proceedings of the city government, during the first year of its existence, relative to the Commissioners of Health, the enlargement of Faneuil Hall Market, the erecting tombs under churches, the lands west of Charles Street and the Common, then called "the ropewalk lands," though taken into consideration, yet having resulted in no action of a general and permanent character, will be stated in connection with the account given of those subjects in the history of the next succeeding administration of the city, when they were each successively and carefully investigated and arranged in new forms, or finally settled on appropriate principles.

The result of the administration of city affairs during this first year had not met the expectations of the inhabitants. They had anticipated from the new charter great changes in the conduct of their municipal concerns. They had flattered themselves that the new form of organization would lead to more efficient, energetic, and responsible measures than could be obtained under the old. Obscure and indefinite hopes had been entertained of improvements in particular localities, which would result in increased accommodation of the inhabitants, and encourage both the growth and enlargement of the city. But when, at the close of the city year, they found none, or but few of these fond anticipations realized, and that their affairs, though conducted with great care, judgment, and fidelity, had received no new impulse from the newly invested powers, but that the course of management had deviated but little from that they had experienced under the ancient form of government, the disappointment was, in a manner, general, and began to be expressed.

The Mayor himself was not insensible to this state of feeling; and so far as he was responsible for it, the circumstances in which he had been placed explained the cause, and were a justification of the course of his administration. Prudence, caution, and conservatism, were his predominating characteristics; and, when called suddenly to a station he had not anticipated, he naturally hesitated to venture upon changes, of which the devising was critical and laborious, and the result uncertain. These tendencies of his mind were increased and strengthened by a state of health, which within one month after the close of his mayoralty, terminated his life.

Few citizens have fulfilled the duties of the respective stations to which they have been called with more fidelity than Mr. Phillips. The evidence of the confidence of his fellow-citizens was continued through a long series of years. He had for more than twenty-five years been, without an omission, elected a member of one of the branches of the state government, and for ten years had been uninterruptedly chosen President of the Senate of the Commonwealth, and in all been distinguished for acceptable and efficient service.

The tribute paid to his administration, by his successor, in his inaugural discourse, it is proper here to quote, on account both of its truth and justice. "After examining," he states, "and considering the records of the proceedings of the city authorities, for the past year, it is impossible for me to refrain from expressing the sense I entertain of the services of that high and honorable individual who filled the Chair of this city, as well as of the wise, prudent, and faithful citizens who composed, during that period, the City Council. Their labors have been, indeed, in a measure, unobtrusive; but they have been various, useful, and well considered. They have laid the foundations of the prosperity of our city deep and on right principles. And whatever success may attend those who come after them, they will be largely indebted for it to the wisdom and fidelity of their predecessors. A task was committed to the first administration to perform, in no common degree arduous and delicate. The change from a town to a city had not been effected without considerable opposition. On that subject many fears existed, which it was difficult to allay, many jealousies hard to overcome. In the outset of a new form of government, among variously affected passions and interests, and among indistinct expectations, impossible to realize, it was apparently wise to shape the course of the first administration rather by the spirit of the long experienced constitution of the town, than by that of the unsettled charter of the city. It was natural for prudent men, first intrusted with city authorities, to apprehend that measures partaking of the mild, domestic character of our ancient institutions, might be as useful, and would be likely to be more acceptable than those which should develop the entire powers of the new government. It is yet to be proved, whether in these measures our predecessors were not right. In all times the inhabitants of this metropolis have been distinguished preëminently for a free, elastic, republican spirit. Heaven grant that they may be forever thus distinguished! It is yet to be decided, whether such a spirit can, for the sake of the peace, order, health, and convenience of a great and rapidly increasing population, endure without distrust and discontent, the application of necessary city powers to all the exigencies which arise in such a community."

Neither the inclination nor the health of Mr. Phillips permitted him to become a candidate for a second election; and his withdrawal being announced, the several parties into which the city was then divided, held, as is usual on such occasions, their assemblies for the selection of his successor. A committee[1] of the deputation from all the wards of the city soon waited upon the individual whom they had agreed upon, and who was finally elected to the office of mayor, and distinctly stated to him, that the municipal affairs of the city had become a subject of more than common solicitude, and that, in communicating to him his selection, by a large meeting of citizens, as the candidate for that office, they deemed it proper to express, as the wishes and expectations of that assembly, that the measures of the ensuing administration should be characterized by great activity and energy, and that a full development should be given as far as

[1] Benjamin Russell, Jonathan Hunnewell, John T. Apthorp.

possible to all the executive powers granted by the charter. To which that individual replied, that should the suffrages of his fellow-citizens result in his election, the affairs of the city should be guided, so far as his influence extended, by the principles and views the Committee, in their behalf, had expressed.[1]

[1] For the members of the City Council from 1822 to 1830, inclusive, see Appendix, M.

CHAPTER V.

CITY GOVERNMENT. 1823-1824.

JOSIAH QUINCY, *Mayor.*[1]

Organization of the City Government — Mayor's Address — Importance of the Official Responsibility of that Officer — Difficulties relative to the Office of Surveyors of Highways — Embarrassments from the Board of Health — Duty of Cleansing the Streets devolved on the Mayor and Aldermen, and how executed — Board of Health discontinued, and their Duties transferred to other Officers.

THE municipal authorities of the City of Boston were organized for the second time on the first of May, 1823, in conformity with the provisions of its charter, in Faneuil Hall, in the presence of a large concourse of citizens. After a prayer by the Rev. James Freeman, John Phillips, the first Mayor of Boston, administered, as Justice of the Peace, the oaths of office to his successor.

The Mayor, in his inaugural address, after paying a due tribute to his predecessor,[2] deduced the spirit of the city charter from its language and the exigencies which led to its adoption, and explained his views of the powers and duties of the office of Mayor, and the principles by which he should endeavor to execute and fulfil them. Among the defects of the ancient town organization, was the division of the executive power among several independent boards, whereby the responsibility of the individual members of each was lessened, and that which did exist could easily be transferred from one board to another. The general superintendence over all the boards, being vested

[1] The whole number of votes were 4,766; of which Josiah Quincy had 2,505. The Aldermen elected were, — David W. Child, Ashur Benjamin, Enoch Patterson, Joseph H. Dorr, Stephen Hooper, Daniel Baxter, Caleb Eddy, and George Odiorne.

The Common Council elected John Welles its President, and Thomas Clark its Clerk. The City Council elected Samuel F. McCleary City Clerk, an office which he now holds, and has held by successive annual elections to this day, (1851.)

[2] See chap. iv. pp. 55, 56.

particularly in no one, the important duty of investigating their relations to one another, and their adequacy to the public service, was either wholly neglected, or performed only occasionally, and in a very irresponsible manner. To remedy these defects, the city charter enjoins on the Mayor, as the executive officer, the performance of these duties, invests him with the requisite powers, and thus renders him responsible, both in character and station, for their efficient exercise and fulfilment; ample security against the abuse or neglect of those powers being provided for in the constitutional control of the City Council and the annual elections by the citizens. With these general views, the Mayor proceeded to state, that he regarded the duties of the executive officer, as resulting from the provisions of the charter, to be the identifying himself, absolutely and exclusively with the character and interests of the city, studying and understanding all its rights, whether affecting property, or liberty, or power, and the maintaining them, not merely with the zeal of official station, but with the pertinacious spirit of private interest. Of local, sectional, party, or personal divisions, he should know nothing, except for the purpose of healing the wounds they inflict, or softening the animosities they excite. The honor, happiness, dignity, safety, and prosperity of the city, the development of its resources, its expenditures, and police, should be the perpetual object of his purpose, and labor of his thought. All its public institutions should be the subject of frequent inspection; and above all, its schools should engage his utmost solicitude and unremitting superintendence. Anticipating the rival projects, individual interests, personal influences, by which an executive officer would be beset in executing the police, protecting the rights, and promoting the prosperity of the city, and that, in proportion to his firmness and inflexibility, his motives and principles would be assailed, the Mayor relied with confidence, that his faithful endeavors to uphold the interests of the city, would receive countenance and support from the intelligence and virtue of the citizens. In relation to his fulfilment of the obligations resulting from the city charter, he promised nothing except a laborious fulfilment of every known duty, a prudent exercise of every invested power, and a disposition shrinking from no official responsibility.[1]

[1] See Appendix B.

The prominence given in this address to the defects of the ancient town organization, and of the remedy provided for them in the powers of the Mayor, was, in his view, made necessary from the particular circumstances of the city at that time, and from the apprehension that the changes those circumstances required, might be the occasion of jealousy and discontent.

Five distinct Boards, — that of Health, of Surveyors of Highways, of the Overseers of the Poor, of Firewards, and of the School Committee, — then exercised powers, of which some were unequivocally executive, and of which all were, under the city charter, without question, properly subject to the general supervision of the Mayor. All these Boards were, more or less, identified with the habits and prejudices of the citizens; the members of many of them had been long in office, and under the town form of government had enjoyed, in their respective spheres, unquestionable authority. Some of them had exercised under the same name the same powers, from very distant, and others from the most ancient periods of the existence of the town. Each had proportions of efficient power and local influence. Each friends, by whom, and circles, within which, the exercise of its particular authorities was deemed useful, and often indispensable. With some, emoluments were connected; and with all, the pleasure of exercising beneficial authority and enjoying useful distinction.

By the provisions of the city charter, the members of some of the boards continued to be chosen directly by the citizens; and thus deriving their authority immediately from the people, were disposed to consider themselves subject to very limited responsibility to the City Council, and as independent of the authority of the Mayor. They were reluctant to acknowledge themselves subject to the inspection of that officer, as this implied they were, in the language of the city charter, "subordinate officers," which, from a natural pride of place, they were not prepared to admit.

The relations of these boards to the city government, rendered the duties of the Mayor, at this juncture, peculiarly difficult and delicate. This division of executive power among independent boards, was evidently incompatible with its efficient exercise and with that personal responsibility which the terms of the city charter had devolved upon the Mayor, and which the people had been led to expect from the individual who might hold that office.

It was apparent, also, that unless the powers of these boards were either immediately modified or abolished, they would be fixed upon the city, with pretensions enlarging with time, until the inconvenience resulting from them should become insupportable. Yet it was easy to foresee that an attempt to abolish institutions long familiar to the people, and with which they had been accustomed to associate the comfort, health, and safety of their families and buildings, would expose the officer who should recommend such measures to suspicions and calumnies tending to affect, if not destroy his influence and popularity. After weighing deliberately all the duties and consequences, the Mayor decided that no personal considerations ought to have any weight in competition with the obvious advantages which must result to the city from the removal or modification of boards, behind which a weak, a cunning, or indolent executive officer might take refuge to hide imbecility or selfishness, or find an apology for inefficiency.

These views of the Mayor were founded on researches and observations relative to municipal governments in Europe and the United States. Either from the terms of their charters, or from a long course of usage and precedents, the powers exercised by mayors were chiefly judicial. Their executive powers were very limited, being chiefly exercised through the medium of boards or of committees; the mayors being deemed little more than presiding or certifying officers, were not held by public opinion more responsible than other members of the board. The power and practical efficiency of this officer consequently degenerated, and the amount of supervision and labor applied to the performance of his duties depended almost wholly on the disposition of the incumbent. As the importance of the office of mayor thus diminished, the qualities essential to a vigilant and efficient exercise of its duties were apt to be disregarded by the community in the selection of candidates. In some places, party spirit gave the office away to its favorite, looking only to his political faith, and not at all to any adaptation of his talents to the fulfilment of its duties. In others, ambition made it a stepping-stone. Here, charity had bestowed it on a needy, popular favorite, honest, but trembling for his bread at every critical exercise of his authority. There, some one of the popular classes, into which every city becomes divided, had placed the head of the class at the head of the city, with no special regard to qualification.

To postpone, and if possible, to prevent the occurrence of such a state of indifference to the essential qualities of the executive officer in the city of Boston, the Mayor elect deemed it his chief official duty to produce and fix in the minds of all the influential classes of citizens a strong conviction of the advantage of having an active and willingly responsible executive, by an actual experience of the benefits of such an administration of their affairs; and also of their right and duty of holding the Mayor responsible, in character and office, for the state of the police and finances of the city.

To bring the responsibility of the executive officer into distinct relief before the citizens, was accordingly a leading principle, by which he endeavored to regulate his conduct in that office. This purpose he avowed, and never ceased to enforce by precept and example, during his administration of nearly six years. And the long continuance of support he received from the citizens, sufficiently evidenced that his views were in accordance with those entertained at that period by a great majority of the inhabitants of Boston.

One of the most urgent duties enjoined on the Mayor, by the city charter, was attention to the health, security, and cleanliness of the city. Immediately, therefore, after the organization of the city government was completed, in May, 1823, the Mayor recommended to the consideration of the City Council the state of the streets, and in what body the care of cleaning them was, or ought to be invested, and what powers and authorities are required to be granted for the purpose of keeping them clean; and also the consideration of the measures which ought to be taken to put the House of Industry into effectual operation.

Each of these recommendations were referred to joint committees in both branches;[1] that in respect of the streets was particularly directed to inquire in whom the powers and duties of surveyors of highways were invested.

[1] That relative to the streets, to the Mayor and Alderman Baxter; and to Messrs. Eliphalet Williams, Silsby, Stodder, Bates, and Dexter, of the Common Council.

That relative to the House of Industry, to the Mayor, Aldermen Odiorne and Child; and to Messrs. Davis, J. K. Williams, Baldwin, Jackson, and Lincoln, of the Common Council

The relations of several of the independent boards, which under the town government had the management of important branches of the public service, were left by the city charter, either obscurely defined or wholly unprovided for. The embarrassments arising from the Surveyors of Highways were the first experienced, and earliest received attention.

Under the town organization, the Board of Selectmen had fulfilled the duties of the Surveyors of Highways. But the city charter had made no special provision for the election of these officers. The power of appointing them was only inferred from the general authority it gave to the City Council "to elect all necessary officers for the good government of the city, not otherwise provided for," and under this clause three Surveyors of Highways were chosen in 1822. Inconveniences arose from the nature of the office and the extent of its powers, which the citizens had been accustomed to have exercised by the whole Board of Selectmen, and the arrangement by which they were transferred to three individuals, dependent on the City Council, was unsatisfactory and unpopular. The Mayor and Aldermen were regarded as the proper successors to the Selectmen, with respect to these powers, but the right of the City Council to confer them on a coördinate branch of the government was doubted. During the first year of the city, the subject attracted the attention of the City Council, and they appointed a committee upon it in October, 1822. But no effectual action resulted. In the mean time, the usual difficulties arising from authorities, intimately affecting the rights and properties of citizens, being exercised by so small a body, began to be felt. The Surveyors of Highways regarded themselves in the light of an independent board. Questions immediately arose, concerning the degree of control the Mayor and Aldermen had a right to exercise in relation to that Board, and the powers intrusted by law to it under the city charter.

In other respects, the state of the several authorities, relative to the highways and streets, were found embarrassing. The great objects of municipal attention, — the street and house dirt and the night soil, and the modes and rules for their removal, had, under the town government, been frequent subjects of question, and even controversy, and early began to appear such under that of the city.

The Surveyors of Highways claimed one species of jurisdiction over the streets; the Mayor and Aldermen another; the Board of Health a third. In consequence of the obscurity of the limits of the divisions of their powers, there was some difficulty, and occasionally something arbitrary in the claims and proceedings touching their respective jurisdictions. Thus, the carrying away of the street dirt was admitted to be within the power of the Selectmen, and now, of consequence, of the Mayor and Aldermen. But of the house dirt, the Board of Health claimed the exclusive jurisdiction, and denied to the Selectmen, and also to the Mayor and Aldermen, the right of intermeddling on that subject. What was house dirt, and what was street dirt, and whether yard dirt belonged to either, and to which, began to be questions of solemn and dividing import. The first year of the city government had witnessed a curious instance of the superiority claimed by the Board of Health over that of the Mayor and Aldermen, and of the conciliatory temper with which the latter Board had received and responded to that claim.

An order was issued by the Board of Health, and duly served upon the Mayor and Aldermen in the following words: —

" *To the Honorable Mayor and Aldermen of the City:* —

" GENTLEMEN, — Complaint has been made at this office that there is collected in the corner, on the westerly side of the T[1] and next to the Long Wharf, a quantity of filthy, putrid, and nauseous substances on the premises belonging to you, or under your direction, and is a nuisance. You will, therefore, appear before this Board on Monday, the seventeenth instant, and show cause, if any exist, why the City of Boston should not remove the same and cut through said T an opening next to the Long Wharf, twenty-four feet wide in the clear, and eight feet deep on a level with the lowest part of the flats, on the easterly side of said T, for the free passage of the tide waters.

" By order of the Board of Commissioners of Health.

" JOHN WINSLOW, *Secretary.*

" 4 June, 1822."

This order was read in the Board of Aldermen, and on the twenty-fourth of June a report was made " that they do not think the city ought to pay any part of the expense, excepting that for removing nuisances." This report was accepted, and no notice taken either of the nature of the claim of jurisdiction or of the manner of enforcing it.

Similar clashing of authority or of opinion occurred between the Surveyors of Highways and the Board of Aldermen, although

[1] A wharf so called.

not enforced by any like tone and official process. The state of uncertainty, in respect of the body, in which both the care of the highways and that of cleansing the streets was left by the charter of the city, led the Mayor, at the commencement of this city year, to regard a settlement of those questions as the most important and urgent in their nature. With respect to the Surveyors of Highways, the change proposed could not be effected without an appeal to the great body of citizens. A general meeting of all the inhabitants, therefore, was called on the fifteenth of May, 1823, on the subject of appointing the Board of Aldermen surveyors of highways. The change proposed readily received their sanction; and the Legislature of the State, on the eleventh of June ensuing, passed an act in conformity with the vote of the citizens, and on the eighteenth of the same month, the City Council elected the Mayor and Aldermen Surveyors of Highways.

In pursuance of this authority, this Board immediately divided the city into four districts, each including three wards, and appointed two aldermen superintendents of each district, by whom the powers thus invested were subsequently exercised without question, and to the general satisfaction of the citizens.

No subject had been pressed upon the Mayor with more earnestness, by private citizens, than the state of the streets and the importance of adopting systematic plans for effectually removing the various accumulations and nuisances in them, which are incident to a populous city. Anticipating, however, that the scale which it would be necessary to adopt, in order thoroughly to effect this object, would lead to a pecuniary expenditure, so far exceeding any thing the citizens had experienced under the town government, the Mayor had, in his inaugural address, endeavored to conciliate their minds, by thus stating the general views he entertained on the powers intrusted to the executive authority on this subject: — "If the powers vested seem too great, let it be remembered that they are necessary to attain the great objects of a city, — health, comfort, and safety. To those whose fortunes are restricted, these powers ought to be peculiarly precious. The rich can fly from the *generated pestilence. In the season of danger the sons of fortune can seek refuge in purer atmospheres. But necessity condemns the poor to remain and inhale the noxious efflu-*

via. To all classes who reside permanently in a city, these powers are a privilege and a blessing. In relation to the city police, it is not sufficient that the law, in its due process, will ultimately remedy every injury and remove every nuisance. While the law delays, the injury is done. While judges are doubting, and lawyers debating, the nuisance is exhaling, and the atmosphere corrupting. In these cases, prevention should be the object of solicitude, not remedy. It is not enough that the obstacle which impedes the citizen's way, or the nuisance which offends his sense, should be removed on complaint, or by complaint. The true criterion of an efficient government is, that it should be removed before complaint, and without complaint."

On examining the powers of the city, relative to these subjects, the Mayor found that the most important were claimed and exercised by Commissioners, called the Board of Health. They had gradually extended their jurisdiction to all subjects, which could, by any fair construction, be brought within the terms of the legislative acts instituting their authority. In respect of these powers, they had acknowledged no subordination to the Selectmen of the town. Collisions had occasionally arisen between them, relative to the removal of nuisances, which had generally terminated in favor of the Board of Health; and they consequently claimed and exercised, at the time the city government was formed, jurisdiction over all subjects which could be comprehended under the terms "causes of sickness, nuisances, and sources of filth, injurious to the health of the inhabitants." The dirt collecting on the surface of the streets, being considered a nuisance, rather in respect of sight, smell, or convenience, than of health, was admitted by those commissioners to be within the jurisdiction of the Selectmen.

By the city charter, the powers and authorities vested by law in the Board of Health were transferred to the City Council, "to be carried into execution by the appointment of health commissioners, or in such other manner as the health, cleanliness, comfort, and order of the said city may in their judgment require." These commissioners, therefore, now held their places, not as formerly, immediately from the people, but by their election by the City Council, and the continued existence of that board depended on its will. Notwithstanding this change in their public relations, these commissioners claimed and exercised as broad and independent a jurisdiction during the first year of the city government, as they had done under that of the town. An instance of their pretensions has just been noticed.[1]

Soon after the commencement of the second administration of the city government, (in 1823,) the Mayor perceived that, so long as this state of things continued, he could not exercise that general superintendence of this important subject which the city charter had made his duty, without troublesome and unprofitable collisions. His powers of inspection were restricted to "subordinate officers;" a relation which the members of that board were not prepared to admit, as applicable to them, so long as they acted under the forms and principles which had been established by virtue of the several acts forming the ancient constitution of that board. In his opinion, there was no department of police for which the chief executive officer of a city ought to be made more strictly responsible, than for that on which the comfort and health of the inhabitants of the city depended. The existence of an ancient board, accustomed to exercise exclusive jurisdiction, and yet claiming a qualified, if not an absolute authority over the subject, would render it easy for a weak, an indolent, or a cunning executive to evade that responsibility, and yet neglect his most imperative official duties.

To prepare the public mind for a new arrangement of these powers, the Mayor, on the day of his inauguration, formally recommended the subject to the notice of the City Council, as already stated; and a joint committee having been appointed, they reported, that "the care of cleaning the surface of the city was, by force of the terms of the city charter, vested in the Mayor and Aldermen; but that the docks, night soil, and house dirt was considered as belonging to the Board of Health, until the farther order of the City Council." In this construction the City Council found that the members of that board would acquiesce; and, being desirous to avoid, or, at least to postpone, all questions which might create collisions, they confined their attention, in the first instance, to the surface of the city, including its streets, courts, and yards.

From inquiries into the antecedent practice of the town and

[1] See page 64.

city, it was ascertained that no general, regular system for cleansing the streets had ever been adopted or executed. All operations had been occasional and local, the result of some particular, urgent necessity. Nor was it found that expenses for such an object had ever, in one year, exceeded one thousand dollars.

The Board of Aldermen and Common Council entirely concurring with the views entertained by the Mayor on this subject, it was determined at once to incur the expense of a general and thorough cleansing of the city. The result, it was anticipated, would so convince the citizens of the benefit, and so habituate them to the comfort of the cleanliness of the city, that it would be impossible for any executive to be negligent in this respect, and long retain his influence and office. To the end that the advantage of the proposed operations might be felt by all the citizens, it was determined to carry them into effect, in every street, alley, court, and household yard, however distant, and however obscure.

For this purpose, the city was divided into four districts, each composed of three wards; and the Board of Aldermen into committees, each composed of two members; the superintendence of the cleansing of one district being assigned to each committee. For the first time, on any general scale destined for universal application, the broom was used upon the streets. On seeing this novel spectacle, of files of sweepers, an old and common adage was often applied to the new administration of city affairs; in good humor by some, in a sarcastic spirit by others.

In the course of a month, the proposed operation was completed, to the very general, if not the universal approbation of the citizens. More than three thousand tons of dirt were removed from the surface of the city, at a cost of about fourteen hundred dollars; and in the first month of this administration, nearly double the sum was asserted to have been thus expended than had ever before been voted, in any one year, to a similar object, since the settlement of Boston. The comfort and pride of city cleanliness was thus brought home to the door and the feelings of every inhabitant, and, for the time, no language was publicly heard but that of approbation; yet, subsequently, this expense constituted one element of clamor, which party spirit did not fail to remember, when the charge of extravagance and the terrors of a city debt were brought to bear upon the popularity of the administration.

The next important question on this subject was, the manner in which the streets should be hereafter cleansed. The old practice was to depend upon the interests of the farmers in the vicinity, who came when they pleased, took what they pleased, in the manner they pleased. The comparative advantage and economy of effecting this object by contract, or by teams and laborers, provided and employed by the city, became a subject of serious debate and deliberation. There were no data on which the principles of a contract could be based and safely adjusted. Neither the value of the sweepings, as manure, nor the quantity which could annually be taken from the surface of the city, could be ascertained. To attain the information the case required, the Mayor and Aldermen advertised for contracts for the work. Among the proposals consequently made, only one embraced all the operations of scraping, sweeping, and carrying away, and including an offer to do the whole work for seven thousand dollars. All the other proposals expressly declined having any thing to do with scraping and sweeping the streets, and confined their offer exclusively to carrying the dirt away. The lowest of these proposals was *eighteen hundred dollars for the year.* All of them were rejected; and it was decided that the city should perform all the operations by its own teams and laborers, and on its own account. This determination being known, the same persons fell in their demands, *from eighteen to eight hundred* dollars. This being rejected, they offered to do it *for nothing.* Even these proposals were rejected; the Mayor and Aldermen being of opinion that the interest of the city required that this work should be done thoroughly, and that the cheapest was not the best, or even the most economical mode of conducting such operations; it being, in their judgment, impossible to do it satisfactorily for any length of time by contract. All the contractors were farmers in the vicinity, whose object it was to obtain manure for their lands, and whose performance would be limited by that interest. Whatever was worthless as a manure would be left. During the months of July and August, when the health and comfort of the citizens required that the work should be most thoroughly performed, it being the busiest season of the year to the farmer, the work in the city would be neglected.

There were also other occasional wants of the city, which rendered the possession of teams and laborers of its own highly expedient and economical. The Mayor and Aldermen, therefore, resolved to take the care of the streets into their own hands; and, having obtained authority from the City Council, proceeded to purchase carts and horses and to hire men, at the cost and on the account of the city.

The expediency of this measure was tested by keeping accurate accounts, during the two first years, of the work done, the expenses incurred, and the incomes obtained; and the experiment resulted in a perfect conviction, that this was not only the most economical, but the only effectual mode, to relieve the citizens from the nuisances incident to streets. The responsibility was thus devolved upon the Mayor and Aldermen. If any cause of complaint occurred, they could not throw the blame off upon contractors. As had been anticipated, great convenience and economy resulted from having horses and teams always at command, and ready to be applied to any sudden exigency which might occur. Exclusive of the first general sweeping, the expenses of cleaning the streets, alleys, and courts of the city amounted, the first year of the experiment, to *three thousand and eight hundred dollars.* After deducting, at the end of the year, the value of the teams owned by the city, and also the value of the city work done by them, not connected with the streets, it was found that twenty-eight hundred tons of manure had been collected, and used on the city lands, and at the city farm at the House of Industry, the value of which was deemed a full equivalent for the whole cost of the operation.

On the succeeding year, the cost of this process was about *six thousand dollars;* from the sales of the manure collected *two thousand dollars* were received. *Fifteen hundred tons* of manure, valued at *a thousand dollars*, had been sent to the city farm at the House of Industry; and the work done for the city by the teams and laborers, exclusive of that on the streets, was estimated to be worth *two thousand dollars;* and the teams on hand at the end of the year were estimated at the value of six hundred dollars. From these general estimates, it was evident that no general mode of removing street dirt, an operation so essential to the health and comfort of the citizens, could possibly combine an equal degree of convenience and economy; and, during the subsequent years of this administration, its expediency was never authoritatively questioned.[1]

In all these arrangements, the Mayor and Aldermen had the benefit of the practical skill and business talents of Enoch Patterson and Caleb Eddy, members of the Board of Aldermen, to whose intelligence, activity, and judgment the city of Boston is greatly indebted for the degree of success which, in the course of this and the ensuing year, was attained in this and other branches of the police services of the city.

The experience of this year of the city government had satisfied the Mayor and City Council that the whole subject, relative to filth and nuisances affecting the comfort and health of the citizens, ought to be taken under their direct control, and could be better managed by a single health commissioner than by an independent board. The satisfactory result of the measures adopted in relation to cleaning the surface of the city, led to the determination that the remaining objects, such as the docks, night soil, and house dirt, should be placed under like control. To prepare the way for this change, a Committee of the City Council, of which the Mayor was chairman, made a report early in February, 1824,—that the Board of Health, in executing the arrangements relative to the internal health regulations, had effected the same by contract, and paid that year nearly three thousand dollars for these objects; that in respect of house dirt the contractors were often remiss; that recurrence to the penalty, although it might punish them, did not effect the chief object in this concern,—the certain convenience of the citizens. Living in the country, they came in heavy ox wagons; were a long

1 1st. The work is done thoroughly and satisfactorily to every inhabitant, in every lane, alley, and court. 2d. It is done responsibly. If it is not so done, the blame falls where it ought to fall, on the Mayor and Aldermen; they cannot throw it off on contractors. 3d. There is great convenience, and often great economy, in having teams and horses at command. The amount of this convenience is great, but difficult to estimate. To the Executive Board, practically speaking, the trouble is nothing in comparison with the gratification they derive, from seeing the streets cleansed of all offensive substances, and a population satisfied with its condition in this respect.

On the 10th of April, 1826, an ordinance was passed by the City Council, prohibiting the removal through the streets, &c. of Boston any house dirt, house offal, or refuse substance, animal or vegetable, unless licensed by the Mayor and Aldermen, on such conditions as they should prescribe. This was unaccountably omitted to be published among the ordinances in the edition of 1827, but was inserted in subsequent editions of those ordinances.

time in loading; and the collections being dragged slowly along the streets, became in the summer season a great nuisance; that the contractors, being farmers, were negligent during the summer months. Besides, being only interested in carrying away the substances which, by their usefulness, would compensate them for the transportation, they often left articles cumbersome, and often noxious to the citizens. The substances carried away were acknowledged by the contractors to be worth, as a food for swine, two thousand dollars, and probably, in fact, were of far greater value.

The Committee recommended that the city should undertake the removal of it on its own account, as they had done in the case of street dirt.

Because, being removed in wagons with horses, they would pass the streets more expeditiously, and being well covered, and the men employed being directly and constantly responsible to the Commissioner of Health, the inconvenience to the citizens would be less, and exactness would be more easily effected; and, if carried to the House of Industry at South Boston, would relieve the city from a great part of the expense; the superintendent of the House of Industry being of opinion that, if applied to the keeping of hogs, the profit on the pork would pay for the transportation, and leave the manure a clear gain to the city.

The Committee then entered into calculations, showing the feasibility, the economy, and the far greater convenience and comfort to the citizens, than the old mode of effecting the same object, by means of contracts with farmers.

Similar views were expressed in relation to the night soil and its removal. This could not well be effected by teams employed by the city. It was unavoidable that the work should be done through the agency of farmers in the vicinity. But the rules adopted, concerning the mode of conducting these operations, the time when the teams should enter and leave the city, the neatness, the silence, and the care with which the work should be performed,—were all circumstances deeply affecting the health and comfort of the citizens, and, perhaps more than any other, ought to be made to rest upon the responsibility of the Mayor and Executive Board.

In consequence of these views and recommendations, the old

mode of managing the concerns of the health department, by the means of a board of commissioners, was abandoned. That board was discontinued. An ordinance was past by the City Council, on the thirty-first of May, 1824, placing the internal police of the city under the superintendence of the City Marshal; the external police, under that of a Commissioner of Health; and that relative to the interment of the dead, under an officer, denominated the Superintendent of the Burial Grounds.

The advantages resulting from these changes became soon apparent, and were acknowledged by the citizens. New contracts on the subject of night soil were made; greater exactness and more regularity in their fulfilment were required, and in case of failure or neglect, rigorously enforced; in some, even to the forfeiture of the contractors' obligations, after very considerable expenditures already incurred by them, for performance of the work during a term of long continuance.

The measures for removing house and street dirt, by means of city teams, were not less satisfactory. In the hottest seasons of the year, the convenience of the citizens was no longer subjected to the interest or caprice of the farmers. Every subject of complaint became the object of the immediate attention of the responsible officer. And when the heat, or any particular urgency, called for additional teams, they were without delay applied to the objects. In reply to a letter making inquiries concerning the result, by one of the city authorities of Philadelphia, the Mayor of Boston thus wrote, on the twentieth of July, 1825: "So well regulated are our city teams and operations, that, notwithstanding the excessive heat of the last week, the whole number of complaints of neglect in carrying away the household dirt, in the whole city, for that week, was but *four*. I do not believe it is possible for any city of equal population to carry into effect this species of cleaning at a less expense, or more thoroughly, or to more general satisfaction."

CHAPTER VI.

CITY GOVERNMENT. 1823-1824.

JOSIAH QUINCY, *Mayor.*

Inconvenient State of Faneuil Hall Market — Difficulties attending its Extension — Measures taken for surmounting them — Invitation to the Proprietors of the Land in the Vicinity to become Associates in the Improvement — Not accepted by them — The Project approved by the Citizens in a General Meeting — Authority obtained from the Legislature — Purchase of the Estates commenced.

THE enlargement of the market under and in the vicinity of Faneuil Hall was one of the first objects to which the attention of the second administration of the city government was directed. The labors and responsibilities the Mayor, Aldermen, and Common Council incurred in accomplishing this great improvement, the extent of their operations, and the extraordinary financial results, are probably without a parallel in the history of any other city. A granite market house, two stories high, five hundred and thirty-five feet long, fifty feet wide, covering twenty-seven thousand feet of land, including every essential accommodation, was erected, at the cost of one hundred and fifty thousand dollars. Six new streets were opened, and a seventh greatly enlarged, including one hundred and sixty-seven thousand square feet of land; and flats, docks, and wharf rights obtained, of the extent of one hundred and forty-two thousand square feet. All this was accomplished in the centre of a populous city, not only without any tax, debt, or burden upon its pecuniary resources, — notwithstanding, in the course of the operations, funds to the amount of upwards of eleven hundred thousand dollars had been employed, — but with large permanent additions to its real and productive property. The proprietors of land in the north section of the city were also enabled by this improvement to open Fulton and Commercial Streets, thus greatly enlarging mercantile accommodations, facilitating intercourse with the great southern wharves, and creating opportunities for the foundation of those noble blocks of granite stores, which have since been erected to the eastward of those streets.

It is due to the men who constituted the city councils at that day, whose intelligence devised, and whose energy effected these great results, and also to the spirit of the citizens, whose votes sustained and encouraged them, through good report and evil report, that the difficulties with which they had to struggle, and the course of measures by which they were surmounted and success ultimately obtained, should be permanently recorded, as an honor to the past and an example to the future.

At the commencement of the second city year, the whole space occupied by stalls in Faneuil Hall market did not exceed fourteen thousand square feet. Even the best of these were inconvenient, and the passages to them obstructed. The dealers in fish and vegetables occupied a wooden shed, without glass windows, and without doors. Their consequent exposure to the inclemency of the winter storms caused premature sickness and death. It was calculated that twenty years changed the whole number of the individuals there employed. The space around Faneuil Hall, devoted to the market, was broken, in its centre, by Odin's Buildings, as they were then called, and was bounded to the eastward by the Roebuck Passage and the Town Dock. The central common sewer of the city opened into the head of this dock, which was also a station for oyster boats, and became consequently a receptacle for every species of filth, and a public nuisance. All the buildings on the north side of the Town Dock were old, and for the most part inhabited by a very troublesome and irregular population. It was impossible to introduce order and systematic arrangement into a market so extremely deficient in local accommodation. The avenues leading to it were in general narrow and crooked, especially the Roebuck Passage, the shortest and most frequented thoroughfare, between the northern section of the city and this central market and the wharves in the middle and southern sections. In a distance of one hundred feet it had three bends, and its width varied from thirteen to twenty feet. Serious accidents had occurred within this inconvenient passage. One child had recently been killed, another had been mutilated, and almost every year petitions had been presented to the town authorities for its enlargement, but without effect. On high market days, Union, Elm, Brattle, Washington, and Exchange Streets were often completely obstructed. Farmers coming from a great distance in the country, were compelled to take their stand along Union Street, as far as Marshall's Lane, and in Washington Street, as far as Court Street. They were thus excluded from the space around Faneuil Hall, where their customers chiefly resorted, and were often obliged to sell their goods to forestallers, greatly to their loss and discontent. Forestalling became, consequently, not only a lucrative but an acknowledged employment. Individuals engaged in it, when prosecuted, were seldom convicted by juries, since, from the many obstructions, arising from the local inadequacy of the market, to all fair competition, forestalling seemed to be indispensable for the interests both of the farmer and the citizens. Such were the general relations and accommodations of the central market of the city, at the commencement of the second administration; and the Mayor, in the first month after his inauguration, having consulted with the Board of Aldermen, decided that the exertions of the city government would be most usefully directed to ameliorate its condition. The general and financial prosperity of the city were favorable to the undertaking. The support of the proprietors of the Long Wharf, and of the inhabitants of the northern parts of the city, were confidently anticipated, since the value of their estates would be enhanced should the project succeed, by the formation of new streets and more commodious water rights, and by the opening of the Roebuck Passage.

These powerful interests and propitious circumstances induced the Mayor immediately to refer the subject of the improvement of the central market to a committee of both branches of the City Council, of which he was chairman. But, so little was the public mind prepared for the extensive plan contemplated, that this Committee could only be induced to assent to a report for the erection of a large vegetable market, thirty-six feet wide, one hundred and eighty feet long, on the north side of Faneuil Hall, which, on the twenty-fifth of June, was accepted in both branches, and fifteen thousand dollars were appropriated for its completion. Those who concurred in the original project were not discouraged by the opposition thus evinced, and, while the report was in discussion, the Mayor took measures, personally, to ascertain the prices at which the estates comprehended within the plan first conceived could be obtained. Some of the principal proprietors refused to sell their estates at any price, and the demands of others were extravagant. But it was evidently for the interest of them all that the plan contemplated should succeed, and not be defeated, or postponed, by the erection of the vegetable market. No obstruction was therefore made to the acceptance of that report; but it was used as an argument, to influence those proprietors to be more moderate in their demands. The policy had the effect anticipated. The appropriation was therefore left untouched and uncalled for; and, on the thirty-first of July, 1823, the Mayor communicated to the City Council his views concerning the improvement contemplated, by a special message, stating the inconveniences of the existing market; the relief which enlarged accommodation and consequent competition would confer, by reduced prices of provisions, on the poorer classes; the circumstances favorable to advantageous purchases; and the necessity of obtaining a power to borrow the sums requisite for the object. The appointment of a committee to take the subject into consideration was recommended, and the Mayor, Aldermen Benjamin and Patterson, and Messrs. E. Williams, Stoddard, Silsby, and Winslow, of the Common Council, were appointed.

It was now thought advisable to postpone further proceedings, until the final terms of the proprietors of the land embraced within the proposed sphere of improvement should be ascertained, and such conditional contracts from them be obtained, as should prevent any one of them falling back from his engagements, after the city should determine to proceed with the project. The Mayor charged himself with this undertaking; and, during the months of August, September, October, and November, he was occupied, during his leisure from other duties, in obtaining plans, forming an acquaintance with the interests, and negotiating with the proprietors. The original scheme embraced all the land between Ann Street and the Mill Creek on the one side, and Butler's Row on the other, limited on the west by the estates on the eastern side of the Roebuck Passage and of Merchants' Row, and extending as far to the east as the flats might reach, which the city, by purchasing the proposed estates in the progress of the improvement, might be able to attain. It was found that, as valued by the proprietors, eight hundred thousand dollars was the lowest sum for which the whole of that property could be obtained. As the advantages of so extensive an improvement were difficult to be made apparent to the citizens in general, among whom there was an instinctive and prevailing dread of a city debt, the Committee postponed the attempt to carry into effect their original project, and for the present, apparently restricted their operations to the space between Ann Street and the street leading to Bray's Wharf, which included about thirty estates, owned by about an equal number of proprietors, and comprising, according to the estimates then made, about one hundred and twenty-seven thousand square feet of ground, inclusive of the docks and passage-ways, and exclusive of the flats in front of the wharves. With two or three exceptions, all the proprietors demanded prices at that time generally deemed extravagant, but which, in the opinion of the Committee, the city might well afford to give, provided it could be made certain of ultimately attaining a title to the whole space. To prevent the scheme being defeated, after the purchase of some estates, by the selfishness and caprice of the owners of the residue, a plan was taken, comprising a general outline of the streets and stores in the contemplated improvement, which at that time it was thought expedient to propose. Estimates having been made, and confidential persons of great practical knowledge having been consulted, the Committee were convinced that an important enlargement of the market might be effected without injuriously increasing the debt or affecting the credit of the city. The Mayor, therefore, proceeded to obtain conditional contracts from the several proprietors, by force of which each bound himself, on the payment of a specified sum by the city of Boston, on or before the first of May then ensuing, to convey his land to the city, with full title and warranty. These negotiations were unavoidably attended with great and peculiar difficulties. Each contract was made separately, often under mutual pledges of secrecy; the proprietors often considering the price they demanded as extravagant, and fearing their estimates might be assumed as a basis of taxation by the assessors. After reducing the price of each estate to its *minimum*, the Mayor took the contract, deeming it essential to success that, after the plan was made public, no proprietor should be able to avail himself of the advantage of a knowledge of the effect of the improvement on his particular estate, or of its special importance to the general design.

By the middle of December, a conditional purchase was effected of almost all the land required. The contracts signed included five sixths of the estates, and amounted to nearly four hundred thousand dollars. The remaining land, it was estimated, might be obtained for less than one hundred thousand dollars. It chiefly belonged to minors, whose trustees or guardians promised to coöperate with the city government, in obtaining authority to sell and invest their title in the city at a fair price.

The most extensive plan the Committee of the City Council dared, at that time, to propose, embraced only the space between the street leading to Bray's Wharf and Ann Street, bounding westerly on a line running in the direction of the eastern side of Merchants' Row, four hundred and twenty feet. The distance to which the parallelogram, of which this line was the base, should extend, easterly, was limited to the east end of Codman's Wharf.

	Feet.
The space between these lines it was proposed to divide into two ranges of store-lots, each 55 feet wide, . .	110
One range for a market house, 50 feet wide, the centre of which was to coincide with the centre of Faneuil Hall, .	50
And two streets, 80 feet wide, on each side of the proposed market house, ...	160
And two streets on the outside of each range of stores, each being 50 feet, ...	100
	420

The subsequent great extension to the eastward, and also that included in the space southward to Butler's Row, and the intermediate estates, according to the original project, were not then by any one deemed possible. Even this plan, so limited in comparison with the one ultimately effected, was condemned, in public and private, as far beyond the resources of the city.

The titles to all the estates in the above space were now invested in, or secured for, the city, with the exception of three fourteenth parts of the estate belonging to the heirs of Nathan Spear, which the proprietors refused to dispose of on any terms. This estate lay, as the annexed plan will show, in the centre of the space required for the proposed improvement; and it was not possible to place the centre of the market house in coincidence with the centre of Faneuil Hall, without crossing that estate, almost in its whole length; and there being some legal questions, applicable to taking lands for a market, which did not apply to taking lands for streets, it was deemed advisable by the City Council to place the market house as far as possible beyond the sphere of the Spear estate. The plan of placing its centre opposite the centre of Faneuil Hall was therefore abandoned, and it was resolved that the northern line of the two edifices should be made coincident; a circumstance often mentioned with regret, as a mistake, by those who are ignorant of the obstacles which rendered the present relative position of the market house expedient. After having entered into contracts, or other satisfactory engagements with all the adult proprietors, whose lands were essential to success, with the above exceptions, and obtained elevations, ground plans, and estimates of a market house and the proposed adjacent stores, on the eighth of December, 1823, the Mayor called together the Committee. Great diversity of opinion was evinced at this meeting; and, after long deliberation, the fear of involving the city in debt prevailed, and it was unanimously agreed, in the first place, to attempt to associate the proprietors of the land in the project, to be effected at common risk and profit. Should this offer be declined, it would be apparent that the improvement must be executed, if at all, by the energy and resources, exclusively, of the city; a circumstance which, it was hoped, would unavoidably produce unanimity among the citizens. With these views, the Mayor, as Chairman of the Committee, made a report of the above date, in which the importance and necessity of the undertaking are stated; the plan and elevations communicated; the impracticability of uniting the opinions of the citizens in favor of purchases to so great an amount, without a previous exposition, asserted; the impossibility of making those purchases on its account, after such development, intimated; and, after declaring the opinion that a full exposition of their plan should be made to the public, proposed to invite the proprietors to become interested in the project, in the proportion of their existing rights; to state what the city would give, in addition to its right in the dock and streets, for the land reserved for streets and a market. Their report concludes with recommending an order, to be passed by the City Council, authorizing a joint committee of that body to enter into a negotiation with the proprietors of the land adjoining the market, and with other citizens, to unite with the City Council in one general plan of improvement in that vicinity, on terms specified in the order.

That order was passed by the City Council on the eighth of December, 1823; and a committee, consisting of the Mayor, and Messrs. Child, Benjamin, and Patterson, of the Board of Aldermen, and Messrs. Dexter, Silsby, E. Williams, Brooks, Russell, Winslow, and Tappan, of the Common Council, were accordingly appointed.

On the tenth of that month the Committee prepared and transmitted to the several proprietors of land three propositions, conformable to the authority given by the City Council. By the first, they were invited to combine and throw their estates into a common stock with the estates belonging to the city, the whole to be appraised at their real value by commissioners mutually to be chosen, who were to be authorized to lay out the estates on a plan specified, and to divide the whole interest into shares, in proportions conformed to the appraisement, and to make sales for the best interests of the concern, the city to be considered as a proprietor for the amount of its estates, but streets and lanes, given or taken, not to be considered in any estimate. The same Commissioners to be authorized to appraise the land reserved for a market, and to decide what the city should pay to the general concern for that interest, considering all circumstances. This sum was to be divided between the proprietors, like the proceeds of the sales, according to their respective shares. The second proposition requested the proprietor, who dissented from the preceding, to state his willingness to sell his land at an appraisement to be made by five or seven disinterested persons, mutually chosen; the city declaring its willingness to consent to such appraisement, upon the single condition that the result should only be obligatory in case of the ultimate success of the general project. The third proposition invited any proprietor, who declined concurring in either of the preceding propositions, to transmit to the Mayor the terms on which he would be willing to sell his land to the city, with the assurance on the part of the city, that either they will be accepted, or a counter-proposition made on its part, limited only by the single condition expressed in the second proposition. The proprietors were requested to give an answer within ten days, and the opinion and earnest wish of the city authorities were expressed, that the whole arrangement might result in uniting the accommodation of the city with the advancement of the interests of the proprietors.

These various propositions were submitted to the proprietors with a view to test their dispositions and to foreclose any future complaints against those measures, to which it might become necessary for the city finally to resort. The prejudices and interest hostile to the prosecution of the improvement by the funds of the city, rendered it expedient to evidence a disposition to admit private citizens into a share in the concern, and particularly the proprietors of the land, should such a disposition be met by a corresponding disposition in any of those individuals, they might be considered and accepted, or rejected, according to their nature. Should no such corresponding disposition appear, then the city authorities would be justified in proceeding on the basis of the city funds and powers, as being obviously the only remaining mode of effecting the improvement.

No proposition was received from any one, on the basis of throwing the estates into a common stock; nor any upon that of selling estates to the city by appraisement. Several of the proprietors, however, expressed their willingness to sell, but the prices demanded by some were deemed exorbitant, and two or three of them refused absolutely to sell at any rate, declaring that they had interests in other parts of the city, which they apprehended would be injuriously affected by the proposed alterations in the vicinity of Faneuil Hall, and that they would enter into no negotiation, nor make any offer upon the subject.

The Committee, therefore, reported on the twenty-ninth of December, 1823, that the prices demanded by the owners of estates in the vicinity of Faneuil Hall Market were generally such as to render it inexpedient to proceed further in an attempt to negotiate, and recommended resolutions, which were adopted by the City Council, appointing a committee to apply to the State Legislature for "such an extension of the powers of Surveyors of Highways, as may enable the city to become possessed of such estates in the vicinity of Faneuil Hall Market as the said Surveyors may deem it expedient for the city to possess for the public use, under such limitations, restrictions, and provisions, as the constitution enjoins, and as regard for the interests of the public, and respect for the rights of individuals shall dictate. Resolutions to this effect were passed in both branches of the City Council, and the same Committee were authorized to apply to the Legislature for such powers.

On the twelfth of the ensuing January, the Committee so appointed made a report, and submitted to the City Council the draft of a memorial to the Legislature, recommending, however, that previously to thus applying to the Legislature, the whole subject should be laid before the inhabitants of the city for their sanction.

This recommendation was made in consideration of the greatness of the effect of this contemplated project on the relations of real property in all that circle of territory, from the Town Dock by the head of Ann Street, and the Mill Creek to Exchange Wharf; the whole of which would be, it was apparent, advantageously affected by the improvement. As the powers about to be asked of the Legislature, though the same in nature with the ordinary powers of surveyors of highways, were yet much more extensive in degree, and would have a direct action upon private rights, and as loans to a considerable amount would be requisite, in case the improvement was authorized, it seemed expedient, considering the great range of these relations, that the real sentiments of the citizens should be formally and satisfactorily ascertained.

The project had thus far appeared to be received with very general approbation; but it was thought that if the result of the proposed appeal to the citizens, in general meeting, should show that they really entertained such views of their own interest, great encouragement and support would be given to the City Council in their future measures. Should, however, the result indicate that the general opinion was opposed to the contemplated improvement, it was desirable that the fact should be known before proceeding farther on the subject.

These views of the Committee were approved by the City Council, and at a general and very full meeting of the inhabitants, on the sixteenth of January, 1824, the following questions were submitted to them. 1st. Is it expedient that Faneuil Hall Market should be extended towards the Harbor, between Ann Street and the street leading to Bray's Wharf, in such direction as the City Council, upon a view of all the circumstances of that vicinity, shall deem most for the public interest; and that the City Council be requested to cause the same to be effected accordingly? 2d. Is it expedient for the City Council to apply to the Legislature for such an extension of the powers of the Surveyors of Highways, as the circumstances of the contemplated project above-mentioned may make necessary, under such limitations and restrictions as the constitution requires, and as respect for private rights may dictate?

At this meeting the subject was debated with warmth, and opposed by several citizens of wealth, talent, and eloquence. In its support, the Mayor stated the views entertained by the City Council, produced a plan of the general improvement contemplated, embracing a ground view and an elevation of the proposed stores and market house;—the former extending no further than to the easterly end of Codman's Wharf, being only four hundred and fifty feet in length, and not passing in an easterly direction beyond the ancient southwesterly line of the dock, and was limited to the space between the lane leading to Bray's Wharf and Ann Street, having the market house fifty feet wide, with a sixty-five feet street on its north side and a sixty feet street on its south side. The market house was proposed to be only one story in height, of wood, open on all sides, supported by a double row of pillars, like the market houses in Philadelphia, and bearing no comparison with the plan which was subsequently executed. It was, however, opposed as being impracticable, from its extent and expense, and was opprobriously denominated "the mammoth project of the Mayor." It was denounced as laying the foundation of a city debt, "which neither the present inhabitants of Boston, nor their posterity, would be able to pay." It was said that schemes of this kind had better be left to the enterprise of individuals, who do them better and cheaper than corporations. It was denied that a great market was wanted.

To these and other arguments adduced in opposition to the project, a very few plain statements were opposed, explaining its necessity, feasibility, and expediency, and showing that it would probably create the means for indemnifying the city for the expenses which its prosecution would occasion. These general considerations, aided by the strong conviction which the embarrassed and inconvenient state of the existing market had impressed on the minds of the citizens in general, seconded by the strong desire prevalent throughout the whole northern section of the city for the widening of the Roebuck Passage, and above all, the certainty that this improvement, from its locality, would, if carried into effect, result in producing important changes, favorable to the value of real estate in that division of the city, caused the arguments in favor of the project to have a weight and influence which neither the talents, nor the respectability of those who resisted the proposition, could successfully counteract. Both questions were carried in the affirmative by great majorities, and as was asserted at the time, by at least three to one.[1]

In conformity with this expression of the public opinion, a full memorial, stating the advantages resulting to the country and the city from the proposed project, was presented to the Legislature, and on the twenty-first of February, 1824, an act was passed "authorizing the extension of Faneuil Hall Market in Boston." The principles of that act were contested, both before the Legislative Committee and in the Legislature itself. At one period the chance of success seemed so dubious, that the Mayor prepared, on his own responsibility, a short pamphlet, and caused it to be distributed to the members of the Legislature, elucidating, very briefly, the questions in controversy. It however finally passed in both branches, with no inconsiderable majorities.

On the first of March, the Committee on the extension of Faneuil Hall Market reported to the City Council the act they had obtained from the Legislature, and suggested the course of proceedings which they now deemed it proper for the City Council to adopt, in the form of distinct resolutions, which were accordingly passed by the City Council on that day. By the first of these resolutions, the conditions of the act of the Legislature, on which the powers granted depended, were complied with by the formal declaration of the City Council, "that the public exigencies required that the limits of Faneuil Hall Market should be extended" between Ann Street on the north, a line drawn from the east end of Faneuil Hall on the west, the south side of Faneuil Hall and the lane leading to Bray's Wharf on the south, and the harbor on the east. By the second, the direction in which the market should be extended, was referred for future consideration. By the third, a joint committee was appointed

[1] *Columbian Centinel*, 17th January, 1824.

to consider whether the land requisite for the improvement should be acquired by purchase or by virtue of the powers granted by the Legislature; and, in the latter case, to report the particular direction in which the extension should be effected. Should the mode of purchase be selected by the Committee, they were then authorized to proceed to make the purchases, three fourths of the Committee concurring in such purchase, and signing a vote to that effect; their powers of purchasing being limited to the sum of five hundred thousand dollars. This sum was inserted in the Common Council, by a majority of only *one*, (yeas 19, nays 18.) By the fourth, the Committee were authorized to borrow, at five per cent., for the payment for the estates purchased, a like proportion of the Committee being required to sanction in writing the terms of any loan. By the fifth, the Mayor and Treasurer were empowered to sign and countersign certificates of such loans; the joint Committee who reported the resolutions being authorized to carry them into effect.

This Committee, consisting of the Mayor and Messrs. Child, Patterson, and Benjamin of the Board of Aldermen, and Messrs. Dexter, Silsby, E. Williams, Brooks, Russell, Winslow, and Tappan of the Common Council, had its first meeting on the sixteenth of March, 1824, and gave a general authority to the Mayor to purchase three of the principal estates (Codman's, Wheaton's, and Miller's) at rates below what those proprietors had previously demanded.

On the twenty-sixth, the Mayor reported the rejection by those proprietors of the offer made by the Committee. The proceedings were then postponed, and the Mayor was authorized to proceed in the negotiation at his discretion, subject to the approval of the Committee.

At this period, great difficulties appeared in the way of the project. Two of the Committee declared themselves decidedly opposed to proceeding on the scale contemplated, and presented calculations to show that the project would result in a debt of at least five hundred thousand dollars. These were met by counter calculations, which were satisfactory to the other members of the Committee; and as on the first of May, the conditional contracts obtained by the Mayor of the several proprietors would terminate, a decisive course of measures now became necessary. On the ninth of April, therefore, the Committee authorized the

Mayor to purchase the estates at the prices at which any of the proprietors were under contract to sell. This authority that officer immediately proceeded to execute, and from this time the operations, with reference to this improvement, were efficiently commenced; a debt of more than forty-eight thousand dollars was now contracted, nearly twenty thousand feet of land, besides wharf rights secured, and a general authority further to negotiate having been vested in the Faneuil Hall Committee, the City Council closed its labors on this subject for the second year of the city.

CHAPTER VII.

CITY GOVERNMENT. 1823-1824.

JOSIAH QUINCY, *Mayor.*

Proceedings relative to the House of Industry — Opposition of the Overseers of the Poor to the Removal of the Inmates of the Almshouse — A House of Correction erected at South Boston — Attempts to Conciliate the Overseers of the Poor — Its Effects — Liberty to use the Cellars of a Church for Burial denied — Department of Police.

AT the commencement of the second administration of the city in May, 1823, it had become apparent that the House of Industry was destined to sustain an unqualified opposition from the Overseers of the Poor, and a decided support from a majority of the City Council.

When the Committee for erecting the House of Industry, under the town government, first visited the Almshouse in Leverett Street, in April, 1821, they were convinced that the edifice and the land round it were wholly inadequate to the present and future exigencies of the community. These facts were admitted by the Overseers of the Poor themselves, and also by the Superintendent of the Almshouse. All the particulars of its want of adaptation to moral effect and discipline cannot here be stated. The Committee, therefore, after obtaining authority and appropriations, purchased, as already stated,[1] sixty-three acres of land at South Boston, and erected the House of Industry, with accommodations to effect a complete separation of the sexes, with every arrangement for the comfort, health, and employment of the respectable classes of the poor, and with distinct apartments for the insane. And they anticipated that the sale of the house and land in Leverett Street would probably indemnify the town for this expenditure at South Boston.

These arrangements of the Committee of the House of Indus-

[1] See ch. iii. p. 38.

try received the sanction of the inhabitants at the last town meeting ever held in Boston. And their opinions and views were confirmed by the Report of the Committee of the first City Council, of which the Mayor, John Phillips, was Chairman.[1] But to the Overseers of the Poor this whole plan was obnoxious. They did not estimate the estate in Leverett Street at so high a value as the Committee, and although they acknowledged the inadequacy of the Almshouse, its location near the centre of business facilitated the performance of their duties, and they did not regard inconveniences to which they had been long inured with the same feelings of disapprobation as did those to whom they were new. They sympathized in the prejudices of the more respectable inmates in favor of the present location, and were unwilling to deprive them of the humble comforts and pleasures obtained, by permission, once a week to stroll about the streets and visit the families and receive the charities of their former friends.

These, and perhaps other motives of a less distinct character, led to a course of opposition, which, during the first year of the city government, prevented the House of Industry from going into operation, and occasioned also a long series of embarrassments to the second administration. On the first of May, 1823, when the Chairman of the Committee of the House of Industry was inaugurated Mayor of the city, he recommended to the City Council to take early measures to carry that institution into effect, and a joint committee[2] was raised on the subject, of which he was appointed Chairman. On the twelfth of May, the Committee reported that it was expedient to put the House of Industry into operation as soon as possible; and eight thousand dollars were immediately appropriated towards its completion.

This report was based upon a statement annexed to it, representing the advantages of supporting the poor on an extent of land sufficient to enable them to raise at least their own provisions, and on the total inadequacy of the Almshouse in Leverett Street to the objects of such an institution, since its restricted limits gave its inmates a pretext to obtain leave to wander about the city every week, where some of them found means to gratify their propensity to intoxication, to beg, or to steal, of

[1] See ch. iv. p. 51. [2] See ch. v. p. 62.

which the records of the Municipal Court contained melancholy evidence.

On the nineteenth of May, in conformity with the act of the Legislature, authorizing the City Council to appoint the Directors of the House of Industry, the first Board[1] was chosen, who proceeded forthwith to complete the arrangements for that institution. And on the twenty-eighth of July, the Directors gave notice that the House of Industry was prepared to receive the inmates of the Leverett Street Almshouse. For the adoption of measures to remove a part of them to South Boston, a joint committee of the City Council,[2] was appointed to meet the Board of Overseers of the Poor. After several interviews it became evident that if the City Council were not to receive a decided opposition to the proposed transfer, they were to have no assistance from the Overseers. It was also found that the inmates of the Almshouse had generally imbibed gross and unfounded prejudices against the House of Industry, in addition to the dislike which paupers, accustomed to be supported in comparative idleness, naturally felt towards an institution in which work was to be required of them.

On the first interview, the Overseers of the Poor declared they had no authority to transfer the poor in the Almshouse to the care of the Directors of the House of Industry, and that they should not coöperate in such removal. On the urgent remonstrance of the Committee, they at length assented to allow to be transferred such of the able-bodied poor as the Master of the Almshouse should declare might be spared from that establishment; and the whole number of the able-bodied poor in the Almshouse being *one hundred and fifty-five*, the Overseers consented to discharge *forty-one*. As the Overseers had set up a claim of exclusive authority on the subject, their decision concerning the number to be transferred to the House of Industry was acquiesced in by the Committee.

But the Overseers, persisting in their determination to give no sanction to the transfer, instead of delivering the paupers over to

[1] The members elected were, — John Bellows, George W. Otis, Henry J. Oliver, Isaac McLellan, Cyrus Alger, Edward Cruft, Samuel Dorr, George Hallet, Benjamin Shurtleff.

[2] This Committee were the Mayor, Daniel Baxter, Joseph H. Dorr, and Caleb Eddy, of the Board of Aldermen; Eliphalet Williams, James Savage, John P. Boyd, Noah Brooks, and Joel Prouty, of the Common Council.

the Committee, called them severally into their room, and, in presence of the Committee, gave to each of the paupers a written discharge from the Almshouse, simply informing them they were now free from that establishment. By this course of proceeding, the paupers were made to understand that the Overseers gave no countenance to their removal to the House of Industry, and that they were at liberty to go or not at their pleasure. The subsequent proceedings of the Committee towards the paupers were, consequently, not authoritative, but persuasive, and they urged upon the *forty-one* able-bodied poor, which the Overseers had consented to spare from the Almshouse, the advantage of taking the bread of the city in the place which the city had provided. The result was, that only *twenty-one* could be prevailed upon to embark for the House of Industry in a boat prepared for their transfer. The rest took the Overseers' discharge; some of them saying, "they did not go into an almshouse for work; that if they wanted to work they could get it out of doors." Thus the first attempts of the City Council resulted in obtaining *twenty-one out of one hundred and fifty-five* able-bodied poor then in the Almshouse for the establishment at South Boston.

The City Council were convinced by this result that temporary and compromising measures must be laid aside, and their determination to carry into full effect the original design of the House of Industry at South Boston should at once be made apparent to the Overseers of the Poor and the inhabitants of the city. And on the twenty-fifth of August, 1823, the Committee made a full report, stating the views of the Overseers of the Poor, regarding their authority and that of the Directors of the House of Industry, and the consequent difficulties they had encountered in their attempts to remove the paupers from the Almshouse to that institution; and then considered the question, whether both these establishments ought to be continued. They argued, that from motives of economy alone, the Almshouse ought to be discontinued, as the sale of the house in Leverett Street would probably be sufficient to defray the expense of all the buildings requisite at South Boston. They then urged that the health and happiness of the paupers required a pure atmosphere, space for exercise, a separation between the sexes and between the vicious and virtuous poor, and opportunity for useful employment; all of which could be obtained in the highest degree at South Boston. They, therefore, recommended that all the inmates of the Almshouse in Leverett Street, which afforded none of these advantages, should be transferred to the House of Industry, and that the estate in Leverett Street should be sold.

The Committee then developed a plan, which the Committee first appointed by the town for the erection of the House of Industry had formed, which was to erect in the vicinity of that institution a house of correction for the reception of rogues and vagabonds, and other proper subjects of restraint and punishment. They urged that the protection and comfort of the poor, who from age, misfortunes, or infirmity, took refuge in the House of Industry, required such a separation, and recommended authority and an appropriation for carrying the same into immediate effect. In conformity with these views they proposed, —

1. That the House of Industry at South Boston should hereafter be the Almshouse of the city, and that the Overseers of the Poor should be directed to cause all the poor to be forthwith transferred to it with certain specified exceptions.

2. That all the furniture, provisions, &c., should be transferred in like manner to the House of Industry also, with certain specified exceptions.

3. That the Overseers of the Poor should be authorized to make temporary provision for the sick and maniacs in the house in Leverett Street.

4. That a committee of the City Council should be appointed to superintend and aid the Overseers in these arrangements.

5. That the Directors of the House of Industry should be authorized to erect a house suitable for a house of correction, and an appropriation of twenty thousand dollars be made for that object.

6. That a joint committee of the City Council should be appointed for the sale of the Almshouse in Leverett Street.

7. That the future admission of paupers into the house in Leverett Street should be prohibited, except in case of necessity, and until they could be removed to South Boston.

8. That the Overseers of the Poor should be authorized to give permits for admission into the House of Industry.

9. That the Mayor and Aldermen, on application of the Overseers of the Poor, should be authorized to provide for the transfer of such poor to South Boston.

This report was accepted, and the votes recommended passed by both branches of the City Council, and the several committees appointed, of each of which the Mayor was constituted Chairman.

By the direction of the Committee, the Mayor communicated these votes to the Overseers of the Poor on the ninth of September; but they refused to comply with the directions relative to the transfer of the poor to South Boston, denying the authority of the City Council and the responsibility of the Overseers to that body.

The Mayor, however, being anxious to prevent, if possible, all collisions between the different city authorities, addressed a letter to the Chairman of the Overseers of the Poor, stating that "*twenty* or *thirty* laborers were now wanting at the House of Industry;" that "he had been informed by one of the Overseers of the Poor that such a number, at least, of able-bodied poor were now in the Almshouse with little or no work;" that "if they could not be obtained, it would be necessary for the city to hire;" and expressing the wish of the city authorities to avoid all public discussions of questions of jurisdiction between coexisting boards, inquired whether, considering the actual relations of things, and also the great respectability in point of character and talent of the Directors of the House of Industry, the Overseers of the Poor, under the expressed wish of the City Council, may not enable that body to avoid the necessity of any discussion, concerning relative powers, by *simply declaring that under these circumstances and relations, they consent that such of the poor as, after consultation by the Committee of the City Council with the Overseers, it shall be deemed expedient to transfer, shall be temporarily placed under the direction and superintendence of the Directors of the House of Industry, until the whole poor shall be transferred, reserving to the Overseers of the Poor the right of visitatorial power, in relation to that establishment, at their pleasure, and of making all inquiries concerning the management there, as they deem expedient, and, in case of any dissatisfaction, of taking such measures as the exigency may require.*"

None of these suggestions were acceded to by the Overseers of the Poor; and on the twenty-third of September, 1823, they made a communication to the City Council, signed by Redford Webster, their Chairman, developing their views of their duties and rights. In this they stated, that as they derived their authority from the people, "*it did not appear that they were, in any respect, the agents of the City Council, or properly subordinate to them;*" that "*they derived their powers from the statute passed in* 1735, *ratified and confirmed in January,* 1789." They then undertook, by a course of reasoning, to show that the city charter effected no change in those powers, and that notwithstanding the acts of the legislature, establishing the Directors of the House of Industry, the Overseers had the right to the care of the Almshouse and the superintendence of its government and the management of the poor.

The Committee of the City Council, thus finding that all attempts to induce the Overseers of the Poor to acquiesce in the measures proposed, were fruitless, submitted a report, marking out a course of measures, which were adopted by the City Council. In this they showed that the claims set up by the Overseers of being "neither agents or subordinates of the City Council," necessarily implied they were either equals or superiors; either of which excluded the idea of responsibility; that if not responsible to the City Council, they were responsible to no one, as the City Council was the only body now invested with the fiscal, prudential, and municipal concerns of the city. The consequences of such a claim by a Board expending annually thirty or forty thousand dollars of the public money was too serious to be passed over without examination; they recommended, therefore, a special committee for that purpose.

In order, however, to avoid all discussions concerning the relations of authority of the City Council and the Board of Overseers, they recommended a course of measures coincident with the views entertained by the Overseers of their own powers, and predicated upon the statute of 1735, which that Board considered as the basis of those powers.

As the statute of 1735 required that "the house for the reception and employment of the idle and poor should be under the regulation of the Overseers of the Poor, and be erected, provided for, continued, or discontinued, as the town of Boston shall find or judge their circumstances require;" and, as the town had no longer a corporate existence, and all the rights of the ancient town were, by the terms of the city charter, vested in the city of Boston; and, as all the administration of the prudential and municipal concerns of said city are, by the same charter, vested in the City Council, the Committee considered that it would not be questioned by the Overseers, or by any one, that it now belonged to the City Council, exclusively, to "judge what the circumstances of the city required, in relation to any such house thus erected."

Upon this ground, following the precise words of the statute of 1735, in all material points, they recommended that votes should be passed of the following import: —

1. That for the present, and until the further order of the City Council, the house in Leverett Street should be the house for the reception and employment of the idle and poor of the city, under the regulation of the Overseers, and be continued, or discontinued, as the City Council shall find or judge the circumstances of the city require."

2. That the Committee of the City Council should proceed to Leverett Street, and, after notice given to the Overseers, "judge what the circumstances of the city require, in relation to said house and the inmates thereof;" and if they judge, in relation to any of said inmates, that "the said house shall be discontinued," it was declared as to them discontinued, and not lawful for the Overseers to apply to such inmates any portion of the public provision; and if they afterwards did so apply it, the amount was ordered to be deducted from their accounts.

3. That, in case the Committee of the City Council should "judge that the circumstances of the city required that the persons, in relation to whom the house in Leverett Street was thus discontinued, should be admitted into that at South Boston, they were authorized to give a certificate to that effect, and the Directors of the House of Industry thereupon should admit them into that institution.

Other votes were also recommended, for appointing a committee to inquire into the powers and authorities of the Overseers of the Poor, under the city charter, particularly with reference to the limitations of expenditure of public moneys, and their responsibility for their disposition of them; also, for the transfer of five thousand dollars of the unexpended appropriation from the Overseers of the Poor to the Directors of the House of Industry; and, finally, giving to the Overseers of the Poor, in conformity with the act of February, 1794, a general visitatorial power, in relation to the treatment of the poor, in the House of Industry. These votes passed the Board of Aldermen on the twenty-ninth of September; and on the first of October, notice having been given of these votes to the Overseers, the Committee attended, on the second of October, at the Almshouse Wharf with a boat, and received from them *thirty-five* of the inmates, who were forthwith transferred to the House of Industry. After this time, the course of measures which the City Council had originally resolved upon were steadily pursued, — to make the house erected at South Boston the refuge of the respectable poor, and the House of Correction, then in progress, the receptacle of the vagrant and vicious.

During the remainder of this city year, the house in Leverett Street was chiefly used for the accommodation of the sick, and for the temporary reception of those who were to be subsequently transferred to South Boston, no further obstructions being offered by the Overseers. An account of their opposition to future measures of the City Council will be given in a subsequent chapter.

The foundation for a building for a house of correction was laid this year, under the superintendence of the Directors of the House of Industry. About five acres of land were also purchased, in its immediate vicinity, for the enlargement of its boundaries.

In this state of progress the relations of that institution stood at the end of the second year of the city government.

In June, 1823, a petition of the proprietors of the church in Bromfield Street, praying for the liberty to erect tombs in the cellars of that edifice, drew the attention of the City Council to a consideration of the expediency of granting such a right. The subject was referred to a Committee of the City Council.[1] The petition was pressed with great urgency, as a common right, and the grant of a like privilege, by the preceding City Council to the churches of St. Paul and Park Street, was relied upon as conclusive. The question presented great difficulties. To grant it, would be to allow all the churches in the city a similar privilege, which, considering the pecuniary advantage resulting, would be likely to be generally used. To deny it, would be to withhold from a nume-

[1] This Committee were, — the Mayor, Aldermen Dorr and Hooper, and Messrs. Page, S. Perkins, Wales, and Bullard, of the Common Council.

rous congregation rights which had, during the last year, been granted to two churches in their immediate vicinity.

On examining into the circumstances under which those privileges had been granted to the St. Paul and Park Street churches, it was found that they had been acquired under a weight of private interests and influences, which rendered it doubtful whether the permanent welfare of the city had been sufficiently considered. The important question, concerning the propriety of allowing cemeteries under churches in the heart of a metropolis, had been brought before the first administration in December, 1822, by a petition of the proprietors of St. Paul's, praying for leave to use the cellar under that building as a place of interment; "and stating that, having erected a church at a great expense, they had incurred a debt, from which they could not be relieved unless their prayer was granted. Among the proprietors of St. Paul's were men of wealth and influence, who were earnestly desirous of securing, not only for their church, but for themselves, the benefit of possessing tombs under it. The proprietors of Park Street possessed similar influences in the community, and were actuated by a similar desire to be relieved from a troublesome debt, by the sale of their cellar for tombs. Members of each society were members of one or the other branch of the city government. This combination of circumstances had a tendency to counteract an unbiased inquiry into the public interest.

The Committee of the first City Council, to whom the petition of the church of St. Paul's had been referred, in 1822, reported, that "learned physicians had given a decided opinion that no injurious effects were to be apprehended from granting such a privilege on the health of the city;" that "persons whose business obliged them to be constantly exposed to the decomposition of animal matter, were as healthy as other classes of citizens;" and that "no danger had arisen from cemeteries under King's Chapel and Trinity Church;" and, "as to nauseous effluvia, tombs might be so constructed as to prevent any inconvenience in that respect;" and after recommending that the City Council should annex it as a condition, that the tombs should be constructed under the direction of a committee of the City Council, and forever subject to their control, they reported the prayer of the petition ought to be granted. This report was accepted in both branches on the thirtieth December, 1822. The Committee who made this report, in answer to the objection, that other societies would claim the same privilege, stated "they had not taken that into consideration, leaving it to the judgment of those who shall have the care of the interests of the city at the time such application may be made." No notice was taken of this statement, or intimation given, so far as could be ascertained, of any intention on the part of the proprietors of Park Street Church, to take immediate advantage of the precedent. Yet, on the twenty-third day of January ensuing, as soon as the principle was settled, by the acceptance of that report, those proprietors presented a petition for a similar right of interment under their church, predicated on the grant to the Church of St. Paul's; and their petition was granted, without even the formality of commitment or any further inquiry.

Other circumstances greatly diminished the confidence of the second administration of the city in the soundness of these permissions, and led them to submit the petition of the proprietors of the church in Bromfield Street to a rigorous scrutiny. On the fourth of August, (1823,) the Chairman of this Committee reported, that the claim of the Bromfield Street Church had no foundation on the ground of common right, each City Council being independent, and not bound to exercise its discretion by precedents set by its predecessors; that if the claim of this church be granted, there would be no resisting similar claims, and that the cellar of every church in the city might be converted into a cemetery; that the temptation to exercise that right, when it was recognized to be universal, would be absolutely irresistible, since Park Street Church had already realized *eight thousand dollars*, and St. Paul's *thirteen thousand*, by sales of tomb rights, under the liberty granted by the first City Council.

Touching the opinions of those physicians, who had declared to the Committee of the first City Council, on the application of St. Paul's Church, "that if tombs under churches were of brick and stone, and arched, there could be no danger to health therefrom;" and that "fevers arise from the decomposition of vegetable, and not of animal, matter;" the Committee of the second City Council remark, that "they have ascertained that other physicians, not less known, of at least equal standing, and as well deserving of confidence, held directly contrary opinions, in which they are supported by facts, and the concurrence of European physicians of eminence;" from which the Committee deemed it at least doubtful, whether any measure so naturally alarming, and, once adopted, if erroneous, so irretrievable, should be predicated on opinions thus equivocally settled among professional men. "But if," they add, "decomposition of animal matter be not obnoxious, why require tombs to be constructed with so much care? The physicians most favorable to such grants declare, there will be no danger if the tombs were properly built, thereby strongly implying there would be danger if they are improperly built. By the very words of these physicians, safety, therefore, depends, not upon the harmlessness of the effluvia, but upon the precautions used. The declaration of one physician, that 'he had never known the slightest offensiveness from tombs under churches,' was distinctly repelled by the deposition of the sexton of King's Chapel, and by the certificate of the Rev. Dr. Freeman, rector of that church; as also by a letter from the oldest physician of the city, Dr. Samuel Danforth, who, for extensive practice, weight of professional character, and intellectual talent, was second to no physician in it; and other certificates, to like effect, might have been obtained from other physicians. In conclusion, the Committee stated, that the evidence of the noxiousness and danger from the effluvia under churches was, in their opinion, established beyond question, and confirmed even by the advocates of that practice; that safety depends upon the tightness of the vaults; and that the impossibility of enforcing requisite precautions by statutory provisions was evidenced by the fact, that the right of erecting tombs under Park Street and St. Paul's Churches was granted on the express condition, '*that they should be built under the direction of the City Council;*' yet, strange as is the fact, *the tombs are built, and no directions of the City Council were either asked or given, so far, at least, as appears by their records.*"

The Committee add, that "a subject of this importance should be decided without regard to private interests. The right of being buried under churches must necessarily be confined to a very few. It is not just, that a small minority of the population should have the privilege of poisoning the air for the great majority. If the right of ancient tombs is to be respected, those rights ought not to be multiplied and extended by the erection of new tombs. It is the duty of the official guardians of states and cities to avoid adopting any policy materially affecting the general health or welfare on the assumption of wavering theories, especially when they contradict the most direct intimations of sense and reason. Instead of advocating the burial of the dead within the city, the great duty of a city government is to adopt rigidly a prospective system, which should ultimately, in some distant time, exclude burial within its limits altogether. The Committee, therefore, recommend a rejection of the petition of the Bromfield Street Church; the prohibition of the erection of new tombs within the ancient peninsula of Boston; the adoption of ' measures ultimately tending to exclude all burials hereafter within the peninsula; and devising measures for applying the only perfect and satisfactory remedy, by adopting some common place of burial for all the inhabitants, selected, if possible, beyond the limits of the city, but certainly beyond that of the peninsula, of an extent sufficient to meet the future exigencies of the population. There let all classes meet together, and let a common interest in the place be fortified and perpetuated by the sympathies and affections common to all, and thus become honored, and protected, and consecrated."

These views were submitted by the Committee in a series of resolutions, and adopted by the City Council.

The church and congregation in Bromfield Street, although denied a liberty which had been granted by the first City Council to the churches of St. Paul and Park Street, and who were thus deprived of an important pecuniary benefit, submitted without a murmur, and in a manner highly honorable and exemplary, to the decision of the City Council.

The tone and policy of this report, made in 1823, have been since sanctioned by the establishment of the cemetery at Mount Auburn by an effective organization of private citizens; and if similar plans are adopted by any future City Council, the main design of the Committee may be in time carried into effect, and burials altogether excluded from the precincts of the city.

The new organization of the city authorities having rendered a more efficient police requisite than had existed under the town government, an ordinance was passed, in June, 1823, authorizing the election and prescribing the duties of the city marshal, to which office Benjamin Pollard was immediately nominated by the Mayor, and appointed by the Board of Aldermen. In constituting this department, a strong feeling was manifested in the Common Council to retain in their hands a concurrent vote in the appointment of the City Marshal, as being the head of the police. But the opinion ultimately prevailed, that this officer was in fact the arm of the executive branch, for which it ought to be exclusively made responsible; that a voice in his appointment, vested in the legislative branch, would essentially and injuriously affect that responsibility. An officer, exercising powers and fulfilling duties like those required of the City Marshal, ought, as far as possible, to be removed from all temptation of fear, on account of his popularity. This office, when faithfully executed, must often cross the interests, and sometimes the passions, of men influential in local spheres. Perhaps no office exposes an individual to greater risks of becoming unpopular. Both from its conspicuousness and its salary, the office would be an object of ambition and intrigue; and that the difficulties of a faithful performance of its duties, from their minuteness, and the general and wide sphere of action to which they were applicable, rendered such performance easily susceptible of mistake and misrepresentation. These considerations were conclusive in the judgment of the Common Council, who passed the bill constituting this department, limiting the responsibility of this officer to the Board of Aldermen, on whom rested the reciprocal responsibility of keeping an unworthy officer in power. The importance of this decision on the character and efficiency of this office cannot be too highly estimated. The qualifications of Mr. Pollard for the office of City Marshal were unquestionable. He was intelligent, well-educated, gentlemanly in manners, acquainted with the laws and with mankind, and of a disposition to fulfil the duties of the office faithfully. It would not have been easy to find an officer combining more requisite qualities, or generally more acceptable.

He performed the duties of City Marshal twelve years, under four successive administrations, until his death, in November, 1835.

CHAPTER VIII.

CITY GOVERNMENT. 1823-1824.

JOSIAH QUINCY, *Mayor.*

Measures for the Suppression of Idleness, Vice, and Crime — A House of Correction — Its Effects — Building provided for Juvenile Offenders — Its Results — Petition for General Meetings in Wards — Loans proposed for City Improvements — Theatrical Licenses — Ropewalk Lands — Islands in the Harbor — Common Sewers.

PECULIAR and difficult duties, relative to idleness, vice, and crime, devolved upon the second administration of the city, which led to measures, during the six ensuing years, resulting in a complete system of institutions adapted to their restraint and reformation.

That class of vicious population unavoidable in a city was, at that time, in Boston, thickly concentrated in a district at West Boston. Twelve or fourteen houses of infamous character were openly kept, without concealment and without shame. The chief officer of the former police said to the Mayor, soon after his inauguration: "There are dances there almost every night. The whole street is in a blaze of light from their windows. To put them down, without a military force, seems impossible. A man's life would not be safe who should attempt it. The company consists of highbinders, jail-birds, known thieves, and miscreants, with women of the worst description. Murders, it is well known, have been committed there, and more have been suspected." He was asked, "If vice and villany were too strong for the police?" He replied, "I think so; at least, it has long been so in that quarter." He was answered, "There shall be at least a struggle for the supremacy of the laws."

These representations of the police officer were not exaggerated; but means of relief were difficult. A house of correction, the legal instrument of control for such offences, had never existed in the town of Boston. Within the inclosure surrounding the Almshouse in Leverett Street, there had been, from its first establishment, a small brick building, called "The Bridewell;" but its accommodations were too limited to restrain or punish even the inmates of the house,[1] and were wholly inadequate as a resource to come in aid of the judicial courts of the county. A sentence to the House of Correction was, in effect, a sentence of confinement to the common jail, where this class of offenders received their punishment, without means of labor, and without other special superintendence or moral influence than tenants of prisons were at that time accustomed to receive, which was comparatively none at all. It accordingly appears, by the official returns of the Municipal Court, in the years 1822 and 1823, that, out of *three hundred and fifty-eight* sentences to confinement, *two hundred and forty-three* were to the common jail, and *not one* to the House of Correction. It was obvious, therefore, that all attempts to give efficiency to the moral police of the city, must be preceded by providing a house of correction.

On inspecting the common jails of the city, in Leverett Street, it was found that, of the two stone prisons there situated, one was amply sufficient for all the usual exigencies of the courts of justice. It was determined, therefore, to convert the other into a house of correction, and employ the inmates in the adjoining jail-yard in hammering stone and like materials.

Accordingly, on the fourth of June, 1823, the Mayor and Aldermen passed an order appropriating the North Prison to that use, and appointed the jailer of the prison its keeper.

Both the sheriff and the jailer opposed this measure. Their objections, representing such a location of the House of Correction, in the vicinity of the common jail, to be incompatible with the safety of the one institution and the discipline of the other, had so much weight, that the Mayor pledged himself, on behalf of the City Council, that the arrangement should be temporary; and, on the recommendation of the Committee, in 1823, the City Council, in December following, authorized a building, destined for a house of correction, to be erected at South Boston.

In October, 1823, the House of Correction was organized in the North Jail, in Leverett Street, under the statutes of the

[1] It was two stories high, forty-one feet long, thirty feet wide, and contained twenty-four locked cells and two other cells.

Commonwealth, by appointing three overseers,[1] and establishing rules and regulations for its government. A Committee of the Board of Aldermen, consisting of the Mayor and Messrs. Odiorne and Child, was also appointed for the general superintendence of the whole subject.

The immediate result of these measures on the moral condition of the city were thus stated by the Mayor, in his inaugural address to the City Council, in May, 1824:—

> "There existed at the commencement of last year, in one section of the city, (West Boston,) an audacious obtrusiveness of vice, notorious and lamentable, setting at defiance not only the decencies of life, but the authority of the laws. Repeated attempts to subdue this combination had failed. An opinion was entertained by some, that it was invincible. There were those who recommended a tampering and palliative, rather than an eradicating, course of measures. Those intrusted with the affairs of the city were of a different temper. The evil was met in the face. In spite of clamor, of threat, of insult; of the certificates of those who were interested to maintain, or willing to countenance, the locating vice in this quarter, a determined course was pursued. The whole section was put under the ban of authority. All licenses in it were denied. A vigorous police was organized, which, aided by the courts of justice and the House of Correction, effected its purpose. For three months past, the daily reports of our city officers have represented that section as peaceable as any other. Those connected with courts of justice, both as ministers and officers, assert that the effect has been plainly discernible in the registers of the jails and of prosecutions.
>
> "These measures did not originate in any theories or visions of ideal purity, attainable in the existing state of human society; but in a single sense of duty, and respect for the character of the city; proceeding upon the principle that, if in great cities the existence of vice is inevitable, that its course should be secret, like other filth, in drains and in darkness; not obtrusive; not powerful; not prowling publicly in the streets for the innocent and unwary.
>
> "The expense by which this effect has been produced has been somewhat less than one thousand dollars; an amount already, perhaps, saved to the community in the diminution of the costs of prosecutions, which an unobstructed course of vice would have occasioned."

The records of the courts of justice soon proved that the House of Correction diminished the inmates of the prison, and its establishment was hailed by those interested in the moral efficiency of the laws, as an era in our municipal history. The Grand Jury of the county, in September, 1824, in their official report, expressed "*their gratification to learn that, after a lapse of*

[1] Thomas Kendall, Jonathan Thaxter, and Edward Dyer.

thirty-six years, measures have been adopted by the government of the city, to erect a suitable house for the confinement and labor of those numerous lewd, idle, and disorderly persons, who, by the vigilance and faithfulness of the Mayor and Police Court, are arrested in their unlawful career."

The beneficial results of the House of Correction were also acknowledged by the citizens in general and the City Council; and in November ensuing, a committee of both branches urged the erection of a stockade fence round the sixty acres attached to the House of Industry, on the ground that the enclosure would soon comprehend the House of Correction, which had already, in its restricted location in the North Jail, by its terrors and discipline, enabled the city authorities so to reduce the number of crimes and offences, as to have their success publicly acknowledged by the justices of both the criminal courts and the keeper of the jail.

In this report, the Committee give the first intimation of the intention of the City Council, which had, from the first establishment of the House of Correction, been entertained by the Mayor and influential members of that body, to make that institution applicable to juvenile offenders, as soon as it had been brought into effective operation at South Boston; by its aid to clear the markets, streets, and wharves of those vagabonds, boys, beggars, and drunkards, who, under pretence of gaining a livelihood, learned the habits of begging, stealing, or gambling, and whose reformation could not be effected without effectual restraint.

Although objections had been made by the sheriff and jailer to the use of the North Jail as a house of correction, experience had induced the latter to wish for its continuance in that location. The Overseers of the House of Correction concurred in this wish, as its superintendence was more easy than at South Boston. Considerable expenses, also, had been incurred for its establishment in the North Prison, which would be lost by a removal. The impending great debt of the city, consequent on the extension of Faneuil Hall Market, was also brought forward to obstruct further appropriations. An opposition was thus raised, which neither influence nor argument could overcome; and after the building for the House of Correction at South Boston had been finished, it was permitted to lay unoccupied for more than a year, so satisfactory had the result of the experiment of its establishment in the North Jail proved.

All attempts for a removal of the House of Correction to South Boston thus being for a time ineffectual, a design was formed to place in the edifice erected for it an establishment for the reformation of juvenile offenders. Accordingly, on the nineteenth of January, 1826, a Committee of the City Council, composed of the Mayor, Aldermen Oliver and Loring, and Messrs. Stevenson, Boies, and Grosvenor, of the Common Council, was appointed to consider the whole subject; and, on the ninth of February, the Committee made a report, stating the importance of the design; the inadequacy of a voluntary association, should it be formed for that purpose; that, although such a house, from its nature, ought to be supported from the resources of the whole community, there was no reasonable cause of expectation that it would be established by the State. The evil being chiefly felt in great cities, the remedy, it was deemed, devolved on the municipal authorities; and that, if a house for the reformation of juvenile offenders was thought necessary, it could only be effected by the power or means of the city.

The Committee then stated the causes and various considerations which had unavoidably postponed, for a time, the removal of the House of Correction to the edifice erected at South Boston, although the growth of the city would render its future transfer inevitable. In this building, the experiment of a house for the reformation of juvenile offenders might therefore be made, with little comparative expense.

The City Council immediately concurred in these views, and authorized an application to the legislature of the State for the requisite powers, which were granted to the City Council, by an act passed in March, 1826. Under this act of the legislature, the east wing of the building at South Boston, originally intended for a house of correction, was authorized to be used for the reception of juvenile offenders, and the Directors of the House of Industry appointed Directors of the new institution. The arrangements for carrying it into effect were made under the disadvantages incident to the circumstances under which it was commenced. There was far from being a universal concurrence in the design, either in the City Council or among the citizens. The expenditures were immediate and considerable;

the advantage distant and problematical. Many were of opinion that it ought to be supported by the resources of the State, and not of the city. It was an experiment, and its success necessarily depended upôn the qualifications of the superintendent, among which zeal and entire devotion to the service are indispensable. Difficulties also occurred from tender-hearted philanthropists, who regarded the length and nature of the restraint as severe, notwithstanding the boys were committed by a court of justice for serious offences. Parents, also, who had been deprived of the services of their sons, made complaints and attempts for their discharge. During the first eighteen months, the institution had about seventy inmates, from nine to eighteen years of age; but its friends, not being entirely satisfied with its success, determined to prove the efficacy of the institution by unquestionable results, or recommend its abandonment altogether. Happily, in November, 1827, the Rev. E. M. P. Wells was appointed the chaplain and superintendent; and entered on the duties of his station with the spirit and energy characteristic of a vigorous mind, a resolved purpose, and a heart zealous and devoted to the objects of the institution. By constant supervision, kind treatment, friendly advice, and strict requirement of obedience, he dispensed with the use of the whip and solitary confinement for punishments, except in highly aggravated offences. He encouraged each individual, as he rose in the moral scale, by privileges, and subjected him to privations, if he fell in it. Strictness without severity, love without indulgence, were the elements of his system of management; regarding the juvenile delinquents rather as "sinned against than sinning," both by parents and society. To secure perfect purity and order, he submitted to the inconvenience of sleeping in a large hall, with the key under his pillow, in the midst of sixty, and, at times, a hundred boys, each in a single bed; several of them possessing physical strength little, if any, inferior to his own. He held the office five years, and produced results sufficient to prove the value and receive the reward, in consciousness of fulfilled duty, of such efficiency and self-devotion. During this period, the annual admission averaged *sixty-two;* the number in the house usually was *one hundred and twenty;* at one time it amounted to *one hundred and twenty-nine.*

The annual average discharge was *fifty-six;* and the whole number over which his care was extended was *four hundred and fourteen. Four tenths* of these juvenile offenders were sent to the institution under the vagrant act; *three tenths* for larceny, forgery, and other crimes; *three tenths* for stubbornness and disobedience. They came, almost without exception, ignorant, lazy, vicious, repulsive and disgusting in external appearance. The work of improvement was general and thorough. After from two to five years' subjection to the discipline of the institution, experience showed that five sixths of those discharged by Mr. Wells might be considered reformed. They were readily received as apprentices by respectable farmers, mechanics, masters of vessels, and gave evidence, by their general conduct, of becoming useful, prosperous, and virtuous members of the community. The excellence of the institution, and the high merits of the superintendent, were universally acknowledged; and a just and well-deserved tribute to both was paid by Messrs. Beaumont and De Tocqueville, Counsellors of the Royal Court of Paris, who came in 1832 to this country, as French commissioners, to inquire into the penitentiary systems of the United States. In their report they state, that the Institution for the Reformation of Juvenile Offenders at South Boston is "admirably conducted; but its success seems to us less the effect of the system itself, than of the distinguished man who puts it in practice," who "exhibits a zeal and a vigilance altogether extraordinary, which it would be a mistake to expect in general from persons most devoted to their duties."

The system of Mr. Wells, comprising, as it does, all the essential and practical elements requisite for a sound moral, physical, and intellectual education, deserves the attentive consideration of the superintendents of all institutions for the reformation of the ignorant and vicious; but, like all systems of government, will be proportionably successful as the individual who conducts it is qualified, by talents and devotedness, for the task he undertakes.

In respect of the general effect produced by the House of Industry, the House of Correction, and that for the Reformation of Juvenile Offenders, on the relations of poverty, vice, and crime, in the citv of Boston, the Mayor, in his address on taking a final leave of the office of Mayor, which he had held for nearly six years, made the following statement, in January, 1829: —

"In respect of what has been done in support of public morals, when this administration first came into power, the police had no comparative effect; the city possessed no house of correction, and the natural inmates of that establishment were on our 'hills,' or on our commons, disgusting the delicate, offending the good, and intimidating the fearful. There were parts of the city over which no honest man dared to pass in the night time, so proud and uncontrolled was there the dominion of crime. The executive of the city was seriously advised not to meddle with those haunts, their reformation being a task altogether impracticable.

"It was attempted. The success is known. Who, at this day, sees begging in our streets? I speak generally; a transient case may occur, but there is none systematic. At this day, I speak it confidently, there is no part of the city through which the most timid may not walk, by day or by night, without fear of personal violence. What streets present more stillness in the night time? Where, in a city of equal population, are there fewer instances of those crimes, to which all populous places are subject?

"Doubtless much of this condition of things is owing to the orderly habits of our citizens; but much, also, is attributable to the vigilance which has made vice tremble in its haunts, and fly to cities where the air is more congenial to it; which, by pursuing the lawless vendor of spirituous liquors, denying licenses to the worst of that class, or revoking them, as soon as found in improper hands, has checked crime in its first stages, and introduced into these establishments a salutary fear. By the effect of this system, notwithstanding, in these six years, the population of the city has been increased at least *fifteen thousand*, the number of licensed houses have been diminished from *six hundred and seventy-nine* to *five hundred and fifty-four*.

"Let it be remembered, that this state of things has been effected without the addition of one man to the ancient arm of the police. The name of the police officer has, indeed, been changed to city marshal. The venerable old charter number, of *twenty-four* constables, still continues the entire array of the city police. And *eighty* watchmen, of whom never more than *eighteen* are out at a time, constitute the whole nocturnal host of police militant, to maintain the peace and vindicate the wrongs of upwards of *sixty thousand* citizens.

"The good which has been attained, and no man can deny it is great, has been effected by directing unremittingly the force of the executive power to the haunts of vice, in its first stages, and to the favorite resorts of crime, in its last.

"To diminish the number of licensed dram-shops and tippling-houses; to keep a vigilant eye over those which are licensed; to revoke, without fear or favor, the licenses of those who were found violating the law; to break up public dances in the brothels; to keep the light and terrors of the law directed upon the resorts of the lawless, thereby preventing any place becoming dangerous by their congregation, or they and their associates becoming insolent, through sense of strength and numbers. These have been the means; and these means, faithfully applied, are better than armies of constables and watchmen."

On the third of January, 1825, a petition by *fifty* qualified voters was presented to the Board of Aldermen for the calling a *meeting of the citizens in wards*, to consider the expediency of having twelve aldermen chosen in each ward instead of eight. The doubts entertained concerning the authority to call meetings of citizens *in wards* on subjects of this nature, were freely stated to the leading petitioners. It was found, however, that they disregarded those doubts, and placed their claim for such a meeting on the basis of right, and denied the authority of the Mayor and Aldermen to refuse, under the language of the city charter, to call any meeting of citizens petitioned for by *fifty* individuals. As the proceedings on this application might form a precedent for future times, the subject was deemed important enough to be referred to a special committee, the Mayor being chairman, who, after deliberate consideration, made a report, of which the following were the leading features, — that the question on this petition did not turn on the general authority of the Board to call meetings of citizens, either in wards or in any other way which they may deem most expedient for the general interest or local convenience; such, for instance, as calling a meeting in wards to choose a vaccinating committee; but the petition was for a very different object, namely, — "*the taking the sense of the citizens on an application to the Legislature for an amendment of the city charter, on the requisition of more than fifty qualified voters, and it prays that the meeting for this purpose shall be holden in wards;*" that the city charter in its twenty-fifth section, specifically provides for three cases, in which, on the requisition of fifty qualified voters, it is imperative on the Board of Aldermen to call a general meeting of citizens, and these are, — 1st. Consultation on the common good. 2d. Giving instructions to representatives. 3d. Taking measures for redress of grievances. That the petition in this case was unquestionable, on subjects specifically included in the above enumeration, for which it was the duty of the Mayor and Aldermen to call a general meeting of the citizens, if that would be satisfactory to the petitioners. But the claim being that the meeting should be *in wards*, the Board decided, that they had "no right, on the requisition of any number of qualified voters, by any authority derived from the charter, to call any meeting other than a general meeting for any of the objects specified in the twenty-fifth section of that charter;" that this section had express reference to the right secured to the people by the constitution of this Commonwealth to assemble, which it was intended to secure according to ancient usage; and which had always been exercised in a "general meeting," and not in ward or sectional meetings. The nature of the subjects provided for by this section, is conclusive against the right of the Board of Aldermen. The questions to which their authority in this respect extends, are of the most grave and weighty character, such as affect *the common good. Instructions to representatives, or redress of grievances*, are subjects which ought to be discussed in general meetings, that every citizen may have the advantage of the counsel and intelligence of every other citizen on a subject of general and common interest. The report, therefore, concluded that the Mayor and Aldermen had no right to call a general meeting of the citizens in wards for any of the purposes specified in the petition. This report was accepted, and ordered to be published in three of the public newspapers, for the information of the citizens.

In November, 1823, the Mayor, by message, recommended a consideration of the expediency of providing, by some general system, of loans, payable by instalments, incurred for objects of permanent improvements, in which posterity were generally and chiefly interested. The motives for this suggestion were stated to be the rapidly increasing population of the city, the proportionate increase of building, involving, as a consequence, a rapid increase in the value of lands; that it was impossible for the Surveyors of Highways to avail themselves of the opportunities daily occurring for widening and extending streets, without exceeding existing appropriations, and without throwing upon the current year burdens greater than was just and reasonable, at the same time that it would be the worst species of economy to suffer opportunities to pass unimproved, which may not occur again for many years, and, possibly, never; or should they occur, could not be availed of but at an expense many times exceeding that at which they now could be made, arising from the certain great increase of the value of land resulting from increasing population. As it respected posterity, therefore, the question was between a light, pecuniary burden of accruing interest and a heavy tax for improvements, which time would show to be unavoidable, together with narrow streets and other inconvenient localities, which the value of the land may hereafter render impossible to change, but which now might be obtained with little comparative expense; all that seemed requisite was, that limitations should be adopted to guard against excess and abuse of this power.

The message was referred to the Mayor and Aldermen Baxter, Odiorne, and Hooper, and in the Common Council to Messrs. Amory, E. Williams, Savage, Shaw, and Lamson. After deliberation, the Committee came to the conclusion, that the apprehension of a city debt, and the difficulty of preventing such a system in after time from abuse, were considerations sufficient to counterbalance the certain expediency of the measure, in its pecuniary effects on the cost of improvements in the city.

The terms and conditions on which theatrical and other licenses should be granted, had been absolutely vested in the Mayor and Aldermen by the city charter. It was important that the first steps taken should be firm and just and well considered, that correct precedents should be established.

A committee, of which the Mayor was chairman, was early raised, and, after great deliberation, reported that licenses were divisible into classes; the principles applicable to each were different, according to their respective natures; that the licenses of theatres were of all the most important, and to be viewed, in respect of morals and finance. The tendency of theatrical exhibitions to draw money from the community, and their effect on morals rendered them proper subjects, not only of revenue, but also of regulation, in respect of morals. The tax upon them ought to have reference to the advantage gained by such license. Where the effect upon morals is unquestionably bad, they should be denied altogether. Where, as in the case of theatrical exhibitions, the good is, to say the least, dubious, it is a reason for raising the tax for the license, to such a degree as, if possible, to reduce the disposition to multiply them, by diminishing the resulting benefit, thereby securing as great a respectability as the case permits, both in the character of such exhibitions, and also of those who engage in such employments. Two principles applicable to the subject result: — 1st. That the tax should be considerable; and 2d. That it should be uniform; that the amount of the tax should not depend on the expenditures incurred to set forth the exhibition, and still less on the smallness of the sum demanded for visiting them. The injury to morals is often great, in a direct ratio to the smallness of such expenditure and of such demand. It is the duty of a municipal authority, in the exercise of such power, to encourage a respectable and responsible theatrical establishment. Such an one cannot long be upheld in any community, if every light, vagrant, and irresponsible company be encouraged to compete with it, on the suggestion that its pretensions were less, and its facilities for public attraction greater. With the same views, bonds of security proportioned to the object, with responsible freeholders as bondmen, should be required to conduct the exhibition with decorum. It should not be permitted, in connection with any licensed tavern, or house for the sale of spirituous liquors. At that period, however, a license to sell them within the walls of the theatre during performance was deemed indispensable; an opinion that increasing moral influences of later times has happily and effectually changed.

This report was accepted, and the votes it recommended passed, — making the licenses annual, the tax seven hundred dollars, and the bonds required to be five thousand dollars.

In January, 1826, a vote passed the City Council, that whatever number of constables or police officers the Mayor and Aldermen shall see fit to appoint for the preservation of order and decorum in any house where theatrical or any other exhibition or public show shall be licensed or had, or in the vicinity thereof, the managers, proprietors, or owners of such exhibition or show shall be liable to pay such expense, and the making such payment shall be inserted as one of the conditions of any bond for such license.

Between Charles Street and the Basin of the Boston and Roxbury Milldam, there lay a large and valuable tract of land, known by the name of "the Ropewalk Lands," which, from its local position, its extent, its capacity of improvement, either for ornament or revenue, was one of the most important interests of the city. This tract had been granted by the town of Boston, in the year 1794, to certain proprietors of ropewalks, situated between Pearl and Atkinson Streets, which had been that year destroyed by fire. The grant was conditional, and had a double motive; sympathy for the sufferers, and the removal of the ropewalks to a distance from the then settled parts of the town; to whose safety such an accumulated mass of combustible materials was deemed dangerous. This land was marsh, or flats, overflowed at high tides by the sea, with the exception of an inconsiderable elevation, called "Fox Hill," which was chiefly valued as a resource for gravel for town purposes. The town, in its grant to the sufferers, by the fire in September, 1794, denominated it "a piece of marsh land and flats, at the bottom of the Common, including such parts of 'Fox Hill' as shall fall within the prescribed boundaries;" the street now called "Charles Street," not being at that time laid out, and these flats being regarded as the boundary of the Common. The grant was made under circumstances of great general feeling and excitement, and without sufficient consideration of its actual intrinsic value and of probable prospective consequences. The rights granted were indeed limited and qualified, but they were in their nature perpetual, and could only be devested by compromise. The ropewalks built upon this tract had been again destroyed by fire, and the proprietors themselves began to realize both the danger of rebuilding five or six long walks of wood in the vicinity of each other, and in the vicinity of buildings, which the increasing population of the city were erecting in their neighborhood. Realizing also the great value of the property, they had, in the year 1822, proposed to the first City Council to negotiate for either the purchase or the sale of the lands which the ropewalks had occupied; offering thirty thousand dollars for a quitclaim from the city, or to release their right to the whole tract, on the payment of eighty-six thousand dollars.

In May, 1823, these proprietors petitioned to the second administration of the city for deeds or a settlement of those lands, and a Committee, consisting of the Mayor, Aldermen Odiorne, Dorr, and Eddy, was appointed, and reported that the interests of those proprietors ought to be purchased by the city, and that no delay ought to occur in making a settlement of that concern. Those interests were now in few hands, but would, probably, by death, transfer, or legal process, soon become subdivided, and should they fall into the hands of minors, great difficulties might arise to the reinvesting the title, free of all incumbrance, in the city. The Committee recommended a reference of the respective claims to discreet and confidential persons, who should decide the amount the city should pay to the proprietors of the ropewalks for their interest in the tract, and that both the city and the proprietors should be bound by their decision. After great deliberation and considerable difficulty, the report was accepted by both the City Council and the proprietors. The reference resulted in an award, that the title of the proprietors should be invested in the city, on the payment of fifty-five thousand dollars. The referees mutually chosen were, — Patrick T. Jackson, Ebenezer Francis, Edward Cruft, Peter C. Brooks, and John P. Thorndike, citizens greatly distinguished for their intelligence, probity, judgment, and acquaintance with real estate; and although some opposition was made to the acceptance of the award by one of the proprietors, all the others accepted it, and the result finally reinvested in the city, free of all incumbrance, that great and valuable tract of land relieved of all the embarrassments which the complicated state of the title had occasioned.

The situation of that tract, and its connection with the health, ornament, and other interests of the city, rendered the future disposition of it a subject of immediate excitement among the citizens. Some contended that these lands were too important to be left unproductive, and that they should at once be put in a state to be sold. Others asserted that those lands were appurtenant to "the Common." And although being flats, and usually covered with water, they had never been embraced within the general idea of "the Common," yet they in fact made part of it, and, by the terms of the city charter, the City Council was expressly excluded from the power of either lease or sale of the Common; and that neither could be done without the sanction of all the citizens. The City Council deemed it most prudent to act in conformity with this last opinion; and to put an end to controversy, which was increasing in the city on the subject, they called a general meeting of the citizens on the twenty-sixth of July, 1824, and required their opinion to be expressed upon the two following questions. First, shall the City Council have authority to make sale of all the lands west of Charles Street, in such way and on such terms as they shall deem expedient? Second, shall they have authority to annex it, as a condition to such sales, that all the lands generally known by the name of "the Common," and lying between Park, Common, Boylston, Charles, and Beacon Streets, shall be kept forever open and free from building for the use of the citizens?

At this meeting, a large committee was appointed by the citizens, of which John T. Apthorp was chosen chairman. This Committee, after many meetings and long deliberation, made, in October following, a report, setting forth the inexpediency of selling the land west of Charles Street, denying the power of selling it under the city charter, and declaring the duty of keeping the space open for a free circulation of air from the west, for the sake of the health of the citizens. This report, which concludes with submitting three other questions for the decision of the citizens, in addition to those submitted by the City Council, was published and distributed, and on the twenty-seventh of December, 1824, the five questions [1] were all negatived by great majorities, except the second, which passed in the affirmative, by a majority of one thousand one hundred and eleven, to seven hundred and thirty-seven in the negative. The result of the meeting was to deny the expediency and withhold the right from the City Council of making sale of the land west of Charles Street.

In November, 1823, the Mayor called the attention of the City Council to the importance of securing Deer and Rainsford

[1] The five questions submitted by the Committee were the following: —

First Question. Shall the City Council have authority to make sale of all the upland and flats owned by the city, lying west of Charles Street, on such terms and at such times as they may deem expedient?

Second Question. Shall they have authority to annex it, as a condition to such sales, that the land known by the name of the Common, and lying between Charles, Beacon, Park, Common, and Boylston Streets, shall be forever after kept open and free of buildings of any kind, for the use of the citizens?

Third Question. Shall the City Council be authorized to bring the question of boundaries between the city and the Boston and Roxbury Mill Corporation to a settlement, and for that purpose be authorized to renew or confirm the former grants and acts of the town, with respect to said corporation, on such terms and conditions as the City Council may deem expedient: Provided that no confirmation or conveyance be made in virtue of their vote, to authorize the erection of dwelling houses or other buildings on any part of the premises?

Fourth Question. Shall the City Council be authorized to prepare for sale, and to convey on such terms and conditions as they may deem fit, so much of the upland and flats as lay southerly of a line beginning at a point on Charles Street, thirteen hundred and fifty feet southerly from the dam belonging to the Boston and Roxbury Mill Corporation, and opposite to the southwesterly corner of the Common, and running westerly at an angle of eighty-five degrees with Charles Street to the bounds of the city flats: Provided there be annexed to all such conveyances a condition that the Common and all the upland and flats lying westerly therefrom shall forever after be kept free from, and unincumbered with all buildings?

Fifth Question. Shall the City Council, whenever, in their opinion, the convenience of the inhabitants require, be authorized to lay out any part of the lands and flats, lying westerly from the Common, for a cemetery, and erect and sell tombs therein, on such terms and conditions as they may deem proper?

Islands from the inroads of the sea. The Mayor, Aldermen Child and Benjamin, and Messrs. Coolidge, Wilkinson, and Oliver, of the Common Council, were in consequence appointed a Committee on that subject, who reported on the nineteenth of November that an examination of those islands, in company with Commodore Bainbridge and General Dearborn, and with other gentlemen skilled in maritime concerns, and particularly acquainted with the influence of tempests and currents on the harbor of Boston, had resulted in a conviction of the importance of taking immediate measures to secure them from the inroads of the sea. Its action had, during late years, done great injury, by gradually washing them away, and thus filling up and shifting the present channels, and diminishing the protection derived from the bluffs and headlands to the great roadsteads of the outer and inner harbor. The operation of these causes, if not attended to in season, threatened to change one of the safest, most commodious, and beautiful harbors in the world, into a sightless, insecure succession of sand banks; the Committee, therefore, recommended an efficient and immediate application to the National Legislature for an appropriation for the preservation of all the important points, on which the safety and convenience of the harbor, and the consequent commercial prosperity depended. They suggested the erecting of a breakwater, and the obtaining from the Legislature a law, prohibiting the taking away ballast from any of the islands. This report was accepted, and the Mayor, Aldermen Child and Benjamin, the President (Wells) and Messrs. Savage, Oliver, and Dexter, of the Common Council, were appointed a Committee to carry it into effect.

On the eighth of December, 1823, the Mayor brought also before the City Council the importance of the immediate purchase of George's and Lovell's Islands, the former being, in the opinion of men of great nautical skill, the bulwark of Boston Harbor, both as being the best site for a fortress, and as affording the only secure anchorage in the lower harbor for ships of war and vessels of every size and description, during easterly gales, when without a pilot. He had ascertained that "those islands, of such inestimable importance to the city, were the property of one individual, who now derives from them an income, by the sale of stone and gravel, and thus assisted the inroads of the sea." By these combined operations, one half of George's Island had been destroyed, and both might be purchased for seven thousand dollars. The City Council were not, however, prepared to adopt the suggestions of the Mayor, and referred the subject for consideration to their successors.

In November, 1824, the Mayor again brought this subject before the City Council, stating that these islands ought to be owned by the city; that although the duty of fortifying the harbor belonged to the United States, the favorable opportunity for vesting the title to them in the city ought not to be lost. The measure would strongly express the opinion of the city government of their importance, and must have a propitious influence on an application to Congress for an appropriation for their protection. This persevering urgency effected its object. The sanction of the City Council was obtained. The Mayor and Alderman Eddy, and Messrs. E. Williams, Wales, and Coolidge, of the Common Council, were appointed a Committee, with full authority; and in March, 1825, they reported that George's and Lovell's Islands had been purchased for six thousand dollars, on terms and conditions to which the City Council immediately acceded.

In the preceding and subsequent negotiation with the General Government, the aid of James Lloyd and Daniel Webster, the Senators of Massachusetts in Congress, was earnestly and successfully given to the views of the City Council. A correspondence was also opened, by the Mayor, with James Barbour, the Secretary of War of the United States, which resulted in a transfer to them of the soil and jurisdiction of George's and Lovell's Islands, and also so much of Deer Island as should be covered by their works, and in an appropriation by Congress of forty thousand dollars for the protection of George's and Deer Islands by a sea wall. This appropriation was, however, exclusively applied to, and exhausted in protecting George's Island.

In November, 1827, the Mayor, therefore, again called the attention of the City Council to the state of the several islands and beaches in the vicinity of the different harbors of the city, stating that the former appropriation made by Congress had been expended, and that additional appropriations were requisite for the protection of our harbor from the inroads of the sea. At the same time he called the attention of the City Council to a petition pending before the Legislature of the State from the town of Chelsea, relative to the jurisdiction over Chelsea Beach, and to the importance of maintaining that Beach in its present state. He adverted also to the practice of taking ballast and sand from Bird Island and from the Bar, extending from the Great Brewster to the Stone Monument, at the entrance of the Narrows. An application to the Legislature was accordingly authorized, and an act obtained, providing against the several injuries which were specified or apprehended.

In February, 1828, the importance of protection to Deer Island, as stated in a memorial from the Boston Marine Society, was laid before the City Council by the Mayor, and a memorial to Congress for an appropriation for that object was authorized, and, in June following, a letter from Mr. Gorham, the member of Congress from Boston, was received, stating that eighty-seven thousand dollars had been appropriated, according to the tenor and request of that memorial, and in the course of the same month, another letter from Samuel L. Southard, Secretary at War, was received by the Mayor, stating that the appropriation had been made, and an engineer directed to proceed in the proposed system of protection. This was accordingly commenced in the autumn of 1828, the city having caused the cession to be made to the United States of the jurisdiction of that part of the island on which the sea wall was erected, as required in like cases by the United States.

The subject of common sewers came early under the consideration of the City Council. Under the town government, the drains were objects of private property, subject to the rules established by law. No person was allowed to open a street for the purpose of laying a new or using an old drain or common sewer, without the consent of the Selectmen. If any inhabitant, with their permission, laid a sewer, every person entering his drain into it, or remotely benefited by it, was held to pay its owner a proportionate part of the charge for its construction and repair, to be ascertained by the selectmen, with an appeal from their decision to the Court of Sessions. In case of subsequent repairs, all persons benefited were held to pay their proportion of the expense. The person opening such drain, being bound to give seven days notice, by advertisement, to all persons interested, to appear and object to it on the day appointed by the Selectmen, whose duty it was to decide whether the drain should be opened, and the person who should bear the expense.

No system could be more inconvenient to the public, or embarrassing to private persons. The streets were opened with little care, the drains built according to the opinion of private interest and economy; and constant and interminable vexatious occasions of dispute occurred between the owners of the drain and those who entered it, as to the degree of benefit and proportion of contribution.

The direction of the drain, and the place in the street selected for laying it, was often guided by the interest of him who first opened it, with little regard to public or general accommodation. An ordinance of the City Council was passed on the seventh of July, 1823, adapted to remedy these inconveniences. It provided that all common sewers should be laid and kept in repair at the expense of the city, under the direction of the Mayor and Aldermen; that persons entering or benefited by them, should be held to pay what they should deem just and reasonable. Their dimensions, size, position, and materials, with which constructed, and all incidental particulars, were subjected to their authority, and they were invested with power to compel any owner of land adjoining to make a sufficient drain into them, and if neglected, to cause the same to be done, and recover the amount of expenses, with ten per cent. damages. Penalties were annexed for entering a drain without a permit, and provisions made for repairing or rebuilding a common sewer, and assessing the cost on those benefited. A plan of each common sewer, embracing its size, its direction, and all particulars to show its local position, was directed to be kept in a book for that purpose.

To carry the system into effect, a superintendent of common sewers was appointed to grant permits, and, under the direction of the Committee of the district, to oversee the opening and repair of common sewers.

Many difficulties at first occurred in carrying this system into effect, from its novelty and from the embarrassments arising from the interference of the city common sewers with the acquired rights of persons. They were, however, surmounted, and resulted finally in the efficient and satisfactory system now in practice.

CHAPTER IX.

CITY GOVERNMENT. 1824-1825.

JOSIAH QUINCY, *Mayor*.[1]

Proceedings of the City Council of the past Year recapitulated — Importance of the Responsibility of the Mayor — Estates purchased for the Enlargement of Faneuil Hall Market — Plan of the New Market — North Block of Stores built and sold — First Plan enlarged — Southern Block of Stores built and sold — Corner Stone of Market House laid.

THE general interest of the citizens of Boston, especially of those who resided in the northern section of the city, that the improvements in progress in Faneuil Hall Market should be carried into effect on the scale in which they had been commenced, conduced to the popularity of the Mayor and Aldermen, who were all reëlected in 1824, almost without opposition.

The Mayor, in his inaugural address, expressed his acknowledgments to the citizens for their continued confidence, and to the Aldermen for their aid in the measures which had been pursued the preceding year. By these, the obtrusiveness of vice had been checked, through the application of a vigorous police; the cleansing of the streets had been taken out of the hands of contractors into the control of the city; thirteen streets had been materially widened, at the expense of nearly twelve thousand dollars; the drains of the city had been transferred from private to public custody; the malls on Charles Street and Fort Hill had been enlarged and improved; the House of Industry had been put into operation; measures adopted to vest in the city the title to the lands west of Charles Street, and to complete the projected improvements about Faneuil Hall.

The Mayor, in this address,[2] justified and explained the necessity of creating a city debt, and the principles by which the exer-

[1] The whole number of votes were 3950, of which the Mayor had 3867. The members of the Board of Aldermen were generally elected by similar majorities.
[2] See Appendix, C.

cise of that power ought to be regulated. He then gave his views of the duties and responsibilities of the Mayor, the qualities the citizens should regard in the selection of a candidate for that office, and the official energy and efficiency they ought to exact from him; and proceeded to show the incompatibility of the powers assumed and exercised by the independent boards, which had originated under the town government, with the responsibility of the Mayor, and the essential authority of the City Council, and the necessity of their removal.

On this principle of responsibility the Mayor, from his first induction in 1823, had taken the place of chairman of every Committee of the Board of Aldermen, appointed on any important interest of the city. As this practice had been openly censured as selfish and assuming, the Mayor afterwards vindicated publicly his course, as essential to a knowledge of the objects of his official duties, which included inspection, superintendence, and recommendation of measures on his responsibility. To an intelligent performance of these duties, the actual investigation of every question, as it occurs, in the course of daily business, is important, as scarcely one can arise among the complicated and often discordant interests of a great city, which is absolutely local and individual. It touches some other, perhaps some rival interest, affects some principle, or creates some precedent, which can be alone detected or rightly understood by being examined in the vicinity, or among the individuals it directly affects. The knowledge thus acquired, must often be all-important to the chief magistrate, who means to place himself in the condition to understand and maintain all the real interests of the city. One of the greatest securities for public virtue and for the exact performance of official duty is a sense of responsibility. Whoever means to be faithful to himself or his trusts will enlarge and multiply occasions for keeping alive this sense in himself and in those whose interests he is called upon to protect.

This course, also, is not merely expedient, but in a degree obligatory. The Mayor is fairly, if not highly, compensated for his services. The members of the Board of Aldermen are uncompensated. On him who receives the salary justly falls the labor and the responsibility. This course, also, has a tendency to give the Mayor a personal acquaintance with the citizens, their interests, prejudices, passions, and characters. The more of such knowledge he acquires, the better is he qualified to shape the measures of his administration so as to promote the satisfaction of individuals and the prosperity of the city.

During the first two years of his administration, the Mayor placed himself, as has been stated, at the head of every committee of a general character, and also of a great majority of those merely personal and local. If, during the subsequent years, he changed, in a slight degree, that course, it was out of respect to the opinion of others, rather than from any perception of difficulty or impracticability. From the recent organization of the city government, and the consequent new arrangement of its powers, and from many new and extensive projects of improvement, there was, during these years, an uncommon influx of questions of great interest and importance; yet the business of the office was efficiently and promptly executed. The practice of this rule of conduct, during nearly six years, did not involve the Mayor in any unreasonable or impracticable accumulation of business; and there is no ground for the opinion that such a rule, and a practice in conformity with it, exceeds the ability of any individual qualified for such a station, who brings into it, as every one ought, a heart exclusively devoted to duty, and a spirit resolved on its faithful performance.

The practice of devolving all, or a principal part, of the duties of the office of Mayor upon committees of the Board of Aldermen ought, therefore, to be received by the citizens with great jealousy.

As the city increases in population and extent, some relaxation of this principle may be required, in relation to merely personal or local questions; but none ought ever to be permitted in respect of those which affect the health, the character, or the general interests of the city. A disposition to evade labor and responsibility is the best criterion of a want of qualification for any office. It is important that this point should be distinctly stated and realized, for a contrary practice is very likely to find advocates in a course of time. Men of talents and high acquirements, who take office only as a stepping-stone to some higher station, will be apt to regard some of its duties as menial; and, consequently, to strive to throw the personal superintendence and examination of the resulting questions upon others, and cast on them the burden and responsibility of inspection and decision.

They will thus be relieved from attention to subjects, often irksome, never, in themselves, interesting, at times disgusting, and, in cases of malignant contagion, dangerous. Above all, an executive officer is thus enabled to escape the odium and unpopularity consequent upon discovering his opinions on questions often intensely interesting to individuals or sections of the city; especially when it happens, as it often must, that the Mayor or his friends are interested in the advancement or prevention of projects or improvements of the city. The practice of devolving responsibility on committees, enables men to do that by influence, which they might be unwilling to do directly. It is so much easier to effect private and personal views by committees, than by direct voice and superintendence, that there is a constant temptation to evade the principle of that official responsibility of the Mayor which tends to place his conduct in frequent and full relief before the citizens.

This principle of executive responsibility, which the Mayor, at his entrance into the office, thus inculcated on the citizens, and which, during the nearly six years of his official tenure, he never ceased both to assume and avow, was unquestionably among the chief causes of whatever success attended that administration. It is, however, unfortunately a fact, that there is in republics a reciprocal tendency, both in executives and among citizens, to keep this principle out of sight. Men are naturally jealous of any disposition to exert powers, even when they exist and are used for their benefit. But if a people require talents in official station, they must exact responsibility in their exercise; for the best, if not the only evidence of talents and qualification for public usefulness is to be found in what is recommended and effected.

The unanimity with which the Mayor and Aldermen were reëlected, in 1824, was, as has been intimated, chiefly owing to the general interest in the improvements then in progress in the great central market of the city.

In constituting the Committee, early in May, to carry into effect the resolutions of the preceding year, relative to Faneuil Hall Market, with the same powers and under the same limitations, the same members of the Board of Aldermen were reappointed; and, as some change had been effected in the other branch, Francis J. Oliver, its President, Messrs. Russell, Curtis,

T. Page, E. Williams, Hastings, and Coolidge, were associated with them, by the Common Council.

The first step taken by this Committee was of a decisive character. A sub-committee[1] was appointed to purchase all the estates within the then avowed sphere of contemplated improvement, provided that the price, including the estates already purchased, should not exceed *five hundred thousand dollars.* All the negotiations, as heretofore, were conducted by the Mayor, the judgment and advice of the other members being occasionally called in aid. By the twelfth of June, 1824, in addition to the estates already purchased, those of Samuel Parkman, of Gore's heirs, of Edward Miller, John Codman, H. G. Otis, and John T. Apthorp were secured, at a price somewhat exceeding two hundred and eighty-six thousand dollars. On that day, the sub-committee made a report of their proceedings, with estimates of what sums would probably be necessary to complete the purchase of the remaining estates, and showing that there could be no question that the whole might be purchased within the sum authorized by the City Council (five hundred thousand dollars.) This report was accepted; votes were passed unanimously, and authority given to carry the several contracts into effect, to examine into the respective titles, and to issue the requisite city stock.

On the twenty-ninth of June, 1824, a sub-committee was raised, consisting of Messrs. Child, Benjamin, and Williams, to consider what measures were requisite previously to a sale of the land purchased. Their report, made on the second of July ensuing, led to votes for notifying the tenants on both sides of the Town Dock, to remove within thirty days; to authorize the extension of the common sewer to the flats; and to locate the sea wall for inclosing the Town Dock. In all these arrangements they were the principal agents. In the mean time, the interest of the city to extend the first project contemplated became evident; and the Mayor informally ascertained the dispositions of Governor Eustis, John D. Howard, and Benjamin Bussey, relative to a sale of their estates. It had become apparent that, by turning the course of the Mill Creek, and extending the project further eastward into the harbor, the space around the proposed market would be greatly enlarged, and a new street

[1] Consisting of the Mayor, Mr. Child, Mr. Benjamin, Mr. Oliver, and Mr. E. Williams.

might be laid out at right angles with the eastern end of the proposed new market house, which would be brought in a line with the westerly end of the stores on Central Wharf, and by removing a few stores on Long Wharf, a straight and most convenient communication would be made with the northern section of the city.

Under these general views, the Committee, having satisfied themselves of the practicability of the plan, immediately authorized the Mayor to purchase Mr. Bussey's estate, and proceed in his negotiation with Mr. Howard and Governor Eustis, and to report the proceedings of the Committee to the City Council, which he accordingly did, on the fifteenth of July, stating to them the estates which had been purchased, and the price paid for them, amounting to four hundred and twenty thousand dollars; communicating, on behalf of the Committee, their great gratification that "they have been able to effect so nearly the purchase of the whole circle of territory necessary for the city to possess, without resort to the exercise of the powers granted by the Legislature;" that "they have deemed it expedient in all cases to yield to the reasonable, and in some, to the extreme, demands of proprietors, rather than to resort to a compulsory process." He then proceeded to detail the particular situation of those estates which had not yet been purchased, by which it appeared that three of the proprietors of the three fourteenth parts of the estate belonging to Spear's heirs were the only owners of estates who had "uniformly declined all negotiation concerning their interest in the contemplated sphere of improvement, and to make any proposal of sale of it to the city; and that the purpose of these proprietors was fixed and unalterable." The Committee, accordingly, recommended a course of proceeding conformable to the act of the Legislature, declaring the public exigencies required that Faneuil Hall Market should be extended in the direction following, namely,—"In an easterly direction, from Faneuil Hall to the harbor, between two lines parallel to the walls of Faneuil Hall, and extending easterly towards the harbor, of which the north line shall be fourteen feet distant from the north side of said hall, and the south line shall be one hundred and eighty feet to the south of said north line." Various other resolves were passed, giving the sanction of the City Council to the several measures proposed by the Committee. This recommendation was adopted by the City Council; and, on the twenty-second of July, the Mayor and Aldermen extended and widened Faneuil Hall Market, in the direction and within the limits prescribed by the City Council; and ordered the proprietors, whose estates had not yet been purchased, to be notified, of a meeting to be holden at a time and place specified in said resolve, and inviting them to submit all questions relative to damages to five disinterested freeholders, as specified in the act of the Legislature.

On the day appointed, the three proprietors declined referring the value of their estates or selling them.

It had always been the anxious wish of the Committee and of the City Council, as has been before stated, to complete this great improvement without resort to the compulsory authority granted by the act of the Legislature. For this purpose, they had given, or offered, in every instance, prices, either satisfactory to the proprietors, or such as, under other circumstances, would have been deemed extravagant. The fixed determination of the three proprietors of the three fourteenth parts of the Spear estate, to stand upon their rights and make no sale of their interests, rendered, however, the resort inevitable. In selecting the lines for the extension of the market, under the authority of the Legislature, the Committee had special reference to the lines of the Spear estate, so that the future interests of the city might be placed in a position not to be embarrassed by any tenacity of purpose of these three proprietors.

The City Council now took the first step towards making preparations for building a market house, by granting an appropriation of twenty thousand dollars for sea walls and drains. The Mayor, Mr. Child, Mr. Benjamin, and Mr. Williams were appointed a Building Committee, with authority to appoint an agent, and the Mayor was authorized to proceed in his negotiation with Governor Eustis for his estate beyond the Mill Creek.

This terminated favorably, and, on the twenty-ninth of July, the Mayor reported that he had closed a contract for that estate for the sum of fifteen thousand dollars. This being accepted, the Committee ordered the Building Committee to cause a new passage for the creek to be cut through Eustis's Wharf, and to fill up the Mill Creek to the southward of the line of the passage-way so cut. At this meeting, the ground plan of the new market was settled, and the walls ordered to be laid in conformity with it, by unanimous vote, Mr. Wright having been previously added to the Committee, in the place of Mr. Hastings, who was absent. Mr. Benjamin was appointed a Committee, to cause a plan to be prepared of the elevation and interior of the new market house.

In the course of the month of August, the estates of John D. Howard and Daniel Vose, and the interest of the minor heirs in David Spear's estate, were obtained, and also the principles, on which that part of the estate owned by the Long Wharf, in and adjoining Bray's Wharf, should be vested in the city, were settled. Arbitrators were also agreed upon, on the subject of the estates taken under the special authority given by the act of the Legislature. The three proprietors of the three fourteenth parts of the Spear estate still continuing fixed in their purpose, not to sell, and alone, of all the proprietors, refusing to refer, according to the election given by said act, —

Messrs. Curtis and Nichols were now employed by the Committee to examine into the whole title of the city and of the proprietors on "the Cove and to the Mill Creek;" and the Mayor was directed to prepare a report on the recent purchases and proceedings of the Committee. This, on the sixth of September, received the approbation of the Committee, and was laid before the City Council on the ninth.

In this report, the City Council are informed by the Committee, that "the interests of the city having further developed themselves, in consequence of a more intimate and accurate acquaintance with, and investigation of, the relations of the estates in that quarter, it was unanimously their opinion, that the extension of Faneuil Hall Market should not be limited by the Mill Creek, as at first contemplated. By the purchase of Eustis's and Howard's wharves, not only a great improvement would result, in the accommodation of the city, but also a great addition to the means of indemnification for its expenditures, from the additional store lots and wharf rights which these new purchases and this new extension would afford. The estate of Mr. Bussey stood in such a relation, both to the Mill Creek and to the passage from Ann Street, as to make its possession by the city extremely important; that the purchases of these estates were necessarily made without any previous public development of their intentions; but, in making them, that the Committee had acted under a distinct pledge from persons of responsibility, that if the City Council chose to disaffirm those purchases, they stood ready to take the estate, and relieve the city from them. The Committee then proceed to state their confidence, that the opinion of the City Council will be in favor of accepting them; their satisfaction that all the purchases will be made within the original estimates; but that the three estates above mentioned, not having been included within the original estimates, an additional appropriation and corrrespondent authority to make loans, would be essential.

This report the City Council accepted, and made an additional appropriation, equal in amount to the costs of those three estates, and the power solicited was granted; making the whole amount of appropriations to this period $547,500.

Between the sixth and thirteenth of September, 1824, the Committee had determined upon the plan and elevation of the new market house, that it should be of stone, and proposed to the City Council the expediency of giving authority for the sale of the store lots on the north side of the new market house.

On the fourteenth, resolves were passed by the City Council, sanctioning the plan and elevation and the sale proposed, and appropriating seventy-five thousand dollars for the erecting of the market house. The sale was directed to be at auction to the highest bidder, and the terms and conditions were to be prescribed by the Committee, three fourths thereof concurring; it being a condition annexed to such sales that a market house should be erected upon the general plan then specified and agreed upon by the City Council.

Accordingly, on the twenty-first of September, 1824, the Committee agreed that the sale should take place on the twenty-ninth of September ensuing; and that the conditions should be, among others, of temporary import,—that no bid less than *seven dollars* per square foot should be taken; the terms ten per cent. in cash; and for the residue, a bond collaterally secured by mortgage on the premises, payable at any period not exceeding thirty years, at five and a half per cent. interest per annum; the purchaser to build on or before the first of July, 1825, a substantial brick store of four stories, conformably to a plan and specification of particulars. A sub-committee was now appointed to settle with the tenants who had been removed, and the Mayor was authorized to negotiate with Samuel Hammond, Esq., relative to the land in the rear of his building, which had its front on Ann Street, and between it and the front line of the proposed new stores.

An authority to raise fifty thousand dollars, by way of loan, at five per cent., was given by the Committee to the Mayor, with the formality required, namely, — ten members signing the record.

On the twenty-seventh of September, the long-continued and difficult negotiation with Samuel Hammond was terminated, by his agreeing to pay thirty thousand dollars for the land and rights conveyed to him by the city. It being a piece of land fifty feet long and fifty-five feet wide, together with the city's right to a passage way; Mr. Hammond to conform to the plan of building required of other purchasers.

On the twenty-ninth of September, conformably to notice, the land for the north block of stores (seventeen in number) was sold; the highest lot producing twenty dollars and eighty-three cents; the lowest seven dollars the square foot; and the gross proceeds of thirty thousand and thirty-seven and a half square feet of land, which, the seventeen store lots included, amounted to the sum of $303,495.42, averaging ten dollars the square foot.

The Sub-Committee on building (Messrs. Child, Benjamin, and Page,) were now directed to proceed in their contracts; and on the fourth of October the City Council authorized the Committee to purchase the estates belonging to the heirs of Henry Bass, and also Jesse Kingsbury's estate, for the purpose of opening a street into Ann Street, and widening the passage back of the store lots. On the fifth of October, Henry Bass's estate was purchased for four thousand seven hundred and fifty dollars, and the plan of the market, as finally built, was signed by the Mayor.

From the commencement of this undertaking, the original design of extending the improvement to Butler's Row had never been lost sight of by the city authorities. The practicability of it was not believed by a majority of the Faneuil Hall Market Committee. Some doubted its expediency. Others could not believe that the estates could be purchased at a sum which would justify the undertaking. The Mayor, however, during the intervening period had negotiated with all the proprietors of land between Parkman's Block and Butler's Row, and had obtained conditional contracts for the purchase within a limited time of all the estates essential to the plan.

The sales of the store lots for the north block had greatly increased the popularity of the plan and sanctioned its success. The practicability of enlarging the accommodations round this great central market, without any important implication of the resources of the city, began to be more generally realized, and the feasibility of the plan to be recognized. The only obstruction to this enlargement was the refusal of the three proprietors to make sale of their three fourteenth interests in the Spear estate. On the thirtieth of September, however, the day after the result of the sale of the north block of stores was known, those proprietors addressed a letter to the Mayor, disclaiming all design "to stand in the way of city improvements," and declaring their "willingness that their land should be embraced in the plans adopted, and sold with the city lands, they receiving for their portion the average of the sales so made." The views of the city's interest, and their duty to it, which the city authorities had long entertained, rendered it impossible to accede to this proposition. The late sales had rendered the propriety of these views more obvious to the Faneuil Hall Committee and to the citizens in general.

By the negotiations the Mayor had now conditionally effected, it was in the power of the City Council to enlarge the plan of improvement to the greatest extent, which the relations of the land between Ann Street and Butler's Row made possible; and on the twenty-sixth of October following, he laid before the Faneuil Hall Committee the practicability of an enlargement of the present improvement, provided the Long Wharf proprietors could be induced to sell to the city an additional extent of Bray's Wharf; upon which he was authorized to enter into a negotiation with those proprietors on that subject, and Messrs. Benjamin, Oliver, and Williams, were united with him to meet any Committee appointed by them on this subject.

On the eighteenth of December, the Mayor laid before the Faneuil Hall Committee plans of an enlargement of South Market Street, and of extending the plan of improvement so as to include all the estates as far as Butler's Row, and also a street forty feet wide. This representation was referred to a sub-committee, consisting of the Mayor, Mr. Child, Mr. Curtis, Mr. Williams, and Mr. Wright, to examine all the plans and calculations, and improve upon them, if practicable, and to report what further measures may be expedient.

Hitherto all the moneys of the Committee had been subject to the draft of the Mayor, and they stood to his credit in the books of the City Bank. The Mayor stated to the Committee that he thought "the power he had over those moneys was not sufficiently restricted and checked, considered as a precedent; he, therefore, proposed a vote, which was adopted, that all payments should be vouched by the Sub-Committees making the expenditure and countersigned by the auditor;" and that all moneys received on account of the Committee should be deposited in bank to the credit of the Mayor, subject to his draft, under the preceding restrictions.

On the twenty-second of December, the Sub-Committee on the proposed extension of the plan of improvement to Butler's Row reported, and the Committee unanimously voted that the proposition for such extension of the improvement ought to be embraced; and the Mayor was requested to call a meeting of the City Council, and state to them that "by the power to apply a sum not exceeding two hundred and twenty thousand dollars, improvements of great importance might be effected, by the purchase of land, without any ultimate cost, and with a certain ultimate gain to the city."

On the twenty-fourth of December following, the City Council were specially convened on this subject, and a message transmitted by the Mayor, which developed all the views entertained by the Committee, and the motives which induced them to recommend the extension of the plan first adopted. As this measure was the occasion of much obloquy at the time, it seems proper that these views should be preserved in the form they were at that time presented to the City Council. That message is therefore subjoined,[1] by which it will be apparent that the motives which actuated the City Council were of the most public and patriotic character; their object being to avail themselves of a propitious moment to effect in the heart of the city an enlargement of the accommodations of its great central market, from a width of sixty to that of one hundred and two feet. The population of the city at that time did not make the necessity and

[1] See Appendix H.

importance of this enlargement as apparent to the citizens in general, as it was to the City Council, and as every day's increasing experience has since made it. No one can pass through South Market Street at the present day (1851) on high market days, without realizing both the importance, and even necessity, of that measure, and perceiving how greatly the advantages of that improvement would have been diminished, had this enlargement not taken place, and this street had been left of the width of sixty feet, as originally proposed.

In consequence of this message, on the twenty-ninth of December, an authority was obtained from the City Council to purchase any land to the southward of the street leading to Bray's Wharf, which they may judge expedient, provided the purchases did not exceed two hundred and twenty thousand dollars, three fourths of the Committee concurring in such purchases and signing such concurrence. On the same day, the vote of the City Council was communicated to the Committee, who unanimously executed an authority to the Mayor and a sub-committee to proceed forthwith to make the respective purchases under the above limitation.

Between the fifth and the eighteenth of January, 1825, purchases were accordingly made of land belonging to Benjamin Adams, Josiah Salisbury, James T. Austin, Thomas Barnes, and the Fifty Associates, for . . . . . . $ 113.347

And, after great difficulties and long negotiation, a final arrangement was made with the Long Wharf proprietors for the purchase of their interest, at 105.000

$ 218.347

The Committee then proceeded to direct, that South Market Street should be laid out not less than one hundred and two feet wide, and the new street, running from Merchants' Row, thirty-five feet wide; that the Mayor and Aldermen be requested to close the street leading to Bray's Wharf, and to open the new street; a select committee was appointed to prepare plans of the new store lots to be sold, determine the conditions of sale, and report; and all the tenants in Parkman's Buildings were ordered to remove in thirty days.

Thus the design of the leading members of the first Committee on Faneuil Hall Market was extended toward the east far beyond their first published plan. The western side conformed, in all material respects, to that plan, except that the market house, instead of being situated between two streets, each eighty feet in width, had a street sixty-five feet in width on the north, and one of one hundred and two feet on the south side. The cause of this unequal division of the space devoted to these streets has already been intimated.

When, in consequence of the ultimate purchases of the chief estates lying between the street leading to Bray's Wharf and Ann Street, the whole of the estate of Nathan Spear's heirs was taken into South Market Street, great complaints were made and indignation expressed, as though unexampled injustice had been done to the proprietors of the three fourteenths of Nathan Spear's estate, by taking in the whole of their interest for a street. It is not, however, apprehended that there was any just cause for such complaint and feeling. Those proprietors had maintained their rights with exemplary firmness, and had vindicated for themselves all the advantages of the increased value of their estates, derived from this city improvement. Their estate, however, was, like those of other citizens, subject to be taken, on indemnification, by the surveyors of highways for public exigencies.

In the process for such indemnification, established by law in such cases, they had the full right of receiving damages, according to the increased value of their estates, as raised by the city; and this principle was acceded to those proprietors, as a matter of law, by the Chief Justice of the Commonwealth, in his charge to the jury[1] who had the duty of assessing damages, and who awarded to those proprietors their proportion of the Spear estate, valued at seventy thousand dollars, which, previously to the commencement of this project of improvement, had never been valued at more than twenty-five thousand. The assertion, that the land was taken by the city as a speculation, was wholly without reasonable ground.

After the extension of the Centre Market, according to the original plan, was thus effected, minor projects were started in connection with it. Some proposed that the new market house

[1] See the *Boston Daily Advertiser* of the twenty-eighth November, 1826.

should be widened from fifty to eighty feet. Others, that the cellar of the market house, which was now, through its whole length, finished and walled, should be taken up and removed, so as to coincide with the centre of Faneuil Hall. The proprietors of the north block of stores on North Market Street also memorialized against the widening of South Market Street, as being injurious to them, and contrary to the faith of the city, pledged to them. Between the eleventh and eighteenth of January, these propositions were considered and rejected by the Committee; the first, unanimously; the second, by a majority of five out of nine. As the decision of these questions involved great responsibility, the Committee, after declaring their opinion, that there was nothing in the proposed widening of South Market Street contrary to the faith of the city, requested the Mayor to state to the City Council the above votes, and communicate their determination to proceed with the market house according to the present location and dimensions, unless the City Council should expressly direct otherwise; and declaring their deliberate judgment, that no other change should be permitted, except that of removing the cellar walls, and erecting it of the present dimensions, with the centre coinciding with the centre of Faneuil Hall, and this only on the condition that the proprietors of the north block of stores consent to pay all expenses consequent on such removal.

The Mayor accordingly communicated to the City Council a very long and elaborate report, showing that the widening of South Market Street was no direct or virtual violation of the faith of the city to the proprietors of the north block of stores; and stating the grounds on which the Committee had seen fit to reject the several projects for an alteration in the existing location and dimensions of the new market.

The City Council concurred in all the views of the Committee, and directed them to proceed in the manner they had before ordered.

At this period, arrangements were commenced for taking down all the buildings purchased to the northward of Bray's Wharf, and for clearing the entire space, preparatory to the sale of the south block of store lots. And, in the course of the month of February, 1825, deeds were received from the proprietors of Long Wharf, and the purchase money for them paid; the claims of tenants who had been removed were settled, and the south lots prepared for sale. The Committee also avowed their intention to recommend to the City Council to make no more purchases of estates in the vicinity of Butler's Row; declaring, at the same time, their opinion, that it would be for the interest of the city if the Mayor could induce private individuals to purchase lands in that vicinity, for further extending the improvement in that direction. This declaration was made with reference to, and in aid of, a plan of David Greenough, which had for its object the entire closing of Butler's Row.

On the seventh of this month, the Committee were deprived of one of its most active and talented members, by the resignation of Mr. Alderman Benjamin, whose practical skill, scientific acquirements, experience, and great judgment, as an architect, had largely contributed to the success and extensiveness of this important improvement, as he had been, in every stage of the building of the new market house, joined in council with Alexander Parris, the employed architect, in devising and improving its original plan.

Mr. Alderman Eddy was elected successor to Mr. Benjamin on the Special Committee.

In the month of March, the Committee purchased the estate of D. Tucker, on the Long Wharf, for the purpose of opening what is now called Commercial Street to the Long Wharf; and, after obtaining the sanction of the City Council, they also purchased, at the cost of thirty-six thousand dollars, the estates of William Welsh, Henry Lienow, and of the heirs of Mrs. Hoffman; the object being to open a thirty-five feet street in the direction of, and including, the Roebuck Passage.

On the thirty-first of this month, the twenty-two store lots, constituting the south block, including thirty-three thousand eight hundred and sixty-five square feet of land, were sold for *four hundred and three thousand eight hundred and fifty-three dollars*, it being *eleven dollars and thirty-two cents* the square foot.

On the twenty-fifth of April, the Faneuil Hall Committee made a report to the Common Council, stating the amount paid for land purchased, and for the streets laid out, for the accommodation of the new market house, with the amount received for store lots; and, on the twenty-seventh of April, 1825, in conformity with previous arrangements, the corner stone of the new market house was laid[1] in the presence of the City Council and a large concourse of citizens, there having been deposited under it, inclosed in a leaden case, a specimen of all the coins of the United States, a map of the city, all the newspapers of the city published on that day, and a silver plate, containing the names of the Mayor, Aldermen, and Common Council, of the President of the United States, and of the Executive of the Commonwealth.

[1] See Appendix I.

CHAPTER X.

CITY GOVERNMENT. 1824-1825.

JOSIAH QUINCY, *Mayor.*

Proceedings relative to the House of Industry — Opposition of the Overseers of the Poor to the Measures of the City Council — Sale of the Almshouse in Leverett Street — The Paupers transferred to the House of Industry — The question of applying to the Legislature for a Modification of the Powers claimed by the Overseers of the Poor, submitted to a General Meeting of the Citizens — Its Result — Death of Alderman Hooper — Claims of Political Parties for the use of Faneuil Hall — Difficulties relative to the Board of Health — Change in that Department — Visit and Reception of General Lafayette.

IMMEDIATELY after the organization of the city government, in May, 1824, a committee, consisting of the Mayor, Aldermen Child, Benjamin, and Eddy, with Messrs. E. Williams, Shaw, Frothingham, Otis, Barry, Upham, and Davis, of the Common Council, were appointed to consider the best mode of disposing of the Almshouse, with authority to sell it, at a sum not less than one hundred thousand dollars.

On the nineteenth of July, the Directors of the House of Industry reported to the City Council their receipts and expenditures on account of that institution, its prosperous state, and the necessity of a stockade fence around it; and a committee, consisting of the Mayor, Aldermen Patterson and Eddy, with Messrs. Wales, Russell, William Wright, and Goddard, were appointed, with full authority to transfer to the House of Industry all the inmates of the Almshouse, with the concurrence of the Overseers of the Poor. This Committee, in repeated interviews with those Overseers, stated the completion and success of the House of Industry; its special adaptation to the class of poor then in the Almshouse, its chief design being to supply them with a varied succession of healthful employment, on the land and in the House, according to the season of the year, their age, sex, and capacity, thus enabling them to do something for their own support, and adding to the comfort of the respectable poor, by a pure atmosphere, a wider space for exercise, and scenes more congenial to the human mind, than an almshouse in the midst of a populous city could afford; that those who had been transferred to the House of Industry the last year with reluctance, were not only satisfied, but grateful and happy in the change.

The Committee requested the Overseers to examine for themselves the correctness of these assertions; and, after stating that the experiment already made had convinced the City Council of the economy, humanity, and acceptableness to the poor of the House of Industry, pressed the expediency of immediately transferring the inmates of the Almshouse to the new, dry, and clean edifice at South Boston, where they might enjoy the comfort and advantage of a residence in the country during the ensuing summer.

The Committee stated that the interest of the city required that the transfer should not be delayed; as a negotiation then proceeding for the sale of the house in Leverett Street would be embarrassed by an opposition to the views of the City Council. They, therefore, proposed an immediate removal of all the poor to the House of Industry, except the sick and the maniacs; for whom suitable attendants would be provided by the city, in the Almshouse in Leverett Street, under the superintendence of the Overseers of the Poor, until that institution could be entirely closed.

They stated that it was not the object of the City Council to deprive the Overseers of their guardianship of the poor, but to render their labors more easy and efficient, by adopting a system of measures suited to the increasing population of the city. From that cause, the office of overseer had become so burdensome, that in one ward three citizens had been recently successively chosen and successively declined. These objections would be lessened when those officers were released from responsibilities relative to the place appointed for the residence of the poor; except those included in their visitatorial power.

The Committee stated that, after the transfer of the poor to South Boston, it was the intention of the City Council that all the poor "in the House of Industry and House of Correction should be under the superintendence of the Directors of the House of Industry; that all other poor within the limit of the city, in the hospital and in families, to be under the care of the Overseers of the Poor, who were to have the exclusive management and distribution of all eleemosynary funds, and of all such as the City Council may provide for the poor out of the house;" considering these services of the Overseers to include an application of time and labor sufficient for any city to claim gratuitously of any individual.

These views were not only repeated by the Committee at several interviews, but were set forth at large by them in a letter to the Overseers, dated the twenty-fifth of June, 1824, and signed by the Mayor, David W. Child, James Savage, and Eliphalet Williams, without any other effect than that which will hereafter be stated.

While the preceding controversy was pending, the Overseers of the Poor raised another difficulty, relative to their accountability to the City Council for the expenditure of public moneys. By the ordinance "establishing a system of accountability in the expenditures of the city," passed on the twenty-second of August, 1824, no moneys could be paid out of the city treasury, unless vouched by the Chairman of the Committee of the Board, under whose authority the expenditure had been made, and unless passed by the joint Committee of accounts of the City Council. The Overseers having drawn an order on the City Treasurer, without regarding the provisions of the city ordinance, which, not being accepted, the Overseers of the Poor on the twenty-fifth of September, 1824, addressed a remonstrance to the City Council, stating that, "under the town, the subscription of the Overseers to the grants and allowances, contained in their draft book, was deemed a sufficient voucher for the Treasurer;" that the delivery of the original bills and instruments, authenticating the claims of the Overseers, "would be a hinderance in the discharge of their official duties, and endanger a loss by the city;" that many of them related to adjustments and transactions between them and the Overseers of the Poor or Selectmen of other towns, and ought to be retained in their hands; that in cases of disbursements made by the Overseers, in their respective wards, to poor persons at their dwellings occasionally, according to their immediate exigencies, many inconveniences were suggested; and measures of the City Council were requested, relieving them from the operation of the ordinance relative to accountability.

This memorial was referred to a committee of the City Council, consisting of the Mayor and Alderman Odiorne, and Messrs. Coolidge, Prouty, and Morse, of the Common Council, who, on the eighteenth of October, 1824, reported that they had an interview with the Overseers of the Poor, and heard and considered all their suggestions, and that they cannot perceive why the particular provisions of that ordinance are not as equally applicable to the expenditures of the Overseers of the Poor as to those of other boards and individuals intrusted with the disbursement of public moneys, and that they see no practical difficulty or inconvenience that will result from the applicability of the ordinance in question to their expenditure; but, on the contrary, in their judgment, it would be productive of great satisfaction. The Committee then proceeded to state the expenditures of the Overseers, during the last current year, to have been upwards of thirty thousand dollars, arranged under four general heads: — 1. Salaries and sums paid for professional services. 2. Payments made to insane hospitals and other towns. 3. Payments of out of door grants and pensions. 4. Payments for articles and provisions purchased for the house. As to the first, amounting to near four thousand dollars, the Overseers could not be subjected to greater inconvenience than that to which other salaried officers were, who are paid by bills certified by the chairman of the committee of the board making the contract. It was obviously expedient that a similar principle should be applied to all accounts for salaries. Indeed the chief objection of the Overseers to the requisition seemed to be the trouble it would occasion them. As to the second head, amounting to upwards of twenty-five hundred dollars, the Committee apprehended no great inconvenience could arise after an account was liquidated and the balance struck, for the account to be certified by the chairman of the board that passed it. The objection made was, that the Overseers would be subjected to unnecessary trouble to go to the office of the auditor, in case of any necessity of recurrence to those accounts. This inconvenience, the Committee apprehended, would be counterbalanced by the great public convenience and security, from having all the public accounts of all the expending individuals and boards deposited in one office, in one systematic arrangement, under the direct superintendence of a committee of the City Council. As to the third head of payments, amounting to upwards of eight thousand dollars, all that would be required was, that a list of the names of all the pensioners, or those to whom grants were made, should be transmitted, certified by the Chairman of the Overseers, that they have been allowed by vote of the Board. And as to weekly distributions of the Overseers in the wards, all that would be required was, a statement of an account by the expending overseer, specifying the names of the person relieved, and a certificate of the Chairman of the Overseers, that the account had been passed by the Board. It was objected by the Overseers, that giving publicity to the name of the person relieved, might sometimes occasion pain to such person. The Committee, however, were of opinion, that it was *the right of society* to know how the public moneys are in such cases applied. Poverty, when it is not the consequence of vice or crime, is no disgrace; when it is the consequence of either, it is not entitled to the consideration which the objection implies. As to the fourth head, amounting to nearly fifteen thousand dollars, the payments made under it are, in every respect, precisely similar to those of other city expenditures, and there can be no reason why they should not be subject to the same system of accountability. The Directors of the House of Industry, whose relations to the city and responsibilities are altogether similar to those of the Overseers (except only that they have no discretionary power to disburse money out of the house) find no embarrassment from the provisions of the ordinance, and the Committee declared their opinion that the experiment in its effects would result in being a great satisfaction to the Overseers of the Poor, instead of an annoyance.

The reluctance thus exhibited by the Overseers of the Poor to be subjected to the same principles of accountability which the City Council had established, with regard to all boards and individuals who had the expenditures of public moneys, made a deep impression upon the minds of the Committee. This was strengthened by their unyielding opposition to the removal of the poor to the institution at South Boston, after the urgent solicitation of the Committee for such removal, expressed in their letter of the twenty-fifth of June preceding; although there were only *eighty* in the class of sick and maniacs out of more than *three hundred* inmates then in the Almshouse. The great majority of these they alleged were not capable of labor and not suited to the mode of relief provided for them in the House of Industry, and accordingly refused to assent to the transfer of more than *forty*. These they discharged in the mode they before adopted, and of this number only *thirty-two* could be persuaded to go to South Boston. It was also soon ascertained that several of these paupers, who, after having been discharged by the Overseers, had refused to go to the House of Industry, and others who had run away from that establishment, wholesome restraint being unsuited to their idle and vicious habits, had been again received into the Almshouse in Leverett Street, without any notice being given to the Directors of the House of Industry and the City Council.

These proceedings were so destructive of the discipline of this institution, that the Committee resolved, on the fourth of September, to make a final attempt to effect, if possible, a transfer of those inmates; and accordingly on that day, had, for that purpose, an interview with the Overseers of the Poor, and received from them a statement that there were *one hundred and forty-four* adults and *ninety-nine* children in the Almshouse, who were neither sick nor maniacs. And when the Committee deemed it their duty to require the concurrence of the Overseers in the transfer of those paupers to the House of Industry, to their surprise that Board, on the tenth of November, passed a vote refusing to concur in the transfer of any of this great number, for the reason that "they were not, in the opinion of the Overseers, in a condition to be discharged from their care and oversight."

The Committee which had been appointed on this subject, on the seventeenth of June, 1824, therefore communicated these facts to the City Council on the fifteenth of November, and, without making any comment on this refusal, declared their opinion that "the whole course of proceedings of the Overseers of the Poor, in relation to the House of Industry and the Almshouse, as well as the great amount of the cash expenditures of that Board, and the obstacles they had thrown in the way of their accountability to the City Council, strongly indicated the necessity and duty of the City Council to obtain, if possible, that the subject of the poor should be placed on a different footing than that which at present exists under the laws of the Commonwealth; that the experience of two years had evinced that a constant succession of embarrassments had obstructed the attempts of the City Council to produce that amelioration in the condition of the poor, and that limitation of the expenditures of that department which was originally intended by the wisdom of the citizens of Boston, when they laid the foundations of the House of Industry;" and they "suggested to the City Council the duty of inquiring whether these embarrassments are not inseparable from the incompatibility of the powers existing in, or claimed by the Overseers, when brought into connection with the powers and authorities now unquestionably vested by the charter of the city in the City Council;" that "by the theory of this charter, the branches which combine its legislative and executive powers, are competent for the management of all the concerns of the city, and among these the care of the poor, one of the most important in point of expense, and one of the most critical in point of interest. By the theory of the Board of Overseers this great concern is thrown into the hands of twelve men, chosen in wards, without much reference to the greatness of the pecuniary trust, and still less to the extent of their claimed powers. Thus, for instance, this Board has, according to their claims, a right to expend what they please, on whom they please, and how they please; sometimes supporting paupers in the house, and sometimes out of the house; sometimes paying them by monthly and quarterly drafts on the treasury; sometimes paying them by cash out of their own pockets, and charging the amount in a weekly or monthly settlement; and in these ways there actually passes through their hands annually from thirty to forty thousand dollars." The Committee in this statement did not include the great annual expenditure of the incomes of eleemosynary funds, amounting, as is asserted, to a capital of more than one hundred thousand dollars, over which the Overseers claimed entire control, and were reluctant authoritatively to give publicity to the exact amount. The Committee, after further commenting on the extreme inconvenience and inexpediency of this state of things, recommended that a Committee of both branches should be appointed, and instructed to consider and report at large on the subject. This report was accepted, and the Mayor, Aldermen Odiorne, Child, and Eddy, and the President, (Oliver) and Messrs. Savage, E. Williams, Prouty, and Curtis, of the Common Council, were accordingly appointed to consider the general relations of the Overseers of the Poor and the city, and report the measures which ought to be adopted on the subject.

This Committee, on the twenty-ninth of November, made a report exhibiting the incompatibility of the existing relations between the Overseers of the Poor and the City Council with the interests of the city, and recommending that the whole subject should be submitted to a general meeting of the citizens, and proposing measures which, if sanctioned by them, would terminate these collisions of authority.[1] To the end, also, that if a board assuming a qualified independence of the City Council should afterwards be permitted to exist, it should be the result of the voluntary act of the citizens, and should not be attributable to any shrinking from, or dereliction of duty on the part of the City Council.

The report was accepted unanimously in both branches of the City Council, and six thousand copies were printed and immediately distributed throughout the city. A meeting of the inhabitants was then called for the sixteenth of December ensuing. At this meeting very warm and exciting debates occurred, occupying the whole morning, and resulting, after several pollings, in a rejection of the measures proposed by the City Council, by a majority of only *thirty-one*, in an assembly casting *eight hundred votes*. The proceedings were then so far reconsidered, as to refer the whole subject to a committee of twelve persons, who were instructed to call, at their discretion, another general meeting of the inhabitants, at which the votes on the report they might submit should be taken by ballot.

This Committee reported at length; and, after dilating on the necessity and importance of the office of overseers of the poor from "the fact, that overseers of the poor are by law trustees of various legacies and donations to certain descriptions of poor, then amounting to ninety thousand dollars, the income of which, the donors, confiding in the humanity, prudence, and integrity of the acting overseers of their day, and justly inferring that the good sense of the people would lead them to elect similar characters as successors in after times, have at various periods placed at the disposal of the overseers so chosen, to be applied in most cases to such as had seen better days, and were not resident in the Almshouse nor partakers of the public bounty in other ways," proceeded to declare their opinion, that "the election of

[1] See Appendix K.

the overseers by the people is not only conformable to the wishes of the citizens, but an ancient practice, which circumstances do not require them to relinquish." In conformity with this opinion, the Committee recommended to the citizens for their adoption, resolutions declaring the inexpediency of complying with the propositions submitted to them by the City Council. The Committee then appointed the nineteenth of May ensuing for a general meeting of the citizens, to take into consideration their report.

On the eighteenth of November, the Directors of the House of Industry again reported to the City Council the state of the institution, congratulated the public on its success, and expressed their strong hopes that great and lasting good would result from it to the morals and interests of the city, and repeated their urgency for an appropriation of five thousand dollars for the erection of a stockade fence, as being advantageous to the present institution, and essential to a house of correction. The appropriation required was immediately granted by the City Council.

The sale of the Almshouse in Leverett Street, in March, 1825, at length put an end to the controversy relative to the transfer of the poor.

The Committee which had effected the sale declared that no delay ought to occur, in compliance with their stipulations relative to clearing the house in Leverett Street of all its inmates; and on their recommendation, two resolves were passed by the City Council, directing all the paupers to be removed to South Boston, on or before the fifteenth of April ensuing, and the members of the former Committee on the subject of the transfer of the poor to the House of Industry were appointed to have an interview with the Overseers, with authority to make such transfer. Accordingly, before that day, the house in Leverett Street was cleared of its inmates, in conformity with the resolve of the City Council; and, on a petition of the Overseers of the Poor, they assigned the southeast chamber of the second story in Faneuil Hall to that board, as a place for their meeting and a deposit of their records. On the eighteenth of April, the Committee charged with the transfer of the poor to South Boston reported to the City Council that it had been effected, and *two hundred and nine* individuals had been removed, making the number now in the House of Industry *two hundred and eighty-one;* and that all the inmates, particularly the aged and respectable females, whose comfort and accommodation deserved particularly to be considered, expressed to the Committee their content and gratitude for the change, and their regret that it had been so long delayed. The City Council, therefore, after all the difficulties with which they had long contended, had the great pleasure and satisfaction of beholding their labors, with regard to the House of Industry, crowned with complete success.

On the sixteenth of September, 1824, the Mayor announced to the City Council the death of Alderman Hooper, a lawyer of great promise, who, by his talents and virtues, had obtained an extensive local influence, which, during the short period he was suffered to remain in public life, he had successfully applied to the advancement of the best interests of the city. A resolve was immediately passed, expressing deep sympathy with his family, and a committee appointed to make arrangements for the City Council to attend the funeral, and to recommend such marks of respect as were justly due to his virtues, talents, and public services.

In November, the vacancy in the Board of Aldermen, which this event occasioned, was supplied by the election of Cyrus Alger.

In March, 1824, the representatives of two political parties, came before the Mayor and Aldermen, each claiming the use of Faneuil Hall on the evening preceding an election, under circumstances which deeply excited the feelings of both. After much deliberation that Board determined that the right should no longer depend upon the priority of application, but hereafter by alternation; and that the claims of the two parties for the ensuing election, being nearly equal, should be decided by ballots, prepared by the City Clerk in their presence; it being declared, that the unsuccessful party should have a right to the Hall on the evening of the next succeeding election. In this decision the representatives of the contending parties acquiesced.

On the nineteenth April, 1824, the joint Committee on quarantine regulations, of which the Mayor was chairman, reported, that, by the city charter, the whole subject relative to quarantine was invested in the City Council; that, in 1822, they had transferred those powers to the Board of Health, who had executed them in the character and with the attributes of an independent board; that doubts had arisen concerning the constitutionality of that transfer; and that this arrangement was not consonant to the spirit of the city charter, nor justified by its provisions; that those powers were a personal and untransferable trust to the City Council; that, although they must be exercised by the agency of others, the body by which they are exercised ought to be so organized that its dependence, in every act of its power, should be felt and acknowledged, otherwise, the City Council have a responsibility without power of control, and the *trust* of the charter is violated or abandoned; that it was a question of great delicacy and seriousness, worthy of the most anxious consideration of the City Council, whether the exercise of those powers by a board like that of the Commissioners of Health, regarding itself as independent, was a fulfilment of the obligations, however wise and respectable might be the members of that board; and that, deeming it their duty to propose a different organization for the exercise of that trust, the Committee recommended the resolutions of the following general tenor:—

1. That there should be appointed, in May, annually, health commissioners, by concurrent vote of the City Council.

2. That they should have power to carry into effect all the powers relative to the quarantine of vessels, the health, cleanliness, and comfort of the city, and the interment of the dead.

3. That there should be, in like manner, appointed a physician for Hospital Island; and also, in case of infectious diseases, three consulting physicians.

4. That there should be a joint committee annually appointed, to prepare rules and regulations and superintend the proceedings of the Commissioners; and, in case of any doubt or question, to submit the subject for the decision of the City Council.

These resolves were adopted in both branches, and the subject left for the action of the ensuing City Council.

Accordingly, on the third of May, in the ensuing city year, the Mayor, Aldermen Child, Eddy, and Hooper, with Messrs. Russell, Morse, Adan, Upham, and William Wright, of the Common Council, were appointed a committee on that subject; and, in pursuance of the policy recommended by these resolves, the agency of the Board of Health was superseded by an ordinance of the City Council, passed on the thirty-first of May,

1824, relative to the police of the city, by which the whole subject was placed under the control of a single commissioner, as has already been stated in this work.[1] On the same day, a vote passed both branches of the city, unanimously expressing their thanks to the members of the late Board of Health, for their faithful and laborious services.

The visit of General Lafayette rendered the years 1824 and 1825 a period of universal jubilee in the United States. Although the testimony of delight at his presence, which cities and states vied with each other in repeating, belong to the history of the nation, yet the proceedings of the municipality of Boston, as the triumphal procession swept through its precincts, requires here a brief notice and distinct reminiscence.

In March, 1824, the Mayor, in compliance with a vote of the City Council, addressed the following letter to Lafayette.

BOSTON, U. S. A., 20 March, 1824.

SIR, — Your intention to visit the United States has been made known to its citizens by the proceedings of their National Legislature. The city of Boston shares in the universal pleasure which the expectation of so interesting an event has diffused; but it has causes of gratification peculiarly its own. Many of its inhabitants recollect, and all have heard of your former residence in this metropolis; of the delight with which you were here greeted on your second visit to this country; and of the acclamation of a grateful multitude which attended you when sailing from this harbor, on your last departure from the United States; and also of that act of munificence, by which in later times you extended the hand of relief in their distress. These circumstances have impressed upon the inhabitants of this city a vivid recollection of your person, and a peculiar interest in your character, endearing you to their remembrance by sentiments of personal gratitude, as well as by that sense of national obligation with which the citizens of the United States are universally penetrated.

With feelings of this kind, the City Council of Boston, in accordance with the general wish of their constituents, have directed me to address this letter to you, and to express the hope that, should it comport with your convenience, you would do them the honor to disembark in this city, and to communicate the assurance that no event could possibly be more grateful to its inhabitants; that nowhere could you meet with a more cordial welcome; that you could find nowhere hearts more capable of appreciating your early zeal and sacrifices in the cause of American freedom, or more ready to acknowledge and honor that characteristic uniformity of virtue, with which through a long life, and in scenes of unexampled difficulty and danger, you have steadfastly maintained the cause of an enlightened civil liberty in both hemispheres.

Very respectfully, I am your obedient servant,

JOSIAH QUINCY, *Mayor of the City of Boston.*

[1] See ch. v. p. 73.

ANSWER OF LAFAYETTE.

To the Mayor of the City of Boston: PARIS, May 26, 1824.

SIR, — Amidst the new and high marks of benevolence the people of the United States and their representatives have lately deigned to confer upon me, I am proud and happy to recognize those particular sentiments of the citizens of Boston which have blessed and delighted the first years of my public career, and the grateful sense of which has ever since been to me a most valued reward and support. I joyfully anticipate the day, not very remote, thank God, when I may revisit the glorious cradle of American, and, in future, I hope, of universal liberty. Your so honorable and gratifying invitation would have been directly complied with in the case to which you allude. But while I profoundly felt the honor intended by the offer of a national ship, I hope I shall incur no blame by the determination I have taken to embark, as soon as it is in my power, in a private vessel. Whatever port I first attain, I shall, with the same eagerness, hasten to Boston, and present to its beloved and revered inhabitants, as I have the honor to offer to the City Council and to you, sir, the homage of my affectionate gratitude and devoted respect. LAFAYETTE.

General Lafayette landed at New York on the sixteenth of August, 1824, amidst those demonstrations of interest and gratitude, which every heart and hand in the United States was prepared to reiterate; and on the twentieth he left that city for Boston, under a military escort. During the whole course of his journey, he received continued evidences of general delight. From the lines of Massachusetts he was attended by the Aids of Governor Eustis, and was received by him at his seat in Roxbury, on the evening of the twenty-third. On the succeeding morning, seated in a barouche the city had provided, he was escorted by a cavalcade of more than a thousand citizens to the lines of Boston, where he was met by the city authorities in carriages, with a large military escort, and was thus addressed by the Mayor, standing in the barouche, in which were seated the Committee of the City Council.

GENERAL LAFAYETTE, — The citizens of Boston welcome you on your return to the United States; mindful of your early zeal in the cause of American independence, grateful for your distinguished share in the perils and glories of its achievement. When, urged by a generous sympathy, you first landed on these shores, you found a people engaged in an arduous and eventful struggle for liberty, with apparently inadequate means and amidst dubious omens. After the lapse of nearly half a century, you find the same people prosperous beyond all hope and all precedent; their liberty secure, sitting in their strength, without fear and without reproach.

In your youth you joined the standard of three millions of people, raised in an uncertain and unequal combat. In your advanced age you return, and are met by ten millions of people, their descendants, who greet your approach and rejoice in it. This is not the movement of a turbulent populace, excited by the first laurels of some recent conqueror. It is a grave, moral, intellectual impulse.

A whole people in the enjoyment of freedom as perfect as the condition of our nature permits, recur with gratitude, increasing with the daily increasing sense of their blessings, to the memory of those, who by their labors and in their blood laid the foundation of our liberties.

Your name, sir, the name of Lafayette, is associated with the most perilous and most glorious periods of our Revolution — with the imperishable names of Washington and of that numerous host of heroes who adorn the proudest archives of American history, and are engraven in indelible traces on the hearts of the whole American people. Accept then, in the sincere spirit in which it is offered, this simple tribute to your virtues.

Again, sir, the citizens of Boston bid you welcome to the cradle of American independence and to scenes consecrated with the blood shed by the earliest martyrs in the cause.

REPLY OF GENERAL LAFAYETTE.

To the Mayor and People of Boston:

The emotions of love and gratitude which I have been accustomed to feel on my entering this city, have ever mingled with a sense of religious reverence for the cradle of American, and let us hope it will be hereafter said, of universal liberty.

What must be my feelings, sir, at the blessed moment, when, after so long an absence, I find myself again surrounded by the good citizens of Boston. When I am so affectionately, so honorably welcomed, not only by old friends, but by several successive generations; when I can witness the prosperity, the immense improvements that have been the just reward of a noble struggle, virtuous morals, and truly republican institutions.

I beg of you, Mr. Mayor, Gentlemen of the City Council, and all of you, beloved citizens of Boston, to accept the respectful and warm thanks of a heart which has, for nearly half a century, been particularly devoted to your illustrious city.

The Mayor then took a seat with Lafayette.

The entrance of Lafayette into the city was announced by raising the American flag on the cupola of the State House and on Dorchester Heights, from whence a salute of one hundred and one guns was fired. The streets were profusely decorated; arches with appropriate mottoes were raised in Washington Street; and during his progress, for more than three miles, all the bells of the city were rung, and he was welcomed by more than seventy thousand inhabitants of the city and its vicinity. Every roof, window, balcony, and steeple, was put in requisition by the excited multitude, which, by its throng, often impeded the progress of the barouche. The day was cloudless, cool, and serene, and every circumstance propitious to general enjoyment. On the Common, Lafayette passed through two lines formed by several thousand children, pupils of the public schools, attired in uniform, and each wearing his portrait stamped upon a ribbon. From the State House, where his reception by the Governor was announced by a national salute from the Common, he was escorted to the mansion at the corner of Beacon and Park Streets, which had been obtained and furnished for his residence, during his visit, by the city authorities; and he afterwards attended a public dinner given by them in his honor. During the week of his continuance in the city, he was escorted by the Mayor and a Committee of the City Council, to visit every object of interest within and around the city, and no testimony of respect and gratitude was omitted.

On the thirty-first of August, the Mayor accompanied Lafayette, on his departure for New Hampshire, to the lines of Boston on Charles River Bridge, where he was received by the aids of the Governor of the Commonwealth and an escort of cavalry.

At parting, he requested the Mayor to assure the citizens of Boston that "it was impossible for words to do justice to the emotions excited in his heart by the distinguished kindness and honor with which he had been welcomed by them; that they would ever be associated with his most precious recollections; and that he warmly reciprocated their expressions of respect and regard."

On the second of September, when Lafayette returned from New Hampshire, an elegant entertainment was given him at his residence in Park Street by the City Council. Lafayette presided at the table, and they dined with him apparently as his guests; and this gratifying arrangement formed an appropriate conclusion to the attention and tributes he received from the city government of Boston.

CHAPTER XI.

CITY GOVERNMENT. 1824-1825.

JOSIAH QUINCY, *Mayor.*

State of the Fire Department — Claims of the Engine Companies — The Result — They surrender their Engines and resign — Other Engine Companies formed — A new Organization of the Fire Department recommended — Measures taken to carry it into effect — Office of Auditor of Accounts established.

DURING the first year of the second administration of the city government, the City Council were restrained by obstacles, apparently insurmountable, from any attempt to improve the then existing system of protection against fire, although great changes in it were evidently requisite. Firewards, engine, and hook and ladder men, with associated friendly fire companies, constituted the fire police. Their efficiency chiefly depended upon the aid of the inhabitants, applied under the authority of the firewards. They formed lanes of bystanders, who, by their direction, passed buckets of water, from pumps or wells in the vicinity, to the engines playing on the fire, and returned them for further supply.

This system of protection had its origin in the relations of the colonial state, when the inhabitants were few, habituated to labor, and respect for the rights of property was general. Dwelling-houses being then separated by gardens or vacant fields, extensive conflagrations were infrequent; yet, being of wood, and the means of insurance unattainable, their occasional loss kept alive the feeling of sympathy in the community. The duty of joining some fire company and assisting at every fire was, therefore, regarded as imperious.

At the time of the adoption of the city government, Boston was in a transition state, and fast advancing to that period, when, by the increase of population, ties of individual interest were diminished. The establishment of insurance offices had, in most cases, transferred the loss upon capitalists; and poverty and crime, multiplying with numbers, began to regard fires as harvests, from the gleaning of which they had not principle enough to abstain.

Although this state of things was obvious, and its effects began to be felt, yet it was long before the duty of aiding the sufferers caused the necessity of imposing restraint on the general interference of the citizens at fires to be recognized. This reluctance to acknowledge the effect of circumstances on the then existing system of protection, was peculiarly strong among the engine companies, in whom the *esprit de corps* was active and general. From the earliest period of the settlement, the members of these companies had been accustomed to regard themselves as the guardians of the city against this element, and took a pride in the consciousness of their power. They were a body of men energetic and fearless. So far from regarding their labors as onerous and looking for their reward in pecuniary compensation, a premium was often paid for admission into the companies, and they deemed themselves recompensed by a small allowance from the town, sufficient for an annual social supper, by exemption from militia duties, and the consciousness of useful and acceptable services to their fellow townsmen. Their engines, found and supported by the town, were without ornament, and valued only for their power. To be first, nearest, and most conspicuous at fires, was the ambition of the engine men; and the use of hose, as it had a tendency to deprive them of this gratification, was opposed. The hostility to any change which should induce its use, was apparently general. The opinion of the efficiency of the then existing system was riveted in the belief, and fortified by the pride of the engine companies. To doubt it, involved with them an inevitable loss of popularity; and the introduction of a hose system was ridiculed and regarded as useless. Although the citizens in general did not coincide in the opinion of the engine companies, and perceived the difficulties of the subject, they were far from being unanimous relative to the improvement the state of the department required. The City Council, therefore, determined to defer until a more favorable moment the desired alterations; and the Mayor prepared for changes which he deemed inevitable, by entering into correspondence with leading members of the fire departments of New York and Philadelphia, whose systems of protection were reported to him as highly efficient.

The fire department was brought under the consideration of the City Council in June, 1823, by a petition of several engine companies for an additional compensation for their services. The Committee to whom it was referred, reported that the remuneration already allowed was sufficient, and gave them leave to withdraw it. The acceptance of this report gave the petitioners great dissatisfaction; and the Mayor soon received notice from the captains of some of the companies that they would never be content with their present allowance, but that at *a proper season* they would renew their application. The Mayor understood, from the terms of this notice, that this renewal would be made in the winter, when their services were most important and arduous, and when, therefore, it would be most difficult to supply substitutes. The City Council consequently, immediately turned their attention to the present organization, efficiency, and equipments of the engine companies, the inducements given to join them, and the power of the firewards. These investigations increased their dissatisfaction, and presented new difficulties. The citizens complained that the firewards did not exercise their authority, despotic for the emergency, with the same energy as their predecessors. The firewards asserted that the citizens no longer aided them in their duties, by becoming members of the fire companies; and that while the classes of population disposed to be inactive or to depredate at fires increased, those who were willing to assist were much lessened. It was, therefore, more difficult to form lanes to supply the engines, and impossible to support them for any length of time. The multiplication of insurance offices, also, by diminishing the losses of the sufferers, weakened the sense of obligation to risk life and health for their relief. The engine companies were also equally loud in their complaints. The increase of population and extent of the city had rendered alarms more numerous and made distances greater. They were often obliged, from a deficiency of water, to drag their engines some hundred feet from the fire to the pump, and then back again, with the loss of half of the water obtained. In this labor and in that of working engines, the citizens were not as willing to aid as formerly. Admission into the engine companies was, indeed, yet regarded as a privilege, for which from *five* to *eight* dollars was paid by each candidate. The companies were accustomed to have four suppers in a year, which exhausted their fees, fines, premiums, and allowance from the city. The fines for failure in the militia service had been so reduced, that exemption from it was no longer a powerful inducement to enter the engine companies. *Four hundred and sixty* men were their full complement, but only *three hundred and twenty* were enrolled, and consequently not one company had its full complement, and one had but *twelve* members. The city owned *sixteen* fire engines, but only *fourteen* were in service. A few of them were of great power, but in general they were ordinary in appearance and workmanship. Only *eight hundred* feet of hose belonged to all the companies collectively. Of these each engine had its proportion for its sole use; and as the screws were not adapted to each other, to act in a conjoined line was impracticable.

Although these facts were well known, no general dissatisfaction existed; and it was dangerous for any man's reputation for sense or patriotism to question the axiom that there was no place whose inhabitants were more distinguished for alacrity and success in extinguishing fires than in Boston. The members of the engine companies, who held most firmly this opinion, were skilful, alert, and vigorous men, experienced in the service and attached to it, and so confident of their ability and popularity, that several of them said to the Committee that if the companies resigned, no individuals could be found in the city willing and able to take charge of the engines. All acknowledged that fires were more destructive than formerly; but this was attributed not to any defect in the system, but to the want of coöperation among the citizens. The remedies proposed and urged were, to revive the ancient volunteer fire companies, to enlarge the supply of buckets, and vest greater authority in firewards. The proposal of a fire department which should exclude, instead of compelling the assistance of citizens, was received with indignation. "Do you think, sir," said one of the captains of the engines, "that the citizens of Boston will ever submit to be prohibited from assisting a fellow townsman in distress. Such sort of laws may be obeyed in despotic countries, or in cities where the inhabitants do not feel for one another; but this is not the case, nor ever will be in Boston. No such system can ever be introduced into this city." When the advantages of the hose system were suggested, it was answered, that it was practicable in Philadelphia, from the abundance and easy command of water; but Boston possessed no such facilities. When it was stated in reply, that in New York the want of a sufficient head of water was supplied by stationing engines at intervals between the water and the fire, which, by playing into each other successively, enabled the nearest to throw a continuous stream upon the fire. The answer of one of the captains was characteristic of the state of the existing prejudices on the subject. "Set enginemen at a distance from the fire! It will never be submitted to. Their desire is always to be in the hottest of the battle. The nearer the fire the higher the post of honor. Their struggle is, who shall get to it the first, and who keep the nearest. It would be more difficult to keep a Boston engine back, in order to play into its neighbor, than it would be to put out the fire." Many thoughtful and intelligent citizens had also doubts concerning the efficiency of the hose system; and the City Council concluded, after much deliberation, that it was most prudent to postpone for a time attempts to introduce improvements obnoxious to so many prejudices.

During the year 1823, the whole damage received by the city from fires did not amount to *five thousand* dollars. And this uncommon exemption from calamity, by diminishing the apprehension of danger, delayed expenditures for protection.

On the seventeenth of September, 1823, the engine companies renewed their petition, demanded the usual premiums for the first and second engines which arrived at the fire, and an annual compensation of fifty dollars for each company, to be disposed of at their discretion. The Committee to whom this petition was referred, were the Mayor, Aldermen Odiorne and Eddy, with Messrs. E. Williams, Oliver, Adan, and Wales, of the Common Council. They had frequent interviews with the captains and leading members of the several companies; but the circumstances of the department, and the temper and language in which their claims were urged, made the course to be pursued very difficult. The season of the year and that which was approaching, were those in which any known general derangement of the engine companies would occasion great alarm among the citizens. The members of those companies had been long in the service of the city. Great confidence was attached to their experience. By many, the safety of the city was deemed to be essentially dependent on their continuance. In their opinion the engine companies were composed of a class of citizens whose claims it was unsafe to deny, and in whatever spirit demanded they ought to be granted.

The claims of these companies were, in fact, pressed in terms indicating their belief that the city could not dispense with their services. The Committee of the City Council were told plainly, that unless their petition was granted, they would unanimously resign their engines. On being asked, whether the companies will not be satisfied with less than *fifty* dollars each, the reply of one of the captains was, "No. We are fixed on that point. *Forty-nine dollars and ninety-nine cents* will not do!"

After this evidence of feeling and opinion, a majority of the Committee came to the conclusion that any grant made under such circumstances would be considered as an "acknowledgment of the dependence of the city upon the individuals who then composed those companies, be attributed to fear, and be only a temporary expedient and a source of future embarrassment; that the permanent safety of a city should never be allowed to be regarded as dependent on the capricious estimate of their own importance by any set of men; but that general confidence should be permitted to rest on no other basis than the conviction that there exists always among the mass of its citizens talents and will adequate to self-protection.

The Committee, therefore, on the twenty-fourth of November made a report, which was accepted by the City Council, that it was not expedient to grant the prayer of the petitioners, the present exemptions and compensations being a sufficient remuneration.

In anticipation of possible difficulty, however, the Aldermen immediately instituted inquiries in their several wards, and ascertained that the citizens generally coincided in the views of the city authorities on these claims, and that if the present companies surrendered their engines, others might be formed without difficulty.

The City Council, however, being unwilling wholly to reject the petition of the engine companies, on the sixth of November, appointed another committee, consisting of the Mayor, Aldermen Patterson, Eddy, and Hooper, with Messrs. Swett, Winslow, Wright, Tappan, and Adan, of the Common Council, who, on the twenty-fourth of that month, made an elaborate report, embracing all the topics of controversy, and after doing full justice to the efficiency of the engine companies, proceeded to show that their present compensation and privileges were greater than those granted to the engine companies of New York, who found no difficulty in keeping their numbers full. To show, however, the appreciation of the City Council of the services of the Boston enginemen, the Committee proposed to increase the premiums of the first and second companies which should arrive earliest at a fire, and an annual allowance of twenty-five dollars to each company, to be used at their discretion, which should have on the first of January in each year a complement of twenty members. This report was accepted in both branches.

When this result was announced to the companies, their captains came before the Mayor, and gave notice that they should deliver up their engines and resign their offices at their respective engine houses on *the first day of the ensuing December.*

Accordingly, at the hour assigned on that day, the captain of each company, at his engine house, delivered its keys, his engine and apparatus, all in good order, to members of the Board of Aldermen, who attended to receive them, and who immediately delivered them into the custody of able and active bodies of citizens, who had volunteered their services on the emergency. On the evening of the same day the Mayor announced to the City Council, that the fire department of the city was in its usual state of efficiency, and, in the course of the month of December, engine companies were organized in connection with every engine.

Such was the system of protection against fires at the end of the second year of the city. These arrangements were the best the state of public feeling and private interest would admit. The Mayor regarded them as temporary; and, being convinced that a radical change must be effected in the whole system, he continued the correspondence he had opened with the chief members of the fire departments of Philadelphia and New York, to satisfy his own mind on the true principles on which an efficient organization of a system of protection on this subject should be established.

The same general views concerning the inefficiency of the existing system were also entertained by the members of the City

Council, and had been confirmed and made evident to the citizens by a conflagration in Beacon Street, on the seventh of July preceding, which continued through the whole day, and consumed fifteen valuable dwelling-houses, the loss being estimated at one hundred and fifty thousand dollars, exclusive of furniture.

The inefficiency of the fire department seemed now to be generally felt and acknowledged; but no evidence was given of such dissatisfaction with the existing system as to justify an attempt to change it altogether. The old complaints, against the firewards, of the want of fire companies and of buckets, and of the indifference of citizens,[1] were reiterated, and the old remedies proposed. The diversity of opinion on this subject, and the force of prejudice was so great, that an attempt to introduce any efficient measures for a change of system was still deemed hopeless, until the seventh of April, 1825, when a conflagration occurred in Doane Street, and extended from State Street to Central Street on the one side, and from Broad Street to Kilby and Liberty Streets on the other, destroying in the course of a few hours fifty-three houses and stores, at a loss of half a million of dollars. The scene, on this occasion, was one of extreme embarrassment and confusion. The lanes, formed by the firewards with great difficulty, were soon broken or deserted, and great depredations were committed on property, brought forth indiscriminately and left unprotected in the streets. From the want of water, the engines were dragged one thousand feet to the dock, and half the water obtained was lost before they could be dragged back again and put into operation.

This calamity made a deep impression upon the citizens. The want of water, and of the means to bring a continuous stream of it on the flames, were apparent; and it became evident, that the change in the habits and sympathies of the population, and the recent and increasing infusion of foreigners, rendered a change in the organization of a system of defence against fire and a more efficient police essential.

The Mayor deemed this a favorable opportunity to exert official influence for the introduction of an independent fire department; and, under the sanction of a Committee of the City Council, consisting of the Mayor, Aldermen Baxter, Odiorne,

[1] See p. 155.

and Patterson, with Messrs. Goddard, S. K. Williams, Frothingham, Haskell, and William Wright, of the Common Council, made, in April, 1825, a report, stating the causes of the existing deficiencies in the system of defence, and the diversity of opinion concerning the remedies, each of which were analyzed and explained. Among these, reliance upon associated fire companies and the aid of the citizens, although, at the time, of all others the most popular and generally acceptable, the report represented as altogether mistaken; and that it would be encouraging false hopes and a false system, if the Committee did not declare their opinion concerning its inadequacy to protection, and did not express themselves decidedly in favor of introducing a supply of water to the engines through the means of hose, instead of by lanes formed of bystanders. The report then submitted eight resolutions for the adoption of the City Council; the four first of which had for their object to satisfy their fellow-citizens, by actual experiment, of the impracticability of reviving the ancient system of fire companies. To test the possibility of this resort, the resolutions proposed an invitation to householders and other citizens, to form themselves into societies for their mutual protection against fire; and a system of organizing such societies, under the sanction of the Mayor and Aldermen, and prescribed the number of buckets, fire bags, and other instruments usual and proper for the service, which each company should provide; and the authority which the members of such companies should exercise at fires; with an assurance that the City Council would apply to the State Legislature to invest them with all requisite powers. This scheme, although carefully devised, when proposed to the citizens, proved an absolute failure. For, although some associations were formed, the attempt evidenced the utter hopelessness of any such reliance. Three of the remaining resolutions proposed the constructing of three reservoirs in suitable places, each containing twenty-five thousand gallons of water; the purchase of two engines, in New York and Philadelphia, of approved power and construction; and also a hydraulion,[1] with the usual quantity of hose attached to each form of engine, as practised in those cities. The last and eighth resolution declared the expediency of adopting a new organization of the fire de-

[1] A small engine, with one chamber, used for forcing water through hose, as a supply to the engines.

partment, on the principle of distinct and individual responsibility; and that a Committee of the City Council should be appointed, for the purpose of arranging and reporting the details of such an organization.

The City Council adopted all the suggestions of the report, and passed the several resolutions it recommended, and appointed the Mayor, Aldermen Blake and Welsh, and Messrs. S. K. Williams, Barry, Boies, and Wales, a Committee on the eighth resolution, to arrange and report the details of a new organization of the fire department. This Committee reported on the twelfth of May two resolutions, which were adopted at once by the City Council.

The first declared the expediency of establishing a fire department, consisting of one chief engineer, and as many engineers, firewardens, engine men, hose men, and hook and ladder men, as may be chosen and appointed by the City Council.

The second requested the Mayor and Aldermen to apply to the Legislature for such powers and authorities, to be vested in the fire department, and also such privileges and exemptions granted to its members, as may be requisite, and in their wisdom deemed expedient.

The Mayor and Aldermen immediately took measures to have two engines, of approved capacity and power, to be built, one in Philadelphia, and the other in New-York. Gentlemen of skill and intelligence, in each city, kindly undertook the superintendence of their construction; and the mechanics employed in each city, being apprized that their work would be brought into direct comparison, under the stimulus of emulation, produced two engines, each of which was pronounced by competent judges to be equal in power, capacity, and workmanship to any engine in either city. Their style of construction, differing from those used in Boston, gave an opportunity to the mechanics of this city to compare, and possibly to improve, the construction of their own engines.

These measures did not pass without animadversion. It was inquired, through the press, "whether the mechanics of Boston were inferior in skill to those in Philadelphia and New York? and why the money of the city was expended in the patronage of the mechanics of other cities, rather than of its own?" But when direct inquiries were made of the Mayor by Boston mechanics themselves, concerning the principles and effects of this policy, the explanation given convinced them of its advantages; and also, that an entire change in the system of our protection against fires would cause expenditures ultimately tending to their benefit.

Such were the first steps taken towards the establishment of a fire department, to act independently of the general aid of the citizens of Boston. At this day, (1851,) after the experience of the advantages of the system, it is impossible for any one to realize the extreme antipathy, and even predetermined hostility, to the measures, evinced by men in other respects of great judgment and sagacity.

Having thus authorized the purchase of two engines and a hydraulion, and the constructing of three reservoirs, each to contain twenty-five thousand gallons of water, the City Council referred the subject of "the organization of a fire department, on the principle of distinct and individual responsibility," to the next City Council, the period of a reorganization of the city government being now approaching.

The inconvenience of leaving city expenditures subject to the control of several boards, some of whom claimed an independence of the City Council, a practice which had been borrowed from that of the town government, began to be seriously felt, and a change was demanded by the plainest dictates of expediency. The Mayor, therefore, in January, 1824, by a special message, recommended to the City Council the consideration of "a more systematic accountability for public moneys, and a more efficient check upon the expenditures of the city." A joint Committee of the City Council was accordingly appointed on the subject, who, in the April following, made a report, stating the system of accountability then practised, representing its unsatisfactory nature, and the reasons for the change it recommended. Four boards were then intrusted with the expenditure of public moneys, namely, — the Mayor and Aldermen, the Overseers of the Poor, the Commissioners of Health, and the Directors of the House of Industry. To each of these various sums were advanced, in the form of appropriations, and expended by votes of the respective boards, under the agency of committees. The members of these committees made the expenditure or the contract, and vouched the bill for the article delivered or the services rendered, including the rate of compensation or the price. A committee from the board, once in each month, examined the account of expenditures of that month, received the vouchers, and, where they agreed, passed the accounts. The course of proceeding was very similar in all the boards. However well suited such a course might have been in the early stage of municipal institutions, when the numbers affected by their authorities were small, and the amounts expended inconsiderable, the Committee deemed that a more systematic and uniform accountability ought to be established to satisfy the increasing demands and expenditures of a city rapidly augmenting in wealth and population.

It seemed to them sufficiently loose and unsatisfactory in point of efficient accountability, that the whole city expenditures should be made by forty or fifty members of four distinct boards, chosen annually for general purposes, with no particular reference to their adaptation to the particular class of expenditures which they were called upon to superintend. That these individuals, acting gratuitously, without compensation, could not be expected to give more than a certain general and occasional oversight to the objects on which expenditures were made; and that, of course, they must act chiefly by minor agents, which, as they multiplied, necessarily increased the chance of mistake and imposition.

The great defect in this organization, with reference to an efficient accountability for public moneys was, in the opinion of the Committee, the fact, that the accountability for the expenditure of each board was to committees of its own; in other words, the power to expend and the power of calling to account was efficiently the same; an arrangement, which, however inconsequential in boards destined for the mere care of property and pecuniary investment, must have important consequences in boards charged with the oversight of great expenditures, relative to objects comprising numerous details, and requiring the employment of many subordinate agents.

The labors of the committee of accounts were lessened by dividing the members of the board into monthly committees, of a number deemed expedient, — usually two.

All the members of the board undertook by turns this labor and responsibility.

The consequence was, that there was no such general superintendence as is implied and effected by accountability to one practical mind, habituated to the rules and routine of a single department. As there was no distinct, uniform rules for proceeding, committees were guided by such principles as on the instant were deemed applicable. Admissions or rejections thus unavoidably often depended upon the particular state or temper of mind of the members of the committees. The circumstances of the individual were often considered instead of the case; and the results were often very different from what they would have been had the same accounts been subjected to the analysis of other members of the same board. No stronger evidence could be given of the incorrectness of these financial arrangements, than the fact that persons having accounts to settle with the city, have been known to inquire who the monthly committee of accounts were, and to postpone presenting their accounts until those they deemed most likely not to sift severely came to exercise the power.

The defects of the system then in practice having been thus set forth, the Committee proceeded to state the remedy they proposed, which consisted in the establishment of an office of "*auditor of accounts*," and in tracing an outline of the duties and rules to which that office should be subjected.

This change was deemed too important to be passed without its being virtually submitted to the decision of the citizens. The Committee, therefore, only proposed that it should be taken into consideration by the then existing City Council, the report to be printed and distributed, recommending the whole subject to the attention of its successors; by whom it was, in August, 1824, revived, the office of auditor established, and a new system of accountability connected with it. In the same month, William Hayden was elected Auditor, and by his great ability and efficiency corrected the irregularity incident to the former system, and introduced principles for checking the facility with which additional appropriations were made, after the annual appropriation bills had been passed by the City Council.

In pursuance of the same general policy, in February, 1828, the City Council adopted a system of *self-restriction*, having for its object to confine the ordinary expenditures of the year within the limits of the ordinary annual incomes, by passing an order of the following tenor: — "That, in the present and every future financial year, after the annual order of appropriations shall have been passed, no subsequent expenditure shall be authorized for any object, unless provision for the same shall be made, by expressly creating therefor a city debt; in the latter of which cases, the order shall not be passed, unless two thirds of the whole members of each branch of the City Council shall vote in the affirmative, by vote taken by yeas and nays."

CHAPTER XII.

CITY GOVERNMENT. 1825.

JOSIAH QUINCY, *Mayor*.[1]

The Citizens accept the Report of their General Committee on the inexpediency of modifying the powers of the Overseers of the Poor — Overseers decline taking Care of the Poor at the House of Industry — Their Rights and Duties submitted to Legal Counsel — Their Report, and consequent Proceedings of the City Council — Measures to introduce a Supply of Fresh Water — Proceedings relative to Faneuil Hall Market — Census of the City — Time of Organizing the City Government changed.

THE organization of the city government was this year transferred from Faneuil Hall to that of the Chamber of the Common Council, and conducted with customary ceremonies. The Board of Aldermen consisted entirely of new members; all those of the preceding year having declined a reëlection.

The Mayor, in his inaugural address, after expressing his gratitude to his fellow-citizens for the unanimity of their suffrages, and paid a well-deserved tribute to the members of the Board of Aldermen of the two preceding years, for their faithful and laborious services,[2] directed the attention of the City Council and his fellow-citizens to the critical question then pending between the Overseers of the Poor and the City Government. After stating, in unequivocal terms, the incompatibility with the public interest of the existence, under a city organization, of an independent Board claiming the right of expending public money without responsibility to the city authorities, he explained the effect upon the character and confidence in the members of that Board, unavoidably resulting from the difference in selecting them, as now practised under the city charter, and as was formerly under the

1 The whole number of votes cast was 1891, of which the Mayor had 1836.
The members of this Board of Aldermen were George Blake, John Bellows, John Bryant, Daniel Carney, John D. Dyer, Josiah Marshall, Henry J. Oliver, and Thomas Welsh, Jr.

2 See Appendix, D.

town government. This development he regarded it his duty to make, notwithstanding that the report of the Committee,[1] appointed by a general meeting of the citizens, in opposition to those views, was about to be taken into consideration by another general meeting of the citizens, to be held on the nineteenth of May, then instant; and no doubt could be entertained that the recommendations of that report would be adopted, so conformable were they to popular habits and prejudices. The City Council, however, took no measures strenuously to oppose the acceptance of that report. They had effected the removal of the poor to the House of Industry, and of consequence felt less interest in the immediate result. They had conscientiously fulfilled their duty to the city, by faithfully explaining to their fellow-citizens the nature and consequences of the relations and claims of that Board in respect of the interest of the city. Whatever ills or difficulties might hereafter result, could not be attributed to any want of firmness or foresight in them. The citizens were left, therefore, to the unbiased exercise of their own feelings and judgment, and the report of their General Committee was adopted without important opposition.

In May, 1825, immediately after the organization of the city government, the Overseers of the Poor addressed a communication to the City Council, asking for a suitable house for the accommodation of the poor, and expressing their readiness to take upon themselves the oversight, care, and government of it. A Committee of the City Council, consisting of the Mayor, and Messrs. Williams, Thaxter, and Elliot, of the Common Council, was immediately appointed, to whom this application was referred, and who reported on the twelfth of May, that a house, such as the Overseers applied for, had already been provided by the city; that it was placed under the care of the Directors of the House of Industry, who were invested by law, in respect of the inmates of that house, with all the powers exercised by the Overseers of the Poor; that they were wisely and efficiently active in their oversight of it, to the content of the poor; and that their superintendence of the moral and physical condition of the inmates was highly satisfactory. The report expressed the gratification the Committee derived from the hope of being

[1] See ch. x. p. 146.

able to avail themselves of the general aid of the Overseers; and the readiness of the City Council to grant all those practical and useful facilities relative to providing for the poor, which, from the tenor of their application, the Overseers appeared to desire; and, in order that the poor of the city might enjoy the benefit and experience of both those Boards, the Committee presented their views in the form of three resolutions, which the City Council unanimously adopted.

By the first, the Overseers of the Poor were authorized and requested to grant permits for admission into the House of Industry of any person, in their judgment, entitled to the support of the city in that house, for which purpose its Directors were enjoined to provide relief and support.

By the second, the Overseers of the Poor were authorized and requested, at their discretion, with or without notice, to visit the House of Industry, to inquire into its condition and the treatment and employment of the poor, and make such representations on those subjects as their wisdom and experience might suggest.

By the third, the Mayor and Aldermen were authorized to provide a suitable vehicle, for conveyance to the House of Industry of such decrepid persons as were incapacitated from going of themselves, and place the same at the disposal of both the superintending Boards.

As soon as these resolutions were received by the Overseers of the Poor, they addressed, on the twenty-third of May, 1825, a memorial in writing to the City Council, stating that "they did not feel justified in relinquishing to the Directors of the House of Industry any of the tasks assigned them by law;" and that "they would not consent to grant the permits contemplated by the above resolves;" and gave notice to the City Council that, "unless a house is provided, to which the Overseers can remove paupers, the city will be exposed to great expense."

This memorial was referred to a Committee of the City Council, consisting of the Mayor, Aldermen Carney, Welsh, and Oliver, with Messrs. Savage, Williams, Thaxter, Elliot, Adan, Tracy, and Ware, of the Common Council; who, on the twenty-seventh of June, reported, that the tenor of the above memorial indicated so great a misapprehension in the Board of Overseers, concerning their rights and duties, as, if acquiesced in, would result in consequences at once serious and embarrassing; and to put those rights and duties, as far as possible, beyond all doubt and question, they had requested the Mayor to lay the whole subject before counsel learned in the law, and for this purpose had selected William Prescott, Charles Jackson, and Daniel Webster, gentlemen possessing the greatest professional reputation, and whose opinion would, it was hoped, be conclusive with the Board of Overseers, and certainly with the public.

The Mayor, accordingly, on the fourth of June, 1825, addressed a letter to those three jurists, and, after stating that an unhappy controversy had arisen, between the Overseers of the Poor and the City Council, in relation to their respective powers and duties, that a Committee of this body, to whom was referred the memorial of the Overseers, dated the twenty-third of the preceding May, had directed him to submit, for their inspection and consideration, certain laws and documents, and subjoin certain inquiries, for their official answer, as counsel learned in the law. The acts submitted were: —

1st. The act for employing and providing for the poor of the town of Boston, passed in the year 1735, and ratified and confirmed in January, 1789.

2d. An act relative to the relief, support, employment, and removal of the poor, passed the twenty-sixth February, 1796.

3d. An act concerning the House of Industry, passed the third February, 1823.

4th. An act concerning the regulations of the House of Correction in the city of Boston, and passed twelfth June, 1826.

5th. An act establishing the City of Boston, passed the twenty-third February, 1822, called the City Charter.

The documents submitted were, —

1. The Vote of the City Council, passed twenty-ninth September, 1823.[1]

2. The Memorial of the Overseers of the Poor to the City Council, without date, but which was committed in this body on the fifth of May last.

3. The Report of the Committee of the City Council on the preceding Memorial and the three Resolves subjoined, adopted and passed on the twelfth of May[2] last.

[1] See ch. vii. pp. 95, 96. [2] See p. 168.

4. The Memorial of the Overseers of the Poor to the City Council, dated the twenty-third of May last.[1]

The inquiries submitted for their official answer were, —

1. Is not the erecting, providing, and endowing the house for the reception and employment of the idle and poor of the city, called the House of Industry, and the appointment of directors thereof, according to the act entitled, "An act concerning the House of Industry," a sufficient and legal exercise of the authority invested in the City Council, under the acts of 1735, of 1794, and of 1822?

2. Does not the authority given to the Directors of the House of Industry to use, regulate, and govern said house, supersede, with respect to all persons sent to it, any authority in relation to them, given by the acts of 1735 and 1794 to the Overseers of the Poor, except so far as the City Council may authorize?

3. Have the Overseers of the Poor any right to appoint a master of said house, or to have the government thereof, or to ordain any rules or regulations concerning it?

4. Does the saving of the act of tenth January, 1789, in the act of 1794, and the continuance in force thereby of the act of 1735, preclude the city of Boston from any of the general privileges of the act of 1794, which are granted by it to the other towns of the Commonwealth; or deprive the City Council, under the transfer of powers made by the city charter, from "directing the way and manner" in which poor and indigent persons shall be supported and relieved, according to the right secured to other towns in the Commonwealth by the act of 1794?

5. Is not the "direction" given by the City Council, as to "the way and manner" in which the poor and indigent shall be relieved and supported, conclusive and obligatory upon the Overseers of the Poor, under and by virtue of the act of 1794?

6. Is not the "direction" given in the vote of the City Council, dated the twenty-ninth September, 1823,[2] full and sufficient in that respect; and have the Overseers of the Poor a right to refuse to exercise that general visitatorial power which that vote provides for and authorizes?

7. After notice given of the passing of the first resolve, on the

[1] See p. 169. [2] See ch. vii. pp. 95, 96.

twelfth of May last,[1] have the Overseers of the Poor a right to refuse to grant permits for admission of the poor and indigent, standing in need of relief, to the House of Industry, who are in other towns of this Commonwealth, but belong to Boston, and to support such persons in other places in said city, or in such other towns?

8. Have the Overseers of the Poor in said city a right to refuse to give permits for admission to the House of Industry of the poor and indigent of said city, standing in need of relief, and to support them in other places in said city?

9. Is there any power and authority in and over the House of Industry which the City Council can vest in the Overseers of the Poor, consistent with the powers and authorities vested by the act of third February, 1823, in the Directors of the House of Industry, other and greater than those invested and specified in the vote of the City Council, passed September 29, 1823,[2] and the second resolve of that body, passed the twelfth of May last?[3]

On these laws, submitted documents, and inquiries, those jurists made the following statement of their opinions: —

"In making up our opinion on the question now pending between the City Council and the Overseers of the Poor, respecting the powers and duties of the latter, we have considered first, the general provisions of the law on this subject; and secondly, the statutes which apply exclusively to the city of Boston.

"By the statute 1793, c. 59, towns may choose any number, not exceeding twelve, Overseers of the Poor, who shall have the care and oversight of the poor, and see that they are suitably relieved, supported, and employed, either in the work-house or other tenements belonging to the town, or in such other way and manner as they (the town) shall direct, or otherwise at the discretion of the Overseers.

"By the city charter (stat. 1821, c. 110,) the City Council now has all the power, in this respect, that was formerly vested in the town. If there were no other statute on this subject, it is evident that the City Council would be authorized to provide a house for their poor, and prescribe the manner in which they should be supported and employed in it; or to cause them to be relieved at their own houses, or in other private houses, or, in short, in any manner which, in the discretion of the City Council, should appear best; and it would be the duty of the Overseers to comply with such directions.

"By the provincial statute, 8 and 9 Geo. II., c. 3, (passed in May, 1735,) the town of Boston was authorized to erect a house for the reception and employ-

[1] See p. 168. [2] See ch. vii. pp. 95, 96.
[3] See p. 168.

ment of the idle and poor, and to discontinue the same if they should think proper; the house to be under the regulation of the Overseers of the Poor, who had power to make orders and by-laws for its government, subject to the control of the town, and to appoint the master and other officers of the house. If there were no other laws but those above mentioned, the City Council might, in their discretion, discontinue their almshouse, and require that their poor should be relieved and supported in some other place or other manner; but as long as the city had a house for the poor, in pursuance of that statute of 1735, the Overseers would have had the regulation and government of it. This last-mentioned statute furnishes the only foundation for the claims of the Overseers; and, although there might possibly be a question whether it has not been virtually repealed, (at least, so far as it relates to the government of the Almshouse,) yet we have thought it more safe and expedient to proceed on the supposition that it remains in force, excepting so far as it has been clearly altered by subsequent statutes. In the year 1823, the city had erected what they called a House of Industry. If this is to be considered as the "house for the reception and employment of the idle and poor," pursuant to the statute of 1735, the Overseers would have had the government of it, if no other provision had been made. But by the statute of the third February, 1822, 1823, c. 56, the Legislature gave the government of this House of Industry to nine directors, to be chosen by the City Council. If, therefore, this is the Almshouse, the government of it is taken from the Overseers and vested in the nine Directors, and the statute of 1735 is so far repealed. The City Council could not, as we conceive, give to the Overseers any control over this house, inconsistent with the authority vested by law in the Directors. On the other hand, if this House of Industry is a distinct establishment, and not such a *poor-house*, as is contemplated in the statute of 1735, it is clear that the Overseers have nothing to do with it. It is equally clear that, whether the house is of one or the other description, the City Council has authority, according to the statute 1793, c. 59, to require that the poor should be relieved, supported, and employed in that house. It may be proper here to remark that, although the law appears to give an unlimited power to towns, to cause their poor to be relieved in any manner whatever, yet there seems to be some limitation, arising necessarily out of peculiar circumstances and from other parts of the law. If, for example, a poor person should break a limb, or be so ill that he could not be moved without endangering his life, the Overseers would be bound to relieve him immediately, without carrying him to the poor-house, or before he could be sent there, notwithstanding the town should have prescribed that as the place for maintaining the poor. There is another kind of exception which, though not required by law, seems to be called for by humanity and benevolence, as well as by a regard to economy, and that is, of those householders and others, who require only partial relief, and who may be rendered more comfortable by a small supply of necessaries at their own homes, than by being wholly supported in a poor-house. And the undersigned would suggest to the City Council, the expediency of passing an order for the relief and employment of the poor in the House of Industry, and of excepting from its operation the two classes of persons above-mentioned.

"As to all those persons who may be lawfully relieved without being sent to the House of Industry, the care of them remains entirely with the Overseers; but as to all who ought by law and the orders of the City Council to be relieved and supported in that place, the Directors have the same powers that the Overseers have to send them there, and have the sole power of governing them after they are admitted.

"If the City Council has a right to require that all the poor, excepting the two classes above-mentioned, shall be supported in the House of Industry, it necessarily follows that the Overseers are bound to send all such poor there for relief; and if they should decline to do so, the remedy would be substantially the same as in any other town in the Commonwealth where the Overseers should refuse to provide for the poor according to law and to the directions of the town.

"These general views of the subject exhibit the opinions that we have formed on most of the points in controversy; but we proceed briefly to give a specific answer to each of the questions contained in the annexed papers.

"To the first, we answer, that, in our opinion, the erecting and providing for the House of Industry, is a valid and legal exercise of authority by the City Council; and we also think that it may be considered such a poor-house as is contemplated by the statute of 1735; though, for the reasons above-mentioned, we have not thought it material to settle the last question. We have no doubt that it is a house in which the City Council may lawfully order the poor to be relieved and employed; and that the poor when there, must be relieved and employed by the Directors, and under their authority.

"To the second, we answer in the affirmative. It is impossible that two distinct and independent bodies should each have the whole of the authority in question, and the statute 1822, c. 56, has given the authority to the Directors.

"To the third; in our opinion, the Overseers have no such right or authority.

"To the fourth; we see nothing in any of the statutes referred to, which could prevent the town, before the charter, or the City Council now, from "directing the way and manner" in which the poor should be relieved, supported, and employed, as any other town in the Commonwealth might do, excepting only that before the statute of 1822, c. 56, if the city had seen fit to build and maintain a poor-house in pursuance of the provisions of the statute of 1735, the Overseers would have had the direction of the house.

"To the fifth; the City Council has, in our opinion, the same authority in this respect that the town formerly possessed, and their votes pursuant to that authority are conclusive and obligatory on the Overseers.

"To the sixth; we see no necessity for the Overseers to exercise any authority over the poor in the House of Industry; and the City Council cannot, as we apprehend, give to the Overseers any authority inconsistent with that which is vested in the Directors by the statute of 1822, c. 56. Of course, we are of opinion that the Overseers cannot exercise any greater authority than that specified in the vote of September 29, 1823. This vote, however, does not appear to be a full exercise of the authority of the City Council, and we would suggest the expediency of their passing a formal order (if there is not such a one in force) requiring that all the poor, with the exception of the two classes above-mentioned, shall be relieved, supported, and employed in the House of Industry.

"To the seventh; if the City Council have passed, or should see fit to pass, an order of the kind suggested in our preceding answer, the Overseers could not lawfully maintain the poor, who come within the terms of the order, at the expense of the city, at any other place than the House of Industry. The Directors of that House have the same power as the Overseers to send there any of the poor persons referred to in this question.

"The eighth is answered in the preceding answer.

"To the ninth; we are not aware of any further measures that can or ought to be taken by the City Council in this respect.

(Signed) WILLIAM PRESCOTT,
CHARLES JACKSON,
DANIEL WEBSTER."

"BOSTON, June 21, 1825.

The opinions of these jurists on the several laws, documents, and questions submitted to them, were received and communicated to the City Council on the twenty-seventh of June, 1825, and, in conformity therewith, the Committee reported the three following resolves, which were immediately passed by the City Council; and, by their order, an attested copy of the report and resolves was transmitted to each member of the Board of Overseers of the Poor.

1. *Resolved*, That the Overseers of the Poor be, and hereby are directed to cause all persons, who, from the nature of the illness under which they labor, or of the accident which has befallen them, are incapable without endangering life to be removed from the place where they are, to be relieved and supported in such place until they are capable of being removed, and as soon as they are capable of being removed, the said Overseers are directed to cause them forthwith to be removed for further relief and support to the House of Industry.

2. *Resolved*, That the Overseers of the Poor be, and they hereby are directed, as it respects those householders and others, who, in their opinion, require partial relief, and who may be rendered more comfortable by a small supply at their own houses than by being wholly supported in a poor-house, to grant such partial relief and small supply of necessaries at their own houses.

3. *Resolved*, That the Overseers of the Poor be, and they hereby are directed to see that all poor and indigent persons, having lawful settlement in the city of Boston, and standing in need of relief, other than those belonging to the classes specified in the two preceding resolves, be suitably relieved, supported, and employed in the House of Industry, according to the regulations and under the superintendence of the Directors of said House.

On the nineteenth of May, 1825, a committee was appointed in both branches of the City Council, to inquire into "the practicability, expense, and expediency of supplying the city with good, wholesome, and soft water." On the thirteenth of June the Committee reported that there was no doubt of its practicability or expediency, and that the only questions were, concerning the expense and the mode by which it could be effected; but that a great diversity of opinion existed, whether it ought to be left to private associations of capitalists, or be done wholly at the expense of the city; they recommended a survey of the most suitable places in the vicinity from which a sufficient supply might be obtained. This was authorized, and an appropriation made of one thousand dollars for the object.

So little were the future wants of the city anticipated, that the Mayor received from a citizen of Boston, perhaps second to none of his time for talents, judgment, and affection for the city, a letter dated June 25, 1825, recommending Stony Brook, in Roxbury, "as the source of supply, and stating, from his own observation, that, during forty years, it had never failed to supply water sufficient for the purposes of the city." Indeed, there was no general deficiency of a supply of water felt at that time, except at fires. On the fourteenth of November, Daniel Treadwell, an experienced engineer, was, however, employed by the city to make a survey of places best adapted to afford such a supply; and, on the twenty-third of the same month, the Mayor received a letter from John C. Warren, then, as now, one of the most eminent physicians in the city, which, after stating "that the introduction of an ample supply of pure water would contribute much to the health of the city, and prove one of the greatest blessings which could be bestowed upon it," concluded with a caution against "any project involving much expense, as being objectionable, and might tend to delay the execution of a more perfect plan, and protract the existence of an evil most important to be removed." Spot Pond, in Stoneham, and Charles River, were the two sources of supply to which Mr. Treadwell's survey related; and the expense to the city from either source was calculated not to exceed six or seven hundred thousand dollars. The public mind was not, however, prepared to incur even this expense for the object; and Mr. Treadwell's report was immediately referred to the next City Council. And in December, a joint committee of both branches were appointed to ascertain on what terms the sources of supply, suggested by Mr. Treadwell, could be obtained.

While these measures were in progress, the Mayor entered into a correspondence with William T. Lewis of Philadelphia, whose superintendence of the waterworks of that city, and instrumentality in constructing them, had highly qualified him to give information on the subject. With great readiness, Mr. Lewis gave his opinion upon all the topics on which the Mayor had inquired, and particularly on that which he regarded as the most important of all others, as to the expediency of effecting the object wholly at the expense of the city, or by the aid of associated capitalists. "On this subject," he replied, "cost is not to be regarded; in London, scarcely a fire of any magnitude happens, without complaints of the deficiency of water; and I have now a paper in my possession, stating a meeting of the Common Council of the city, inquiring into its cause. This it does not require much consideration to answer. It is from the fatal error of suffering interested individuals to have the supply of an article of the most indispensable nature, and, without which, health and comfort cannot be enjoyed. Expense is comparatively no object. If a company supply your city, they will expect to profit by it, and this profit may as well be saved to your corporation. If it be a losing business, individuals should not suffer by forwarding a great public object; and if they do, the citizens will be sure to feel it by a pinched and partial supply. In Philadelphia, we have expended vast sums of money, yet I firmly believe that were the question submitted to the citizens, to sell to a company the whole cost, with interest, that not one tenth part of the population would agree to it. The increased security from fire, the abundant supply for washing the streets, the copious streams afforded for baths for cleanliness, and, in short, many other advantages, are such, and so well appreciated, that no money would tempt them to make sale of the works." These views were deemed by the Mayor conclusive on this point; and a very powerful association being, at that time, forming, to introduce water into the city, he came to the resolution to throw his whole official influence against it.

During this year the building of Faneuil Hall Market was pursued with great vigor. On the second of May, a committee of both branches[1] was raised on the subject, who appointed a sub-committee[2] for its superintendence, and David W. Child, the active superintendent of the work. None but ordinary supervisory attentions were required; and the year closed with reports to the City Council, concerning the expenditures of the year, and the outstanding claims of proprietors of the land.

In October, 1825, a resolve passed the City Council, vesting the Mayor with authority to take a census of all the inhabitants of the city. In order to give perfect satisfaction to the citizens, the Mayor, after consulting the Board of Aldermen, selected two individuals for each ward of the city, and for that part of ward No. 12, called South Boston, two additional persons, all well qualified for the task; and after a thorough research, it resulted that the population of the city in the year 1825, was *fifty-eight thousand two hundred and eighty-one;* making an increase in the five years succeeding the last census in 1820, of *fourteen thousand three hundred and eighty-one.*

In January, 1825, a request, signed by sixty citizens, was made in writing to the Mayor and Aldermen, for a call of a meeting of the citizens *in wards*, to apply to the Legislature for such an alteration in the city charter, that the Board of Aldermen shall consist of twelve members, one of whom should be chosen in each of the wards, the vote on the question to be taken by ballot. This application was soon followed by a remonstrance of other citizens, denying the authority of the Mayor and Aldermen to call ward meetings for such a purpose. The subject was referred to a committee, of which the Mayor was chairman; and a report,[3] stating their views of the authority vested in the Mayor

[1] The Committee were, — the Mayor, Aldermen Blake, Marshall, and Bryant; and of the Common Council, Oliver, (its President) Coolidge, Curtis, Williams, Hastings, Adan, and Boies.

[2] The Sub-Committee were, — the Mayor, Marshall, Bryant, Williams, and Boies.

[3] The following is a condensed statement of this report: —

That antecedent to the amendments of the constitution of the Commonwealth in 1820, the power to call public meetings of the inhabitants in wards was never exercised or attempted to be, *other than for the choice of officers;* and that the power of constituting a city and organizing its government by ward elections was first obtained under the second article of the amendments to that constitution; and that by the terms of that amendment that power is vested in the General Court, with the power of prescribing the manner of calling and holding public meetings of the inhabitants in wards or otherwise; so that the powers of the city authorities to call meetings *of the inhabitants in wards, depends solely on the grant of the legislature,* and do not extend beyond the terms of that grant.

and Aldermen, was made, accepted, and a resolve passed in both branches of the City Council, that, in their opinion, "the Mayor and Aldermen are not authorized by the city charter to call meetings of the citizens in wards, on the application of any meeting of citizens whatsoever, for any purpose, except those expressly provided for in said charter."

In May, 1825, a petition, signed by more than sixty persons, was presented to the Mayor and Aldermen, requesting that a general meeting of the citizens should be called, to give their ballots by yea and nay, on the following proposition, namely,— "Shall ten hours faithful labor be considered hereafter as a day's work for journeymen mechanics in this city." Which, being read and considered, it was resolved to be inexpedient to pass the same, "the Board deeming the subject not within the provisions of the city charter."

The city charter had made no provision for filling any vacancy which might occur by death or resignation in the Board of Aldermen. This defect was remedied in June, 1824, by a special act of the Legislature of Massachusetts.

The inconvenience of organizing the city government so late in the season as the month of May, had been generally felt by the members of the City Council. And in November, 1824, a committee, of which the Mayor was chairman, made a report on the expediency of applying to the Legislature for an alteration in the city charter, so as to enable the citizens to organize the city government at an earlier period of the year, stating that the two first months of the year were those of the greatest leisure, and would give the new government enlarged opportunities to review the proceedings of their predecessors, and to digest their own; more ample time to make the necessary contracts for the service of the year, before the business season commenced, and greatly facilitate the operations of the city; concluding with a recommendation that a meeting of the inhabitants of the city should be called, for the purpose of obtaining their authority to apply to the Legislature for such a change in the city charter, that the municipal elections should take place annually, in the

Now there is no clause in the charter of the city giving any color to the exercise of a power to call any public meeting of citizens in wards, except in cases specifically enumerated, in which it is not pretended that the meeting for which that now requested to be called is included.

month of December, and the municipal year commence on the first Monday in January. The sanction of the inhabitants having been obtained, the Legislature, by an act passed on the twenty-seventh of June, 1825, authorized the proposed alteration of the charter; and this city year included, of consequence, but eight months.

CHAPTER XIII.

CITY GOVERNMENT. 1825.

JOSIAH QUINCY, *Mayor.*

An Act authorizing a New Organization of the Fire Department applied for and obtained from the State Legislature — Sanction of the Act by the Citizens — Measures pursued to carry it into effect — Sites for Engine Houses selected — Reservoirs constructed — Lafayette revisits the City — Measures adopted on the Occasion by the City Council.

SOON after the organization of the city government, in May, 1825, a joint committee of the City Council, consisting of the Mayor, Aldermen Blake, Marshall, and Bryant, and of Messrs. Oliver, Parker, Rice, Dyer, Fisher, Wells, and Elliot, of the Common Council, was raised on the fire department, according to the recommendation of the preceding City Council. On their report a vote was passed, that a new organization of it was expedient, and another, authorizing the Mayor and Aldermen to apply to the Legislature of the State to invest the officers of the proposed fire department, when elected, with such powers and authorities as might be requisite.

The Mayor, in reply to his inquiries, received a letter from Thomas Franklin, who had been for twenty years Chief Engineer of the Fire Department of the city of New York, of the following tenor: "Relative to our system of extinguishing fires, *I believe, from long experience,* IT IS THE BEST THAT CAN BE DEVISED; and I respectfully recommend, that a suitable person be appointed to visit and examine our fire department, and see the operation thereof. I am persuaded it will be more effectual than any written communication."

In consequence of this suggestion, the Committee of the City Council commissioned George Darracott, a citizen of Boston, — who had been one of its firewards, and who was highly qualified by experience, energy, and practical skill, — to visit New York and Philadelphia, and inquire into the organization of their fire department, and to examine into the construction, size, and power of their engines.

Mr. Darracott immediately visited those cities, and received in both every facility for becoming acquainted with their whole system of fire police. On the first of June ensuing, he addressed a letter to the Mayor, minutely replying to all the particulars included in his commission, with precision and with practical statements and reflections, resulting in an unequivocal expression of opinion, that "such is the advantage of the system in use in those cities, that it could not be too early pressed upon the attention of the city authorities of Boston;" adding, that "although the firemen of Boston possessed as much intrepidity as any men, and risked readily both their property and persons, yet they have not been accustomed to regard favorably the hose system, and seldom make use of hose, except when they cannot play from the pipe. The reverse of this is the case in New York. It there frequently happens, when a fire originates in narrow passage-ways, where engines cannot operate to advantage, that they are placed in the centre of one of their large squares, entirely out of view of the fire, and the hose is led through stores and houses in the vicinity. This, with the efficient organization of the various component parts of the department, and the playing of the *whole* under the supreme command of *one*, is what, in my opinion, after a minute and careful inspection of the whole system, gives the firemen of New York, such a decided superiority over those of any other place. To this conclusion my mind has been irresistibly led. I have always felt a degree of pride in the character of our Boston firemen, and never would concede the point, that fires were not better managed here than elsewhere. But recent events have caused doubts in my mind. Those doubts are now confirmed. The fault lies not in the men, but in the system." This letter was immediately published for the information of the citizens, and a petition at once presented to the State Legislature, conformably to the authority given by the City Council, for powers to organize a fire department in Boston, on the principles which have been stated.

There was, however, reason to fear, that such was the inveterate animosity of certain individuals to the system proposed, some of whom were members of the Legislature and of the Boston seat, that their influence would be thrown in favor of rejecting the application altogether, without giving the citizens opportunity to express their opinion upon it. The Mayor, therefore, to cast upon the opponents of the system the responsibility of such total rejection, caused the following address to be immediately printed and transmitted to each member of the Legislature.

TO THE MEMBERS OF THE BOSTON SEAT, IN THE LEGISLATURE OF MASSACHUSETTS.

BOSTON, 12th June, 1825.

GENTLEMEN: — Understanding that doubts are entertained, concerning the principle of the bill, relative to a fire department, and that too by members of the Boston seat, I deem it my duty not to permit that bill to fail, without distinctly explaining the views of the City Council upon the subject. If the city is again made subject to destruction by the inapplicability of our present system to the existing state of population, I am desirous that the City Council shall escape the responsibility of such misfortune.

The principal object of the bill, is to vest in the City Council *the power of constituting an efficient fire department, and, for this purpose, that they should have the appointment of the officers of that department and the distribution of their duties. The power to appoint and to prescribe the duties is the simple object.* If it fail, there can be no organization of an efficient fire department, and the consequences I need not portray.

The present system is, from the nature of things, inapplicable to the existing state of population, and it cannot be made applicable.

At present, thirty-six members compose a board of firewards, and as many more as the City Council may determine. They are chosen in wards. Their power consists, —

1st. In requiring, during fire, assistance in extinguishing it, or in removing goods or guarding them, and in suppressing tumults or disorders.

2d. In directing and appointing the stations and operations of engines and enginemen, and of all persons in extinguishing fires.

This power is supported by the sanction of a penalty of ten dollars, on refusal or neglect to obey their orders.

This system had its origin in, and from the nature of things *is solely applicable* to comparatively small towns.

The authority of firewards, though called *power*, is in fact *influence.* Of what possible use toward an efficient extinguishment of a fire is the recovery of ten dollars the next day on a delinquent? Of the thousand neglects and refusals which occur at every fire, how many are prosecuted? Comparatively speaking, not one!

The efficient authority of firewards, under our present system is *mere influence.* And, as such, the highest and the most influential citizens, who could be persuaded to take the office, it was the practice to make firewards; to the end that the individuals whom they required to assist, might be unwilling to refuse, either through shame or respect.

This was the real efficient power of the present system. But it is obvious that the whole of this power is annihilated, when a city is grown to such a size, as that not one in ten of the firewards, let him be ever so respectable, can be known to the attendant multitude, when that multitude are, for the most part, assembled not from sympathy for the sufferers, but from idle curiosity, and many from worse motives; when, from the practice of insuring, and the belief prevalent that the loss will be borne by the capital of insurance offices, indifference to them becomes more prevalent, and disinclination to incur the labor and hazard of assisting in extinguishing them more general; and that too in those very classes of the community whose weight of character and property used formerly to constitute the strength of the 'influence' of firewards, by coöperating in their exertions.

Is it wonderful, in such a state of population and of feeling, that the scenes which every man has witnessed of late at fires should occur? The surrounding multitude have neither shame nor fear, in refusing the fireward, and running away in masses as soon as he is seen with his badge of office advancing towards them; or if a few yield a reluctant assent temporarily, yet quitting the lanes, or leaving the work assigned them, as soon as the fireward's back is turned.

The result of this state of things is as undeniable as it is inevitable, and the consequences and duties resulting from it are equally plain and unquestionable.

The system of depending upon the aid of the surrounding multitude must be abandoned, and with it the system dependent upon mere influence or solicitation of sympathies.

A system must be adopted, suited to a large population, which every day is growing more mixed and less sympathizing with each other; in other words, discipline, subordination, and a well-marshalled arrangement, in which success is made to depend upon the organization of the department and its own efficiency, and not upon the reluctant aid of those who happen to be present.

In other words, Boston, like New York and other great cities, must have a fire department based upon the principle of being adequate to self-protection, in which the assistance of the mass of the citizens, so far from being solicited, is in fact prohibited; a system not of influence, but of self-dependent power.

If it be denied to the present earnest application of the City Council, there needs no spirit of prophecy to foretell that it will, at no great distance of time *be burnt into us.*

This system, as it exists in New York, is founded upon the use of suction and distributing hose, in filling their engines, instead of buckets; by which it is proved that *every hundred feet of hose* is as effectual as the presence of *sixty men* with buckets; whereby the presence of the multitude is not rendered necessary. The discipline of the department applies only to those who belong to it. Great efficiency and energy is the result. And a system of influence is abandoned, and one of efficiency substituted.

To the introducing of this system, the City Council have already authorized a great expense for engines and hose, and must incur more.

In order to make it effectual, discipline must be introduced, subordination established, practice in the use of the hose apparatus encouraged. For this purpose it is absolutely essential that the power proposed by this bill should be invested in the City Council.

Thirty-six men, coequal in power, excludes the idea of organization or subordination. How absurd is it to any efficient responsibility, that the body of men which are intrusted with the power of supplying the means and instruments should be denied the power of selecting the agents and organizing the department which is to make use of them! How fruitful in disputes and controversies must be such an attempt.

This system is not theory. It is now in existence, practised and satisfactory. I subjoin extracts [1] from a letter from the late Chief Engineer of New York, concerning the excellence of their system. Above all, I subjoin an extract from a letter of George Darracott, Esq., formerly a fireward of this city, who has been sent on by the city authorities to examine the actual state of things in this respect in New York.

I entreat the gentlemen of the Boston delegation so far to obtain the bill, if possible, as to be subject to the acceptance or refusal, by ballot of the citizens of Boston, at a general meeting.

Considering this measure to be of the most vital importance to the prosperity and safety of this city, I have taken the liberty to address this letter to you, gentlemen, and to give it publicity, to the end that the views of the City Council might not be misapprehended, and that if this measure fail, it shall not be attributable to any neglect, indifference, or shrinking from official responsibility in them.

Very respectfully, yours,

JOSIAH QUINCY.

The course thus adopted proved successful. The purpose of at once absolutely rejecting the system was not pursued; and on the eighteenth of June, 1825, an act was passed by the Legislature "establishing a fire department in the city of Boston," dependent for its final adoption on the votes of the citizens. A general meeting of the inhabitants was thereupon called, to vote on the subject on the seventh of the then ensuing July.

Notwithstanding these statements and exertions, the hostility to the proposed system was not allayed.

The private interests it opposed, and the attachment to old customs which it thwarted, rendered final success dubious. The ward rooms rang with patriotic harangues on the infringement of the ancient liberties of the people, by depriving them of the power of electing firewards; and the press, with warning voices on the usurpation of powers, which, it was asserted, could best be exercised by the body of the citizens. The attempt to deny citizens the right of assisting each other in distress, was indignantly reprobated; and it was publicly declared, that "it would not be submitted to by the fire-proof brethren of the North End."

[1] For these extracts, see pp. 182, 183.

The idea of efficiency in a hose system, and of engines putting out fires, by playing into one another, was treated as ridiculous.

Language of this kind began to be used, not only by the violent and prejudiced, but even by men from whom a higher knowledge and better feelings might have been anticipated. In this state of the controversy, the Mayor wrote and distributed, on his individual responsibility, on the day previous to the general meeting, the following address, explanatory of the views of the City Council, and urging the citizens to attend the meeting and give in their ballots, by all the considerations he thought calculated to awaken and to influence.

TO THE CITIZENS OF BOSTON.

PERCEIVING that the acceptance or rejection of the 'act establishing a fire department' is a subject of some discussion in the public prints, and being desirous, whenever that question is taken, that, whatever may be the event, its real nature and consequences may not be misapprehended by my fellow-citizens, I deem it my duty, in the relation I stand to the city, to make a distinct development of the subject. Considering also its nature and the circumstances connected with it, I cannot deem this duty fulfilled as it ought to be, unless I annex my name to this elucidation.

It will not be necessary to use any words to prove that our present system of protection against fire is, for some reason or other, not satisfactory to the citizens of this metropolis.

It will only be necessary to recall, on this point, the recollection of our fellow-citizens to the deep discontent manifested at the conduct and result of both the last great fires, — that in Beacon and that in Central Street.

On both these occasions, the inadequacy of our means of protection, or the insufficiency of their application was palpable, and the discontent expressed little short of universal.

Great difference of opinion, however, was manifested as to the causes of the confusion, disorder, and inefficiency exhibited on these occasions. Some lamented the want of water. Some the want of buckets. One set of men complained of the want of power in the firewards to command. Another of the want of willingness in the multitude present to obey. And all, of the general want of fire clubs, and of those ancient associations for mutual protection on occasion of fire.

In this state of sentiment and feeling, which notoriously existed, it was the duty of the City Council to ascertain the real causes of the evils of which all complained, and apply remedies suited and adequate to the nature of the case.

Now, it was impossible to reflect upon this acknowledged state of things, with the seriousness which a sense of duty and of responsibility imposed on the City Council, without coming to the conclusion that all these wants or deficiencies were, more or less, founded in fact, and the resulting want of protection was not so much, if at all, attributable *to the men*, who had the control of the present system, as to that system itself; in other words, that the evils of which all complained, were attributable chiefly, if not solely, to *the inapplicability of our present system of protection against fire, to the present state and relations of the population of our city.* And as this population was every day increasing with great rapidity, our present system was every day with like rapidity growing more inadequate to effect that protection the citizens had a right to demand.

A very transient reflection on the acknowledged state of things will, I think, satisfy my fellow-citizens of the justice of this conclusion.

And first, of the complaint of the want of water. A deficiency in this respect is unquestionable, and means are in train for remedying it, under the auspices of the City Council. Yet the truth is, that we have as much water now as we ever had in the city, and as we had in those times when the conduct of fires gave great and just content in our city. Assuredly also, the deficiency of water in the vicinity of Beacon Street or of Central Street, could not be considered as the cause of the confusion, disorder, and inefficiency which all complained of on both those occasions.

On the contrary, if our present system be sufficient, a manifest deficiency in the article of water would be a reason for order and regularity, rather than a cause of disorder and confusion.

Our present system presupposes either *a will* in the surrounding multitude at fires, to aid in forming lanes to pass water to the engines, or *a power* in the firewards to compel them to form such lanes.

Now, just in proportion as water in the vicinity of any fire is deficient, is the necessity apparent that it should be brought from a distance; and, of course, that the efficiency of the will, or the power to make lanes, should be manifested. If our present system be, therefore, in this respect, sufficient, the alacrity to form lanes and to preserve order in the multitude present, and the facility with which the firewards are enabled to form the one and preserve the other, will be increased rather than diminished, by the existence of so great an exigency. How it was on both occasions, can best be answered by the firewards and the citizens present.

Again, — are the evils of which we complain to be attributed to the want of buckets, of fire clubs, or of any of the ancient associations for mutual protection? What is the reason of this? Why are we deficient in buckets? Why are the members of fire clubs greatly diminished? Why those ancient associations abandoned or grown into disuse? There can be but one answer. The state of things is changed in this respect. With the greatness of population, a different state of feeling and of modes of protection have grown up.

Formerly, one could not open the front door of the highest or the richest citizen, without having his eye greeted with at least two buckets, containing fire bags and a bed key, all duly labelled, indicating to what fire society he belonged. The same was true in relation to the house of almost every citizen, except those of the poorest class.

At this day, how many doors can you open and behold the same sight? I answer, within bound, not one in fifty. Why is this? If you ask the owner, and he answers truly, nine times in ten it will be, — 'I am insured; why should I keep fire buckets? Why subject myself to the rules and customs of fire clubs? Or why turn out to fires at all? I go to the expense of protecting myself. I ask no protection from others, and I mean to incur no voluntary expense; and, much more, will not incur the risk of health and life in protecting them.'

However cold, selfish, or calculating this language may seem, it is the practical language of men in all great cities. In such cities, the influential classes of citizens, the householders, and men of property of every description, grow more in the habit of protecting themselves, more unwilling to incur the risk and the labor which aiding at fires makes necessary; and the number of those who are indifferent on such occasions, or who are willing to make profit by the misfortunes of others, is increased. The consequence is, that in all cities, after they have attained a certain point of greatness, the system of depending upon the aid of all the citizens has been abandoned, and a system, self-dependent, and which, so far from requiring the aid of all the citizens, excludes that aid, has been adopted.

The substantial question, therefore, presented to the citizens of Boston is this, — having become a city, with a great population, will you adopt a system conformable to the state of things in which you exist? or, with a great population, will you adhere to a system adapted only, and which can be efficient only, in a city with comparatively a very small population? Whatever prejudices may exist upon the subject, and whatever interests or feelings may be affected by the avowal, it is my duty to state, as the result of all the researches made under the authority of the City Council, on the subject, that *the present system of firewards is not, and cannot be made, an efficient system of protection against fire, with a population such as at present exists in this city.* The fault is not in the men, but the system.

Thirty-six men are annually chosen, in wards, all equal in power; and in cases of fire, *any three have precisely the same power with every other three.* I lay aside all questions concerning the effect of choosing in wards, rather than by general ticket. I take it for granted, that the men, thus chosen, are the best thirty-six men that exist in the city for this purpose, and that they always will be the best.

I ask, then, what are the efficient powers of such firewards, in relation to commanding aid on these occasions, considered in the light of substantial protection? The answer, and only answer that can be given, is, that '*they can require the assistance of all persons present to aid in extinguishing fires.*' But, suppose the persons required refuse or neglect to obey? What then? They are liable to be prosecuted the next day for ten dollars!

The penalty, indeed is heavy; but what is it as it respects efficient protection?

Of the thousands, which, at every great fire, either refuse or neglect to obey the fireward, and shrink from him, or go away as soon as he approaches, how many have ever been prosecuted, and paid their ten dollars. Comparatively speaking, not one.

This *great authority* of the fireward, on which so much reliance is placed, when looked to for efficient protection, turns out to be nothing more than *the good will* of the persons present. The fireward orders, and *if the person ordered wills, he obeys; if he does not so will, he lets it alone.* And this is the whole matter. For, unless in the case of some flagrant insult or outrage, he never hears any more of the business. Nor can there be any blame cast on the fireward.

Amidst darkness and confusion and hurry, how can he identify the individual, much more arrest and keep him in custody?

The efficient authority of firewards turns out then to be, after all, *mere influence;* and the whole system is predicated upon its *being influence, and nothing else.* It is a sufficient system in an early stage of society, and in a limited extent of population. But when society advances, when a population becomes numerous, the weight of personal character and influence is little felt; comparatively not at all. And the consequence is, that a system of influence must be abandoned, and one of efficiency adopted.

Now a system, to be efficient, must be *self-dependent;* not relying upon whim, caprice, or the accidental presence of well-disposed individuals; but possessing within itself, and by the inherent force of its own organization, the capacity of affording the protection required. By the aid of hose, of suction, and supply engines, such a system supersedes the necessity of lanes, and, by the power of machines, renders only a very small number of persons sufficient for protection. This is the system of New York. The surrounding multitude, instead of being solicited to aid, are prohibited from interfering. The engineers, the firemen, and hosemen, and hook and ladder men, are competent to manage all the machines. The efficiency of this system is not a matter of speculation. The following extracts of letters, although already published, deserve to be here inserted, for the sake of those who have *not seen* them.[1]

The question, then, now presented to the citizens of Boston, is a question *between two systems.* And, on this point, in order that there may be no mistake in this matter, and no deception, I wish it to be distinctly understood, that the existence and present relations and powers of firewards *is wholly incompatible with the system recommended, and in practice in New York; and that, so long as these relations and powers subsist, this system cannot be introduced.*

For, although firewards make a component part of the system in New York, yet their relations and their powers are very different from those of firewards in this city. One great business, for instance, of firewardens under our system, is *to make citizens assist at fires.* Whereas, one great business of firewards in New York, is to 'keep persons at a distance from them.'

I know that it is urged with great warmth and vehemence in the public prints, that the object of the City Council is, 'to wrest from the citizens the election of firewards.'

The truth, however, is, that the object of the City Council is of a much higher and more consequential character than the poor acquisition of any such elective power. It is an endeavor to place the safety and protection of the city against fire upon the basis of a self-dependent, efficient system; one that does not claim from age, or manhood, or boyhood, as a duty, to turn out and give protection against fires, at the exposure of health, and often of life. On the contrary, it takes the protection of the city on itself. It asks of the citizens, not immediately interested, only to keep away. It depends on its own discipline, practice, force of machinery, and engines; and relies not at all on the reluctant aid of casual bystanders.

This system is inevitable in a full-grown state of society. If our citizens do

[1] For these extracts see pp. 181, 182.

not realize, or will not admit the necessity of it *now*, the adoption is only postponed. Come it will. The great teacher, calamity, which has already spoken once and twice, will speak again and again, until its voice is heard.

If, then, the effect of the bill is to vest in the City Council the choice of the firewards, it is because that the powers and relations of firewards, in a system destined to give protection without calling in the aid of the multitude present, are different from their powers and relations in a system like our present one, based upon depending on the aid of that multitude altogether.

Thirty-six men, coequal in power, every three of whom have a right to command, are wholly incompatible with a system, which is of the nature of an organized force, having a head and members subordinate to each other; and in which responsibility is precise, direct, and individual.

It will, therefore, be seen by my fellow-citizens, that the real question to be decided by them, on the acceptance and rejection of the bill, relates to the two systems, — that which now exists, and that which is recommended.

So far as the question affects the elective franchise, it depends upon another question; and that is, whether the City Council, the constitutional and responsible representative of all the citizens, be, or be not, the proper body to be intrusted with the organization of the fire department of the city?

Upon the general expediency of retaining the present system, which is founded on the practicability of commanding the aid of the whole multitude present at fires, I ask my fellow-citizens to consult not only recent experience, but also to reflect on the actual relations of our population. Is it not becoming every day less and less homogeneous? By emigration and the constant infusion of foreigners, are not the sympathies among citizens, considered merely as such, diminishing? Has not an increased disposition to take advantage of fires, as occasions for plunder, been manifested of late years? Must it not be inevitable in every city with an increasing population? What right has this city to expect an exemption from the common lot of humanity in great cities?

In making this elucidation, I am sensible that I have exposed myself to the charge of unsuitable obtrusiveness. But I am willing to submit to this, or to any other like censure, rather than to have the conviction, which I should otherwise have felt, that I had failed in my duty to a people to whom I owe so ma obligations for the confidence they have reposed in me.

My great purpose will be answered, if I can draw the attention of my fellow-citizens to the real nature of the question; and that, when decided, an unequivocal expression of their opinion should be given by the number of their suffrages; and that it should not be left, as some questions have been of late, to the decision of a few individuals in the vicinity of the Hall, or who had a particular interest in the subject.

The question deeply interests the fate of the whole city. Only let then the voice of the whole city be heard.

Your fellow-citizen,

4th July, 1825. JOSIAH QUINCY.

The responsibility thus assumed by the Mayor was received with those opposite demonstrations, of censure and praise, which, in a republic, every public officer may expect who throws openly his personal or official influence into the scale, on questions deeply agitating contending parties. By one set of men, it was characterized as "obtrusive," "busy," "meddlesome," "using his short-lived authority to augment the power and perpetuate the influence of his office." By another, it was denominated "a noble spirit of independence in a chief magistrate, who, holding his office by the popular voice, intrepidly takes the hazard of lending publicly all his influence to a measure which he believes will be attended with important and salutary consequences, regardless of the manner in which it may affect his personal popularity." The result proved the propriety and necessity of these measures. The meeting, on the seventh of July, as was anticipated, proved one of great struggle and excitement. Upwards of *twenty-five hundred votes were cast;* and, so powerful and general was the opposition, that the question in favor of adopting the system was decided by a majority of only *one hundred and eighty-three votes!* On so critical an issue did a question, thus vital to the safety and prosperity of the city, turn!

Thus, after an open and active struggle, the organization of an independent fire department received the support of the citizens of Boston; and, from that time, a systematic course of measures was steadily pursued for carrying the projected organization into effect, with the general coöperation of the citizens, without any obstruction, except by attempts to injure the apparatus of the department, by cutting the hose, by a few unknown and unprincipled individuals. A committee of both branches of the City Council, consisting of the Mayor, Aldermen Blake and Welsh, and Messrs. Williams, Barry, Boies, and Wiley, of the Common Council, was appointed to prepare an ordinance in conformity with the act of the Legislature. But difficulties yet lingering among some classes of citizens, rendered delay expedient; and the details of this ordinance were not conclusively settled and sanctioned by the City Council until the end of December. Time was also required to obtain the engines and apparatus ordered from New York and Philadelphia, which postponed the final organization of the fire department until the ensuing municipal year, now, for the first time, about to commence in January.

During the controversy on the new system, the Committee of the City Council selected sites for engine houses; not on the principle of economical and temporary expediency hitherto chiefly regarded, but such as were best adapted to facilitate easy communication with the most exposed or populous parts of the city. With these views, they selected a site on Pemberton Hill, now No. 9, Tremont Row, a location in the vicinity of the elevated streets on Beacon Hill, nearly opposite the entrance of Hanover Street and other avenues descending to the north, by which aid could be easily extended to sections of the city the most populous and exposed to conflagration. They also desired to widen and improve the great thoroughfare over Pemberton Hill, then steep and inconvenient, and in the winter season often dangerous. These objects were regarded so important, that the City Council authorized an offer of twenty-five hundred dollars for about five hundred feet of land, which the proprietor rejected. The price of the land was therefore deemed an insurmountable obstacle to the project. An unanticipated transaction, however,[1] enabled the city authorities to obtain the space the improvement required *for nothing*. The proprietor of the remaining land, therefore, was now induced to accept an offer of three thousand dollars for an adjoining lot, on which an engine house was erected of granite, on the model of the Choragic monument at Athens, and the engine and hydraulion purchased at Philadelphia were placed in it. The cost of this edifice was justified, in the opinion of the city government, by the circumstances under which the improvement and purchase had been effected; by the satisfaction a building so ornamental to the street gave to the proprietors of estates in the vicinity, who had objected to the erection of an engine house in their neighborhood; and, above all, by the consideration that, such were the peculiar facilities of that location for the protection of the city, that its future alienation[2] was deemed improbable, and its appropriation to that object would, therefore, be permanent.

In October, 1825, the City Council appropriated fifteen hundred dollars for the construction of two reservoirs. Notwithstanding their utter insufficiency for the requisite supply of water, they were all that could be obtained. Pumps, buckets,

[1] The facts relative to this transaction were officially stated in the *Boston Courier*, of the 9th of November, 1825.

[2] This lot and the building has been recently (1851) sold, in cash, for eleven thousand four hundred and fifty dollars

and lanes of citizens continued to be considered, by many, as more efficient for the supply of the engines than hose. They regarded the new fire department as an experiment, and of very dubious result. In this opinion, some even of the City Council coincided. A destructive fire which, on the tenth of November, 1825, occurred in Court Street, awakened the citizens again to the existing deficiency of water, and of the inadequacy of the ancient means of applying it with efficient force to the flames; and a committee of the City Council, of which John Bellows was chairman, reported a resolve, which was accepted in both branches, by which an adequate appropriation was made for the building of *thirteen* reservoirs, in addition to the *two* already authorized, each to be of a capacity to contain *two hundred and fifty hogsheads;* which was immediately carried into effect.

In January, 1825, information was received, that General Lafayette had accepted an invitation to be present and aid in laying the corner stone of the Bunker Hill Monument; that he would, in consequence, revisit Boston, and probably be in the city on the anniversary of national independence. By a committee of the City Council, appointed to take suitable measures on the occasion, the Mayor was requested to address a letter to General Lafayette, expressing the gratification of the City Council at receiving this information, and the universal satisfaction of the citizens of Boston at the anticipation of his presence at that interesting ceremony. Lafayette, in reply, announced his intention to be present at Bunker's Hill on the seventeenth of June; but that a recent family bereavement placed it out of his power to be present on the fourth of July at the city celebration. Information was also received from another source, that Lafayette had accepted the invitation of the Hon. James Lloyd, a senator from Massachusetts in the Congress of the United States, to reside in his family during his visit to the city.

Notwithstanding this information, on his arrival in Boston, in the month of June, a vote passed the City Council, authorizing the Mayor and Aldermen "to make such arrangements for his honorable reception and entertainment, during his residence in the city, as they may deem expedient and proper." Under another vote of the City Council, both branches of the city government waited on Lafayette, on the sixteenth of June, at the mansion of Mr. Lloyd, to offer their respects and congratulations on his return to Boston, after his auspicious and successful progress through the United States.

In March preceding, the Mayor had been authorized, by a vote of the City Council, to procure a portrait of General Lafayette, "to be taken at such time as will suit his convenience, and to draw his warrant for the amount."

To this application of the Mayor, Lafayette replied, that it would not be in his power to comply, during the short period he expected then to remain in the United States; but that, after his return to France, should it be desired, he would with great pleasure obey the wishes of the city. At the same time, he observed to the Mayor, that it was hardly possible for a better likeness to be obtained than that which had been recently taken of him by P. Schæffer, one of the first artists in France, just before he commenced his visit to the United States, fine engravings from which were then of common and easy attainment.

In July, 1824, a Committee of both branches, consisting of the Mayor, and Alderman Benjamin, with Messrs. Prouty, Russell, and Hartshorne, of the Common Council, was raised to consider the expediency of authorizing the Surveyors of Highways to cause a prospective plan and elevation of all the streets in the city, to be made, to comprehend, as far as possible, all future improvements, as opportunities may occur.

This Committee reported, in September following, expressing their opinion, that it would be greatly for the public interest if such a system of surveys should be adopted; that the present course of proceeding originates in, and is limited by, the immediate exigency of the particular estate on which any owner proposes to build; that the Mayor and Aldermen, after surveying the estate, only decide how far the street shall be widened by taking from *that* estate. In doing this, they have no authority to lay out a prospective plan of any street, and to guide their proceedings by an enlarged view of the greatest improvement which the general relations of the street would permit, so as to become obligatory on their successors; they are therefore reduced to the prudential course of widening each street to such a reasonable line, as no future Board of Aldermen would hesitate to adopt, in relation to other estates, when an opportunity of further widening should occur. The consequence of which is, that the widening of streets, not being governed by any established prospective plan, amounts, for the most part, only to the cutting off angles and removing occasional projections, and results in leaving, after all is done, a sightless, irregular outline; and that, often in cases where, if a bolder line could be taken with the assurance of its being completed, improvements of an important character might be made, with the acquiescence of the landholder, and with ultimate gain, in point of expense, to the city.

The tendency of the present system is as little calculated to give satisfaction to the owners of estates, as to promote the improvement of the public streets. For, in general, owners of estates would readily acquiesce (on being compensated) in very considerable reduction of their lands, for the sake of widening streets, provided they could have the assurance that, in future time, the particular specified line to which their estates were cut down, should be from time to time extended, and become the permanent line of the streets.

An established prospective plan, such as is suggested, would also be greatly beneficial in reducing the claims for compensation, on the taking of such lands by the public. For, the particular line of the street, being established by the city authorities, recorded, and published, every subsequent purchaser of an estate bounding on such street, would acquire it with full notice of the fact, and could have no claim or pretence of damages on account of calculations made, or prices given, in ignorance of the intention of the city authorities.

In conformity with these views, the Committee reported three resolutions, which were, in March, 1825, adopted by the City Council, in the following terms: —

Resolved. That the Mayor and Aldermen cause surveys of the streets of the city to be made on a prospective plan, embracing, in relation to each street, as far as possible, the greatest ultimate practical improvement of such street, both as it respects widening and elevation; and that they cause such plan of each street, as it shall be completed, together with a plan of the particular estate affected by such proposed improvement, and the estimated expense for carrying the same into effect, to be laid before the City Council; and that they continue such surveys until a complete prospective plan of the streets of the city shall be made and established.

Resolved. That, when such surveys shall be approved by the City Council, the same shall be entered in a book, to be kept for that purpose, to be entitled, " The Book of the Prospective Plans for the Improvement of the Streets of the City of Boston."

Resolved. That, whenever such prospective plan of improvement in any street shall be approved and recorded, it shall be the duty of the Mayor, for the time being, to give public notice thereof in two at least of the newspapers published in this city, that all persons may know the same and govern themselves accordingly.

Surveys of the streets, on the principles of this report, were immediately commenced, and early steps taken to carry its provisions into effect.

CHAPTER XIV.

CITY GOVERNMENT. 1826.

JOSIAH QUINCY,[1] *Mayor.*

Prosperity of the City — Measures for introducing Water — Views of the Mayor on the Subject — Proceedings of the City Council — Powers of the Mayor in the Suppression of Riots — Petitions for a general Contribution for Relief by Sufferers from Fire — The Result — Progress of Faneuil Hall Market — Final Settlement of the whole Improvement — Organization of the new Fire Department — Celebration of the Fourth of July, 1826 — Death of John Adams and Thomas Jefferson — Tribute to their Memories.

THE Mayor, in his inaugural address,[2] noticed the difficulty of satisfying the conflicting passions and interests always existing in a great community, and the happy effects of the wisdom, harmony, and public spirit of former city councils on the prosperity of the city. It appeared from the recent city census that, during the past five years, the comparative increase of its population equalled that of any of our maritime cities, on the basis of its previous numbers. While the aggregates of property valuation had increased, the ratio of taxes had diminished. Although advancing wealth and population had unavoidably augmented the amount of taxes, yet there had been, in every successive year since the existence of our city government, a decrease in the amount of uncollected taxes. The expenditures, in respect of their objects, had been apparently satisfactory to a majority of the citizens; and the establishment of the office of auditor of accounts had introduced an order, simplicity, and correctness in that department highly creditable and advantageous. The attention of the City Council was now directed to the importance of obtaining for the city "a never-failing supply of pure river or

[1] The whole number of votes cast were 1395, of which Josiah Quincy had 1202. The Aldermen were Daniel Carney, John Bellows, Josiah Marshall, Thomas Welsh, Jun., Henry J. Oliver, John T. Loring, Francis Jackson, and Edward H. Robbins, Jun.

[2] See Appendix, E.

pond water," which had been enforced by the urgency of physicians; and the Mayor, having received information that an association, formed for that purpose, contemplated an application to the Legislature for the requisite powers, expressed a hope that the project would be met by the City Council "with the most decided and strenuous opposition, and with a corresponding spirit and determination to effect the great object solely on the account and with the resources of the city;" at the same time, "declaring it explicitly to be his opinion that, on that subject, the city ought to consent to no copartnership."

Four days after these views had been thus publicly expressed by the Mayor, Patrick T. Jackson, a citizen commanding, by his talents, character, and enterprise, the entire confidence of the community, associated with other individuals of wealth and influence, petitioned the City Council to assist them in obtaining from the Legislature an act of incorporation, giving them authority "to construct an aqueduct, for the purpose of conveying into the city a sufficient quantity of fresh water for the use of the inhabitants, and for the extinguishing of fires." This petition was referred to a committee, consisting of the Mayor, Alderman Welsh, and Messrs. Bassett, Hallett, and Brooks, of the Common Council. The Committee and City Council, coinciding in the views of the Mayor, the application received a decided negative. Nothing effectual was done in consequence of this movement. The Committee charged with the subject held various meetings, in which discussions were had concerning Neponset and Charles Rivers, as sources of supply; and the Mayor, on his own authority, obtained contracts securing conditional rights of purchase, for the city, of a majority of the lower water rights on both those rivers, at stipulated prices, dependent upon the sanction of the City Council within a limited time. The impression concerning the importance of the subject, though generally acknowledged, was far from being universal; and no willingness to increase the city debt, for the attainment of the object, was manifested. The claims of the proprietors of the sources of water were regarded as too extravagant to be presented for consideration to the City Council. The Mayor, therefore, having, as he thought, sufficiently impressed the City Council and the citizens with the importance of retaining the right of introducing water from the resources of the city alone, without the instrumentality of private associations; and deeming it best for its interests to wait for times when the urgent wants of the inhabitants should counteract the prevailing apprehension of a city debt, forbore any further to urge the subject upon the attention of the City Council.

During the year 1825, the Mayor was called upon to suppress riots on two occasions. On the first, the object of the exertion of his official authority had no precedent. After consulting the Board of Aldermen, in order to be able, in case of any similar emergency, to justify before a legal tribunal such exercise of authority as circumstances might require, he submitted to counsel learned in the law the nature of the powers vested in the office of Mayor by the city charter, applicable to such occasions. The result of their opinion being, that riots, routs, and unlawful assemblies were only cognizable under the laws of the Commonwealth; and that the course of proceeding, and the persons intrusted with their execution, were expressly pointed out in those laws, among whom the Mayor of the city was not included; and that, although it was his duty, in the language of the charter, "to cause all laws for the government of the city to be duly executed and put in force;" yet, that it was a question of some doubt how far his authority extended in respect of the general laws of the Commonwealth, the execution of which was intrusted to other authorities. It was therefore deemed most safe and prudent for the Mayor to act as "justice of the peace throughout the Commonwealth," concerning whose powers in such cases there could be no possible question. Accordingly, the Mayor, in that capacity, with a strong police, assisted by well-disposed citizens, who volunteered their services, proceeded to the scene of riot, and dispersed the assembly in the course prescribed by the statutes of the Commonwealth, arresting some of the offenders and sending others to prison.

On a subsequent occasion, in the case of a disturbance at a theatre, the Mayor, on finding that a justice of the peace was in actual fulfilment of the duties of that office, with all the powers vested in him by law, refused personally to interfere, deeming it for the interest of the city that the views he entertained of the powers of his office should be distinctly and practically manifested to the citizens and the public, to the end that, if the Mayor was to be held responsible to act in all such cases, his powers might be accurately defined and his duties prescribed by law; deeming himself as much bound to abstain, as Mayor, from assuming to exercise powers not vested in him by his office, as it was to exercise those with which he was intrusted.

These views he accordingly spread before the City Council in this inaugural address.

In January, 1826, petitions from several towns in the State of Maine, whose inhabitants had suffered from fires, praying that a general contribution might be authorized by the City Council for their relief, were referred to the Mayor and Alderman Robbins, with Messrs. Morey, Torrey, and Howe, of the Common Council.

After examining into the circumstances of the conflagration and of the sufferers, the Committee decided that the City Council were not justified in resorting to the mode of relief sought by the petitioners. Their report stated, that the distinguished liberality of the citizens of Boston, being unquestionably the cause of frequent applications for relief, the city government should consider it their duty not to permit the charity of their fellow-citizens to be unduly or unseasonably called upon, particularly in the form of authority, and under the sanction of an official act; and that their public recommendations of a general contribution should be restricted to cases of great and extensive calamity, which call for the interposition of a great community. This report was read and accepted in both branches of the City Council.

After the organization of the city government, in January, 1826, a committee[1] on the extension of Faneuil Hall Market was appointed to carry into effect the resolutions of the three last City Councils, with the same powers and authorities, and subject to the same limitations, as the former committees. On their recommendation, the City Council authorized the purchase of the land of William Welsh, the price not to exceed twenty thousand dollars, but without any appropriation, the cost of the land being reimbursed, as was anticipated, by the sale of the city lots. A street lying at the north of the north block of stores, (now called Clinton,) and extending to Exchange Wharf, was,

[1] The Committee were the Mayor, Aldermen Bellows, Marshall, and Robbins, and Messrs. Adan, (President of the Common Council,) Curtis, Hastings, Boies, Lodge, Grosvenor, and Barnard.

by the effects of this purchase, obtained without cost to the city. In July, this Committee discussed the arrangement of the stalls in the new market house; settled the terms on which they should be leased, and then voted that the leases should be sold at public auction, unless the tenants of the old market house chose to take them at the appraisement. This they readily did; and, on the twenty-sixth August, 1826, the new market house was opened, for the first time, to the public.

An order was then passed by the Common Council, that the further use of Faneuil Hall, as a market house, should be discontinued. This was nonconcurred by the board of Aldermen, who requested the Mayor to lay before the City Council a statement of the obligations of the city, resulting from the gift of Peter Faneuil, and from the votes passed by the town of Boston in reference to that donation. The Mayor, accordingly, made a full report, in conformity with that request, in which, after recapitulating all the chief facts already detailed in this history,[1] and stating that, after the edifice had been erected on the town's land, by Mr. Faneuil, in 1742, and accepted as a market house by the inhabitants, they repeatedly shut it up, and did not use it for the purpose for which it was given; and that, it having been destroyed by fire in 1761, it was rebuilt at the expense of the town, and the inhabitants voted "that the lower part of the building should not be improved, as a market, until the further order and determination of the town." The Mayor, therefore, declared that, in his judgment, no obligation rested upon the city, which could affect any use of the land covered by the building called Faneuil Hall the City Council should deem expedient; and votes in conformity with this opinion were passed in concurrence with the order of the Common Council.

On the ninth of November, the superintendent for building the new market reported, that all the bills and accounts for erecting it,—for labor, materials, and services, were paid, and the whole concern in a state to be closed. The Committee then requested the Mayor to prepare a final report on their proceedings; which, on the thirteenth of November, he accordingly submitted to them, detailing in it the origin of the project, the difficulties which had attended its execution, the various changes

[1] See p. 12.

of plans and views which had occurred in its progress, the amount of the moneys which had been under their control, their expenditures, the debt created, and the property vested in the city by their operations; concluding with this gratifying result, that "this *noble improvement had been completed, not only without any addition to the present taxes or burdens of the citizens, but also without the possibility of any addition in future time, on this account, to their taxes or burdens; and, on the contrary, that it has augmented, in no inconsiderable degree, the real and productive property of the city.*"

This report was accepted by the Committee and by both branches of the City Council unanimously.[1]

[1] The opinion having been at the time assiduously spread, that this Committee had created a debt, which it had left no adequate funds to discharge; and even at this day (1851) the belief being still entertained by some, that its proceedings laid the foundation of the present city debt, it is due to the memories of the members of that Committee, that the actual result of their operations should be stated from unquestionable documents.

By the official reports of William Hayden, Jun., the City Auditor in 1826, it appears that the Committee which erected the market had under their control, derived from every source .		$1,141,272.33
That of this amount they paid, from sources obtained exclusively from their own operations, .		532,797.33
Leaving an *apparent* debt on the city of . .		$608,475.00
The same Auditor's report shows that the Committee delivered over to the City Treasurer unquestionable demands, amounting to	$4,560.92	
And also good notes on interest, of a like unquestionable nature, amounting to	219,709.82	
Constituting an aggregate fund, of which the city has since availed itself in full, of . . .		224,270.74
So that the real debt left on the city was only .		$384,204.26
The annual interest on 608,475 dollars, paid by the city on the *apparent* debt, was . . .		$31,622.95
And the annual interest on $219,709.82, the available notes delivered the city, was . .		11,109.23
It results that the annual interest the city has ever had to pay was only		$20,513.72

As an offset for this debt, and to pay this interest, the Committee vested in the city the new market house, with the land it covered (27,000 feet); also, certain tracts of land, lying to the north of the north block of stores on North Market

All the preparatory steps being taken, and the principles settled for the establishment of a Fire Department, in the preceding year, the present City Council, immediately after its organization, took measures to carry it into effect. And, in January, 1826, they appointed Samuel Devens Harris chief engineer, and all the other engineers and firemen required by the city ordinance.

Street, containing upwards of 26,000 feet of land, valued by them at $100,000; also, 142,000 feet of flats and lands, lying at the eastward of the New Market House, estimated at the value of another $100,000 by the Committee, in their report.

Concerning the product to the city of these three species of property, it appears, by an official statement of Elisha Copeland, the present (1851) City Auditor, that, during the last twenty-five years, (1826 – 27 to 1850 – 51, inclusive,) the incomes of the city market, *after deducting every payment made on its account, including salaries and all expenses for carrying it on*, amounted to the net sum of . .	$562,460.66
And that, during the same period, the incomes of the City Wharf, which had been built in 1831, at an expense of $18,856.75, on the flats, vested in the city by the Committee, *after deducting the cost of its erection, above-mentioned*, and adding the incomes from the tracts of land lying to the north of the North Market Street block, amounted to the net sum of	162,002.86
So that the net incomes of the property, during twenty-five years, therefore, (*without including the value of the last-mentioned tracts of land, which was received in full by the city, by sales and application of it to city uses*,) amounted to	$724,463.52
Equivalent to an annual income of	$28,970.00
To discharge the annual income of the debt created, amounting, as above stated, to . .	20,513.72
Leaving to the city an annual surplus of interest, amounting to	$8,456.28
And, by way of equivalent or offset for the debt of $384,204.26, created for the city by the Committee, they vested in the city the new market, which never has been estimated at less than	$500,000.00
And the City Wharf and flats, which, although usually estimated much higher, can, at this day (1851), without fear of contradiction, be valued at	400,000.00
This being the fund provided, by way of offset, for a debt of about $384,000	$900,000.00

There were circumstances which rendered th acceptance of the office of chief engineer by Mr. Harris of great importance, at the first organization of the department. He was a man of known judgment and prudence; of tried ess; a soldier in spirit; and, as far as the events of his life had permitted, by education. He distinguished himself as a cavalry officer, in almost every battle on the Canadian frontier, in 1814; and was generally regarded as singularly qualified to introduce order and subordination into the department. The state of his health rendered him, at first, unwilling to accept the office, as it would subject him to great exertion and exposure; but he at length yielded to the solicitations of the Mayor and City Council. Soon after entering upon the duties of the office of chief engineer, Mr. Harris requested the Mayor not to bring the subject of his salary before the City Council; assigning as a reason for this request that, having the command of a department consisting wholly of uncompensated volunteers, he thought his usefulness would be disadvantageously affected by his acceptance of a salary.

Mr. Harris held his office nearly three years; and all the anticipations which occasioned his appointment were realized. A spirit, in every respect noble, fearless, and disinterested, characterized his whole conduct at the head of the department; and, as he never asked, he never received any compensation for a long series of invaluable services.

In the course of arrangements attending the new organization of the fire department, troubles of various kinds occurred, and

In addition to which, the Committee vested in the city, free of expense, six streets, as follows, namely: —

	Feet.		Feet.
1. South Market Street, of the width of	102	and containing	53,843
2. North Market Street . .	65	"	34,080
3. The street leading from Long Wharf, now constituting part of Commercial Street .	65	"	30,100
4. Clinton Street	40	"	20,490
5. The Roebuck Passage, now part of Merchants' Row, .	35	"	5,120
6. Chatham Street . . .	40	"	20,560
			64,193

several evidences of hostility were manifested. One engine company refused to communicate water at fires with another engine company, because it was composed of minors, though they were full grown and of sufficient strength. Another, whose captain had been dismissed by the Mayor and Aldermen, voted that, notwithstanding his dismissal, they should consider him their captain, and, as such, obey his orders. In both cases, the companies were dissolved, the engines taken from them and committed to new companies, which were immediately formed. Two of the city engines were disabled, in the night time, and their hose cut. This occurred several times at fires; and, although a reward of five hundred dollars was offered for detection of the offenders, it was without effect. Other dispositions to embarrass the operations of the new department were manifested. All the arrangements for carrying it into full efficacy were not completed until the twenty-fourth of April ensuing; when the Mayor issued his proclamation, declaring the fire department of the city duly organized, and that it would go into effect on the twenty-ninth of that month, which it did accordingly.

Votes of thanks were passed by the City Council to those citizens who had volunteered their services to take the engines when they were thrown up by the old companies; and "to the members of the late Board of Firewards, for their faithful, active, and disinterested services in support of the measures for organizing the fire department." This last acknowledgment was highly deserved by the old firewards. Notwithstanding its necessary effect was to put an end to the existence of their own board, the support they gave to the new department was uniformly open and decided, and their influence largely contributed to its ultimate success.

Owing to the defective state of the old engines, the great deficiency of hose, the necessity of fitting up all the engines and engine houses, in a style of greater neatness and convenience than had been before customary, as also, the constructing of reservoirs, the amount of expenditure exceeded twenty thousand dollars. But the efficiency manifested by the department was so universally felt and acknowledged, that the call for adequate appropriations was met by the City Council with readiness, and by the citizens without complaint. To check, as far as possible, an excess of expenditures, to which a department involving so many and such a diversity of claims was peculiarly liable, the Mayor recommended, and the City Council ordained, that they should be placed under the special superintendence of a joint committee of the City Council, without whose authority no expenditure exceeding fifty dollars should be incurred. By the course of measures above specified, a spirit of zeal and activity was infused into the fire department, chiefly resulting from the exertions, judgment, and fidelity of the chief and assistant engineers, which gradually introduced into it harmony and subordination, highly honorable to them and satisfactory to the citizens.

In April, 1826, the Rev. Henry Ware, Jun., was appointed the city orator for the then ensuing fourth of July, which he accepted; but the state of his health compelled him, on the nineteenth of June, to decline fulfilling his engagement. The Committee of the City Council appointed on this communication reported, that "an invitation should be given to the Hon. Josiah Quincy to pronounce the address on that anniversary; that the brief period now allowed for preparation seemed to preclude the probability of any of the younger gentlemen from accepting the delivery of the address, which, with the singular interest attached to the fiftieth anniversary, rendered it peculiarly proper that the appointment should be made of a citizen who, from his age, may be presumed to have witnessed some of the events, and to have imbibed the spirit which led to our Revolution. Your Committee believe that the zeal and interest the Mayor is known to feel and manifest in every thing relating to the city will induce him, notwithstanding his multiplied official avocations, to accept this appointment, if such should be the wish of the City Council."

A resolution, in conformity with this report, was passed unanimously by both branches.

The Mayor, having delivered an oration on the same occasion in 1798, was anxious to avoid a repetition of the effort; but finding that the short time for preparation,—the remaining days allowed,—was an insuperable obstacle to every citizen solicited to take the appointment, he deemed it his official duty, and acceded to the request of the City Council.[1]

[1] See Appendix L.

This anniversary was rendered memorable by the death of John Adams and Thomas Jefferson, both of whom had been signers, on that day fifty years before, of the Declaration of Independence, and both having filled the office of President of the United States.

On the fifth of July, at a special meeting of the Mayor and Aldermen, the record states: "This Board, having received notice of the afflictive dispensation of Divine Providence, in the death of the Hon. John Adams, formerly President of the United States, on the fourth of July instant, thereupon,

Resolved, That Aldermen Bellows, Marshall, Welsh, Oliver, and Loring, with such as the Common Council may join, be a committee to consider and adopt such measures as they may deem expedient, to express the sense of the eminent worth and public services of the deceased entertained by the citizens of Boston, in common with their fellow-citizens of the United States; and also, their sorrow at this bereavement, which has deprived this State of one of its most honored and cherished sons, and the American nation of a most eminent patriot and distinguished statesman."

The Common Council, in concurrence, joined, on its part, Messrs. Curtis, Grosvenor, Gray, Waters, Lodge, Hallet, and Rice.

This Committee reported: "That it would be proper for the Mayor and Aldermen and Common Council, accompanied by their Clerks and City Marshal, to attend the funeral of their distinguished fellow-citizen at Quincy; that the bells of the city should be tolled on that day from four to five o'clock; that it be recommended to the masters and owners of the vessels in the harbor, to cause their colors to be hoisted at half mast; and the citizens to close their places of business on the afternoon of said day, as a mark of respect for the deceased."

On the tenth of July, when news first reached the city of the death of Thomas Jefferson, a joint committee, of which Alderman Bellows was Chairman, was raised to consider what measures were proper to be adopted on the occasion. This Committee reported as follows: —

"The Joint Committee, who were charged to consider and report what measures it would be proper for the City Council to adopt, expressive of the respect entertained by the city for the eminent services of the late John Adams and

Thomas Jefferson, have the honor to report, that they view the almost simultaneous decease of these distinguished statesmen as a dispensation of Divine Providence, which will be deeply felt by the whole American nation.

"That these venerable champions of liberty should have commenced their political career at the same time; should have sustained the same important trusts and high offices; should have each contributed so essentially to the achieving of our independence; should have lived to see their children's children realize the blessings of that independence which, fifty years before, they jointly risked their lives to secure to them; and should at last be summoned, on the same day, and almost at the same hour, to receive the reward of their virtue and patriotism, constitute a coincidence without parallel in the history of the world.

"That either of these ancient men should have been spared to witness his nation's *jubilee*, was not to be expected in the usual course of human events; but that both should attain to that felicitous moment, enjoying such a degree of health, as not only to be conscious of their privilege, but to participate in the general exultation of that day, is an event which seems to mark the hand and special presence of that Being by whose unerring wisdom we are governed, and by whose beneficence we are protected and sustained. The lives of these great men have been no less distinguished than their deaths are remarkable; and your Committee are of opinion, that they ought to be commemorated by a discourse delivered on this solemn and impressive occasion; and they have reason to believe that, if it was known to be the wish of his fellow-citizens, an individual, eminent for his talents and public services, in whom the confidence and pride of this city are justly centred, would be induced to undertake the performance of this honorable but delicate trust.

"The Committee, therefore, recommend the adoption of the following resolutions: —

"1. *Resolved*, That it is due to the eminent patriotism and distinguished public services of the late John Adams and Thomas Jefferson, that their lives and characters should be commemorated in a public discourse.

"2. *Resolved*, That it is the wish of the City Council, that this discourse should be delivered by the Hon. Daniel Webster; and the Mayor is hereby authorized and requested to invite that gentleman, in the name and on behalf of the authorities of this city, to pronounce the same, as early as his convenience will permit.

"3. *Resolved*, That the Mayor and Aldermen and Common Council will unite with their fellow-citizens in the solemn exercises of the day (to be appointed); and that the citizens be requested to close their several places of business, and masters of vessels to display their colors at half mast, during the movement of the procession and the performance of the exercises."

This report was accepted, and the resolutions adopted unanimously, in both branches; and an order was passed, appointing the Committee who reported these resolutions to make the necessary preparations for the reception of the audience in Faneuil Hall, to arrange the order of procession, and with authority to make such arrangements as they shall deem suitable and proper for the occasion.

Daniel Webster having accepted the invitation of the city authorities, they, with distinguished public functionaries invited on the occasion, among whom were the President of the United States and the Governor of the Commonwealth, the officers of various public institutions, and the citizens in general, formed a procession, on the second of August, 1826, from the State House to Faneuil Hall, which was hung and carpeted with black and appropriately decorated, where, in presence of a numerous audience, after prayers by the Rev. Dr. Lowell, Mr. Webster delivered an eloquent discourse on the character and services of John Adams and Thomas Jefferson.

The bells of the city were tolled; minute guns fired; the shipping lowered their flags to half-mast; the stores were closed; business suspended; and no demonstration of respect was omitted.

CHAPTER XV.

CITY GOVERNMENT. 1827.

JOSIAH QUINCY, *Mayor*.[1]

General Relations of the City — Views concerning the City Debt — The Location of a City Hall — The Responsibility for the Correctness of the Voting Lists — General State of the Schools — Proceedings of the City Council in Relation to them — School Committee object to their Interference, and claim Independence — Opening of the Hancock School — High School for Girls established as an Experiment — Its Result — The School discontinued, and the Privileges of Females in the Common Schools extended — The Relation of the Mayor to the School Committee.

THE Mayor, in his inaugural address,[2] stated the general relations of the city; its increasing population; the advance of its improvements; and the indications given of the satisfaction of the citizens with the general conduct of their affairs. Since the government had been changed from a town to a city, its debt had been increased, in round numbers, from one hundred thousand to one million of dollars. The wisdom and fidelity of the public agents who incurred this debt must be tested by the permanent and important character of the objects attained by its creation. These were the acquisition of the lands west of Charles Street, and the property vested in the city by the Committee for the extension of Faneuil Hall Market. The value of the property thus acquired was equivalent to the discharge of the whole of the then existing city debt, besides adding a large surplus to its revenues. Nearly half a million of dollars had been expended during the same period in improvements of a permanent and prospective usefulness, having a direct influence on the future convenience and prosperity of the city. No public debt could be

[1] The whole number of votes were 2629; of which the Mayor had 2189.
The Aldermen were James Savage, Thomas Kendall, Phineas Upham, John T. Loring, Robert Fennelly, John Pickering, James Hall, Samuel T. Armstrong.

[2] See Appendix, F.

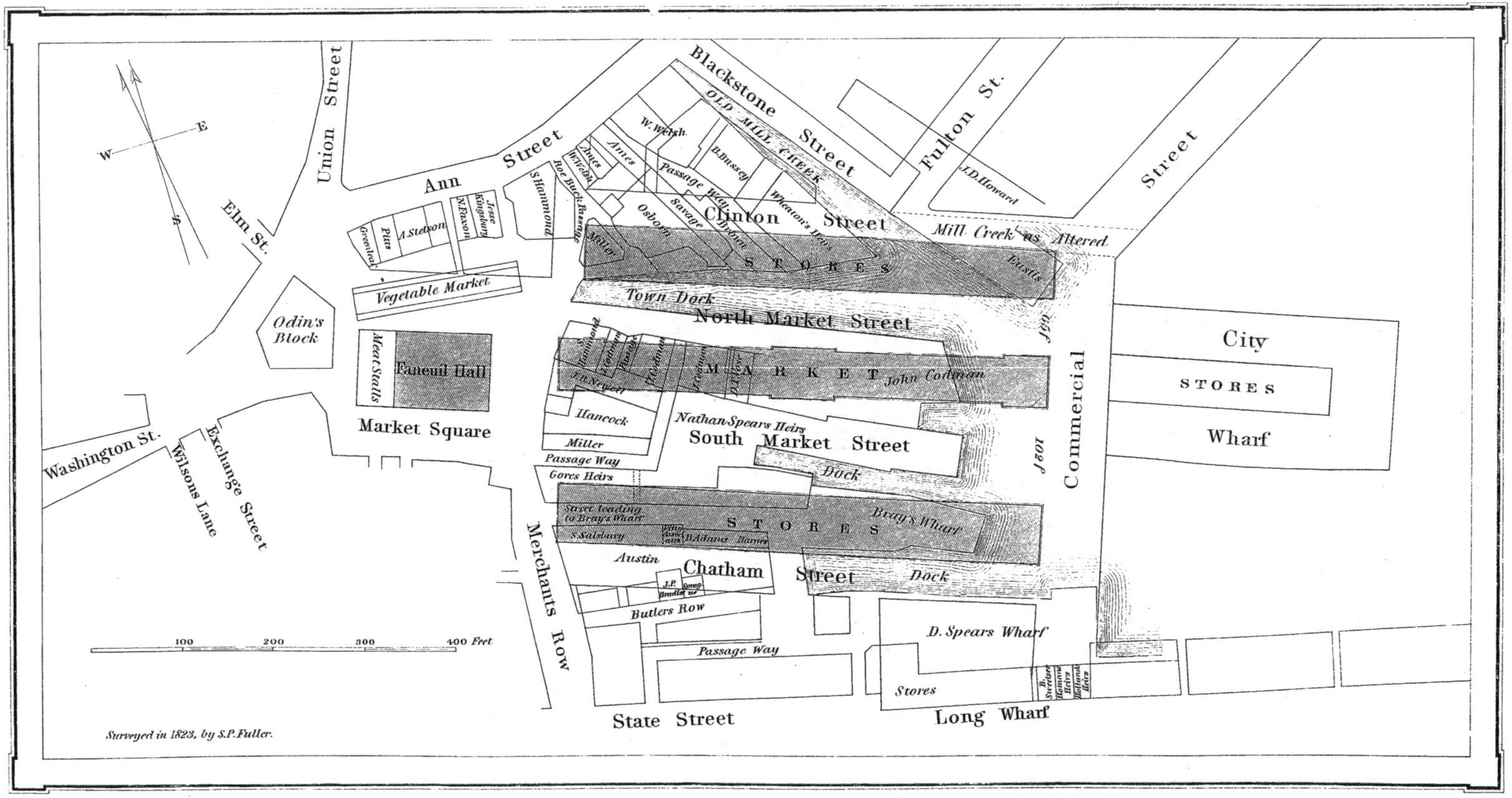

Union Street
Elm St.
Ann Street
Blackstone Street
Old Mill Creek
Fulton St.
Street
J.D. Howard
W. Welsh
B. Bussey
Ames
Ames
W. Welsh
Passage Way
Wheaton's Heirs
S. Hammond
Roe Buck Passage
Jesse Kingsbury
N. Faxon
A. Stetson
Pitts
Greenleaf
Osborn
Savage
Bryant
Clinton Street
Mill Creek as Altered
Miller
Stores
Eustis
Vegetable Market
Town Dock
North Market Street
Odin's Block
Meat Stalls
Faneuil Hall
S. Hammond
Codman
Passage
Codman
Codman
D. Tyler
J. R. Newell
Market
John Codman
City
Stores
Wharf
Commercial
Hancock
Nathan Spears Heirs
South Market Street
Miller
Passage Way
Gores Heirs
Dock
Market Square
Washington St.
Wilsons Lane
Exchange Street
Merchants Row
Street leading to Bray's Wharf
S. Salsbury
B. Adams
Barnes
Stores
Bray's Wharf
Austin
Chatham Street
J.P. Bradlee
Dock
Butlers Row
Passage Way
D. Spears Wharf
Stores
B. Sweetser
Homans Heirs
Hollands Heirs
State Street
Long Wharf
100 200 300 400 Feet
W E S

Surveyed in 1823, by S.P. Fuller.

GROUND PLAN OF THE MARKET HOUSE, ERECTED IN 1826, AND OF THE SPACE INCLUDED IN THE IMPROVEMENT.

justified on stronger grounds than that which the city government, with a fearless and independent spirit, and in a just confidence in the judgment and intelligence of their fellow-citizens, had incurred. Their arrangements had already lessened to a comparatively narrow sphere the necessity of future expenditures; and the remaining duty was to finish the improvements, to correct existing establishments, and to apply the means in their possession to the gradual extinction of the city debt. To this object, the Mayor recommended the specific appropriation of the whole property and its incomes, transferred to the city by the Committee for the extension of Faneuil Hall Market; it being, in his judgment, not proper to consider property, thus obtained, as a subject of complete ownership, until the debt for which it was incurred is paid. For this purpose, he recommended that those funds should be placed under the supervision of commissioners, composed of public officers, *ex officio*, appointed by the City Council.

The erection of a new court house and a city hall were, at this time, subjects of discussion and controversy. The Mayor, deeming it greatly for the interest of the city, that the intercourse between the departments should be convenient and easy, recommended Faneuil Hall as the most suitable location for their accommodation. His views, were, however, at variance with interests, opinions, and views of citizens, in different parts of the city, and resulted in a still further postponement of the concentration of the city offices in one building.

At this period, great complaints existed on the subject of the voting lists; and the question was agitated with some warmth,—whether the responsibility for their correctness rested, as it did under the town government, on the Assessors; or whether it was not devolved upon the Mayor and Aldermen, by the terms of the city charter. The discussion ultimately resulted in the opinion, that the labor of making out the voting lists, of comparing them with their books, and certifying their correctness, were the duties of the Assessors; but that the Mayor and Aldermen were responsible for the time, form, and manner in which it should be done. In conformity with this result, the Mayor and Aldermen constituted the Mayor a sub-committee, to superintend the making out the voting lists; to resort, in cases of difficulty for advisement to the whole Board; it appearing to them, that the duty of general superintendence and direction, and the exercise of a sound judgment, concerning all the great municipal relations of the city, particularly those which immediately affected the elective franchise, was devolved on the Mayor and Aldermen, by the express terms of the city charter.

For three years after the organization of the city government, no important addition was made to the number or expenses of the public schools, except the erection of the Hancock School, under the administration of Mr. Phillips, and its completion under his successor. By a report of the School Committee, made in October, 1822, it appears that "the general state of the schools was satisfactory;" but regret was expressed, that "many parents were indifferent as to sending their children to school;" "and that, with regard to regularity of attendance," the negligence of both parents and children was excessive.

In the last year of the town government, (July, 1821,) a school for mutual instruction had been established by the votes of the inhabitants. In August, 1822, on the petition of several citizens, stating that "the experiment had succeeded admirably;" and that, in their opinion, more intellectual activity, a greater degree of interest in studies, of readiness in learning, and of punctuality, may be produced under that than under the prevailing system; that the expense would be less; the present cost for the instruction of each scholar being *twelve dollars and fifty cents* per annum, while that proposed would be less than *four dollars*,—the School Committee voted that the Hancock School should, until otherwise ordered, be appropriated to give the system a fair trial.

These proceedings were not acceptable to the City Council, who, on the twenty-first of October, 1822, voted, that "it was not expedient to make the alterations in the Hancock School contemplated by the School Committee." This vote, and also an order, passed by the City Council, in May preceding, "authorizing the School Committee to elect instructors for the public schools, to remove them, and fix their salaries," were regarded by the School Committee as "an interference with powers delegated to them by the citizens;" and, on the twenty-first of November, 1822, a sub-committee of that body, in a labored report, maintained that, by force of the nineteenth section of the city charter, the care and superintendence of the public schools were vested in the School Committee; that the power thus granted ought to have a reasonable construction, implying incidental powers, to make such superintendence effectual, — such as appointment and removal of masters, fixing their salaries, selection of books, and regulating the studies of the schools; that the exclusive right to make appropriations of public moneys, possessed by the City Council, was the proper and only check held by that body over the proceedings of the School Committee, and was applicable only to extreme cases, and not involving the power of making their proceedings nugatory; they not being the agents of the City Council, but a distinct and independent body, deriving their powers, delegated to them by the citizens, under the provisions of the city charter.

These proceedings were the chief measures of a general character adopted on this subject by the city government. During these two years, no material alteration took place in the condition or system of the schools. Some complaints were, indeed, at that time made, by parents against masters, for undue severity to their children; and by masters against parents, for indulging their children in want of punctuality, or for keeping them from school in their private service. There were other practices, and some disposition thought to be evidenced to keep men, who were deemed unqualified, in office. And, in June, 1823, on the first opening to the public of the Hancock School, the Mayor, at the request of the School Committee, delivered, and subsequently, also, at their request, published an address, from which extracts, relative to topics of permanent interest and frequent recurrence, and deeply affecting the success of the schools, are here inserted, as follows: —

There are two mistakes into which parents are chiefly apt to fall in this connection. First, — they are too ready to imagine, that school education and discipline can supply the want of discipline and instruction at home; and they often throw blame upon the masters which, in justice, belongs to themselves. If, therefore, the child of any parent returns from school shamed or corrected; if he make little or no improvement; or if the tendency of his temper be wayward or vicious; before blaming the master, or finding fault with the discipline of the school, let such discontented parent set himself seriously to inquire into the manner in which he himself has, in past life, performed, or how he is, at the present time, performing his duties to his child; what principles he has inculcated; what habits he has permitted; what example he has set. School education can do but little without domestic discipline and example. The father, and mother, form and influence, more than any masters, the characters of children. Let no parent, then, listen hastily to complaints, unless he is himself conscious of being guiltless of having given any countenance or encouragement to that conduct which he condemns, and which masters, in their fidelity, must punish.

A second mistake of parents, affecting these institutions, is, — that they are apt to imagine, because schools are provided by the public, it is the right of individuals, and of themselves as well as of others, to use or neglect them at pleasure, according as any whim, caprice, temporary interest, or convenience may dictate.

The consequence is, that they send children to school only occasionally, when they please, or at what time they please, without any regard to the order and regulations of the school, or the interest of their child.

Now, the usefulness of all schools, in a great degree, depends upon strict habits of punctuality and order; and on regularity in the master's performance of his established routine of duties. Now, no master can thus perform his duties, if children are permitted by parents to loiter on their way, or delay, or neglect going to school; or if they are kept after school hours engaged in work, or on errands, and thus, by coming late, break in upon the regularity of the school.

The rights of parents are, in this respect, precisely like and parallel with all the other rights of civil life. So use your own rights, as not to injure the rights of others; above all, so use them as not to injure the general interest. It is the duty of masters to exact punctuality of attendance from their scholars; and for this purpose, as a chief means, to be most minute and critical in their own punctuality. And as to those parents, who will not submit to a principle so essential to the success of this great interest of the republic, they must not complain, should those who have the care of that interest exclude altogether from the enjoyment of these privileges those delinquents who, by such injurious neglect, show they are unworthy to possess them.

The relation of master and usher is still more important and critical to these institutions. Their duties are, all of them, of a nature so simple and obvious, that to allude to them would imply a possibility of ignorance, or deficiency, which ought not to be admitted, even by way of supposition.

There are duties, however, resulting from their relation to one another and to this Board, on which it may be useful to touch; and the rather, because difficulties have heretofore arisen from misapprehensions on those subjects.

The relation, then, of the master and usher, of the same school, ought to be understood to be, in the nature of things, a relation of subordination, and not of equality. It is one of the chief duties of him who is second, to support and strengthen the hands of him who is first; and, for this purpose, to study on all occasions to elevate his character, to extend his influence, to facilitate his labors, and promote his respectability, both in school and in the world. There is no surer mark of unworthiness for a higher station, than an unwillingness to submit to the requisitions, or to yield the deference, which is due from a lower. All espionage, all disputes of authority, all petty cavils, of the inferior in relation to the superior, are to be avoided; being assured that such conduct can receive no countenance from this Board; with the certainty that, though its effect may be to injure him whom it affects, that it cannot fail to disgrace him who condescends to the practice.

This principle, however, must not be understood to extend to the concealment of any notorious vice or fault in the masters, or to any open or habitual violation in him of the rules established for the government of the school by the School Committee. Failure openly to represent this to the proper authority, is a failure in duty, for which the usher is, and will be, considered responsible.

On the other hand, the duty of the master towards the usher is not less plain and imperious. In the order of things, he is, indeed, superior; but then, he should always remember that it is only superiority of station, which does not necessarily imply individual superiority. The relation in which masters and ushers stand to each other is that of gentlemen; of men under joint obligations to promote the interests of the school, and the improvement of the scholars; and the great study of both should be, so to coöperate in their labors, as mutually to aid each other in effecting this joint object.

From both instructors, the public have a right to expect, and it will be the endeavor of the present School Committee to enforce, punctuality, exclusive devotion to the interests of the school, and strict obedience to the rules established for its government.

The habit of punctuality, instructors should consider as a primary and essential duty. They should be, by system, as true to the fixed time of opening and closing their school as the shadow of the style is true to the sun dial.

So, also, with respect to an exclusive devotedness to the interests of the school. It may be questioned whether either, — and certainly, whether the principal instructor, — ought to be permitted to engage in any other business or employment, the object of which is pecuniary emolument. But it cannot be questioned, that neither of them ought to be permitted to carry any engagement or other pursuit into school hours. The whole of the prescribed time belongs to the public. During its continuance, instructors have no right to do any thing else, or think of any thing else. Whatever part of the time is not occupied in instruction, is sufficiently well employed in superintendence of order and decorum.

Lastly, gentlemen of the School Committee, in this reference to the duties of others, which I have thus made, at your suggestion, you will permit me, also, to notice some which belong to ourselves. In the organization of this Committee, distinguished men, drawn for the most part from the learned professions, are added to the higher branches of the city authorities. It must generally be expected, that the Mayor and Aldermen will be men of business, rather than of science, and better acquainted with the rules and measures of active life, than with those of schools and seminaries of learning. This part of the Committee have, therefore, a natural right to look to the superadded members for advice, direction, and for a vigilant and active superintendence, in this particular department. And while the Mayor and Aldermen will extend to this great concern all the protection which the extensive nature of their other duties will permit, it is to the members of the Committtee, who do not belong to this Board, that the city authorities have a right to look for a severe and scrutinizing investigation of the state of the schools, and of the manner in which masters and ushers, as well as parents and children, fulfil their respective obligations.

The great difficulty with which we have to contend is that disposition which is innate in all, to avoid painful responsibilities, when the exercise of authority affects particularly and directly the hopes and prospects of an individual, and only generally and remotely the interests of the community. But, gentlemen, in assuming this office, we have undertaken a duty for which we are responsible, not only to our country, but to Heaven. If men obviously weak, or inefficient, or inadequate, are maintained in office, merely through reluctance to exercise power which our station devolves upon us, and which, by accepting the trust, we have solemnly engaged to fulfil, I need not explain to wise, honorable, and thoughtful men the nature and consequences of such failure, to fulfil an important and voluntarily incurred obligation. This city has a right to have efficient and capable men in all its departments; especially in its schools. The worst of all charities is that which supports imbecility in official station, merely from reluctance at depriving it of official emoluments. And, however this may be pardonable in relation to offices affecting only personal or local interests, it is, in relation to such as are of the nature of public instructors, little less than criminal.

I repeat it, this city has a right to have, in every department of this great concern, none but adequate men. The liberality for which the inhabitants of Boston have been distinguished towards public instructors, in all times, has afforded this Committee the means and the power of selecting the best, and of excluding the bad or the indifferent from those offices. If, through our weakness, carelessness, or fear, the rising generation in any school district be dealt by unfairly, and do not reap its equal share of the advantages which this city, by the liberality of its public provisions, endeavors to secure to all its citizens, the fault and the shame will lie upon those who, being intrusted with the power, and having accepted of it, shrink from their duty, under the influence of a false and mischievous sympathy.

Early in the year 1825, the School Committee accepted a report of one of their sub-committees, recommending an establishment of a high school for girls, and an application to the City Council for an appropriation for that object. The plan proposed was, that girls who were qualified should be admitted when *eleven*, and not more than *fifteen* years of age; and that the course of studies should occupy *three* years, and embrace all the branches of education usually taught in colleges, except Greek and Latin. There being at that time a very general desire in the School Committee to test the usefulness of monitorial or mutual instruction, it was proposed that the school should be conducted upon that system; and, in respect of expense, the report supposed that *one large room* would be sufficient, at least for the first year.

The adoption of the report was pressed with great earnestness by several members of the School Committee, and the success of the High School for Boys, was urged as conclusive in favor of a similar school for girls. The High School for Boys had been in operation *five years*, and no additional school for them was required or anticipated. *The applicants for admission to it had never exceeded* NINETY; *the greatest number ever admitted to it in one year was* EIGHTY-FOUR; *and, at that time, the number was only* ONE HUNDRED AND FORTY-SIX. The number, also, in the High School for Boys regularly diminished every successive year, as parents found places for their sons, as apprentices and in counting-houses; so that the greatest number of those who continued through their whole course was *seventeen;* and they belonged to a class consisting originally of *seventy* members. Those members of the Committee, however, who considered the difference between the occupation and preparation for active life, of girls and boys, between the ages of eleven and fifteen years, doubted if the result of the High School for Boys was a criterion to be relied upon for a high school for girls. It was certain that the inevitable effect of this school would be to attract from the common schools all the most ambitious and intellectual scholars, and of consequence deprive those schools of the girls best qualified by attainment and example to excite the spirit of emulation, to raise their standard, and to take, in them, the place of monitors. Apprehensions of this kind added force to the doubts concerning the expediency of establishing it.

There existed, at this time, a general opinion in favor of extending and enlarging the advantages enjoyed by females in the public schools. The project was therefore in unison with this prevailing desire, and popular with parents whose daughters were of an age to take advantage of it, and the appropriation of two thousand dollars, recommended by the School Committee, was granted by the City Council with great unanimity. The anticipations of difficulty were, however, so strong and plausible, that it was adopted expressly "as an experiment;" "if favorable, to be continued, if adverse, to be dropped of course." With this understanding, the project being sanctioned by the City Council, the twenty-second of February, 1826, was appointed by the School Committee for the examination of candidates for admission into the High School for Girls; the largest and most commodious room owned by the city having been assigned for it, and fitted up, at a considerable expense, to the satisfaction of the Committee.

But before this examination occurred, it became apparent that the result of a High School for Girls would be very different from that of the High School for Boys; and that, if continued upon the scale of time and studies the original project embraced, the expense would be insupportable, and the effect upon the Grammar or Common Schools positively injurious.

Instead of *ninety* candidates, — the highest number that had ever offered in one year for the school for boys, — it was ascertained that nearly *three hundred* would be presented for the High School for Girls. The spacious room provided for the school would not accommodate more than *one hundred and twenty;* and it was evident that, either *two high schools for girls must be established the first year*, or that more than one half of the candidates must be rejected, to the great disappointment of their parents and instructors.

In this dilemma, a special meeting of the School Committee was called, on the twenty-first of February, the day previous to that appointed for the examination; and, after much deliberation on the course to be pursued, they resolved to keep the number to be admitted under their own control; and for this purpose passed a vote, that the Sub-Committee, appointed as examiners, should report to the School Committee "*the names, ages, and standing of all the candidates they should find qualified for admission, that* THIS COMMITTEE MAY DETERMINE WHAT CLASSES OF THEM SHALL BE ADMITTED."

Under the influence of this vote, the examination was accordingly conducted. *Two hundred and eighty-six candidates* presented themselves for examination. And, on the twenty-eighth of February, the Sub-Committee of Examiners, from motives of prudence, *did not report to the School Committee the names of those they found duly qualified, but only the ages of each candidate, with a table of the marks, from one to twenty, put opposite each, under each head of examination, and the general result;* and, to bring the admission of applicants within the extent of the accommodations which had been provided, they recommended that the School Committee "*should strike from the list of applicants all between eleven and twelve years of age; and that, of the remainder, all who had received the numbers of thirteen and a half and upwards, should be admitted as members of the school.*"

The School Committee adopted the course suggested by the Sub-Committee of Examiners, and regulated their admission of candidates by the principles they recommended. The consequence was that, of the *two hundred aud eighty-six candidates, about one hundred and thirty were admitted, and one hundred and fifty rejected.* Parents, friends, and instructors of these unsuccessful candidates regarded these proceedings as unjust, and the rule of selection as arbitrary. Complaints of favoritism were not uncommon, — the natural consequence of extreme disappointment. The course, however, pursued by the School Committee was unquestionably the best the circumstances in which they found themselves placed permitted. This feeling of discontent was not, however, generally allayed, although, from particular considerations, the vote for striking out all between eleven and twelve years of age from the list of applicants was subsequently rescinded, and seven candidates between those years were admitted.

Notwithstanding the number of candidates offered far exceeded all anticipation, the High School for Girls was put into operation under very favorable auspices. The master was talented, earnest, and assiduous; and members of the Committee, some of whom had daughters enjoying its advantages, superintended its course with marked and critical interest. The girls who were admitted were the *élite* of the Grammar Schools, and were among the most ambitious and highly educated of them and of *private schools*, from which a majority of those admitted were derived. It was impossible that a school thus conducted, superintended, and composed, should not be highly advantageous to the few individuals who enjoyed its benefits; and its success was a subject of congratulation among their parents.

In August, 1826, a report was made to the School Committee, setting forth the necessity of a further provision for its support, enlargement, and accommodation; and stating, by way of information, the following facts: — "*That the present number of the school was one hundred and thirty; that few, if any, could be excluded the present year; that, according to the best calculations that could be made, the number of the candidates for admission at the then next ensuing examination, would be four hundred and twenty-seven, who, if they were all admitted, and those now in the school retained, it would be necessary that five hundred and fifty-seven members of it should be provided for.*" The Sub-Committee, however, suggested that, probably, not more than *two hun-*

dred would be found qualified; a suggestion unsupported by any data.

This report unavoidably brought under the consideration probably of every member of the School Committee, and of the city government, the practicability of a system of schools, including such an extent of time and course of studies as the plan of this school originally embraced. It was obvious that the result of the High School for Boys was no criterion by which to estimate that for girls, who were not compelled to prepare for active life between the ages of eleven and sixteen, and to whom a high classical education was extremely attractive; and, being confined to the best scholars in all the schools, private as well as public, by its select and necessarily exclusive character, obviated the objections of many parents to public schools. The effect of this circumstance was apparent in this "experiment." Of the number admitted into it, *sixty-two* were from private schools, and only *fifty-nine* from the public. And it was ascertained, that if the school should be maintained upon the extensive plan of time and studies embraced in the original project, that there would be a far greater influx into it from the private schools. Those, therefore, whose property enabled them to educate their children at private schools, would occupy the greatest proportion and receive the chief benefit from the High School for Girls. No circumstance could show more effectually that the school was chiefly for the advantage of the *few, and not of the many;* and those, also, the prosperous few. Again, this first experiment showed, in another respect, the entire difference in result of the school for girls and of that for boys. In the latter school, as has been already stated,[1] the number of scholars regularly diminished every year, so that the far greater proportion of those who entered it quitted before the expiration of the three years; whereas, of all those who entered this High School for Girls, *not one*, during the eighteen months it was in operation, voluntarily quitted it; and there was no reason for believing that any one admitted to the school would voluntarily quit it for the whole three years, except in case of marriage. It was ascertained that the whole number of girls, between eleven and fifteen years of age, then in the Grammar and High Schools was about *seven hun-*

[1] See page 217.

dred; and that in the private schools the number was greater. Of consequence, there would be a great total, of at least, *fourteen hundred* girls every year; the number, also, increasing with the population, to whom the benefit of this collegiate course was annually to be proffered; and, considering the uncommon and desirable privileges thus offered, it was probable that at least one third would qualify themselves for the benefit, and that not one of those, once admitted, would quit the school for three years. It was evident, therefore, that at least two High Schools for Girls must at once be established; and that, if the whole number of anticipated applicants should be admitted, that three such schools would be required, with a prospective certainty of the increase of this number every year. It was apparent to all who contemplated the subject disinterestedly, that the continuance of this school would involve an amount of expenses unprecedented and unnecessary; since the same course of instruction could be introduced into the Grammar Schools, to the far greater benefit of the greater number of females, and those, too, of a class for whom it was the chief duty and interest of the city to provide a high education. The opinion, therefore, became general, if not universal, that, if the school was continued, some change in its principles must be adopted. Two schemes only were suggested, by those who wished to continue the course three years:— 1. That the High School should be confined to girls educated in the Grammar Schools. This could not be sustained for one moment. For, in addition to the common right, which would be inherent in all parents, to send their children to schools supported at the public expense, the tendency would be to bring back to the Grammar Schools a class of children, from the education of whom the city was now relieved, by the predilection or pecuniary ability of parents. 2. That the qualifications for admission should be raised, and the course of three years be continued. This last was the favorite scheme of those most desirous of continuing the school for the term of three years, according to the original project. A single objection seemed, however, conclusive against this scheme. In proportion as the qualifications for admission are raised, the school becomes exclusive. Although nominally open to all, it will be *open only to the few, and shut to the many.*

Actuated by these general views, a sub-committee was appointed by the School Committee, to whom the report made in the August preceding[1] was referred, to consider the expediency of making further provision for the High Schools for Girls, on the same basis of extent, of time, and of studies as the original project embraced. This Committee, after long deliberation, and inquiring of the several masters of the Grammar Schools, as to the effect upon the character and prospects in those schools produced by the High School for Girls, found there was a diversity of opinion. Some of the masters regarded the effects as beneficial; others thought them prejudicial. Removing the best and most exemplary scholars damped the ardor of the girls who remained, and took away the materials from which monitors were selected, and reduced the standard of the Common Schools from the highest to a secondary grade. The Committee, therefore, on the seventeenth of November ensuing, made a report, stating those facts, and that new principles ought to be adopted in relation to the qualification for admission and time of remaining in the High School for Girls; and unanimously recommended the following modifications of the system of that school. These were immediately adopted by the School Committee, namely,—that the age of admission should be *fourteen, instead of eleven;* that continuance in the school should be only for *one year, instead of three;* and that the requisitions for admission should be raised, so as to include all branches taught in the public Grammar and Writing Schools; and that no female should be admitted after the age of *sixteen.*

These modifications, in which the School Committee and City Council generally concurred, so greatly diminished the advantages the original plan of the school proposed, that much of the interest which its creation excited was also diminished. It became apparent, that a school thus limited, of which the advantages could be enjoyed only for *one year*, would not be, as the original scheme professed, for the benefit of *the many;* but, in fact, for the exclusive advantage of *the few*, and, for the most part, of those whose private resources were fully adequate for the education of their own daughters. The higher the qualifications required, the more exclusive the school. The daughters of educated men, of lawyers, clergymen, and physicians, who had

[1] See page 219.

leisure themselves, or those who had fortunes sufficient to give their daughters the high preparatory education, would, unavoidably, be preferred on examination. To them, the advantages of the school would principally result, and not to the daughters of the mass of the citizens.

The school, however, was permitted to continue, subject to this modification, until November, 1827, when a committee was raised to consider the expediency of continuing it; which, on the eleventh of December following, reported that, in their opinion, "it was expedient to continue it." This report was the occasion of much debate; and several modifications were proposed, on which the Committee was equally divided, when a motion was made for the postponement of the question to the next School Committee, which, in the course of that month, was to be elected. On this question, the votes being equal, — "six and six," — the Mayor, after declaring, that his opinion was so decidedly adverse to the continuance of the school, that he could not vote in its favor; yet, regarding the question of great importance, and that the continuance of it was a subject of much public and popular animadversion, and that the School Committee then about to be elected, coming immediately from the citizens, would be better qualified, from their acquaintance with the general feeling and sentiments of the people, to decide the question most satisfactorily, postponed the subject to the next city year by his casting vote.

This decision having been made the subject of much popular animadversion, the Mayor did not deem his official duty fulfilled without presenting his views distinctly to his fellow-citizens; and, accordingly, in his inaugural address to the city government, in January, 1828,[1] expressed, in a direct and unequivocal manner, his opinion, that the standard of public education ought to be raised to the greatest practicable height in our Common Schools; that the effect of the High School for Girls was, in his judgment, far different from that which popular opinion entertained; that, instead of being for the benefit of the children of the whole community, it was, in fact, comparatively for the benefit of those of a very few, and that, too, a class who were best qualified, by intelligence, education, and wealth, to provide for the high instruction of their own children.

[1] See Appendix, F.

Leading members of the City Council coincided in these general views; and at a meeting, early in January, 1828, at the suggestion of the Mayor, the succeeding School Committee took into consideration the subject referred to them by the preceding Board; and when under discussion, say the records, "James Savage remarked that, though he had, as a member of the Common Council, voted an appropriation to the High School for Girls, it was mainly with a view to make a public experiment of the system of mutual instruction; that he was opposed to the High School for Girls, and to the whole system of instruction, as regards females; he therefore moved, that a sub-committee be raised to consider, —

"Whether the High School for Girls shall be continued, and the basis on which it shall be established; —

"Whether the girls may not well be allowed to remain at the Grammar Schools throughout the year; —

"And, whether the time of their continuance at these schools may not be advantageously extended."

This motion being adopted, the following Sub-Committee was appointed for its consideration, namely, — the Mayor, John Pickering, Samuel T. Armstrong, William B. Fowle, Samuel Barrett, Zabdiel B. Adams, and Amos Farnsworth.

This Committee made, on the twelfth of February, an elaborate report unanimously, in which was set forth, in detail, all the chief views and arguments connected with the subject; and declared their opinion, that the High School for Girls "ought not to be reëstablished upon the basis of embracing the extent of time and the multiplied objects of education which the original plan of that school contemplated;" and that it ought not to be continued "on the restricted basis, as to time and objects, to which it was reduced by the vote of the seventeenth of November, 1826;"[1] but that "it was far preferable to arrange all our Grammar and Writing Schools so that the standard of education in them may be elevated and enlarged, thereby making them all, as it respects females, in fact, high schools, in which each child may advance, according to its attainments, to the same branches recently taught in the High School for Girls. The Sub-Committee then entered upon a wide survey of the whole school system; and closed their report by recommending

[1] See page 222.

a series of resolutions, which, after undergoing some modifications, were adopted by the School Committee unanimously, in which the opinion of the School Committee was declared, that it was for the interest of the city, that the mutual or monitorial system of instruction should be introduced into the Boylston and Bowdoin Schools; that an appropriation be requested of the City Council, for preparing the school houses for this purpose; and the Sub-Committee, who made the report, were reappointed to carry the resolutions adopted into effect. On the third of June ensuing, " Mr. Savage moved that the girls be permitted to remain in the English Grammar Schools throughout the year." This motion being adopted, and measures taken for carrying into effect the views thus sanctioned, the project of the High School for Girls was abandoned, and the scale of instruction in the Common Schools in the city was gradually elevated and enlarged.

This result, and the distinctness with which the Mayor had made known his opinion, concerning the inexpediency of establishing such a High School for Girls at the expense of the city, in opposition to the views and interests of a body of citizens of great activity, and of no inconsiderable influence, gave origin to party assaults upon the motives and conduct of that officer, which he noticed in his final address to the Board of Aldermen, on taking leave of the office, in January, 1829.[1] The soundness of these views, and their coincidence with the permanent interests of the city, seem to be sanctioned by the fact, that twenty-three years (1851) have elapsed, and no effectual attempt, during that period, has been made for its revival, in the School Committee, or in either branch of the City Council.

A question growing out of the relation of the Mayor of the city to the School Committee, of which, by the city charter, he was officially a component part, ought not, perhaps, to be omitted in this history, although of no other general importance than as preserving a remembrance of the different construction made of that charter, and of its having temporarily been the occasion of party animadversions. When, under the town government, the School Committee was established, there was no individual elected by the vote of all the inhabitants as chief officer or head of the town. The Selectmen, as the Executive Board, was

[1] See page 269.

accustomed to elect annually a chairman; but his authority and official character were derived solely from their election. The School Committee, therefore, considering, justly, that the power of electing a chairman of the Selectmen did not include the power of electing a chairman of the School Committee, notwithstanding the Selectmen were component parts of that Board, provided, in their first organization, "that, at the first meeting in each year, the Board should organize itself by choosing a chairman." And this was the uniform practice, until the adoption of the city charter. It was manifest that the relation of things was materially changed by this charter. Like the Selectmen, the Mayor and Aldermen were made a component part of the School Committee; but the Mayor was not chosen by the Board of Aldermen, but elected head of the city by the body of its citizens; and, by the force of that relation, it was the opinion of many, and, at the commencement of the new government, apparently of all, that, *ex officio*, he had the right, and that it was his duty to claim the station of chairman of all the boards of which, *ex officio*, he was a component part. This opinion was so strong and so general, that it does not appear that, during the first seven years after the organization of the city government, that any question was raised, or any doubt expressed on the subject. John Phillips, the first Mayor, with the Aldermen met, on the sixth of May, 1822, the other members of the School Committee, and took the chair, as Mayor of the city, and the School Committee proceeded immediately to organize themselves by the choice of a secretary. Neither the record nor any document indicates that the proposition to choose him or any one chairman was either made or thought of by any member of the School Committee. The same was the case with his successor, during the nearly six years to which his administration extended. The first intimation of any discontent existing in the Committee, for their omission to elect a chairman, occurred on the twelfth of February, 1828, more than a month after the School Committee had been that year organized in the usual course.

On that day, the record states, that "it was suggested by Mr. Bowdoin," (the Secretary of the Committee,) "that, in examining the rules of the Board now in force, with a view to his duties as secretary, he had found a provision requiring, as a part of the organization of the Board, the annual choice of a chairman, at its first meeting in January; that the organization, by such choice, was not completed at the late meeting; and, adverting to the words of the preamble to the rules, that *the School Committee is a constituent branch of the city government, by the charter,* added that, as it was a part of the duty required of those elected by the several branches, he doubted whether they could dispense with the responsibility of that part of the organization.

"After some debate on the subject, in which it was said by the Mayor, who disclaimed all *personal* motives, that 'he considered the person holding the office of Mayor as being chairman by force of the city charter,' it was voted that a committee of five be appointed to take into consideration a revision of the rules; and the Mayor, accordingly, appointed Messrs. James Bowdoin, John Pickering, Samuel T. Armstrong, Joseph Head, the Rev. C. P. Grosvenor, for the purpose."

The course and conduct of the Mayor, on this subject, having been animadverted upon in pamphlet and newspaper, as "assuming" and "selfish," in order that no obscurity might rest on his opinions and motives, he immediately addressed a letter to the Board, in the following terms:—

TO THE SCHOOL COMMITTEE OF THE CITY OF BOSTON.

GENTLEMEN,—At your last meeting, Mr. Bowdoin called the attention of the Committee to its organization, by the choice of a chairman, and stating "*the doubts he entertained if, when meeting as a Board, they could dispense with the responsibility of that part of the organization.*"

As this suggestion and these doubts have reference to the relations of the office which the subscriber has now the honor to hold, and are in repugnance to the uniform practice and course of proceedings ever since the organization of the city government, the subscriber deems it his duty to that office, and to all who may be his successors in it, to state openly his views, resulting, as they do, from the terms of the city charter, now, for the first time, authoritatively questioned, to the end, that no obscurity may rest upon their nature and foundation.

The School Committee is constituted by the last clause in the nineteenth section of the city charter, which is in these words:—"And the said citizens shall, at the same time, and in like manner, elect one person in each ward to be a member of the School Committee for the said city; *and the persons so chosen shall* JOINTLY, WITH THE MAYOR AND ALDERMEN, *constitute the School Committee for the said city, and have the care and superintendence of the public schools.*"

From the terms of this section it is apparent,—

1. That the Mayor and Aldermen are part of the School Committee, *ex officio.*

2. That the term, "Mayor and Aldermen," is not a designation of the *individuals*, but of their office and relation.

Had that term been intended to designate *the individuals*, to whom the persons so elected were to be joined, the expression would have been different, namely, — "*and the persons so chosen shall, jointly, with the persons who shall be chosen Mayor and Aldermen*," &c. As the expression of the charter now is, the persons so chosen are *joined to the office and relation*, and not to the persons as such. In corroboration of which reasoning, it is apprehended that it will not be questioned, that an Alderman resigning his seat at that Board, or the Mayor resigning his office, would, by that act, vacate his seat in the School Committee.

From the above reasoning, it follows, necessarily, that the Mayor and Aldermen compose a part of the School Committee, when it meets, *ex officiis;* that is, as "Mayor and Aldermen," and in no other capacity, right, or relation.

By the tenth section of the city charter, it is declared, "that the *Mayor and Aldermen*, thus chosen and qualified, SHALL COMPOSE ONE BOARD, AND SHALL SIT AND ACT TOGETHER AS ONE BODY, AT ALL MEETINGS OF WHICH THE MAYOR, IF PRESENT, SHALL PRESIDE.

From both these sections the conclusion is, in the opinion of the subscriber, unavoidable, that the Mayor and Aldermen cannot meet, *ex officiis, but as one board;* at all meetings of which the Mayor, if present, must preside.

If to the Mayor and Aldermen, for a particular purpose, as in this case of schools, other citizens are joined, they are, by force of the terms of the charter, so joined, as all citizens are joined, when they are connected with the Chief Executive Board of the Corporation; that is, *modified by the organization of that Supreme Executive Board, as established in the charter.*

The subscriber requests, that this claim of official right may be put on file and on record, to the end that the nature and foundation of it may be understood, and that those who may hold this office hereafter, may have none of their just official claims compromitted, by any neglect or want of vigilance on his part.

Very respectfully, Gentlemen,

I am your obedient servant,

JOSIAH QUINCY, *Mayor.*

BOSTON, 21 February, 1828.

No report appears by the records to have been made by the Committee thus appointed; but the records of the next succeeding year state, "that the Board proceeded to elect a chairman by ballot, and the Mayor was unanimously chosen; a practice which has continued to the present day; notwithstanding, in the year 1835, by act of the Legislature, the Board of Aldermen were excluded, and the Mayor of the city constituted a component part of the School Committee. The course thus adopted being probably deemed important to maintain the independence of that board of the city government.

CHAPTER XVI.

CITY GOVERNMENT. 1828.

JOSIAH QUINCY, *Mayor.*[1]

General Relations of the City in respect of Debt — Health — Protection against Fire — Its Duty in respect of Education — Effect on its Prosperity by the Principle of Arbitrary Valuation without Relief — Principles of Proceeding relative to the Voting Lists — Indemnity of City Officers for Acts of Official Duty — Sale of Spirituous Liquors prohibited on the Common — Inexpediency of Selling the Flats to the Eastward of the New Market House, and the Result of the Measures taken on that Subject.

THE municipal prosperity of the city, and the decisive evidences of the content of the citizens with the conduct of their affairs, were noticed in the inaugural address of the Mayor,[2] and the chief causes of these results were recapitulated. The apprehensions of a city debt had been allayed by the rigid economy enforced, and by the fact, that none of the appropriations made at the beginning of the year had been exceeded. Success had attended the measures adopted for the reduction of the city debt, and at the close of the current financial year one hundred thousand dollars of it would be discharged. The general order of the city had been well maintained, and the number of complaints in every branch of the police diminished. The advantageous effect of the new arrangements in the Health Department were apparent. The general vaccination adopted under the authority of former city councils, and the vigilance of the Health Physician and police officers had been so effectual, that only one case of the smallpox, within the city, had been known or suspected, although it had spread with activity in towns in the immediate vicinity. Tables, founded on the bills of mortality, showed that, from 1824 to 1827 inclusive, the annual ave-

1 The whole number of votes cast, were 2629, of which Josiah Quincy had 2189. The Aldermen elected were, — John T. Loring, Robert Fennelly, James Savage, Thomas Kendall, James Hall, John Pickering, Phineas Upham, Samuel T. Armstrong.

2 See Appendix G.

rage proportion of deaths to population had not only been less than that in any antecedent year, but it was believed to be less than that of any other city of equal population on record. These facts and calculations were stated, to show the wisdom of persevering in that systematic cleansing of the city from noxious animal and vegetable substances, which was commenced in 1823, and had been since regularly pursued. The occasion was taken to press upon the minds of the citizens the duty of holding the executive officers of the city directly responsible for the right conduct of this branch of police, more than for any other, and the certainty that it can never, for any great length of time, be executed well, except by agents, whose labors it can command at all times and apply to all exigencies, and to the ever-varying requisitions of a city.

The establishment of a fire department had created a sense of security, and reduced the rates of insurance against fire on the real property within the city *twenty per cent.* This reduction, the Presidents of several insurance offices had authorized it to be stated, was solely the effect of the efficiency of that department.

The duty and interest of society, with regard to public education, was stated to be best fulfilled by establishing such public schools as would elevate as highly as possible the intellectual and moral condition of the mass of the community. To this end, every necessary branch of elementary instruction should be put within the reach of every citizen. If other and higher branches of instruction are to be added to these, it should be to our common schools, and enjoyed on the same equal principles of common right, and as common property. Every school, the admission to which is based upon the principle of requiring higher attainments, at a specified age, than the mass of children in the ordinary course of school instruction, at that age, can attain, is, in truth, a school for the benefit of the few, and not of the many. In form, it may be general; but in fact, it will be exclusive. The Mayor closed this address, by presenting views concerning the effect upon the prosperity of the city, of "assessing taxes on the principle of an arbitrary valuation without relief."

To these views, the attention of the city government was early called, by a petition of Jesse Putnam and a number of other citizens of wealth and respectability, stating that the inequality produced by the present system of taxation, was apparently unwise and unjust and disadvantageous to the prosperity of Boston, in comparison with the effects of the system pursued in other cities.

The Mayor, having been previously informed of an intention to bring this subject under the consideration of the City Council, had, in the December preceding, addressed letters to the Mayors of New York, Baltimore, and Philadelphia, where modes of assessment were practised more generally satisfactory than those adopted in Massachusetts; from each of whom a reply was received.

The Mayor of New York[1] stated that "the mode of assessing taxes in that city was considered *the best that can be adopted.*" Lists from every individual of the amount of his estate are not required. To many persons engaged in mercantile business, a fair exhibit is impossible, and might be injurious. Two assessors are chosen by the people in each ward at the annual election in November. They are under oath to make a fair and equitable assessment of all estates, real and personal, in their respective wards, excepting such lands and buildings as are exempted by law from taxation. The Assessors commence business early in May, and complete it by the first of July. They then advertise to hear appeals. For ten days, any one may apply and view the assessment. If they consider the amount too high, they may make oath to the Assessors of the value of their property, which is conclusive. The books are afterwards returned to the Mayor, Recorder, and Aldermen, who examine whether the wards are assessed in a just proportion to each other, and they have power to lessen one ward and augment another, so as to produce an equitable apportionment.

The Mayor of Baltimore[2] stated that "although their system of taxation was not free from objection, he was perfectly free to say that it gives general satisfaction." The Assessors, who are under oath to make a just valuation of all assessable property, apply together to the residence of each taxable person, and obtain a statement of their property, and assess or value the same to the best of their judgment; where they have reason to suspect deception or imposition in rendering an account of their property, they have the power of requiring an oath. A bill

[1] William Paulding. [2] Jacob Small.

of particulars is required to be made out by the Collector, and delivered to each person assessed, on or before the first of July in each year, which, if not paid within three months, the Collector is authorized to enforce.

The Mayor of the city of Philadelphia[1] stated that "the assessments were made by fifteen assessors, annually elected, one for each ward. Triennially, two assessors are elected in each ward to make a new assessment; but every year the assessment is examined and corrected by each assessor in his own ward; and the new assessments are compared and equalized by a general meeting of the Assessors. These returns are made subsequently to county commissioners, who, under the law, are bound to fix certain days of appeal, before whom any citizen, who is aggrieved or injured in the valuation of his real estate, may appear, and have the valuation altered. No lists of valuation of property or estate are demanded of owners or occupants. The Assessors affix the value of the premises and owner's name, as they pass from door to door, and if they err in obtaining the proper owner's names, the Collector gets it right on a duplicate. There never has been, to my knowledge, with a view to taxation, any estimate of the personal property of an individual or corporation. I am not aware of any dissatisfaction as to the manner of assessment, or of inequality in the affixed valuation."

The petition of Jesse Putnam, with the accompanying documents, was referred to the Mayor, Aldermen Pickering, Upham, and Armstrong, and to Messrs. E. Williams, Simonds, Appleton, Gibbens, Dyer, Gray, and Ward, of the Common Council, who referred the subject to a sub-committee, of which John C. Gray was chairman, with instructions, in conformity with the petition of Jesse Putnam, to "investigate the system of apportioning the taxes as now pursued in the city, and to consider of a modification of them." This Sub-Committee reported in March following, that "by the laws establishing this system, every individual is compelled to exhibit an exact statement of his property, personal as well as real, or in default thereof, to be doomed by assessors, according to the best of their knowledge and judgment. In a community so active and wealthy as ours,

[1] Joseph Watson.

there must be obviously serious embarrassments in carrying such a system into complete execution. In such a community there must be great and manifest objections on the part of numerous individuals to the first branch of the alternative offered by our laws, namely, — a complete disclosure of their property. In the first place, such a disclosure is often impracticable. The capital of an individual may be employed, for instance, in foreign trade, and may be materially affected by events which are unknown to the possessor at the time of his making his statement. Secondly, there are very many who cannot expose the state of their affairs without embarrassment or ruin. These circumstances, and others of equal importance, which have frequently been stated to the public, have produced a general unwillingness among the inhabitants of this city, and it is believed of other towns in the Commonwealth, to exhibit accurate lists of their possessions. Nor, perhaps, is this fact to be greatly regretted. By demanding such lists, we invite each individual to become *a witness in a case in which he has the most immediate and direct pecuniary concern.* Can it be questioned, that if the practice of exhibiting lists should become general, that the minds of individuals must, in many cases, be biased by their interest; that statements of very different degrees of exactness and fairness might be rendered by persons possessing an equal amount of property; that a strong temptation would be offered, if not to falsehood and perjury, at least to dangerous prevarication; and that the Assessors might, in the end, be far from arriving at the exact truth, which it was the object of this provision to secure? This general omission of our fellow-citizens, to give accurate statements of their property, however little to be regretted in a moral, or even an economical point of view, renders it the duty of the Assessors to doom all property to the best of their knowledge; and this is a task which is attended with much difficulty and embarrassment, so far as respects personal property. Their means of knowledge must be, in many cases, exceedingly limited, and their opinions founded merely on report or conjecture. Their power, therefore, no matter how wisely or conscientiously exercised, is, to a great degree, an arbitrary power; and such it must always be under our actual system of taxation. Hence we find that a tax on personal property in general, is considered by the best writers on political economy, as one which can never

20*

be imposed without serious disadvantage, except in communities of very small size and very limited capital. These circumstances have led many of our fellow-citizens to inquire, whether some radical change could not be made in our present system of taxation." Having stated these views on this subject, the Sub-Committee forbore to pursue further the questions arising at that time, as whatever change was effected must be made by the Legislature of the Commonwealth, and confined their attention to a change in the number and to varying the compensation of the Assessors, which they recommended in the form of an ordinance, which was, on the fourteenth of April, passed by the City Council; who, in accepting this report of the Sub-Committee, in view of the extent and importance of the resulting questions, postponed them for future deliberation, and, finally, in December following, referred them, with all the documents, to the next City Council, in which they were not revived.

The state of the voting lists and the repeated applications of citizens to have their names inserted in them on the day of election, and after they had been delivered to the Inspectors, having been frequent topics of discussion during the course of the second administration of the city government, and the subject being of annual occurrence and permanent interest, it has been deemed useful, in addition to the statements already made in this history, that the chief principles and measures, successively adopted in relation to it, should be recapitulated and brought into one view.

In March, 1824, a question arose, concerning the mode of admitting the name of voters to be placed upon the voting lists, the inspectors, in some of the wards, having taken upon themselves to place names on those lists after they had been delivered to them by the Mayor and Aldermen. It was deemed important to put an early stop to practices so irregular and contrary to the charter. And a committee was appointed, consisting of the Mayor, Aldermen Child and Hooper, and Messrs. E. Williams, Wilkinson, Wright, and Davis, to inquire into "the propriety and expediency of adopting some uniform mode of admitting the names of voters to be placed on the voting lists." This Committee reported that the duty of making out the lists of the citizens qualified to vote in each ward, was, by the twenty-fourth section of the city charter, expressly devolved upon the Mayor and Aldermen; that the list they had prepared, it was their duty to deliver to the City Clerk, to be used by the Warden and Inspectors; and the charter was express, that "no person shall be entitled to vote at such election, whose name is not borne on such list;" and that it was the special duty of the inspectors "*to take care that no person should vote whose name is not borne on such list;*" and a resolve was accordingly passed, declaring that the inspectors had no right to admit any person to vote who was not on the list delivered to the City Clerk by the Mayor and Aldermen, and also a resolve, that ten days previous to any election, three copies of the lists made out by the Mayor and Aldermen should be deposited in three public places in each ward, so as to give full opportunity for every citizen, if he saw fit, to ascertain if his name was borne thereon, and have the mistake rectified.

In April of the same year (1824) a person who had not been taxed the preceding year, and whose name was, of consequence, not upon the voting lists, voluntarily procured himself to be assessed, and brought a certificate of the fact to the Mayor and Aldermen, demanding that his name should then be inserted in the voting lists. They refused to insert his name, and passed a vote, declaring that they had no authority so to do, under those circumstances.

In April, 1826, the errors which had occurred in the voting lists, as delivered to the Mayor and Aldermen by the Assessors, had been so numerous, that the Mayor made a special recommendation to the City Council for a more specific provision against such occurrences in future. The Committee raised on this recommendation, reported that, owing to the great press of business and the sickness of one of the Assessors, a greater number of errors had occurred in the voting lists than was usual; that this temporary cause of inaccuracy might, and would be prevented, by increasing the number of assessors; but that there were causes of a permanent nature, for which the remedy lies wholly with the citizens themselves, and consists in their own vigilance. Mistakes in the voting lists, being for the most part detected in the heat, and under the excitement of an election, give rise to suspicions of intentional omissions utterly unfounded. The citizens should remember that, from the complexity and intrinsic difficulties, perfect accuracy is unattainable. Citizens who change their residence from one ward to another, and who have recently come of age, are peculiarly subjects of such errors. Even fixed inhabitants may sometimes be omitted, either in copying or printing the voting lists, including eight or ten thousand voters. It is true, such errors seldom occur; but the safe principle for every citizen to adopt is, that there is no absolute certainty that his name is on the lists, except it be ascertained by previous personal inspection. The Assessors' lists, which they are obliged by law annually to make out and deliver to the Mayor and Aldermen, are, substantially, the evidence of the right of the citizen to vote at any election. Their correctness depends upon their coincidence with the books of the Assessors. Of this coincidence, the Assessors are the legal certifying officers. The revision and correction of those lists by the Mayor and Aldermen must depend upon the evidence adduced by the individual citizens whose names have been omitted. Without such evidence, the Mayor and Aldermen have no authority to correct them. Between the lists and books of the Assessors, there is no reason to anticipate important variance; nor yet between the written and printed lists of the Assessors. In both respects, comparison is the duty of the Assessors, who are responsible for their accuracy.

The chief sources of error are in the books of the Assessors, and are attributable to various circumstances incident to the subject, and not wholly to be prevented by any vigilance. Of these the following are the most common: —

1. In the manner in which the inquiries, on which the books of the Assessors are founded, are unavoidably made in families, where, when the head is absent, the information given by domestics is often incorrect, the Christian name mistaken, or surnames misspelt, particularly in the case of temporary residents in boarding-houses, or boarders or domestics.

2. Changes of residence after the Assessors have finished their perambulation.

3. Persons moving into the city, or, who coming of age, after such perambulation is finished. Such persons, if their names are not on the lists, have none to blame but themselves.

4. A very common source of error is the withholding at boarding-houses, through ignorance or wilfulness, the Christian names of the boarders; so that only their surnames are inserted

in the books of the Assessors; and although, when the tax is collected, the Collectors ascertain the Christian names, it is often too late for entry on the voting lists.

The remedy proposed for correcting these errors, and which received the sanction of both branches of the City Council were, — 1st. The increase of the number of the Assessors. 2d. A systematic preparation and printing of the voting lists, as early as the first of March, so that the intermediate time before election should be employed in their revision and correction. 3d. A more general and impressive sense, on the part of the citizens, of the duty of inspecting each for himself the voting lists previous to elections, particularly previous to that in April, when the lists being new, inaccuracies are more likely to occur.

In December, 1826, the duty of superintending the voting lists was devolved by the City Council on the Mayor, with the aid of the Assessors, subject to the revision of the Board of Aldermen; to whom, on the nineteenth of March, 1827, he reported the revised lists, and recommended that public notice should be given to the following persons, concerning whom errors in the lists were most likely to occur; — those doing business in other wards than those in which they live; those taxed without their Christian names; those taxed within two years, who had become inhabitants since the first of May; those who have come of age, or changed their place of residence since the same period. Notice was at this time given, that all who had not paid taxes within two years would have their names stricken from the voting lists.

In April, 1828, complaints were made by the Warden and Inspectors of one of the wards, of the imperfection in the voting lists, and suggesting the expediency of investing the Warden and Inspectors with power to insert names in those lists. The City Council, desirous that the nature and causes of the obstacles to obtaining correct voting lists should be well understood, postponed any report until the new lists, taken under the knowledge of the previously existing complaints, should be tested by some strongly controverted election. This occurred on that of mayor on the eighth and fifteenth of December of this year; and the Mayor, on the twenty-second of the same month, as Chairman of a Committee of the City Council, made a report, which was accepted in the Board of Aldermen, and printed by the Common Council, but ultimately referred in that branch to the next City Council. In this report, the Committee stated, that " at no previous election had the satisfaction with the voting lists been more general; that few errors had occurred, although the names on the lists amounted to *twelve thousand.* The Committee then proceeded to state " minutely the errors for which the officers making out the voting lists were responsible: — 1st. Such as *neglecting to place the name of an inhabitant on the tax books*, so that it does not appear on the voting lists. These errors, when they occur, are often the effect of accident, the inhabitant not being at home, or his house shut up, or wrong name given, when the Assessors called. These accidents most frequently occur to boarders, or men not heads of families, concerning whom wrong names are often given at the boarding-houses; for these errors the Assessors are without blame. 2d. *Neglect to transfer members of firms from the ward where they do business to the wards where they reside.* This, when it occurs, often results from misinformation. 3d. *Erasing the name by accident* from the tax-books, so that it is not inserted in the voting lists. This is so rare as scarcely to deserve notice. 4th. *Errors in printing the voting lists.* These are more likely to happen in printing the voting lists than in printing any other work, from mistakes in chirography, as it respects names, and there being no connection of sense, whereby the intention of the writer can be ascertained. The above are generally all the errors for which the Assessors are responsible.

Those errors, for which the Assessors are not, and cannot be responsible, are the most numerous. Such are, — 1. Ignorance of the voter himself of the ward in which he resides. 2. Removal after the first of May, without taking care to have his name inserted on the lists of the ward to which he has removed. 3. Absences in May from the city, of consequence not taxed, and thus the name not entered on the lists. 4. Having one's name transferred to a wrong ward, or by a wrong name, by officious friends. 5. Not having paid a tax, neither for the preceding nor for the current year, the name of such person having no right to be borne on the voting list. 6. Impracticability to obtain the Christian name of the person taxed, and the name, in such case, being not usually inserted in the voting lists. 7. Aliens taxed, but not naturalized, and so not entitled to vote. 8. Aliens naturalized, and their naturalization not made known to the Assessors. 9. Persons coming of age subsequently to the first of May, or to the perambulation of the Assessors. 10. Persons living in boarding-houses, or young persons not heads of families, whose names are not given to the Assessors by the families in which they reside. 11. Names of tenants or taxable inmates, whose names are given wrongly by domestics.

From experience, it appears that *four out of five* of the errors which occur, are of the nature of those last enumerated, for which the Assessors are not responsible, and for which there is no practicable remedy, except *by personal inspection of the voting lists previous to the day of election.*

In order to throw light on a subject of some complexity, and to guard voters against mistakes, they were reminded "*that new voting lists are made out every year from the tax books of the Assessors ; that these tax books have reference to the state of residence on the first of May ; and that a voter, not found in any ward in May by the Assessors, will not be taxed, and will not be upon the voting list of that year.*"

An ignorance of this fact is one of the principal causes of discontent. Men shun taxes and seek the polls ; but he who has received no tax bill has no right to expect that his name is on the voting lists. Old inhabitants are apt to imagine that, because their names are on the list of the preceding year, they must be on the new lists ; but it should be remembered *that the only foundation of the voting lists in any year is the tax books of that year.* The unavoidable difference between the lists of any former and any present year, from changes of residence, death, coming of age, and the like general causes, probably amounts every year to *a difference of more than one half of all the names on the voting lists.*

No facts can more impressively urge upon every voter *the duty of ascertaining for himself, whether his name is inserted on the voting lists.* As to the suggestion of the expediency of investing the Warden and Inspectors with power to insert names on the voting lists, the Committee stated that it was not consistent with the laws of the Commonwealth ; that if attempted, it would be calculated to introduce errors into the voting lists, confusion at the polls, and charges of favoritism and corruption against the Inspectors. These officers have now but *one single and simple duty;* that is, TO THE ADMITTING ALL TO VOTE WHOSE NAMES ARE BORNE ON THE LISTS AND TO THE EXCLUDING OF ALL OTHERS.

Should the Warden and Inspectors be allowed the right to insert names on the voting lists, every inducement, and even necessity, of making the lists accurate, previously to election day, would be taken away. It had been urged, that inspectors might be authorized to insert names of those who produced their tax bills; but nothing would prevent the same tax bill from being presented in more than one ward at the same election; the right to vote being often in a ward different from that specified in the tax bill. The questions arising, relative to this right, are often very complex, depending on various circumstances; when made before the Mayor and Aldermen, with great clamor and sense of right, they are often ascertained to be of a dubious character, and sometimes wholly unfounded. If made in the heat of an election, and in the midst of impassioned electors, it would give rise to much excitement and charges of favoritism. The possession of such a power by the Wardens and Inspectors would also cause the selection of these officers to be made with reference to party spirit, rather than to general character. In some wards the Inspectors are changed every year; and the mistakes made by them, amidst the occasional confusion of the election, notwithstanding the exceeding singleness and simplicity of their present duties, sufficiently indicate that no greater power ought to be intrusted to them.

Thus, names have been checked off by mistake; men, unconsciously by the Assessors, have been admitted to vote by an assumed name; and often voters have been turned from the polls, and denied the right to vote, whose names were actually borne on the voting lists, being overlooked by the Inspectors in the haste and hurry of a contested election. From this cause alone, *there were, at one election, more cases of rejection, than from all the other causes taken together;* there having occurred more than THIRTY instances of rejection, from this cause alone, of persons whose names were borne on the lists. Notwithstanding the general good intentions and fidelity of the Warden and Inspectors, the above errors to which they are now exposed are sufficient to show that their duties should not be augmented.

So long as no person's name can be placed on the voting

list, except by the Mayor and Aldermen, no one can lose his vote, unless he has been so indifferent as to neglect the inspection of the voting lists once in each year. It is surely better, that the citizen who will not take so small a trouble for so great a privilege, should lose his vote, than that a system should be adopted, which, by establishing *twelve distinct tribunals*, should introduce controversies and party spirit, leading to confusion and to all the difficulties above stated at the polls. The Committee concluded, by stating the course adopted, previous to the last election, had produced such an approximation to correctness, that, during it, *not more than four errors in the lists had occurred* which it was possible for the Assessors to have corrected. Considering the great interest and importance of the subject, the above abstract of this report, being the result of several years experience and careful observation of facts by the Mayor, has been deemed important enough to be here distinctly preserved; and the more so, because early under the succeeding city administration, a similar attempt was made to enlarge the power of the Inspectors, and Mr. Otis, as Mayor and Chairman of a Committee on this subject, in a report made to the City Council, expressly referred to the report, of which the above is an abstract, as an "elaborate exposition of facts and principles on the subject."[1]

On the fourteenth of April, 1828, Charles P. Curtis, the City Solicitor, stated to the Board of Aldermen that an application had been made to him to defend a watchman for an alleged assault and battery, who, justified under color of his office. The Solicitor requested that he might receive instructions in this and similar cases; and that a general rule might be established also in regard to advancing fees and expenses of witnesses. The communication was referred to Aldermen James Savage and John Pickering, to consider and report, who accordingly reported that it was expedient to instruct the Solicitor to defend the watchmen at the expense of the city, and to make all necessary advances during the progress of the action. With respect to other similar cases, it was difficult to lay down any invariable rule for the government of the Solicitor, in respect of actions brought against any officer of the city. From the great number

[1] See p. 290.

of those officers, of various degrees of intelligence and discretion, of various dispositions and temperaments, and selected from different classes of citizens, it is obvious that occasions for groundless suits will be as likely to occur among them as among individuals of a similar character, who are not city officers; and if a spirit of litigation should be encouraged, as it would be by indemnifying the officers in all cases, the consequence would be extremely injurious to the peace and welfare of the city. But, on the other hand, it is the duty of the city to protect faithful officers in the proper execution of their duty, and to indemnify them when they are compelled to defend themselves in the discharge of their official duties. The Committee, therefore, reported the following order for the government of the City Solicitor, namely, — "That in all the actions and suits described in the ordinance passed on the eighteenth of June, 1827, against any officer of the city, such officer shall, in the first instance, prosecute and defend, at his own expense, and, if it shall be found, either by verdict or otherwise, in the opinion of the Solicitor, that such officer did so prosecute or defend for good cause, and that he ought to be indemnified for his expenses in such suit, then the City Solicitor shall certify accordingly, and such officer shall be so indemnified; otherwise, such expenses shall be borne by the officer himself.

This report was read and accepted accordingly.

In May, 1828, a few weeks before the general election day of the State, which, at that period, occurred annually on the last Wednesday of this month, a petition signed by Isaac Parker, Chief Justice of the Commonwealth, and about fourteen hundred citizens, was presented to the City Council, praying that the selling of spirituous liquors on the Common, on public holidays, should be prevented. An order accordingly was issued, directing the Constables to prosecute any person, who, in the Common, or in the malls and streets in its vicinity, should sell any spirituous or mixed liquors, of which part was spirituous, or who should in any of those places play cards, dice, or with any implements of gaming, on the days of general election, artillery election, and the fourth of July. Notice of this order was published immediately in the city newspapers, and the Constables directed to make it known to all who should have permission to erect booth, tent, or table on those days.

The expediency of selling by auction or otherwise the right which the Faneuil Hall Market Committee had secured for the city to the eastward of that Hall, was, in the autumn of this year (1828) brought before the City Council. This right embraced an extent of flats equal to *three hundred and fifteen* feet in length, and on the west line *one hundred and ninety-eight* feet, and on the east *one hundred and sixty-eight* feet, and included *fifty-seven thousand six hundred and forty-five feet square of wharf*, besides the right of dockage on three sides of the said proposed wharf. The subject was referred to a Committee of the City Council, consisting of the Mayor, Aldermen Loring and Upham, and Messrs. Moody, E. Williams, Means, Pickman, and Pratt, of the Common Council, who, on the sixth of October, reported at large, stating the importance of this space to the city as a possession, its prospective, increasing value, and that its local relations were such, that there seemed to be no possible state of things in which it could be wise for the city to abandon the control of it, which it now possesses by its right of property. Lying at the head or junction of five of the most thronged and busy streets of the city, now called Commercial, Clinton, North and South Market, and Chatham Streets, the efficient and permanent control of that space was deemed peculiarly important to be retained in the city government, from its very location, with reference to the general business of that part of the city; but when, in addition to this, the fact is considered that it contains the whole space lying between the New City Market and the Channel, and that this is the only space within which the market itself can be extended, or the accommodations of those doing business in it enlarged, should the increasing greatness of the city render it necessary, it seemed to the Committee, that on this account alone, the city could not, in any state of things, be justified in divesting itself of the fee it had acquired in this property. The idea of selling these wharf rights could not, therefore, be entertained. The expediency of leasing them to others, rather than to undertake filling them up on the account of the city, having been urged upon the Committee, they declared that, in their opinion, the relation of this property was such, that its value and importance, either as a property or a possession, could not be well understood previously to its being filled up and actually occupied; and the control of it, in their judgment, ought not, even temporarily, to be put out of the power of the city, until its value and importance should be tested by actual experience. They, therefore, recommended that measures should be adopted without delay by the city, for filling up the space on its own account, before entering upon any consideration of the subject of leasing it; and they entered into statements and reasonings, showing that the cost of filling up the proposed space of wharf in the most substantial manner, could not exceed *twenty thousand dollars*, and that when filled up, the annual receipt would probably be at least *eight thousand dollars*, and could not be less than *six thousand.* The Committee therefore recommended two resolutions, — the first authorizing the filling up the wharf rights, with authority to borrow, not exceeding twenty thousand dollars, for that purpose; and the second, directing that the income hereafter derived from these wharf rights should be placed in the hands of the Committee for the reduction of the city debt, until the said income should equal the amount of debt created under the first resolution. This report was accepted, and the resolutions passed unanimously in both branches of the City Council; and the Committee who reported the resolutions were authorized to carry them into effect.

There were at this time active influences without doors at work to induce the City Council to make sale of these wharf and dockage rights. Capitalists see early and clearly the value of choice locations for business and investment. And, in relation to city property, if the City Council can be prevailed upon by temptations of a higher price than, at the time the average rate of land in the vicinity commands, by the desire to diminish the amount of taxation for the passing year, or to reduce the city debt, the more important consideration of the permanent value of precious localities to the general interests of the city is apt to be disregarded, when weighed in the scale against temporary advantage or popularity. In this case, the sale of these flats was pressed upon the Mayor and other members of the Committee with urgency. The idea of ever obtaining an income from them of *eight thousand dollars* was ridiculed. The popularity to be obtained by an immediate large reduction of the debt incurred by erecting the New Market was set forth in strong lights. The actual result will be the best comment on the wisdom and firmness of the City Council. The flats were filled up at an expense of less than *nineteen thousand dollars;* and in September, 1832, the then City Council leased the wharf and dock rights for twenty years on an annual rent of *ten thousand dollars*, on condition that *ten* substantial brick stores, to the acceptance of the City Council, should be built thereon, and kept insured and in good order, and should revert to the city in fee simple at the end of the lease. In September, 1852, this wharf, dock rights, and stores will consequently revert to the city, and thus a property, which, in 1826, the City Council did not venture to estimate higher than *one hundred thousand dollars*, has, by the wisdom and foresight of successive City Councils, risen, at this day, to the value of at least *four hundred thousand dollars*.[1]

[1] See page 203.

CHAPTER XVII.

CITY GOVERNMENT. 1828.

JOSIAH QUINCY, *Mayor.*

The Annexation of South Boston to the Ancient City, and the Difficulties attending it — Project of Semi-Annual Sales of Domestic Manufactures in the City — The Hall over the New Market appropriated for the Object — Question concerning the Eligibility of Members of the City Council to City Offices — State and Progress of the Fire Department — Resignation of the Chief Engineer — His Gratuitous Services — Vote of Thanks to him by the City Council — Prosperous State of City Affairs — The Mayor declines being a Candidate for Reëlection — Harrison Gray Otis chosen Mayor.

AT the commencement of the present century, the tract of land, now called South Boston, was a part of the town of Dorchester, and inhabited by a few families, chiefly engaged in agriculture. At that period, it was purchased by a number of enterprising citizens, most of whom were capitalists, who obtained from the inhabitants of Boston a vote authorizing an application to the Legislature of the State for its annexation to that town. As the original project contemplated the erection of a bridge from South Street, or Sea Street, to South Boston, a violent opposition to the plan arose among the proprietors of wharves lying above the proposed site. After warm discussions in the public newspapers and town meetings, the proposition resulted in a compromise, fixing the locality of the bridge above most of the wharves, whose proprietors were thus relieved from the apprehended obstruction of the channel; but, at the same time, the expectations of immediate profit formed by the original associates in the project were materially diminished. To carry into effect the compromise, three acts were passed by the Legislature of the State on the same day (sixth of March, 1804.) By the first, the part of Dorchester now called South Boston was annexed to Boston. By the second, the proprietors of the purchased lands were constituted a corporation, with authority to erect a bridge from the southwesterly part of Boston to Dorchester Neck. By the third, the proprietors of certain lands at the south part of Boston were authorized to open a street from Rainsford Lane to the proposed site of the new bridge.

The several powers granted by these acts were executed, in conformity with the compromise. The population of South Boston gradually increased until the year 1822, when the project of building a bridge from South or Sea Street revived, and constituted one of the most important and exciting topics of discussion during the two first administrations of the city government. All the bitter animosities and apprehensions were renewed, which the compromise of 1804 had allayed. No efficient support was, however, obtained for the measure until March, 1824. A petition from the inhabitants of South Boston was then presented to a general meeting of the inhabitants of the city, and a vote was passed, after several days debate, by a great majority — 2,487 in the affirmative, 779 in the negative — requesting the City Government to petition the Legislature for liberty to erect the proposed bridge. The City Council prepared and presented a petition, in conformity with the vote of the citizens; but the conflicting passions and interests the subject excited succeeded in postponing any conclusive measure until the twenty-fifth of February, 1825. A bill then passed the Legislature, authorizing the city to build a bridge, to be free of toll from or near Sea or South Street to South Boston. This act was referred in the City Council to the Mayor, Aldermen Baxter, Odiorne, and Child, and to S. K. Williams, Russell, Ballard, Lodge, and Lincoln of the Common Council. They reported, that the City ought not to erect the bridge, but recommended that a committee should be appointed to advertise for proposals to build it, indemnify the City from all expenses, and compensation for damages, and to comply with all the requisitions of the act of the Legislature. The Committee who made this report were authorized by the City Council to issue such proposals. On the sixteenth of May, they stated to that body, that they had issued and advertised for proposals, but no application of any kind had been received in reference to the object; and, therefore, recommended to the City Council to take no farther measures on the subject. This report was accepted in both branches.

Other attempts to harmonize these conflicting interests, such as appointing commissioners, and endeavoring to purchase South Boston Bridge by means of subscriptions, were wholly unsuccessful. The friends of the original project, therefore, applied to the Legislature, and, by an act passed in March, 1826, obtained a repeal of the act of February, 1825, and an authority for the petitioners, with others, to build the proposed bridge, provided it should be done in such manner as the city of Boston should approve; — the corporation, thus constituted, to be subject to all damages resulting from its erection, light it, keep it in repair, and provide facilities for raising the draw, until the city of Boston should assume the care of it, when the corporation was to be relieved from all these obligations. The act contained also a provision granting to the city of Boston the right to build the bridge, if they availed themselves of the privilege within three months. As the corporation could not proceed until the decision of the city was known, they immediately submitted the act to the City Council, and asked a conference on the subject. This application was referred to the Mayor, Aldermen Bellows, Marshall, and Loring, who, after deliberation and conference with the applicants, reported, that it was inexpedient for the City Council to take any order in relation to the right and liberty to build the bridge conferred on the city by the act.

The subject remained in this state until January, 1827, when the corporation communicated to the city government their intention to build the bridge; and, after stating the material of which they proposed to construct it, submitted the mode and the manner of constructing it to the decision of the City Council, and inquired whether the city would assume the care of the bridge and the obligation to keep it in repair, light it, and provide facilities for raising the draw, after it should be constructed.

This application was referred to the Mayor, Aldermen Bellows, Welsh, and Boies, and to Messrs. James, Morey, Russell, Phillips, Hallett, Howe, and Dyer, of the Common Council. In this committee were discussed all the questions growing out of the inquiries of the corporation; also, whether it should proceed from South Street or Sea Street, and how the expense attending the enlargement of it, which was contemplated, should be disbursed; and whether it should be accepted by the city even after it should be built in the manner prescribed by the City Council. All these questions were debated with great zeal by the respective parties. Several meetings were held, — times and places were appointed, at which all persons interested might appear before the Committee; and upon most of them the Committee were nearly equally divided. A sub-committee had made a report at large, and concluded in favor of the bridge's proceeding from South Street, by a majority of *three* out of *five*. This report the Committee rejected, and substituted Sea Street for South Street, by a majority of *seven* out of *twelve*. And on the twenty-second of February they reported, by a like majority, that the bridge should be built from Sea Street; and that, if made and finished in such manner as the City Council should direct, it would be expedient to accept the bridge, light, keep it in repair, and provide facilities for the draw, so long as South Boston should remain a part of the city of Boston. This report was accepted in both branches of the City Council, and a series of resolutions passed, in conformity with the recommendation of the Committee, specifying the mode in which the bridge should be built, and the terms on which it would be accepted, and a committee of the City Council and a competent engineer to superintend building the bridge, and to see that the terms were complied with, were appointed.

Notwithstanding these precautions, when, in June, 1828, the bridge was offered to the City Council for their acceptance, opposition to the measure revived, and remonstrances against its acceptance were presented. The City Council, however, early in July, discharged the Superintendent, and the Common Council voted to accept the bridge. In this, however, the Mayor and Aldermen did not concur, and appointed a committee, who made a report, accepted by the Board of Aldermen, and non-concurred in the Common Council. The disagreement between the two branches was finally brought to a close by the appointment of a joint-committee, consisting of the Mayor, Aldermen Loring, Fennelly, Pickering, Upham and Armstrong, and of Messrs. Betton, Seaver, Paine, Howe and Pickman of the Common Council, with full powers, to accept the free bridge, and to submit all differences to the arbitration of three persons mutually to be chosen, with powers also in the Committee to carry their award into effect, and report the result to the City Council.

Loammi Baldwin, Samuel Hubbard, and Willard Phillips were appointed referees, in conformity with this authority; and on the seventh of October, 1828, the Committee reported to the City Council the award of these referees, which was, in effect, that "the public convenience required that the city should forthwith accept the said bridge, and, in consequence of its unfinished state, that the corporation should pay to the city sixteen hundred and seven dollars, and deliver to it certain enumerated deeds." The Committee recommended, that a vote should be passed by both branches of the City Council, authorizing a fulfilment of the conditions of the award. A vote was passed in conformity with this recommendation; and this long, perplexing, and exciting controversy was thus brought to a final conclusion.

The apparent intimate connection between the prosperity of the city and of that of the manufacturing interests of the State and vicinity, led to the expression of a general desire, that an attempt should be made to foster those interests, by an exhibition and sale of domestic manufactures annually within the city. The Mayor, coinciding with these views, in October, 1825, recommended, by special message, the subject to the attention of the City Council, and suggested the adaptation of the hall over the New Market to this project, and the policy of appropriating it in whole or in part to carry it into effect. This communication was referred to the Mayor, Aldermen Bellows, Marshall, and Bryant, and to Messrs. Williams, Hallett, Parker, Barry, and Boies, of the Common Council.

In consequence of this movement, various plans and propositions were made and discussed between the Committee or its members, and persons interested in manufactures; and in January, 1826, on the petition of Patrick T. Jackson, in behalf of an association, for the public exhibition or sale of domestic manufactures, the Committee reported that the petitioners should have, for the purposes of such exhibition and sale, the use of so much of the upper story of the New Market House as they might require for the present year, not exceeding twenty days in the spring and twenty days in the autumn. Their report was accepted in both branches.

And in the ensuing July, on the petition of the Society for the promotion of Manufactures and the Mechanic Arts, the entire hall over the New Market, or as much as might be necessary or convenient for them, was devoted to their use, during the months of September and October, for the purposes of exhibition and sales of domestic goods and mechanic inventions, free of all charges; and, on the twelfth of September, the first auction sale under this grant was holden. In January and July, 1827, the New England Society for the promotion of Manufactures and Mechanic Arts petitioned for the same privilege, and the City Council granted the use of the hall for the exhibition and sale of domestic manufactures and wool, for twenty days in March and twenty days in August.

The success of these exhibitions and sales led to a petition, in the ensuing November, having for its object to place the accommodation they had received from the use of the hall on a more permanent footing, which, being referred to the Mayor, Aldermen Loring and Savage, and Messrs. Dorr, Russell, Parker, and Ward, a report was made by them, stating that the sole object of this Society was to effect, through the means of semi-annual auction sales of domestic manufactures a change in the course of business, by bringing foreign purchasers to the domestic market, and thus relieving our manufacturers from the necessity of seeking a market in other States and countries; that the Society had few funds, and derived no emolument whatever from its labors; that the effect of such semi-annual sales could not but be highly advantageous to the progressive prosperity of the city, and the advantage, in the opinion of the Committee, was a sufficient justification and inducement to the City Council for such an appropriation of the hall over the Market as the petitioners solicit. Thus far, the experiment of these auction sales had been as successful as could reasonably have been expected; the gross proceeds of all the three semi-annual sales had amounted to upwards of $956,000. The tendency of them to bring foreign purchasers, at the season of these sales, to this metropolis, and the effect on its prosperity, direct and incidental, were so obvious and unquestionable, that the Committee could not hesitate to recommend such an acquiescence in the prayer of the petition as will place the subject, at all times, under the control of the City Council, and yet give the petitioners the assurance of the permanent patronage of the institution by the City Government, until a future City Council should take a different view of the interests of the city. The Committee recommended that the New England Society for the promotion of Manufactures and Mechanic Arts should have the hall for the purpose of their annual sales from the fifteenth of March to the fifteenth of April, and from the fifteenth of August until the fifteenth of September, until the further order of the City Council, and that six months notice should be given to the Society of the rescinding of this privilege.

This report was accepted in both branches of the City Council.

These semi-annual sales not only produced those advantages to the city, which had been anticipated, but proved highly beneficial to the manufacturing interests; all the various classes of which were well represented in them. They were numerously attended by traders from all parts of the United States. Some of the best purchasers from the South and West were attracted by them to the city, some of whom became subsequently regular customers. The prices obtained were generally quite satisfactory to the owners of the goods, and advantageous to all parties. Between September, 1826, and March, 1832, there were twelve of such sales. The total amount of the proceeds cannot be at this day (1851) exactly ascertained; but they cannot be estimated at less than from five to six millions of dollars; since two only of the auctioneers[1] employed in those sales, disposed of more than $4,645,000 in value. Notwithstanding this success, these semi-annual sales were discontinued in 1832; for reasons never, it is believed, officially stated, but generally attributed to the influence of certain large commission merchants and jobbers, who imagined that these sales interfered with their particular interests. This discontinuance was, however, in direct opposition to the opinion of many of our most intelligent merchants and manufacturers, who regarded these sales as among the most effective means of advancing and prospectively giving a great impulse to the prosperity of the city, as well as promoting the manufacturing interests of the State. In these views the late Patrick T. Jackson zealously concurred; and no citizen, at that period, watched over the interest of both with a more practical, philosophic, and patriotic spirit.

In June, 1827, a question was raised in the Common Council, whether a member of the City Council could be legally appointed by them a surveyor of boards and lumber. The subject was referred to the Mayor and Alderman Savage, and to

[1] Whitwell, Bond & Co.; Coolidge, Poor & Head.

Messrs. Gray, James, and Morey, of the Common Council, who reported, —

That there are two clauses of the city charter, which restrict the eligibility to office of members of the City Council; the one contained in the *twenty-first*, and the other in the *twenty-second* section of that instrument. The former is in these words: "Provided, however, that no person shall be eligible to any office, the salary of which is payable out of the city treasury, who, at the time of his appointment, shall be a member either of the Board of Aldermen or Common Council." As the salary, or compensation of a surveyor of boards and lumber, is not payable out of the city treasury, the eligibility to this office of a member of either branch of the City Council is not affected by the proviso. The remaining clause is in these words: — "And neither the Mayor, nor any Alderman, or member of the Common Council, shall, at the same time, hold any office under the City Government." The Committee were of opinion, that the office of surveyor of boards and lumber, not being created by the City Government, nor the officer responsible to it, is not such an office as a member of the City Council is prohibited from holding under the above recited clause of the twenty-second article of the City Charter.

The Report was accepted by both branches of the City Council.

During the years 1827 and 1828, the spirit in which the Fire Department had been in the preceding year instituted was sustained and invigorated. Mr. Harris had been in each year successively reëlected to the office of chief engineer, unanimously, in both branches of the City Council. The discipline of the department had been maintained by him and the other officers and members. In 1826, one company of enginemen had been dismissed for insubordination; and in 1827, another discharged for remissness in their duty as enginemen. In both instances, new companies were readily formed. Engine-houses were enlarged; the accommodation of the engine companies increased. The great deficiencies of the old engines, in respect of active service, were supplied. These improvements, and the almost entire change of apparatus, in order to adapt it to effective operations under the new system, led unavoidably, as has already been stated, to great expenditures, wholly without precedent in the previous system of protection against fire.[1] In a report, made by a committee of the City Council, the nature and causes of these expenditures were detailed and explained. Under other circumstances, the amount would have probably given rise to severe popular animadversions; but the efficiency of the new system, and the general satisfaction with its success, silenced complaint. The requisite appropriations were always passed, in both branches of the City Council, without difficulty, and almost without cavil. At this period, the number of active members of the department, officers of all ranks included, amounted to twelve hundred strong, chiefly young men, under the command of one chief, and twelve assistant engineers; all selected, with great care, from men of suitable age and characteristic activity.

The whole Fire Department being in this state of high discipline and preparation, on the eighth of October, 1828, the Chief Engineer addressed a letter to the Mayor resigning his office, on account of the inadequacy of his health to its duties; and, after expressing "his obligations to the officers and members of it, for their prompt and willing coöperation in bringing the new system into efficiency," added, "that the department was adequate to all the purposes of its establishment, and possessed a body of men, whose alacrity, zeal, and devotedness could not be surpassed." The Mayor postponed communicating this resignation to the City Council, and made various endeavors to induce Mr. Harris to withdraw it, all of which proved fruitless. On the eighth of December, therefore, having communicated the resignation of the Chief Engineer to the Board of Aldermen, and it having been accepted by them, the Mayor transmitted to the City Council a message stating that "it was now nearly three years since Colonel Harris had been appointed to that office, and that during this period an entire renovation had been effected in that department, the number of its members greatly increased, and a spirit of harmony, subordination, and efficiency introduced into it highly honorable to those who compose it, as well as to the city, and, it was believed, universally satisfactory to our fellow-citizens.

"In all the arrangements connected with these improvements, the zeal, intelligence, and firmness of Samuel Devens Harris, in

1 See page 205.

the office of Chief Engineer, had been conspicuous, and eminently contributed to their adoption and success. At the time of his appointment, the expectation was generally entertained, that a salary would be annexed to that office, and the principle on which the new organization of that department was advocated and adopted, in both branches of the City Council, amounted to an assurance that an adequate compensation would be fixed for his services. He had, however, held the office but a short time,[1] before he particularly requested the Mayor not to bring the subject of his compensation before the City Council, assigning as a reason, that, having the command of a department consisting wholly of volunteers, he was of opinion that his influence and usefulness would be disadvantageously affected by his acceptance of a salary. The conduct of this officer, in every thing relative to the discipline, orderly arrangement, and efficiency of the department, had been so exemplary and disinterested, that the Mayor deemed it his duty to recommend the subject to the consideration of the City Council, that such an expression of their sense of his services may be made, as they should deem just and suitable."

This message was referred to a joint committee, consisting of Aldermen Loring and Hall, and Messrs. Oliver, Everett, Means, and Aspinwall, of the Common Council. On the twenty-second of December, this Committee reported the following order for the adoption of the City Council:—

"Whereas, the City Council hold in high estimation the services rendered this city by Samuel Devens Harris, late Chief Engineer of the Fire Department, and are convinced that the general spirit of harmony, of subordination, and efficiency, which characterize that department, and render it highly honorable to those who compose it, and useful to the city, is to be attributed, in a great degree, to the intelligence, the zeal, and active exertions of its late chief,—

It is therefore Ordered, That the thanks of the City Council be, and they hereby are, presented to Samuel Devens Harris, for the faithful, arduous, and highly useful services, gratuitously rendered by him for nearly three years, in the office of Chief Engineer of the Fire Department."

This Report, being read and accepted, the Order was passed, by a unanimous vote, in both branches of the City Council.

The seventh year of the city government (1828) had passed

[1] See page 209.

with great apparent unanimity and general satisfaction. The measures, which had been devised and commenced by the several succeeding City Councils, during the preceding years, were either completed or in successful progress. The New Market had been finished, and all the accounts connected with that improvement were settled; provision for the gradual payment, by instalments, of the debt it had created, had been made; and also for the final discharge of that debt and its accruing interest out of the proceeds of the real estate, consisting of land and wharf rights, and other funds, which the wisdom of those City Councils had acquired. During these years, besides the expenditures connected with the purchases and improvements about the New Market, many streets, which were great thoroughfares in various parts of the city, had been widened. The Fire Department had been put into efficient operation, to the apparent satisfaction of all. A House of Correction, and a House of Reformation of Juvenile Offenders had been established; the House of Industry had been completed and the poor transferred to it, to the acknowledged improvement of their condition, and the manifest benefit of the city. The title to the lands lying west of Charles Street, called the Ropewalk Lands, had also been obtained and secured. Deer Island had been effectually protected by a sea-wall from the action of the elements; appropriations for that object having been solicited by the city and granted by Congress. George's and Lovell's Islands had been purchased, and the title to them transferred by the city to the United States; for whom also the jurisdiction of those islands had been obtained from the Commonwealth. These prospective measures led, in subsequent years, to the erection of those efficient fortifications which now command and protect the outer harbor of Boston.

And in relation to the incomes and expenditures of the City for the preceding financial year, William Hayden, the City Auditor, in his official report, dated the fifteenth of May, 1828, stated that "the aggregate amount of the incomes of the city had exceeded the aggregate amount of its expenditures; and that the results afforded a practical illustration of the wisdom and spirit of economy, which characterized the proceedings of the last City Council, and led to the adoption of a system of self-restriction in regard to appropriations, and of confining the ordinary expenditures of the year within the limits of its ordinary annual income." And the City Auditor closed this report by the following remarks: — "It is believed, that the results of the financial operations of the last year, while they must be highly satisfactory to those, in whose hands the citizens have placed the control of their public funds, will have a tendency to sustain that confidence, which the people of this city have reposed in its government; for they show conclusively, that while those great improvements which the public interest seemed most obviously to demand, have been originated and matured, the city government had not lost sight of that point, at which a system of economical restriction should commence."

In this state of general prosperity and satisfaction with the affairs of the city, the municipal year drew towards its close. No other than those general objects of attention, which are incident to every condition of municipal relation, appeared, at the moment, to be subjects of general anticipation or desire. No special cause of public discontent had occurred within the year. To apply wisely and faithfully the resources of the city to those exigencies which time must produce, and a rapidly increasing population rendered unavoidable, embraced apparently the whole sphere of duty for the ensuing City Councils.

The office of Mayor had now been sustained almost six years, by the same individual. The novelty of the office, the diversity of opinions relative to its powers, extensive public improvements, and many new institutions, had rendered his administration one of peculiar trial and difficulty. It had been, however, powerfully supported, and to general satisfaction, as the results of six successive elections evidenced.

At the usual period of municipal election, in 1828, after two trials, on the eighth[1] and fifteenth[2] of December, it appeared that the Mayor had not received the majority of votes, which the law required for his reëlection, although in both the number

[1] The whole number of votes cast on this trial was . . 4,082
Requisite to a choice, . . . 2,042
Of which Josiah Quincy had 1,959

[2] The whole number of votes cast on this trial was . 5,253
Requisite to a choice, . . . 2,627
Of which Josiah Quincy had . . . 2,561

closely approximated to it. As soon, therefore, as the last result was known, he sent to the press the following note: —

TO THE CITIZENS OF BOSTON.

After the result of the recent elections, I deem myself at liberty to decline, — as I now do, — being any longer a candidate for the office of Mayor.

To the end, that no future candidate may be deprived of votes, cast in my favor, I deem it proper to state, that no consideration will induce me again to accept that office.

Very respectfully,

I am your fellow citizen,

JOSIAH QUINCY.

BOSTON, 16th December, 1828.

On the ensuing twenty-second of December, Harrison Gray Otis was chosen Mayor without opposition.

CHAPTER XVIII.

CITY GOVERNMENT. 1828.

JOSIAH QUINCY, *Mayor*.

Address of the Mayor on taking final Leave of the Office — His Acknowledgments to the Members of the Board of Aldermen, Common Council, and his Fellow-Citizens — Measures and Results of the Past Administration: for Protection of the City against Fire; and of the Islands against Storms; for the Health of the Inhabitants; for Public Education; in Favor of Public Morals; for increasing the Financial Resources of the City and reducing its Debt — Principles on which his Conduct in Office had been guided. Tribute to his Successor.

THE circumstances which caused the Mayor to decline being again a candidate, led him to consider it due to his associates and himself to state publicly the views and principles which, during nearly six years, had guided the administration of the city government.

Having given intimation of this intention to the Board of Aldermen, they passed an order to the City Clerk "to give notice to the President of the Common Council, that the Board of Aldermen stood adjourned to Saturday, the third of January, 1829, at one o'clock, at which time and place it is expected that the Mayor will address the Board, previous to his leaving the Chair, in order that any gentlemen of the Common Council may attend if they see fit."

Accordingly, on that day, in the chamber of the Common Council, in the presence of its members and of other citizens, the Mayor delivered the following address to the Board of Aldermen, who, after retiring to their room, *Voted*, "To request a copy of it for the press, and that the whole Board wait upon him for that purpose."

GENTLEMEN OF THE BOARD OF ALDERMEN: —

HAVING been called, nearly six years since, by my fellow-citizens, to the office of their chief magistrate, and having, during that period, been six times honored by their suffrages for that station, I have endeavored, uniformly, to perform its duties to the best of my ability, with unremitting zeal and fidelity. At the late election it was twice indicated, by a majority of those who thought the subject important enough to attend the polls, that they were willing to dispense with my services. According to the sound principles of a republican constitution, by which the will of a majority, distinctly expressed, concerning the continuance in office of public servants, is, to them the rule of duty, I withdrew from being any longer a cause of division to my fellow-citizens; declaring that "no consideration would induce me again to accept that office." These were not words of passion, or of wounded pride, or temporary disgust; but of deep conviction, concerning future duty, in attaining which, my obligations to my fellow-citizens were weighed as carefully as those which I owe to my own happiness and self-respect.

I stand, then, to this office, in a relation final and forever closed. There are rights and duties which result from this condition. It is an occasion on which acknowledgments ought to be made, feelings to be expressed, justice to be done, obligations to be performed. To fulfil these duties, I have thought proper to seek and avail myself of this opportunity.

And first, gentlemen, permit me to express to you that deep and lasting sense of gratitude which is felt for all the kindness, support, and encouragement with which you have lightened and strengthened official labors. In bearing testimony to the intelligence, activity, and fidelity with which you have fulfilled the duties of your station, I but join the common voice of your fellow-citizens. With me, your intercourse has been uniformly characterized by a willing and affectionate zeal; leaving, in this respect, nothing to be desired; and resulting, on my part, in an esteem which will make the recollection of our association in these duties among the most grateful of my life. Accept my thanks for the interest and assiduity with which you have aided and sustained endeavors to advance the prosperity of this city.

I owe also to the gentlemen of the Common Council a public expression of my obligations for the candor and urbanity with which they have received and canvassed all my communications. It is a happy omen for our city, that, for so many successive years, the intercourse between the branches and members of its government has been distinguished for gentlemanly character, not less than for official respect. The collisions which are naturally to be expected in a community where rival interests and passions exist, have never disturbed the harmony of either council. When diversity of opinion has arisen, a spirit of mutual concession has presided over the controversy. Happy! if in this respect, past years shall be prototypes of those which are to come.

To my fellow-citizens who, for so many years have supported or endured an administration conducted on none of the principles by which popularity is ordinarily sought and acquired, I have no language to express my respect or my gratitude. I know well that recent events have given rise, in some minds, to reflections on the fickleness of the popular will, and on the ingratitude of republics. As if the right to change was not as inherent as the right to continue; for the just exercise of this right, the people being responsible, and to bear the consequences. As if permission to serve a people at all, and the opportunity thus afforded to be useful to the community to which we belong and owe so many obligations, were not ample recompense for any labors or any sacrifices made or endured in its behalf. Is it wonderful, or a subject of reproach, that, in a populous city, where infinitely varying passions and prejudices and interests and motives must necessarily exist, an individual who had enjoyed the favor of its citizens for six years should be deprived of it on the seventh? Is it not more a matter of surprise, that it has been enjoyed so long, than that it is lost at last?

At no one moment have I concealed from myself or my fellow-citizens, that the experiment of a new government was one very dubious in its effects on continuance in office. Who that knows the nature of man, and the combinations which, for particular ends, at times take place in society, could hesitate to believe that an administration which should neither court the few, nor stand in awe of the many, which should identify itself exclusively with the rights of the city, maintaining them not merely with the zeal of official station, but with the pertinacious spirit of private interest; which, in executing the laws, should hunt vice in its recesses, turn light upon the darkness of its haunts, and wrest the poisonous cup from the hand of the unlicensed pander; which should dare to resist private cupidity, seeking to corrupt; personal influence, striving to sway; party rancor, slandering to intimidate; — would, in time, become obnoxious to all whom it prosecuted or punished; all whose passions it thwarted; whose projects it detected; whose interests it crossed? Who could doubt that, from these causes, there would in time come an accumulation of discontent; that, sooner or later, the ground swell would rise above the landmarks with a tide which would sweep it from its foundations?

In the first address which, nearly six years ago, I had the honor to make to the City Council, the operation of these causes was distinctly stated, almost in the terms just used; and the event which has now occurred was anticipated. Nothing was then promised except "a laborious fulfilment of every known duty; a prudent exercise of every invested power; a disposition shrinking from no official responsibility; and an absolute self-devotion to the interest of the city."

I stand this day in the midst of the multitude of my brethren, and ask, without pride, yet without fear, Have I failed in fulfilling this promise? Let your hearts answer.

Other obligations remain. A connection which has subsisted long and happily is about to be dissolved, and forever. To look back on the past, and consider the present, is natural and proper on the occasion. I stand indebted to my fellow-citizens for a length and uniformity of support seldom exemplified in cities where the executive office depends upon popular election. They have stood by me nobly, and with effect, in six trials; in the seventh, though successless, I was not forsaken.

To such men I owe more than silent gratitude. Their friendship, their favor, the honors they have so liberally bestowed, demand return, not in words, but in acts. I owe it to such goodness to show that their confidence has not been misplaced; their favor not been abused; and that their friendship and support, so often given in advance, have been justified by the event.

What then has the departing city administration done? what

good has it effected? what evil averted? what monuments exist of its faithfulness and efficiency?

If, in the recapitulation I am about to make, I shall speak in general terms, and sometimes in language of apparent personal reference, let it be understood, once for all, that this will be owing to the particular relation in which I stand at this moment to the subject and to my fellow-citizens; and by no means to any disposition to claim more than a common share of whatever credit belongs to that administration. This, I delight to acknowledge, is chiefly due to those excellent and faithful men, who, during successive years have, in both branches of the City Council, been the light and support of the government; by whose intelligence and practical skill I have conducted its affairs full as often as by my own. The obligations I owe to these men I mean neither to deny nor to conceal. Speedily, and as soon as other duties permit, it is my purpose, in another way and in a more permanent form, to do justice to their gratuitous labors and unobtrusive fidelity.

Touching the measures and results of the administration which will soon be past, I necessarily confine myself to a few particular topics; and those, either the most vital to our safety and prosperity, or, in my apprehension, the most necessary to be understood. Time will not permit, nor, on this occasion, would it be proper to speak of all the various objects of a prudential, economical, restrictive, or ornamental character, which, in adapting a new organization of government to the actual state of things, have been attempted or executed.

I shall chiefly refer to what has been done by way of protection against the elements; in favor of the general health; in support of public education; and in advancement of public morals.

The element which chiefly endangers cities is that of *Fire*. It cannot at this day be forgotten by my fellow-citizens with what labor and hazard of popularity the old department was abolished, and the new established. From the visible and active energy which members of a fire department take in the protection of the city against that element, they always have been, and always must be, objects of general regard. Great as is the just popularity at present enjoyed by that department, the same public favor was largely enjoyed by their predecessors. Those who at that time composed it were a hardy, industrious, effective body of men, who had been long inured to the service, and who, having the merit of veterans, naturally imbibed the errors into which old soldiers in a regular service are accustomed to fall. They were prejudiced in favor of old modes and old weapons. They had little or no confidence in a hose system; and above all they were beset with the opinion that the continuance of their corps was essential to the safety of the city. More than once it was said distinctly to the executive of the city, that "if they threw down the engines, none else could be found capable of taking them up." Under the influence of such opinions, they demanded of the city a specified annual sum for each company. It was refused. And in one day all the engines in the city were surrendered by their respective companies; and on the same day every engine was supplied with a new company by the voluntary association of public-spirited individuals.

From that time, a regular, systematic organization of the Fire Department was begun and gradually effected. The best models of engines were sought. The best experience consulted which our own or other cities possessed. New engines were obtained; old ones repaired. Proper sites for engine houses sought; when suitable locations were found, purchased; and those built upon; when such were not found, they were hired. No requisite preparation for efficiency was omitted; and every reasonable inducement to enter and remain in the service was extended.

The efficient force and state of preparation of this department now consists of twelve hundred men and officers; twenty engines; one hook and ladder company; eight hundred buckets; seven thousand feet of hose; twenty-five hose carriages; and every species of apparatus necessary for strength of the department, or for the accommodation of its members.

In this estimate, also, ought to be included fifteen reservoirs, containing three hundred and fifty thousand gallons of water, located in different parts of the city, besides those sunk in the Mill Creek, and the command of water obtained by those connected with the pipes belonging to the aqueduct.

Of all the expenditures of the city government, none perhaps have been so often denominated extravagant as those connected with this department. But when the voluntary nature of the service, its importance, and the security and confidence actually attained are considered, it is believed they can be justified.

In four years, all the objects enumerated, including the reservoirs, have cost a sum not exceeding sixty thousand dollars, which is about forty-eight thousand dollars more than the old department, in a like series of years, was accustomed to cost. The value of the fixed and permanent property now existing in engine houses and their sites, engines and apparatus, and reservoirs, cannot be estimated at less than twenty thousand dollars. So that the actual expenditure of the new department beyond the old, for these four years, cannot be stated at more than five thousand dollars a year, or twenty thousand dollars. Now it will be found that, in consequence solely of the efficiency of this department, there has been a reduction of *twenty per cent.* on the rate of insurance within the period above specified. By this reduction of premiums alone, there is an annual gain to the city on its insurable real estate of ten thousand dollars; the whole cost remunerated in two years. In this connection, let it be remembered how great is the security, in this respect, now enjoyed by the city; and that, previously to its establishment, two fires, — that in Central, Kilby, and Broad Streets; and that in Beacon Street, — occasioned a loss to it, at the least estimate, of *eight hundred thousand dollars!*

Unquestionably, greater economy may be introduced hereafter into this department, in modes which were impracticable at its commencement and in its earlier progress. Measures having that tendency have been suggested. These, doubtless, future city councils will adopt, or substitute in their stead such as are wiser and better.

All the chief great expenses, necessary to perfect efficiency, have been incurred; and little more remains to be done than to maintain the present state of completeness in its appointments.

Under this head of protection against the elements, may be justly included the preservation of our harbor from the effects of waves and tempests. By the vigilance and successive application of the city government, the protection of the two great islands, on which depend the safety of our internal and external roadsteads, has been undertaken by the General Government; and works are finished, or in progress, of a magnitude and strength exceeding all antecedent hope or expectation.

In relation to what has heen done in favor of general health, when this administration came into power, of the two great branches on which depend the health of a city, the removal of street dirt, and of that which accumulates in and about the houses of private families, the former was almost entirely neglected, and the latter was conducted in a manner exceedingly offensive to the citizens. So great was the clamor and urgency of the citizens, and so imperious was deemed the duty, that the records of the Mayor and Aldermen will show that the present executive, on the first day of his office, indeed before he had been inducted into it an hour, made a recommendation to the City Council on the subject. From that time to the present, the arrangement of those subjects has been an object of incessant attention and labor. It was, until early in the present year, a subject of perpetual struggle and controversy, — first, with the old Board of Health, who claimed the jurisdiction of it; then with contractors, whose interests the new arrangements thwarted; then with the citizens, with whose habits, or prejudices, or interest they sometimes interfered. The inhabitants of the country were indignant that they could not enjoy their ancient privilege of carrying away the street dirt when they pleased, and the offal of families as they pleased. The inhabitants of the city, forgetting the nature of the material, and the necessity of its being subjected to general regulations, were also indignant, because they "could not, as they did formerly, do what they would with their own." For three years the right of the city to control this subject was contested in courts of law; and it was not until last April, that the city authority overcame all opposition, and acquired, by a judicial decision, complete jurisdiction in the case.

Since that time, the satisfaction of the citizens with the conduct of this troublesome concern, indicated not only by direct acknowledgment, but also by evidence still more unequivocal, has equalled every reasonable wish, and exceeded all previous anticipation. I state as a fact, that in a city containing probably sixty-five thousand inhabitants, and under an administration inviting and soliciting complaints against its agents, — during seven months, from May to November, both inclusive, amidst a hot season, in which a local alarm of infectious fever naturally excited great anxiety, concerning the causes tending to produce it, — the whole number of complaints from citizens, whose families were neglected by the agents of the city, made, or known to the Mayor or to any officers of the city, amounted only to the number of *eight in a month, or two in a week*, for the whole city! and four fifths of these, it is asserted by the intelligent and faithful superintendent of the streets, were owing to the faults of domestics rather than to his agents, — a degree of efficient action on a most difficult subject, which it is the interest of the citizens never to forget, as it shows what may be done, and, therefore, what they have a right to require.

I refer to this topic with the more distinctness, because it is one of vital interest, not only to this, but to all populous cities. I know not that the practicability of establishing an efficient system for the removal from populous cities of these common and unavoidable nuisances has anywhere been more satisfactorily put to the test. Nor has the evidence of the direct effects of such efficiency, upon the general health of the population, been anywhere more distinctly exhibited by facts. I speak before citizens who have enjoyed the benefits of these arrangements; who now enjoy them; who see what can be effected; and what is reasonable, therefore, for them in this respect to claim at the hands of their public agents.

I cannot close this head without referring to the tables connected with, and the facts stated in, the address I had the honor to make to the City Council at the commencement of the present year.

It is there stated that the city authorities commenced a systematic cleansing of the city, and removal of noxious animal and vegetable substances, with reference to the improvement of the general health and comfort, in the year 1823.

"That the bills of mortality of this city, and calculations made on them for the eleven years, from 1813 to 1823 inclusive, show that the annual average proportion of deaths to the population was about *one* in *forty-two*."

"Similar estimates on the bills of mortality of this city, since 1823, show that this annual average proportion was, for the four years, from 1824 to 1827 inclusive, less than *one* in *fifty*; for the two years, from 1826 to 1827 inclusive, less than *one* in *fifty-five*."

It now appears, that, on the principles stated in these tables, for the *three* years just terminated, 1826, 1827, 1828, the annual average proportion of deaths to population was less than *one* in *fifty-seven.*

Upon the usual estimates of this nature, a city of equal population, in which this annual average should not exceed *one* in *forty-seven*, would be considered as enjoying an extraordinary degree of health.

From the facts thus stated, it is maintained that this city does enjoy an uncommon and gradually increasing state of general health; and that for the four last years it has been unexampled. And although the whole of this important improvement in the general health of the city is not attributed to the measures of the police, yet since, in the year 1823, a system was adopted expressly for the purpose of preventing disease, by an efficient and timely removal of nuisances, it is just and reasonable to claim for that system a portion of the credit for that freedom from disease, which, subsequently to their adoption, has resulted in a degree so extraordinary.

The residue of what was then said upon this topic, I repeat, as being important enough to be reiterated.

"I am thus distinct in alluding to this subject, because the removal of the nuisances of a city is a laborious, difficult, and repulsive service, requiring much previous arrangement and constant vigilance, and is attended with frequent disappointment of endeavors, whence it happens there is a perpetual natural tendency in those intrusted with municipal affairs, to throw the trouble and responsibility of it upon subordinate agents and contractors; and very plausible arguments of economy may be adduced in favor of such a system. But if experience and reflection have given certainty to my mind upon any subject, it is upon this; that upon the right conduct of this branch of the police, the executive powers of a city should be made directly responsible, more than for any other; and that it can never, for any great length of time, be executed well, except by agents under its immediate control; and whose labors it may command at all times, in any way which the necessities, continually varying, and often impossible to be anticipated, of a city, in this respect require."

"In the whole sphere of municipal duties, there are none more important than those which relate to the removal of those substances whose exhalations injuriously affect the air. A pure atmosphere is to a city what a good conscience is to an individual,— a perpetual source of comfort, tranquillity, and self-respect."

In relation to what has been done for the support of public education, considering the multiplied and pressing objects of attention, necessarily occurring in the first years of a new organization of government, I know not that a greater degree of support of this branch of public service could have been justly given or reasonably expected than has occurred. Under our ancient institutions, the scale of appropriations for this object was, of all others, the most liberal and complete. It was found, in 1823, with an annual expenditure of forty-four thousand five hundred dollars. It is left, at this day, with one of fifty-six thousand dollars. In the interval, two schoolhouses have been built and sites purchased at an additional direct expenditure of upwards of fifty-five thousand dollars. In addition to which the House of Reformation of Juvenile Offenders, which is, in fact, a school of most important character, has been established and supported at an expense already incurred of upwards of sixteen thousand dollars.

But the High School for Girls has been suspended. As, on this topic, I have reason to think very gross misrepresentations and falsehoods have been circulated in every form of the tongue and the press, I shall speak plainly. It being in fact a subject on which my opinion has at no time been concealed.

This school was adopted declaredly as "an experiment." It was placed under the immediate care of its known authors. It may be truly said that its impracticability was proved before it went into operation. The pressure for admission at the first examination of candidates, the discontent of the parents of those rejected, the certainty of far greater pressure and discontent which must occur in future years, satisfied every reflecting mind that, however desirable the scheme of giving a high classical education, equal about to a college education, to all the girls of a city, whose parents would wish them to be thus educated at the expense of the city, was just as impracticable as to give such an one to all the boys of it at the city's expense. Indeed, more so, because girls not being drawn away from the college by preparation for a profession or trade, would have nothing except their marriage to prevent their parents from availing of it. No funds of any city could endure the expense.

The next project was so to model the school as that, although professedly established for the benefit of *all*, it might be kept and maintained at the expense of the city for the benefit of the *few*. The School Committee were divided equally on the resulting questions. The subject was finally postponed by the casting vote of the Chairman. As all agreed, that if the school was to be maintained according to its original conception, new and great appropriations were necessary, the Chairman was directed to make a report on the whole subject to the City Council. The report indicated that, in such case, appropriations were indispensably necessary, but did not recommend them, because a majority of the Committee were not favorable to the project. That report was printed and circulated throughout the city. A year has elapsed, and not an individual in either branch of the City Council has brought forward the question of its revival by moving the necessary appropriations.

No shield has ever before been protruded by the individual principally assailed as a defence against the calumnies which have been circulated on this subject. It has now been alluded to, more for the sake of other honorable men, who have, for a like cause, been assailed by evil tongues and evil pens, than for his own.

In all this there is nothing uncommon or unprecedented. The public officer who, from a sense of public duty, dares to cross strong interests in their way to gratification at the public expense, always has had, and ever will have, meted to him the same measure. The beaten course is, first, to slander, in order to intimidate; and if that fail, then to slander, in order to sacrifice. He who loves his office better than his duty will yield and be flattered as long as he is a tool. He who loves his duty better than his office will stand erect and take his fate.

All schools requiring high qualifications as the condition of admission, are essentially schools for the benefit, comparatively, of a very few. The higher the qualification, the greater the exclusion. Those whose fortunes permit them to avail themselves of private instruction for their children, during their early years, — men highly educated themselves, who have leisure and ability to attend to the education of their own children, and thus raise them at the prescribed age to the required qualification, — will chiefly enjoy the privilege. To the rest of the community, consisting of parents not possessing these advantages, admission to them is a lottery, in which there is a hundred blanks to a prize. The scheme to reduce the school to an attendance of one year, seems to be a needless multiplication of schools and of expense; as it is plainly far better that a year should be added to the continuance in the common schools, and their course of instruction proportionably elevated.

The great interest of society is identified with her common schools. These belong to the mass of the people. Let the people take care, lest the funds which ought to be devoted exclusively to the improvement and elevation of these common schools, thus essentially theirs, be diverted to schools of high qualification. Under whatever pretence established, their necessary tendency is to draw away, not only funds, but also interest and attention from the common schools. *The sound principle upon this subject seems to be, that the standard of public education should be raised to the greatest desirable and practicable height; but that it should be effected by raising the standard of the common schools.*

In respect of what has been done, in support of public morals, when this administration first came into power, the police had no comparative effect. The city possessed no house of correction, and the natural inmates of that establishment were in our streets, on our "hills" or on our commons, disgusting the delicate, offending the good, and intimidating the fearful. There were parts of the city over which no honest man dared to pass in the night time; so proud there and uncontrolled was the dominion of crime. The executive of the city was seriously advised not to meddle with those haunts, their reformation being a task altogether impracticable.

It was attempted. The success is known. Who at this day sees begging in our streets? I speak generally; a transient case may occur. But there is none systematic. At this day, I speak it confidently, there is no part of the city through which the most timid may not walk, by day or by night, without cause of fear of personal violence. What streets present more stillness in the night time? Where, in a city of equal population, are there fewer instances of those crimes to which all populous places are subject?

Doubtless much of this condition of things is owing to the orderly habits of our citizens, but much also is attributable to the vigilance which has made vice tremble in its haunts and fly to cities where the air is more congenial to it; which, by pursuing the lawless vender of spirituous liquor, denying licenses to the worst of that class, or revoking them as soon as found in improper hands, has checked crime in its first stages, and introduced into these establishments a salutary fear. By the effect of this system, notwithstanding in these six years the population of the city has been increased at least *fifteen thousand*, the number of licensed houses has been diminished from six hundred and seventy-nine to five hundred and fifty-four.

Let it be remembered that this state of things has been effected without the addition of one man to the ancient arm of the police. The name of police officer has indeed been changed to city marshal. The venerable old charter number of *twenty-four* constables still continue the entire array of city police; and *eighty* watchmen, of whom never more than *eighteen* are out at a time, constitute the whole nocturnal host of police militant, to maintain the peace and vindicate the wrongs of upwards of *sixty thousand citizens.*

If it be asked why more have not been provided, I answer, it has frequently been under consideration. But, on a view of all circumstances, and experience having hitherto proved the present number enough, there seemed no occasion to increase it, from any general theory of its want of proportion to the population, seeing that practically there seemed to be as many as were necessary.

The good which has been attained, and no man can deny it is great, has been effected by directing unremittingly the force of the executive power to the haunts of vice in its first stages, and to the favorite resorts of crime in its last.

To diminish the number of licensed dram-shops and tippling-houses; to keep a vigilant eye over those which are licensed; to revoke without fear or favor the licenses of those who were found violating the law; to break up public dances in the brothels; to keep the light and terrors of the law directed upon the resorts of the lawless, thereby preventing any place becoming dangerous by their congregation; or they and their associates becoming insolent through sense of strength and numbers;—

these have been the means; and these means, faithfully applied, are better than armies of constables and watchmen. They have been applied with as much fearlessness as though the executive office was not elective; without regarding the fact, that the numerous class thus offended, their landlords, dependants, and coadjutors, had votes and voices in city elections. So far as these classes had any influence on a recent event, and it must have been small, the cause is not a matter of regret, but of pride.

Without pressing these topics further into detail, and without stating how the condition of things was found at the coming in of this administration, — because the faithful men who executed the ancient town government did as much as the form of organization under which they acted permitted, — I shall simply state, in one view, how the city affairs, in respects not yet alluded to, have been left.

Every interest of the city, so far as has come to the knowledge of the city government, has been considered, maintained, and, as far as practicable, arranged. All the real estate of the city surveyed and estimated; plans of it prepared; the whole analyzed and presented in one view for the benefit of those who come after. The difficulties of the voting lists laboriously investigated, and the sources of error ascertained, and in a great degree remedied. The streets widened, the crooked straightened, the great avenues paved and enlarged. They and other public places ornamented. Heights levelled. Declivities smoothed or diminished. The common sewers regulated and made more capacious. New streets of great width and utility, in the centre of population, obtained without cost to the city. Its markets made commodious. New public edifices, in the old city and at South Boston, erected; the old repaired and ornamented.

These things have been done, not indeed to the extent which might be desired, but to a degree as great, considering the time, as could reasonably be anticipated.

But then, — "the city debt," "the taxes," — "we are on the eve of bankruptcy." "The citizens are oppressed by the weight of assessments produced by these burdens." Such are the hollow sounds which come up from the halls of caucusing discontent!

The state of the city debt has recently been displayed by official authority; by which it appears, that, after deducting funds in the hands of the Committee for the reduction of the city debt, and also the amount of bonds, well secured by mortgages, payable to the city, the exact city debt amounts to $637,256.66; concerning which subject, I undertake to maintain two positions:—

1st. It has not been, and never can be, a burden; that is, it has not been, and never will be, felt in the taxes.

2d. So far from city bankruptcy, the state of its resources is one of enviable prosperity.

It may be stated, with sufficient accuracy, that the present city debt is entirely the result of operations which obtained for the city the New Faneuil Hall Market, the City Wharf, and land north of the block of stores on North Market Street; and of those which gave it, free of incumbrance, the lands west of Charles and Pleasant Streets.

Now, this property *thus newly acquired* by these operations, for which the city debt was incurred, may be exchanged, no intelligent man can doubt, at any hour, in the market, for an amount equal to the entire city debt.

The property *thus acquired*, now in actual, unincumbered, undisputed possession of the city, consists,—

1. Of the New Market and its site, estimated by its annual incomes, ($26,000,) which are in their nature permanent, and must increase rather than diminish, at . . .	$500,000
2. City Wharf, estimated by some at $100,000; on this occasion it is put down at	75,000
3. Eight thousand five hundred and twenty-eight feet of land on both sides of the Mill Creek, and the new streets now completing in that vicinity; on this occasion estimated at, as an unquestionable price, although its real value probably greatly exceeds	12,000
4. Twenty-eight acres and a half of land west of Charles and Pleasant Streets, exceeding 1,200,000 square feet, estimated only at ten cents; which, how far it is exceeded by the fact, my fellow-citizens understand, is set down at . . .	120,000
	$707,000

Thus it appears the city is possessed of a real estate, of an unquestionable value, exceeding *seven hundred thousand dollars*, as an offset for a debt of *six hundred and thirty-seven thousand dollars.*

It may confidently be said, that no capitalist of intelligence and resources, equal to the purchase, would hesitate an hour to contract, on condition of a transfer of that property, to assume the whole city debt. Should I say, he would give a hundred thousand dollars as a *bonus* for the bargain, I should probably come nearer the truth. Am I not justified, then, in my position, that the marketable value of the real estate acquired and left to the city by that administration, greatly exceeds the amount of debt it has left? The scales are not simply even; they greatly preponderate in favor of the value of the property above the debt. It is no answer to this, to say, that the property *thus newly acquired* is of a nature or value so important to the city, that it ought never to be disposed of. This is probably true; at least of a very great part of it. But what of this? Does not the fact show, that greatly as the marketable value of the property exceeds the debt, the value of it, in its interest or importance to the city, greatly exceeds even that marketable value? After this, have I not a right to assert, according to the usual and justifiable forms of expression, under circumstances of this kind, that, *so far as respects the operations of the administration, now passing away, they have left the city incumbered with* NO DEBT; because they have left it possessed of a newly acquired real property, far greater in marketable value than the whole debt it has incurred?

Again, it has not only done this; but when this subject is considered with reference to annual income received, and annual interest to be paid, it will be found that this administration leaves the city with a property, in real estate and bonds and mortgages, the income and interest of which amounts to *fifty-two thousand dollars*, while the annual interest of the debt which it leaves is only *forty-seven thousand dollars.*

If, then, the annual income of the property left be now, and ever must be, far greater than the annual interest of the debt incurred; if the newly acquired real estate is, and always must be, far greater in marketable value than the whole amount of that debt, has not this administration a right to say, that, *so far as respects its financial operations, it has left the city incumbered with* NO BURDEN AND NO DEBT.

If there is no debt, then there is no bankruptcy. Whatever estate the city now has, over and above that which is above specified, is so much clear and unincumbered property, to be used or improved for its advancement or relief in all future times and emergencies, according to the wisdom and fidelity of succeeding administrations. Unless, indeed, that wisdom direct, as it probably will, that the property above specified, obtained for the city by this administration, shall be kept as the best possible investment of city capital, and the proceeds of the other lands applied to the discharge of the debt incurred for the purchase of the property thus acquired.

Now, what is that clear, unincumbered city property which remains, after deducting that *thus newly acquired?* It consists of nothing less, as appears by the official report of the Committee on Public Lands, than upwards of *five million three hundred thousand* feet of land on the Neck and in different parts of the city, — capable of being sold, without any possible objection; — *lands* belonging to the House of Industry, amounting to sixty acres; and a township of land in the state of Maine, being neither of them included in this estimate.

Without taking into consideration, then, the encouragement given to our mechanic interests; to the influx of capital and population, which have been necessarily the effect of the activity of capital induced by the measures of the city government; and confining myself to the single consideration of the amount and unincumbered state of the real property of the city, am I not justified in the assertion, that IT IS, IN RESPECT OF ITS FINANCIAL RESOURCES, ONE OF ENVIABLE PROSPERITY ?

But "the taxes," "the taxes" are heavy beyond all precedent! In answer to which, I state, that *the taxes have not increased in a ratio equal to the actual increase of property and population.* The Assessors' books will show, that the ratio of taxation has been *less* in every year of the seven years in which the city government has had existence, than was the ratio of any year in the next preceding seven years of the town government, one year only excepted; and even in this it was less than in one of those next preceding seven years above-mentioned. Comparing the average of the ratios of these two periods of seven years together, it will be found, that while the average of the ratios of these seven years of the town government was *eight dollars and fifteen cents*, the average of the ratios of the seven years of the city government has been only *seven dollars and twenty-seven cents.*

I might here close. But there have been objections made publicly to this executive, which, although apparently of a personal nature, are, in fact, objections to the principles on which he has conducted his office. Now, in the particular relation in which that executive stood to his office, it was his duty well to consider those principles, since they might become precedents, and give a character and tone to succeeding administrations. He has uniformly acted under a sense of this relation, and of the obligations resulting from it; and intentionally has done nothing, or omitted nothing, without contemplating it. On this account, it may be useful to state those objections, and answer them. And first, it has been said, "The Mayor assumes too much upon himself. He places himself at the head of all committees. He prepares all reports. He permits nothing to be done but by his agency. He does not sit solemn and dignified in his chair, and leave general superintendence to others; but he is everywhere, and about every thing, — in the street; at the docks; among the common sewers; — no place but what is vexed by his presence."

In reply to this objection, I lay my hand first on the city charter, which is in these words: — "It shall be the duty of the Mayor to be vigilant and active at all times, in causing the laws for the government of said city to be duly executed and put in force; to inspect the conduct of all subordinate officers, in the government thereof, and, as far as in his power, to cause all negligence, carelessness, and positive violations of duty to be duly prosecuted and punished. It shall be his duty, from time to time, to communicate to both branches of the City Council all such information, and recommend all such measures as may tend to the improvement of the finances, the police, health, cleanliness, comfort, and ornament of the city."

Now let it be remembered, that to the performance of these duties he was sworn; and that he is willing to admit that he considers an oath taken before God as a serious affair; and that having taken an oath to do such services, he is not of a spirit which can go to sleep or to rest after shifting the performance of them upon others.

As to his "seeing to every thing," who has a better right than he, who, at least by popular opinion, if not by the city charter, *is made responsible for every thing?*

Besides, why is it not as true, in affairs of police as of agriculture, that "the eye of the master does more work than both his hands."

If those who made these objections intended "by doing every thing," that he has been obstinate, wilful, or overbearing in respect of those with whom he has been associated, I cheerfully appeal to you, gentlemen, how willingly, on all occasions, he has yielded his opinion to yours; and how readily he has submitted whatever he has written to your corrections. If he took upon himself generally the character of draughtsman of reports, it was because your labors were gratuitous, and for his a salary was received. It was because he deemed it but just, that the "hireling" should bear the heat and burden, both of the day and the labor.

Great assiduity and labor did appear to him essential requisites to the well performance of duty in that office. He could not persuade himself that the intelligent and industrious community which possess this metropolis could ever be satisfied in that station with an indolent, selfish, or timid temper, or with any one possessed of a vulgar and criminal ambition.

I cannot refrain, on the present occasion, from expressing the happiness with which I now yield this place to a gentleman[1] possessing so many eminent qualifications; whose talents will enable him to appreciate so readily the actual state of things; who will be so capable of correcting what has been amiss; changing what has been wrong; and of maintaining what has been right. May he be happy! and long enjoy the honors and the confidence his fellow-citizens have bestowed!

And now, gentlemen, standing as I do in this relation for the last time, in your presence and that of my fellow-citizens, — about to surrender forever a station full of difficulty, of labor, and temptation, in which I have been called to very arduous duties, affecting the rights, property, and at times, the liberty of others, concerning which, the perfect line of rectitude, though desired, was not always to be clearly discerned, — in which great

[1] Harrison Gray Otis.

interests have been placed within my control, under circumstances in which it would have been easy to advance private ends and sinister projects; under these circumstances, I inquire, as I have a right to inquire, — for, in the course of the recent contest, insinuations have been cast against my integrity, in this long management of your affairs, whatever errors have been committed, and, doubtless, there have been many, — have you found in me any thing selfish, any thing personal, any thing mercenary?

In the simple language of an ancient seer, I say, "Behold, here I am. Witness against me. Whom have I defrauded? Whom have I oppressed? At whose hands have I received any bribe?"

Six years ago, when I had the honor first to address the City Council, in anticipation of the event which has now occurred, the following expressions were used: — "In administering the police, in executing the laws, in protecting the rights and promoting the prosperity of the city, its first officer will be necessarily beset and assailed by individual interests; by rival projects; by personal influences; by party passions. The more firm and inflexible he is in maintaining the rights and in pursuing the interests of the city, the greater is the probability of his becoming obnoxious to the censure of all whom he causes to be prosecuted or punished; of all whose passions he thwarts; of all whose interests he opposes."

The day and the event have come. I retire, — as in that first address I told my fellow-citizens, "if, in conformity with the experience of other republics, faithful exertions should be followed by loss of favor and confidence," I should retire, — "rejoicing, not indeed with a public and patriotic, but with a private and individual joy; for I shall retire with a consciousness, weighed against which all *human suffrages* are but as the light dust of the balance."

CHAPTER XIX.

CITY GOVERNMENT. 1829.

Harrison Gray Otis, *Mayor*.[1]

Circumstances recalling the Mayor from Private Life — Tribute to his Predecessors — Views concerning the City Debt — On the Supply of Pure Water — The Importance of Railroads — Political Relations of the State and Union — Flats to the Eastward of the New Market — Attempts to authorize Inspectors to place Names on the Voting Lists — Tribute to the Directors of the House of Industry — Chief Engineer of the Fire Department appointed — Resignation of all the Assistant Engineers — Petitions to extend Wharves to the Channel — Relief to Sufferers by Fire in Georgia — Petitions for a General Meeting of Citizens on Railroads, and for a Grant of Land for their Accommodation.

On the fifth of January, 1829, the organization of the city government was this year transferred from the chamber of the Common Council to Faneuil Hall; it being the era of a new administration of its affairs. After the usual solemnities, the Mayor delivered, in the presence of a large assembly of citizens collected on the occasion, the following inaugural address: —

GENTLEMEN OF THE CITY COUNCIL: —

Nothing could be more unexpected by me than the circumstances by the result of which I find myself in this place. After nearly thirty years of occupation in public affairs, with but short intermissions, I resigned my seat in the National Legislature with an intense desire, and, as I thought, unalterable purpose of passing the few years that might remain for me, in a private station. The objects for which I became a humble actor in the political scene were attained. The tempest which uprooted the

[1] The whole number of votes cast were 4,546, of which Mr. Otis received 2,977.

The Aldermen were, — Henry J. Oliver, John T. Loring, Samuel T. Armstrong, Benjamin Russell, Thomas Kendall, James Hall, Winslow Lewis, and Charles Wells. Eliphalet Williams was President of the Common Council.

institutions of the Old World had subsided. The broils which had agitated and endangered our own country, and kept the minds of all who took part in them in a state of discomfort were extinguished. The constitution was preserved, the government wise, and the people happy. Opportunity had been afforded of supporting, by my feeble aid, an administration which, under a different aspect of affairs, I had opposed. The public favor and confidence, both in measure and duration, had exceeded my estimate of my own pretensions; and though it was not to be dissembled that this favor was in the wane, I carried into retirement the consolation that if my services had not been valuable, neither had they been expensive to my country; as I had never sought nor lingered long in any office of emolument. And I indulged the hope that, having done nothing to forfeit the approbation of my friends, the rigorous judgment formed of my conduct by those from whose political system I had formerly the misfortune to dissent, would not follow me beyond the tomb, and that the candid and charitable portion of them would not finally withhold from my motives and intentions the justice which I have never been consciously backward to render to theirs. From this retirement I have been called by my fellow-citizens for a short season, under circumstances which make it a duty to obey their will. Their invitation was the more grateful as it was spontaneous. And great indeed will be my gratification, if, by coöperating with you, I shall be considered as having, in any reasonable measure, requited a demonstration of good-will from my fellow-citizens so flattering and honorable to me.

It is now my province, and it will soon become my duty to communicate to you such information as may be requisite, and to recommend such measures as may seem to be conducive to the best interest of our city. But I stand merely upon the threshold of an office, with the interior of which most of you are more familiar than myself. I can touch only upon general topics, assuring you, however, that I will apply my entire time and attention to master the business of this department, and to apprise you of such details as you have a right to expect. And the utmost exertion of my faculties shall not be wanting in constant and united effort to cherish and extend the prosperity of the interesting concerns committed to our charge. It is indeed fortunate for us all, that the administration of this department has hitherto been conducted under the auspices of those, whose different qualifications were eminently adapted to the varying exigencies of the station which they successively occupied. The novel experiment of city government was commenced by your first lamented Mayor with the circumspection and delicacy which belonged to his character, and which were entirely judicious and opportune. He felt and respected the force of ancient and honest prejudices. His aim was to allure, not to compel; to reconcile by gentle reform, not to revolt by startling innovation; so that while he led us into a new and fairer creation, we felt ourselves surrounded by the scenes and comforts of home. His successor entered upon office with the characteristic energy of his distinguished talents. He felt that the hour had arrived for more radical reformation, and that the minds of the citizens were ripe for greater change and more permanent improvements, and he devoted an assiduity that can never be surpassed, to a development and application of the resources of the city, which have materially contributed to its ornament, comfort, health, accommodation, and in all respects lasting advantage. We are surrounded on all sides with the monuments of this enterprising, disinterested zeal. But they could not be consummated without expense. This affords to some a serious subject of speculation on the future, and to others of complaint. But, after such cursory examination of the state of our finances, as time and opportunity have enabled me to make, since I found it to be a duty, I perceive indeed the necessity of strict economy, but no just cause for uneasiness or complaint. Documents just made public, show the outstanding, funded debt (after deducting the amount of good and convertible securities) is about six hundred and thirty-seven thousand dollars. For the gradual extinguishment of this debt, provision is made by standing regulations, appropriating fifteen thousand dollars annually from the city tax; the balances in the treasury at the end of the year, moneys arising from the sales of real estate, and payments made on account of the principal of bonds and notes. This process may be accelerated at your pleasure, by providing for a more rapid sale of the city lands. A subject on which I will be better prepared than I am at this moment to give an opinion. The appropriation for the expense of the current financial year, which begins in May, was three hundred and twenty-eight thousand, six hundred and twenty-five dollars, of which the assessed tax constitute an amount of two hundred and thirty-five thousan dollars. It is not perceived, at present, that this sum can diminished. But while unceasing attention is due to the devi ing of ways and means for alleviating taxes, there is encourag ment to presume, that if this cannot be effected by lessening t nominal amount, an increasing population and resources, bringing to the support of the burden a greater contribution strength, will diminish its pressure on the individual.

In relation to the debt itself, it should be remembered that retain, in a great measure at least, the value received. O money has not evaporated in airy speculations, or been lavish in corrupt expenditures. Works of permanent utility have be established. The Market House, House of Industry, Priso Schools, and other substantial monuments have been erecte Our crooked paths have been made strait, and widened, a new avenues have been opened. The benefit of these and some other improvements will extend to many generations y to come, and those which immediately succeed should be co tent to share a fair apportionment of the equivalent paid, shou it be necessary or convenient to procrastinate a total redempti of the debt. It is possible that the scale on which some of the improvements were projected is somewhat in anticipation future exigencies. But it is doubtful whether great plans, wit out this ingredient, would deserve to be regarded as impro ments, supposing the city destined to advance in prosperity. the other supposition, no great plan would, in fact, be improvement, for none such should be undertaken. If a mark would barely accommodate those who resort to it this ye inconvenience would arise the next year. The same remark applicable to school houses, streets, and, in a degree, to all pu lic buildings. We must proceed (certainly with discretion) the presumption that population and wealth have not come a stand; and if none of us would now be ready to surren these appendages in return for the price of the purchase, th consideration should go far towards reconciling us to the con tions on which we have obtained them.

From the great improvements which were required by t necessities of the city, two inconveniences have arisen whi were unavoidable, and will, it is believed, be temporary. Fi a sudden transfer of value from some parts of the city to others, by which the proprietors of old estates have been injured, while, by the increase of accommodation beyond the demand, the purchasers of the new have failed to realize the fair profits of their investments. Secondly, the city became a purchaser of lands to sell again, and thus far a competitor with individuals in private enterprise. Probably, therefore, the time has come when prudence may recommend a pause from great and expensive attempts, and it may be incumbent on us who are intrusted with this year's administration, to look rather to the preservation and completion of what has been finished or commenced, than to new undertakings. There is, however, wanting to the city a convenience of which, it is ventured to assert, it should never lose sight, — an abundant supply of wholesome water. The object has been placed before the City Council on a former occasion by my predecessor in striking relief; and I am free to avow my conviction of the correctness of the views by him exhibited in relation to it.

Another object, however, is lately brought into view by the spirit of the age we live in, the importance of which, if within the reach of the city, it would not be easy to exaggerate, — a communication with the country by railway. This city, from its earliest foundation, has been advancing in a regular progression of populousness and wealth. And though, in both these respects, it has not kept pace with other cities, yet the population has increased in a ratio sufficiently indicative of its prosperous tendencies, and wealth continues to bear a greater proportion to population than is perhaps elsewhere to be seen. So long as these advantages shall continue, the growth of our sister cities will furnish no cause of envy or regret. The time which has elapsed since the treaty of Ghent, enables us to form a sufficiently correct estimate of the probable operation of circumstances on the interests of this city in any other period of peace of the same duration. We have experienced all the vicissitudes of business which arise from a transition from war to peace, and the efforts made by commerce, both external and internal, to adjust themselves to new positions, and to surmount the embarrassments and consequences inseparable from such change. Among these, may be reckoned the fluctuation of trade with foreign countries, the perplexities growing out of their commercial regulations, and, on the whole, its sensible diminution. The effects of excessive exports and imports; the occasional drains and refluxes of specie; the corresponding increase of the coasting trade; the alternation of scarcity and surplus in the money market, by the operation of the banking system; the rise and progress of the manufacturing interests, and the variations in the employment afforded to the middling and laboring classes of our fellow-citizens. The result of these mutations proves the condition of our city to be sound and vigorous. Great fortunes are no longer accumulated; but judicious enterprise and honest industry are generally rewarded by competent gain. The mechanic is employed, and the laborer receives his hire. This state of things demands our highest gratitude to the Giver of all good, and justifies the inference, that if we can maintain our natural resources and connections, we shall find no cause for despondence. But it is not to be disguised, that these connections are menaced with interruptions and diversions, requiring exertion and vigilance to obviate their effects. All parts of the Union but New England are alive to the importance of establishing and perfecting the means of communication by land and water. The magic of raising states and cities in our country to sudden greatness, seems mainly to consist in the instituting of canals and railroads. The choice, therefore, is not left to us of reaping the fruits of our natural resources, and from abstaining from all part in these enterprises. The state and city must be up and doing, or the streams of our prosperity will seek new channels. We must preserve our intercommunication with each other and with our sister States by the methods which they adopt, or we shall be left insulated. Our planet cannot stand still, but may go backward without a miracle. The question will arise, and we must prepare to meet it, not whether railroads are subjects of lucrative speculation, but whether they be not indispensable to save this State and city from insignificance and decay. It would be quite premature to enlarge in a dissertation on particulars connected with this subject. Unless the surveys and calculation of skilful persons employed in this business are fallacious, there is no doubt that a railroad from this city to the Hudson may be made with no greater elevation in any part than is found between the head of Long Wharf and the Old State House; and that the income would pay the interest of the capital employed. Reports and documents from commissioners appointed by the Legislature, may, it is believed, be expected at an early day. Should they be as favorable as is anticipated, to the practicability of the undertaking, they will present to our citizens and to us materials for more grave consideration than can arise from any other subject. I will not trust myself to express the joy I should feel in ascertaining that the undertaking is not only feasible, but within the compass of the resources of the State or city, or of enterprising individuals, or of all united, and that they would be so applied. These feelings, however, will never, I trust, stimulate me to recommend measures that shall not have undergone and been found equal to sustain the closest scrutiny. It is now intended, merely by general allusion, to invite you to turn your thoughts to the subject, and to familiarize yourselves to reflect upon the probable (I may say) certain effects of a communication which, by connecting this city with the Hudson, would open a market to the regions beyond it, and be realized in their immediate influence in every house, wharf, store, and workshop. Nor would the consequences be less propitious to the country through which it would pass; converting its wastes into villages, its forests into fields, its fields into gardens, and the timber and granite of its mountains into gold. While, on the one side, public attention will be attracted towards facilitating intercourse by land, great advantages would result on the other, from an extended plan of steam navigation to Maine and to the British Provinces and to the Island of Nantucket. The apathy hitherto prevailing, in relation to this scheme, is unaccountable. But as the success of it can be expected only from individual enterprise, it is mentioned merely for the sake of respectfully commending it to the patronage of your separate opinions and influence out of doors.

Gentlemen, I will now bespeak your indulgence for a few moments upon a matter which, though not directly appertaining to the municipal sphere, may not, when candidly weighed, be regarded as misplaced and unseasonable on this occasion. It is quite apparent to all our fellow-citizens, that the honor of the chair which I now occupy, is not the fruit of any party struggle. With the friends of former days, whose constancy can never be forgotten, others have been pleased to unite (and to honor me with their suffrages) who hold in high disapprobation the part I formerly took in political affairs. Their support of me on this occasion is no symptom of a change of their sentiments in that particular. I presume not to infer from it even a mitigation of the rigor with which my public conduct has been judged. But it is not presumptuous to take it for granted, that those who have favored me with their countenance on this occasion, confide in my sense of the obligation of veracity, and of the aggravated profligacy that would attend a violation of it, standing here in the presence of God and my country. On this faith, I feel myself justified by circumstances to avail myself of this occasion, the first, and probably the last, so appropriate, that will be in my power, distinctly and solemnly to assert, that, at no time in the course of my life, have I been present at any meeting of individuals, public or private, of the many or the few, or privy to correspondence, of whatever description, in which any proposition, having for its object the dissolution of the Union, or its dismemberment in any shape, or a separate confederacy, or a forcible resistance to the government or laws, was ever made or debated; that I have no reason to believe, that any such scheme was ever meditated by distinguished individuals of the old federal party.

But, on the other hand, every reason which habits of intimacy and communion of sentiments with most of them afforded, for the persuasion that they looked to the remote possibility of such events as the most to be deprecated of all calamities, and that they would have received any serious proposal, calculated for those ends, as a paroxysm of political delirium. This statement will bear internal evidence of truth to all who reflect that among those men were some by the firesides of whose ancestors the principles of the Union and independence of these States were first asserted and digested; from which was taken the coal that kindled the hallowed flame of the Revolution; from whose ashes the American eagle rose into life. Others who had conducted the measures and the armies of that Revolution, — Solomons in council, and Samsons in combat. Others who assisted at the birth of the federal constitution, and watched over its infancy with paternal anxiety. And I may add, to the best of my knowledge and belief, that all of them regarded its safety and success as the best hope of this people, and the last hope of the friends of liberty throughout the world. Are treasonable, or disloyal plots or purposes, consistent with these relations? It would seem to be hardly conceivable; yet it is possible. The lost archangels caballed and revolted against the government of heaven; favorites, rioting in the sunshine of royal favor, have turned traitors to their king; and republicans, sickening with the higher glory of the love and confidence of the people, have enslaved them to factions and sold them to tyrants. Such foul conspiracies may have been in our time. But should they be credited without evidence proportioned to their probable enormity? without doings as well as sayings? without any evidence whatever? Secret cabals and plots are the constant theme of suspicion and accusation in times of political excitement; and they can be disaffirmed only by the simple negation of the parties accused, until the proofs are adduced. Are unguarded slips of the tongue, or passionate invectives, proofs which ought to satisfy impartial minds? Surely, it is not for the honor or prosperity of this city or of any party, that it should be stigmatized as the head-quarters, not of good principles, but of treasonable machinations. The discredit of the malaria once fixed would affect the reputation of all. The distinction between leaders and led, so insulting to freemen who are supposed to come under the latter denomination, will not be recognized; and if you are known to come from the infected district, those who hold their nostrils and avoid you will not stop to inquire, whether the plague were in your own family.

I again express my hope, that these remarks will not be considered ill-timed. They are a testimony offered in defence of the memory of the honored dead, and of patriotic survivors who have not the same opportunity of speaking for themselves. Their object is not personal favor, though I am free to admit, that I am not indifferent to the desire of removing doubts and giving satisfaction to the minds of any who, by a magnanimous pledge of kind feelings towards me, have a claim upon me for every candid explanation and assurance in my power to afford.

Moreover, the harmony of our fellow-citizens may be promoted by a right understanding of these matters. The history of republican states and cities is soon told. Parties grow up from honest difference of opinion on the policy of measures. In process of time, the subject of controversy dies a natural death; and if personal animosities could be buried in the same grave all would be well.

In that event, the people would have a respite from party struggle, and when new contests and dissensions should arise, they would again choose sides from principle, and take a new departure from each other, free from the fetters and irritation of former alliances. The virulent humors of the body politic would not collect in the old wounds, but be again dispersed and cured by the course of nature. But this happy termination of political strife, with its original causes, seems not to accord with experience. The names and badges and attitude of parties are preserved; antipathies become habits. Men resolve to differ eternally, without cause, for the mere reason of having once differed for good cause. One portion of the people is excluded by the other from the public service. Parties become factions. The torch of discord blazes while the fire of patriotism expires, and the fierce and unholy passions which have rent the Republic survive its ruin. May our beloved city prove an exception to these sad examples.

Gentlemen, the duties on which we are about to enter are not classed with those of high political dignity; but if they are less fascinating to the ambitious, they are not without attraction to the benevolent.

We are intrusted with the care of institutions which have a daily bearing upon the morals, education, health, and comfort of our fellow-citizens. Our population exceeds that of more than one State at the time of admission into the Union. Its interests are not the less precious, because they are condensed in one spot. While the political government are occupied with counsels which look to the wealth and safety and glory of the nation, what better can we do than to consult together for the happiness of those among whom many of us were born and all of us live, and which is indissolubly linked to our own.

On you, gentlemen, I shall rely for concurrence, in whatever may tend to this object, and I will refer by messages to your intelligence and consideration all matters that, by the charter, require that direction.

On the twelfth of January, the subject of the flats lying to the eastward of Faneuil Hall Market came under the consideration of the City Council, and a committee was raised and invested with full authority to fill them up; and to borrow money for that object, on the terms and on the conditions and restrictions contained in the vote on that subject of the preceding City Council. In October, the superintendent of these operations reported them to be finished, and the cost of filling the flats up as having been *seventeen thousand three hundred dollars.*

On the nineteenth of the same month, a petition from a number of citizens was presented, praying for such an alteration in the city charter, that the warden and inspectors in the respective wards may have the right to receive the vote of any person duly qualified, though his name be not borne on the voting list. The subject was referred to a committee of both branches of the City Council, of which the Mayor was chairman, who, on the second of February, reported that "it would not be expedient to grant the right prayed for, to the warden and inspectors, as it would be giving them the power of deciding upon the qualifications of voters amid the urgent business of an election; that such a power would be liable to great interruption in its exercise, under such unfavorable circumstances; would produce disputes and delay, and give rise to different decisions in different wards under similar circumstances and evidence, tending also to render the lists of the voters imperfect, and in the end useless, as the citizens would be remiss in procuring their names to be entered, knowing that the remedy could be done at the polls. On the whole subject, the Committee refer to a report made December twenty-second, 1828,[1] to the last City Council, (which was then printed and distributed,) "for an elaborate exposition of facts and principles relative to this subject." It is on the whole believed, that whatever improvement can be made in the means of enabling the citizen to ascertain whether his name be inserted on the list of voters, and to enable him to have it thus placed, prior to the election, ought to be adopted; but that no government is bound to protect its citizens against wilful negligence and inattention to their own privileges. By this report two resolutions were submitted, the first requesting and directing the Assessors to take proper measures for making out the voting lists, in each ward, by noting the names of the qualified voters at the time of making out the tax lists, so that the voting lists may be completed in each ward as near as may be at the

[1] See page 237.

same time with the tax lists of such ward; and that they prepare and transmit to the Mayor and Aldermen, corrected voting lists of all the wards, on or before the first day of October, in each year.

The second, declaring it to be the duty of the Mayor and Aldermen, as soon as they shall have received a certified transcript of the voting lists, pursuant to the preceding resolution, to cause a copy thereof to be posted in some public place in each ward, and to give public notice, in one or more newspapers of the several places in which such lists shall be posted. The above report was accepted, and the resolutions passed, in the City Council.

On the second of February, 1829, a committee of the City Council was appointed on the memorial of the Directors of the House of Juvenile Offenders, of which the Mayor was Chairman, who reported, that "they had repaired to the site of the institution for the purpose of inspection, and examining into the state of its discipline, government, and general condition, and had a full conference and comparison of views with the Directors and Superintendents of said House and of the House of Industry, with which the same is in some measure connected; and after due examination into the premises, the Committee are gratified in expressing their approbation of the fidelity, industry, and ability, which are manifested in the administration of the affairs of the institution, by the Directors and other officers, and their persuasion of the real advantages resulting and promised to the City and Commonwealth from the system established and enforced by those who have the management of it, in all the departments; and that the thanks of the community are specially due to those individuals who have devoted, and persevere in devoting, their time and attention to the advancement of its interests, with no other reward but that of conscious benevolence, and a regard to the cause of humanity." The Report concluded with a recommendation to the City Council to carry into view the measures suggested by those Directors, which were presented in the form of a bill, defining more precisely the powers and duties of those Directors, and of the other officers of the institution.

On the ninth of February, the Mayor nominated Thomas C. Amory, Chief Engineer of the Fire Department, which was concurred in by the City Council; and on the same day all the Assistant Engineers of the last year were nominated, and appointed by unanimous vote of that body. And on the twenty-ninth of the same month the Assistant Engineers all presented a memorial to the City Council, "requesting that measures may be taken, as soon as consistent with the convenience of the city authorities, to elect others to supply their places; and that in the mean time they will act as heretofore, and give all the aid and assistance in their power in subduing the common enemy." On the twenty-fifth of March ensuing, a vote passed the Board of Aldermen, giving their thanks to the late Assistant Engineers of the Fire Department, for the fidelity and alacrity uniformly manifested by them in the discharge of their arduous duties, with an assurance of the sense entertained by the Board of the value of their services and example, in promoting the efficient organization of that department. On the same day, the vacancies thus created were filled by electing twelve other citizens to constitute a new board of Assistant Engineers. And on the first of April ensuing, the salary of one thousand dollars for the Chief Engineer was established by the city authorities, to be computed from the sixteenth of the preceding February, and paid quarterly. Until this time the services of the Chief Engineer had been gratuitously rendered.

In February, 1828, petitions having been presented to the Legislature of the State by the proprietors of wharves at the northerly part of the city, for permission to extend them into the channel of the harbor, the Mayor, apprehensive that such a permission might injuriously affect the free navigation of the channel, requested the Legislature to suspend its proceedings, and by special message brought the subject before the City Council, as being obviously of great importance; stating that, although it is quite conceivable, that, in certain situations, wharves may be extended to some reasonable length into the channel without detriment to the harbor, yet it may be expected, that privileges granted to one set of proprietors, will be claimed with great importunity by others; and that embarrassment may arise to the city government from precedents, established without due consideration; that it by no means follows of course, that, because a license may be granted to extend a wharf in a place where the channel is wide, and where the current would not be injuriously affected, a similar permission should be given in other cases, to which the dimensions of the channel and the effect on the current would present serious objections. Caution and deliberate examination by impartial judges, seemed to him requisite to make proper discrimination, to preserve limits and terms to every such license, as well as to the mode of carrying it into effect. In some positions, wharves erected on piles might be tolerated, which, if of solid construction, would be formidable nuisances. The Mayor, therefore, suggested the expediency of appointing commissioners, composed of merchants and others acquainted with the circumstances of the harbor, to examine and report upon every such application, such facts and opinions as may guide the city government in deciding on its merits; and that every permission granted by the Legislature should be on condition, that the work be executed in a mode satisfactory to the agents of the city government. This recommendation resulted at first in the passing, by the Board of Aldermen, of two resolutions, requesting the Mayor to present a remonstrance on the subject, in behalf of the City Council, and suggesting the expediency of having the entire power over the whole subject delegated to the city authorities. These resolutions were, however, non-concurred in the Common Council, and an order passed proposing a joint committee of the City Council, to take such measures as they may deem proper to protect the rights and interests of the city, in the extension of wharves into the channel of the harbor, with power to appear before the Committee of the Legislature that had the subject in hearing; and, if necessary, to employ the City Solicitor to maintain the rights of the city in the premises. In this resolution the Mayor and Aldermen concurred.

In April, 1829, the Mayor communicated a letter from a committee appointed by the citizens of Augusta, in the State of Georgia, stating "that that city had recently suffered greatly in consequence of a tremendous conflagration," which had consumed about two hundred houses, and deprived more than fifteen hundred persons of a house, and praying relief. The City Council accordingly ordered, that a copy of the letter should be sent to each of the pastors of the several churches in Boston, and authorized the Mayor to recommend, in behalf of the Board, a contribution thereon for the relief of those sufferers. On the twenty-fifth of May, Alderman Armstrong, as Treasurer of the contributions of the several churches in the city for the relief of the sufferers of Augusta, stated, that the amount collected was two thousand two hundred and forty-seven dollars and fifty-eight cents, which the City Council authorized the Mayor to transmit to the Committee appointed by the sufferers to receive contributions, which was immediately done, and in June following, the receipt of that amount was acknowledged by the Committee, in a letter to the Mayor, "expressing the grateful feelings with which so acceptable a benefaction had been received, heightened by the reflection, that neither distance nor the absence of intimate relations could repress an exercise of liberality so honorable to his fellow-citizens." This letter was ordered by the City Council to be entered at large on their records, and be published.

In May, 1829, it having been represented to the Mayor, that causes were slowly but certainly operating unfavorable effects upon the navigable waters of the inner harbor, and that the part of the channel extending from the Long Wharf, or thereabouts, southerly to the new bridge at South Boston, is gradually becoming more shallow from various causes; that vessels lying at the wharves in that space are endangered by easterly and northeasterly storms; and that there is no position, in that quarter, which can safely be occupied by steamboats, owing to the peculiarity of their construction, he presented the subject by special message to the attention and care of the city government, stating that if the flats, lying in the channel, (beyond the reach of individual claims,) were the property of the city, improvements might be made upon them by means of breakwaters or island wharves, that would afford effectual protection to the wharves and harbor in that quarter, and obviate the increasing shallowness of the channel; that such improvements might be made without expense to the city, and possibly on contracts that would afford some ultimate revenue; that the flats are manifestly not, and can never become, of value to the Commonwealth, except indirectly, as they may be subservient to the safeguard and navigation of the harbor; and that it could not be doubted, that upon suitable application on behalf of the city to the Legislature, a cession might be obtained of the flats above-mentioned, and which, being in possession of the city, might, under their direction and authority, be converted to th public benefit; that it would seem more proper and necessar that these flats should become the property of the city, ina much as memorials are frequently presented to the Legislatu for private grants and immunities, by the proprietors of wharv and estates lying in that neighborhood, (and others may anticipated,) of the reasonableness or injurious tendency which, as well as of the limitations and regulations to whic if granted, they ought to be subjected, the city governme would possess the most competent means of deciding, t premises being constantly under their observation. The May therefore, suggested the appointment of a committee, with f powers to apply to and endeavor to obtain from the Legis ture a grant of the premises, or of a portion thereof, sufficie for the purposes above expressed. These views of the May were immediately carried into effect in the City Council, appointment of a committee for the purposes expressed in t message.

In June following, the Committee reported, that the vie presented by the Mayor were correct, and confirmed by t opinion of the Boston Marine Society, who had investigated t subject at their request; and resolutions were reported a passed by the City Council, authorizing the Mayor to apply the Legislature for a grant of the flats specified, and the Sen tors and Representatives of the city were requested to aid obtaining the grant.

In February, 1829, on a petition signed by the requis number of qualified voters, a warrant was issued by the C Council for a general meeting of citizens, on a day appoint for that purpose, to give in their ballots, by yea and nay, on t following resolutions: —

1. *Resolved*, That in our opinion it is expedient for the Co monwealth to construct a railroad, on the most eligible rou from Boston to the western line of the county of Berkshire, that, in conjunction with the authorities of the State of N York, it may be extended to the most desirable point on t Hudson River, near Albany or Troy; and also from Boston the Pawtucket River, at or near Providence, in the State Rhode Island.

2. *Resolved*, That in case the Legislature should deem

expedient to construct said railroads, wholly at the expense of the State, that the city government be authorized and requested to apply to the Legislature for an act to enable any cities, towns, or bodies corporate, or individuals, to subscribe for such portion of said stock as may not be taken by the State, on such terms and conditions as may be deemed expedient.

On the day appointed, a general meeting of the citizens of Boston was holden in Fanueil Hall, and both resolutions were passed by upwards of three thousand votes in the affirmative to less than sixty in the negative.

An application to that effect was immediately made by the City Council to the Legislature, in conformity with those resolutions.

In November, a number of citizens petitioned the City Council, praying them to appropriate a suitable piece of land on the flats between the Western Avenue and Boylston Street, in aid of, and as a convenient terminus for warehouses, and a depot for a railroad, then proposed from the city to Brattleborough, in Vermont. This petition was referred to the Mayor and Alderman Loring, and to Messrs. Everett, Ellis, and Rayner, of the Common Council.

This Committee, in December following, reported, "that the establishment of railroads connecting the city with the interior country, is of such vital importance to the prosperity of the former, as to leave no room to doubt, that the city government will ever be actuated by a disposition to promote the success of these operations, (when plans for them shall be matured,) by all reasonable aid and means within the limits of their constitutional authority. The location of land for the termination of such railroads in the city, appears to the Committee to involve many important considerations, which, in the present incipient stage of the business, the City Council are not competent to examine and weigh. It is a measure, also, upon which any company obtaining a charter would reserve the right of deciding for itself; and a premature assignment of lands for the proposed object might not only be rejected by such company, but prevent subscriptions to the stock by individuals, who would be dissatisfied in perceiving the adoption of views, which might preclude them from an entire freedom of voting and deciding upon what might be deemed a very essential feature in any enterprise of this kind." The Committee, therefore, recommended the passage of a resolve: — "That it is not expedient for the City Council to make any grant or assignment of land for the accommodation of railroads, until one or more charters of incorporation shall be obtained for the construction of such railroads, and the City Council shall thus be enabled to act upon distinct information of all circumstances, in reference as well to the provisions of such charters, and as to their authority to make such grants under the charter of the city and the laws of the Commonwealth." This resolve was passed in concurrence by both branches of the City Council.

CHAPTER XX.

CITY GOVERNMENT. 1830.

HARRISON GRAY OTIS, *Mayor*.[1]

Prosperous State of the City — Embarrassment of the Manufacturing Interests, and its Causes — Completion of the City Wharf — State of the City Debt — Sale of Public Lands — Condition of the Flats to the West of the Neck — State of the Court-Houses — Protection of our Outer Harbor — Centennial Celebration resolved upon — Grant of the City Hall for Sales of Domestic Manufactures Rescinded — Sale of Spirituous Liquors on the Common Prohibited — Old State House to be called "The City Hall" — Centennial Celebration of the Settlement of Boston.

THE records of the Mayor and Aldermen on the fourth of January, 1830, state, that "a message was received from the Mayor, expressing his regrets that indisposition prevented his having the honor of meeting the gentlemen of the Board of Aldermen and Common Council in their own chambers; and, therefore, he respectfully requested their presence at his house, at such hour as might be agreeable to them, to qualify for their respective functions. The members of both branches of the City Council then proceeded to the mansion-house of the Mayor, where the government was organized with the usual solemnities; after which, the Mayor delivered the following inaugural address: —

GENTLEMEN OF THE CITY COUNCIL: —

The season has returned, in which we who are chosen by our fellow-citizens to administer their municipal concerns for the current year, are expected to enter upon the discharge of our respective functions.

Our acknowledgments are due to the Great Disposer of all events for having preserved to our constituents, throughout the

[1] The whole number of votes were 1,966; of which the Mayor received 1,844. The Aldermen were Henry J. Oliver, John F. Loring, Samuel T. Armstrong, Benjamin Russell, Winslow Lewis, Charles Wells, Moses Williams, John B. M'Cleary.

past year, the possession of the principal blessings, on which depend the welfare and comfort of populous cities. The healthiness of the city, always unrivalled, has been preserved at least to its usual standard. With the advantages of health have been united those of plenty. Our markets and magazines are filled to exuberance with all that is needful for sustenance, or conducive to comfort and luxury, at reasonable and reduced prices. We live also in a state of peace, which seems not to be threatened with approaching interruption. The public concerns of the State and nation are thus far well-administered, and no indication is manifested, in the communications of the executive government of the United States, of plans or schemes of policy calculated to inspire apprehensions of measures unfavorable to the interests of this community. These circumstances seem to embrace all that is requisite for the prosperity of an industrious and enterprising people. They have, however, for the last two years, been counteracted by others, which have opposed serious impediments to our advancement. The capitalists and merchants of this city, influenced by the strong demonstrations manifested in other parts of the Union in favor of the manufacturing policy and by the patronage of government, and allured by fallacious estimates of great profits made by others, in violence of their natural predilections and habits, have invested an undue portion of capital in manufacturing establishments. Their example was followed by those whose capital consisted wholly in their spirit of enterprise. Hence ensued a disastrous competition. The establishments bottomed on substantial funds were stimulated to launch forth beyond the natural and reasonable limits of those funds. They could not renounce the market without ruin, and their rivals could not maintain themselves in it without sacrifices, that must end in ruin. This crisis was eagerly seized by the British manufacturers as furnishing an occasion to extinguish, perhaps forever, the manufacturing spirit in this country; and they inundated our market with the redundancy of their own. Hence resulted an excessive plethora, and consequent depreciation of value, loss, and sacrifice by forced sales. Owing to these incidents, combined with the unwise and improvident system of our legislation as respects manufacturing corporations, and with the uncertainty of the future policy of the government, disturbed by the vehemence of opposition to the protecting system originating here, hence extending to other States, and brought back by violent reaction — add to these the panic which always aggravates calamitous events — it has happened, as might be foreseen, that property vested in manufactures has for a time become valueless as a medium of exchange, or a foundation for credit or accommodation in any form. By these means, many of our worthy citizens are ruined, others cramped and embarrassed, and our whole community become less able to embark in other enterprises, which would augment the wealth and resources of the city. There is, however, a cheering prospect that the fierceness of this storm has overblown; that our affairs, in common with those of other parts of the world, will gradually find their level, with less of injury to the city than our fears would seem to justify; and that, after the struggle of half a century, in peace and in war, our nation will have secured the privilege and the faculty of manufacturing for itself. Neither the state of public sentiment, nor the condition of our treasury at the close of the year, authorized the expectation that appropriations would be made for expensive public buildings, or improvements of any description. Accordingly, nothing in this line has been attempted. The City Wharf has been completed, and promises a revenue, which, after a few years, will reimburse its cost, and be then applicable to other objects. Two new engine-houses, two school-houses, and a cottage for the resident Physician on Hospital Island, are the only new buildings erected the past year. Five new reservoirs have also been completed.

The amount of the city debt, on the first of May last, was $911,850. Of which the sum paid by the Committee on the reduction of the public debt, beyond the amount of moneys borrowed to be applied to that object, is $54,100. There was also borrowed for the payment of debt to the Mercantile Wharf Corporation, and for the completion of Faneuil Hall Market, the sum of $25,880.75. So that the true deduction from the amount of the debt as it stood in May last, up to this day, is $28,219.25. Thus leaving the aggregate amount of the city debt at this time, $883,630. The only personal assets on which reliance can be placed, as a partial offset against this debt, are bonds and securities due to the city, of $257,341.42.

Apart from these, the only fund available for the reduction or extinguishment of this debt, must be found in the city's lands; and it follows, of course, that in the judicious management and disposal of these lands can be found the only resources for public credit, and for the ultimate improvement of the city, without resort to direct taxation, and that no object can be more worthy of our constant vigilance.

I have great faith in the intrinsic value of these lands, which, owing to the vesture in which they are permitted to remain, is not sufficiently appreciated. They certainly will not take care of themselves. It is essential to any project for the lucrative sale of them, that a prospective plan should be adopted and established, so that purchasers may calculate with reasonable certainty upon future, as well as present advantages. It is also indispensable to the success of such project, that moderate appropriations should be made, from time to time, to enable the commissioner, under instructions from the Mayor and Aldermen, at the sole expense of the city, or by coöperating with other proprietors, (as the case may be,) to make such drains, dikes, and canals, as may put certain parts of the land in a marketable condition. I am far from recommending the expenditure of large amounts upon uncertain speculation; but am also satisfied, that, without some disbursement, nothing valuable can be effected. For this purpose, the needful sums might be borrowed as wanted, reimbursable from the first sales; thus making a nominal temporary addition to the debt, for the sake of its sure, effective, and ultimate payment. There could be little danger of serious aberration in this procedure. These lands are in some places contiguous to those of individual proprietors, whose well-directed sagacity and enterprise have converted premises possessing no supereminent advantages into populous streets and squares, and at rates, which, realized by the city, would not only extinguish its debt, but contribute an ample fund for future improvements, and relief from our annual burden.

Nothing is perceived to inhibit those intrusted with the sale of your lands from looking over the shoulders of these wise stewards and profiting by their experience, but funds necessary for occasional advances. In this connection it is my duty to state, that the condition of the flats west of the neck is regarded by eminent physicians as becoming pregnant with danger to the health of the city. It is an unwelcome truth, that the intermittent fever is no longer confined to those regions, to which it was until lately regarded as endemial, but occasionally appears in more northerly latitudes, which were thought to be happily exempted from that scourge. Our own State, (so far as I am informed,) and certainly our own city, are, under Providence, strangers to this afflicting and enervating disease, which is rarely dislodged from positions which it once occupies. But, if such be the predisposition of the atmosphere of the country around us, we are admonished by it not to set danger at defiance, by fostering upon our borders an immense morass, circumvented with solid dikes, and from its position a receptacle of the seeds of disease.

The state of our principal court-houses and of the land connected with them, and of other county property, demands serious investigation, and is not free from embarrassing circumstances. This land, lying in the centre of the city, is of great value in itself; but, cut off from streets by the public buildings, it could not be sold for a fair equivalent. These buildings are not only altogether ill adapted to the exigencies of the city, but the principal court-house is of a construction so defective as to have been condemned upon a regular survey as unsafe. It is now shored up in some parts by buttresses. It is believed, that no alternative will remain to the city but to sell all the land and buildings, and to apply the proceeds, as far as they will go, to the purchase of another site, suitable for the accommodation of all our courts, and city government, and officers. It is not my intention to recommend this measure definitively at this time. But, under a deep conviction that it will bear examination, and be found at no distant period consistent with true economy, and essential to the public accommodation, I shall crave your permission, in due time, to submit to your inspection the details of a plan for this purpose, not yet quite matured. To some share in these lands and buildings, the town of Chelsea, as a portion of the county, is understood to have a claim. The best interest of the city requires that this claim should, on some equitable principles, be adjusted and extinguished; and that with it should terminate the existing connection between Chelsea and this city. It seems, at first blush, preposterous, that this city should be compelled to maintain the organization and formalities of a county jurisdiction, in consequence merely of this connection. It is attended with great additional embarrassment, and the expense of it is not subject to the ordinary revision and control of the city government. Its dissolution must be preliminary to any substantial and salutary reform in the organization of our courts, and the administration of justice.

The affairs of the Houses of Industry, Reformation, Correction, and the Jail, have been conducted in the most meritorious manner by their respective Overseers, and Superintendents, according to their means. But so much is wanted to place them on a footing commensurate with the claims of humanity and the feelings of the age — so much beyond our present resources — that I refrain from enlarging on the subject; expressing merely the hope, that some cheap provision may be made, by temporary buildings for the more effectual separation of the insane from the children of vice, and the least atrocious of those from hardened offenders; and that the time is approaching, when the unfortunate debtor will not be domiciliated or confounded with either of these classes.

From undoubted information it is ascertained, that the danger of our harbor, from the alluvion of some of the islands, and the breach of the sea over the beaches, is constantly increasing. A confidence is felt, that the national government will continue its aid, to secure us against the more formidable inroads of the sea in our lower harbor. But additional protection is wanted for the interior positions, and for the existing wharves. A large surface of flats in the southeasterly quarter of the city, beyond the limits of those appendant to the upland, and entirely useless for any but the proposed object, would serve as a foundation for breakwaters; and, if, owned by the city, might be ceded for that purpose to companies who would erect them. Application has been made to the Commonwealth for a release of any claim they may have to the premises, and no objection is foreseen to their granting what is of no value in its present circumstances, but in the benefit of which the State would participate, when made useful to its metropolis.

A copious supply of fresh water is a convenience, the want of which becomes constantly more imperative. If, upon due consideration, it should not be determined expedient for the city to erect hydrants on its own account, the propriety of granting that immunity to a company will naturally engage and command the attention of the city government.

The transcendent success of the railroad system in England, as well as the encouraging result, so far as it has been attempted in this country, support the hope, that Massachusetts will not linger in the rear of that enterprise, from the issue of which no other State has more to expect than herself.

GENTLEMEN OF THE COMMON COUNCIL, — It is peculiarly your province to devise all practicable means for alleviating the weight of taxation, and retrenching the expenses of the city government. I have anxiously reviewed the ordinary heads of expenditure, with a desire to suggest to you any savings that may be made, consistently with the accustomed wants, habits, and expectations of our fellow-citizens. I regret to say, that I can discern none of much importance. The population of the city is increasing. The support of the School and Fire establishment is expected to be maintained in full energy. The city is at present defectively lighted, though additions are constantly making to the number of lamps and quantity of oil. Many streets are unpaved, the claims of whose inhabitants to equal accommodations with their neighbors, are extremely importunate. Occasions constantly present themselves for the widening of streets, which, if not improved, will not recur for many years. It is my own opinion, that the cleaning and the sweeping of the streets are practised to a needless and pernicious extreme; but such hitherto seems to be the pleasure of our fellow-citizens, to which I have consequently instructed the Superintendent of Streets to conform. Of the sums appropriated for the current expenses of this year, more than nineteen thousand dollars have been paid to meet the arrearages of the last financial year, arising from outstanding contracts and demands. It is confidently believed, that no such items will appear to trench upon the appropriations for the current service; still, it is apprehended that no very important reduction can be made in our annual expenditure.

On the subject of salaries, I have but a single remark, that can be made with decorum. Should a general reduction of the salaries of your city officers be decided on, I shall not avail myself of the protection provided by charter for the Mayor's salary during the period for which he is elected; but shall conform to what I may discern to be the public sentiment.

Nothing remains for me but to renew to you all my sincere expression of the good wishes inspired by the associations of the season, and to assure you of the great pleasure I shall derive in my humble attempts to give effect to your ordinances.

H. G. Otis.

January 4, 1830.

On the eighth of February, 1830, the Mayor communicated a letter from the Hon. John Davis, Thomas L. Winthrop, James Savage, and the Rev. Dr. Thaddeus M. Harris, a Committee of the Massachusetts Historical Society, "respecting the expediency of celebrating the second century of the foundation of Boston, which happens the present year," which, being read, was referred to a committee, consisting of the Mayor, Aldermen Russell and Lewis, and Messrs. Bigelow, Minns, James, Eveleth, and Gregg, of the Common Council, to consider and report.

On the first of March ensuing, this Committee reported, that the seventeenth of September next will be the commencement of the third century, since the name of Boston was first conferred upon this city by the Court of Assistants then held at Charlestown, and that there would be a propriety in the public celebration of that day by the citizens of Boston and their government; that a public address commemorative of that event and its all-important consequences be, on that day, delivered at some suitable place in this city; that a committee of arrangements be authorized to engage an orator for that day, and to make such other dispositions for the honorable notice of it as they may deem proper.

The report being accepted in both branches, the Mayor and Benjamin T. Pickman, President of the Common Council, and the other members who constituted the Committee that made the above report, were appointed a Committee of Arrangements to carry the same into effect.

This Committee invited Josiah Quincy, then President of Harvard University, to deliver the oration, and Charles Sprague, Esq., a distinguished citizen of Boston, to deliver a poem on that occasion, both of whom accepted the appointment.

On the eighth of March, 1830, an order was passed by the Board of Aldermen, "that notice be given to the New England Society for the promotion of Manufactures and the Mechanic

Arts, that, after the expiration of six months, the vote which passed the City Council on the nineteenth of November, 1827,[1] granting the exclusive use of the hall over the Market for the purpose of their semi-annual sales, from the fifteenth day of March to the fifteenth day of April, and from the fifteenth day of August to the fifteenth day of September, free of rent, until the further order of the City Council, and that six months' notice should be given to the said Society of the rescinding of this privilege, be and the same is hereby rescinded." This being passed by the Board of Aldermen, was, on the twenty-second of March, non-concurred by the Common Council; and on the twenty-ninth, a committee of conference was appointed, consisting of the Mayor, and Alderman Armstrong, and Messrs. Waters and Winslow Wright, of the Common Council, on the subject of the difference between the two Boards. On the third day of May, this Committee reported, that the privilege granted to the New England Society was experimental and a temporary accommodation; that a diversity of opinion existed among those interested in manufactures, as to the advantage of persevering in these semi-annual sales; that whatever course the manufacturers might adopt on the subject, the "true inquiry of the city government was, whether the advantage indirectly accruing to the city itself, from their continuance, was equivalent to the emolument which may reasonably be anticipated directly to result from another mode of disposing of the premises. Your Committee are unable to discern that that is the case. The manufactures of this part of the country have now attained so good a standard, and to such celebrity; that whenever the supply throughout the United States does not exceed the demand, they will be sought for by customers, whether to be had at private or public sales. The use of the building is of little or no value to those who fabricate the goods. The amount of the storage thus saved (if in fact it be saved) averaged on the whole quantity of goods sold, cannot be felt in the price of the goods, either by the individual seller or the purchaser; nor can the accommodation be very important to the auctioneers, all of whom have capacious warehouses. On the other hand, the state of the city and its finances impose upon its

[1] See p. 251.

government the duty to avail themselves of every fair source of revenue in its occupation of its property." The Committee declared their belief that a fair rent might be obtained for the use of the hall; and that if the New England Society should be inclined to persevere in their public sales, there might be a disposition to allow them the use of Faneuil Hall in lieu of that in their present occupation. The Committee, therefore, recommended that the Common Council recede from their vote of the twenty-second of March, *non-concurring* with the order of the Board of Aldermen, passed on the eighth of March, and that they concur in passing the same; and that the Mayor and Aldermen be authorized to lease the hall over the Market, heretofore used by the New England Society, upon the best terms they can obtain.

This report was accepted, and the order passed in both branches of the City Council.

In May of this year, a Committee of the Society for the Suppression of Intemperance petitioned the Mayor and Aldermen to cause a band of music to be stationed on the Common on the afternoons and evenings of the General Election and Fourth of July, such a practice having, in their judgment, a tendency to promote order and suppress an inclination to riot and intemperance, which, on the report of a committee, was ordered, and an adequate appropriation was voted.

Orders at the same meeting were passed similar to those issued in 1828, directing the constables of the city to prosecute any person who should sell on the Common, in the malls, or in any of the streets contiguous thereto, spirituous liquors or any mixed liquors; or who should, upon any of said places, play at cards, or dice, or with any implements used in gaming, on the day of General Election, Artillery Election, and the Anniversary of the Declaration of Independence; and before granting permission to any person to erect booths, notice to the above effect should be given, and also by publishing copies of this order in the newspapers and in suitable public places.

On the twenty-fifth of June, the Mayor, by special message, after referring to the relations and interests of the city, in respect of the public buildings at its command, for public purposes, recommended the giving to the Committee charged with the alteration and repairs of the Old State House, full power to prepare in that building chambers for the accommodation of the Mayor and Aldermen and Common Council and such of the city officers as could be conveniently provided for in those premises. This recommendation was immediately sanctioned by the City Council, and the arrangements having been made as suggested in that message, the City Council first met in the chambers prepared for their accommodation on the seventeenth of September, 1830, the day assigned for the centennial celebration of the foundation of the city, and the two branches being assembled in Convention, the Mayor announced to them the name "by which the edifice" (called the Old State House) "shall hereafter be called, namely, — CITY HALL," — and then made to the Convention an address; "after which," the records state, "the two branches went in procession to the Old South Church, escorted by the Ancient and Honorable Artillery Company, where an address was delivered by the Honorable Josiah Quincy, President of Harvard University, and a poem by Charles Sprague, Esq., and other services were performed in commemoration of the close of the second century from the first settlement of Boston."

On the twentieth of September, votes were passed by both branches of the City Council, with customary expressions of interest and respect to Mr. Otis and Mr. Quincy for their respective addresses, and to Mr. Sprague for his poem; and copies of each were requested for the press. They were published accordingly, and constitute the remaining and final chapters of this history.

CHAPTER XXI.

CITY GOVERNMENT. 1830.

HARRISON GRAY OTIS, *Mayor.*

Address of the Mayor to the Members of the City Council, on the Removal of the Municipal Government to the Old State House, on the Morning of the 17th of September, 1830.

GENTLEMEN OF THE COMMON COUNCIL: —

I HAVE the honor to announce to you, that the Mayor and Aldermen have concurred with your request to change the name of this building, and to order that it be henceforth called and known by the name of the *City Hall.*

GENTLEMEN OF THE CITY COUNCIL: — The intimations which I have received from many individuals of your body, have left me no room to doubt of your general expectation, that this first occasion of our meeting in this chamber should not be permitted to pass away without something more than a brief record of the event upon your journals. The spot on which we are convened is patriot ground. It was consecrated by our pious ancestors to the duties of providing for the welfare of their infant settlement, and for a long series of years was occupied in succession by the great and good men, whom Providence raised up to establish the institutions and liberties of their country.

There are none, who have paid even a superficial attention to the process of their perceptions, who are not conscious that a prolific source of intellectual pleasures and pains is found in our faculty of associating the remembrance of characters and events, which have most interested our affections and passions, with the spot whereon the first have lived and the latter have occurred. It is to the magic of this local influence that we are indebted for the charm which recalls the sports and pastimes of our childhood, the joyous days of youth, when buoyant spirits invested all surrounding objects with the color of the rose. It is this which brings before us, as we look back through the vista of riper years, past enjoyments and afflictions, aspiring hopes and bitter disappointments, the temptations we have encountered, the snares which have entangled us, the dangers we have escaped, the fidelity or treachery of friends. It is this which enables us to surround ourselves with the images of those who were associates in the scenes we contemplate, and to hold sweet converse with the spirits of the departed, whom we have loved or honored in the places which shall know them no more.

But the potency of these local associations is not limited to the sphere of our personal experience. We are qualified by it to derive gratification from what we have heard and read of other times, to bring forth forgotten treasures from the recesses of memory, and recreate fancy in the fields of imagination. The regions which have been famed in sacred or fabulous history; the mountains, plains, isles, rivers, celebrated in the classic page; the seas traversed by the discoverers of new worlds; the fields in which empires have been lost and won, are scenes of enchantment for the visitor who indulges the trains of perception, which either rush unbidden on his mind, or are courted by its voluntary efforts. This faculty it is, which, united with a disposition to use it to advantage, alone gives dignity to the passion for visiting foreign countries, and distinguishes the philosopher, who moralizes on the turf that covers the mouldering dust of ambition, valor, or patriotism, from the fashionable vagabond, who flutters among the flowers which bloom over their graves.

Among all the objects of mental association, ancient buildings and ruins affect us with the deepest and most vivid emotions. They were the works of beings like ourselves. While a mist impervious to mortal view hangs over the future, all our fond imaginings of the things which "eye hath not seen nor ear heard," in the eternity to come, are inevitably associated with the men, the events and things, which have gone to join the eternity that is past. When imagination has in vain essayed to rise beyond the stars which "proclaim the story of their birth," inquisitive to know the occupations and condition of the sages and heroes whom we hope to join in a higher empyrean, she drops her weary wing, and is compelled to alight among the fragments of "gorgeous palaces and cloud-capp'd towers," which cover their human ruins; and, by aid of these localities, to ruminate upon their virtues and their faults, on their deeds in the cabinet and in the field, and upon the revolutions of the successive ages in which they lived. To this propensity may be traced the sublimated feelings of the man, who, familiar with the stories of Sesostris, the Pharaohs, and the Ptolemies, surveys the pyramids, not merely as stupendous fabrics of mechanical skill, but as monuments of the pride and ambitious folly of kings, and of the debasement and oppression of the wretched myriads, by whose labors they were raised to the skies. To this must be referred the awe and contrition which solemnize and melt the heart of the Christian who looks into the Holy Sepulchre, and believes he sees the place where the Lord was laid. From this originate the musings of the scholar, who, amid the ruins of the Parthenon and the Acropolis, transports his imagination to the age of Pericles and Phidias ; — the reflections of all not dead to sentiment, who descend to the subterranean habitation of Pompeii, — handle the utensils that once ministered to the wants, and the ornaments subservient to the luxury of a polished city, — behold the rut of wheels upon the pavement hidden for ages from human sight, — and realize the awful hour when the hum of industry and the song of joy, the wailing of the infant and the garrulity of age, were suddenly and forever silenced by the fiery deluge which buried the city, until accident and industry, after the lapse of nearly eighteen centuries, revealed its ruins to the curiosity and cupidity of the passing age.

These remarks, in which you may think there is more of truth than of novelty, have been suggested by the experiment, which, a few days since, I attempted, to condense in the compass of a short address a few ideas appropriate to this occasion. Beginning to think upon matters connected with the old Town House, I found my mind confused, and overwhelmed with the multitudinous associations of our early history which it naturally induced. To indulge them to a great extent, would trench upon the province and the hour assigned to another, whose eloquence will furnish the principal gratification of the day. It is, therefore, indispensable, to confine myself to a few observations, and consequently to do but imperfect justice to my feelings and the subject.

The history of the Town House, considered merely as a compages of brick and wood, is short and simple. It was erected between the years 1657 and 1659, and was principally of wood, as far as can be ascertained. The contractor received six hundred and eighty pounds, on a final settlement in full of all contracts. This was probably the whole amount of the cost, being double that of the estimate — a ratio pretty regularly kept up in our times. The population of the town, sixty years afterwards, was about ten thousand; and it is allowing an increase beyond the criterion of its actual numbers at subsequent periods, to presume that at the time of the first erection of the Town House, it numbered three thousand souls. In 1711, the building was burnt to the ground, and soon afterwards built with brick. In 1747, the interior was again consumed by fire, and soon repaired in the form which it retained until the present improvement, with the exception of some alterations in the apartments made upon the removal of the Legislature to the new State House. The eastern chamber was originally occupied by the Council, afterwards by the Senate. The Representatives constantly held their sittings in the western chamber. The floor of these was supported by pillars, and terminated at each end by doors, and at one end by a flight of steps leading into State Street. In the day time, the doors were kept open, and the floor served as a walk for the inhabitants, always much frequented, and during the sessions of the courts, thronged. On the north side, were offices for the clerks of the supreme and inferior courts. In these the judges robed themselves, and walked in procession, followed by the bar, at the opening of the courts. Committee-rooms were provided in the upper story. Since the removal of the Legislature, it has been internally divided into apartments and leased for various uses in a mode familiar to you all, and it has now undergone great repairs. This floor being adapted to the accommodation of the city government, and principal officers, while the first floor is allotted to the post-office, newsroom, and private warehouses.

In this brief account of the natural body of the building, which it is believed comprehends whatever is material, there is nothing certainly dazzling or extraordinary. It exhibits no pomp of architectural grandeur or refined taste, and has no pretensions to vie with the magnificent structures of other countries or even of our own. Yet it is a goodly and venerable pile; and, with its recent improvements, is an ornament of the place, of whose liberty it was once the citadel. And it has an interest for Bostonians who enter it this day, like that which is felt by grown children for an ancient matron by whom they were reared, and whom, visiting after years of absence, they find her in her neat, chaste, old-fashioned attire, spruced up to receive them, with her comforts about her, and the same kind, hospitable, and excellent creature, whom they left in less flourishing circumstances. But to this edifice there is not only a natural but "a spiritual body," which is the immortal soul of Independence. Nor is there, on the face of the earth, another building, however venerable for its antiquity or stately in its magnificence, however decorated by columns and porticos, and cartoons, and statues, and altars, and outshining "the wealth of Ormus or of Ind," entitled in history to more honorable mention, or whose spires and turrets are surrounded with a more glorious halo, than this unpretending building.

This assertion might be justified by a review of the parts performed by those who have made laws for a century after the first settlement of Boston; of their early contention for their chartered rights; of their perils and difficulties with the natives; of their costly and heroic exertions in favor of the mother country in the common cause. But I pass over them all, replete as they are with interest, with wonder, and with moral. Events posterior to those growing out of them indeed, and taking from them their complexion, are considered by reflecting men as having produced more radical changes in the character, relations, prospects, and (so far as it becomes us to prophesy) in the destinies of the human family, than all other events and revolutions that have transpired since the Christian era. I do not say that the principles which have led to these events originated here. But I venture to assert that here, within these walls, they were first practically applied to a well-regulated machinery of human passions, conscious rights, and steady movements, which, forcing these United States to the summit of prosperity, has been adopted as a model by which other nations have been, and will yet be propelled on the railroad which leads to universal freedom. The power of these engines is self-moving, and the motion is perpetual. Sages and philosophers had discovered that the world was made for the people who inhabit it; and that kings were less entitled in their own right to its government than lions, whose claims to be lords of the forest are supported by physical prowess. But the books and treatises which maintained these doctrines were read by the admirers of the Lockes and Sidneys and Miltons and Harringtons, and replaced on their shelves as brilliant theories. Or, if they impelled to occasional action, it ended in bringing new tyrants to the throne and sincere patriots to the scaffold. But your progenitors who occupied these seats first taught a whole people systematically to combine the united force of their moral and physical energies; to learn the rights of insurrection, not as written in the language of the passions, but in codes and digests of its justifiable cases; to enforce them under the restraints of discipline; to define and limit its objects; to be content with success, and to make sure of its advantages. All this they did; and when the propitious hour had arrived, they called on their countrymen as the angel called upon the apostles, — "Come, rise up quickly, and the chains fell from their hands." The inspiring voice echoed through the welkin in Europe and America, and awakened nations. He who would learn the effects of it, must read the history of the world for the last half century. He who would anticipate the consequences must ponder well the probabilities with which time is pregnant for the next. The memory of these men is entitled to a full share of all the honor arising from the advantage derived to mankind from this change of condition, but yet is not chargeable with the crimes and misfortunes, more than is the memory of Fulton with the occasional bursting of a boiler.

Shall I then glance rapidly at some of the scenes and the actors who figured in them within these walls? Shall I carry you back to the controversies between Governor Barnard and the House of Representatives, commencing nearly seventy years ago, respecting the claims of the mother country to tax the Colonies without their consent? To the stand made against writs of assistance in the chamber now intended for your Mayor and Aldermen, where and when, according to John Adams, "Independence was born?" and whose star was then seen in the East by wise men. To the memorable vindication of the House of Representatives by one of its members? To the "Rights of the Colonies," adopted by the Legislature as a text book, and transmitted by their order to the British Ministry? To the series of patriotic resolutions, protests, and State papers, teeming with indignant eloquence and irresistible argument in opposition to the stamp and other tax acts? To the landing and quartering of troops in the town? To the rescinding of resolutions in obedience to royal mandates? To the removal of the seat of government, and the untiring struggle in which the Legislature was engaged for fourteen or fifteen years, supported by the Adamses, the Thachers, the Hawleys, the Hancocks, the Bowdoins, the Quincys, and their illustrious colleagues? In fact, the most important measures which led to the emancipation of the Colonies, according to Hutchinson, a competent judge, originated in this house, in this apartment, with those men, who, putting life and fortune on the issue, adopted for their motto, —

> "Let such, such only tread this sacred floor
> Who dare to love their country and be poor."

Events of a different complexion are also associated with the Boston Town House. At one time it was desecrated by the King's troops, quartered in the Representatives' chamber, and on the lower floor. At another time, cannon were stationed and pointed toward its doors. Below the balcony in King Street, on the doleful night of the fifth of March, the blood of the first victims to the military executioners was shed. On the appearance of the Governor in the street, he was surrounded by an immense throng, who, to prevent mischief to his person, though he had lost their confidence, forced him into this building, with the cry "to the Town House! to the Town House!" He then went forth into the balcony, and promising to use his endeavors to bring the offenders to justice, and advising the people to retire, they dispersed, vociferating "home! home!" The Governor and Council remained all night deliberating in dismal conclave, while the friends of their country bedewed their pillows with tears, — "such tears as patriots shed for dying laws." But I would not wish, under any circumstances, to dwell upon incidents like these, thankful as I am that time, which has secured our freedom, has extinguished our resentments. I therefore turn from these painful reminiscences, and refer you to the day when Independence, mature in age and loveliness, advanced with angelic grace from the chamber in which she was born into the same balcony, and holding in her hand the immortal scroll on which her name and character and claims to her inheritance were inscribed, received from the street, filled with an impenetrable phalanx, and windows glittering with a blaze of beauty, the heartfelt homage and electrifying peals of the men, women, and children of the whole city. The splendor of that glorious vision of my childhood seems to be now present to my view, and the harmony of that universal concert to vibrate in my ear.

Such, gentlemen, is the cursory and meagre chronicle of the men and the occurrences which have given celebrity to this building. And if it be true, that we are now before the altar, whence the coals were taken which have kindled the flame of liberty in two hemispheres, you will realize with me the sentiment already expressed, that the most interesting associations of the eventful history of the age might rise in natural trains, and be indulged and presented on this occasion without violence to propriety.

We, gentlemen, have now become, for a short period, occupants of this temple of Liberty. Henceforth, for many years, the city government will probably be here administered. The duties of its members are less arduous, painful, and dignified than those of the eminent persons who once graced these seats, and procured for us the privilege of admission to them. Yet, let not these duties be undervalued. They are of sufficient weight and importance to excite a conscientious desire in good minds, to cultivate a public spirit, and imitate with reverence great examples. There is ample scope for dispositions to serve our fellow-citizens in the department of the city government. It is charged with concerns affecting the daily comfort and prosperity of sixty thousand persons, a number exceeding that of several of these United States at the time of their admission into the Union. The results of their deliberations have an immediate bearing upon the morals, health, education, and purse of this community, and are generally of more interest to their feelings and welfare than the ordinary acts of State legislation. It is a community, which any man may regard as a subject of just pride to represent, rivalled by none in orderly and moral habits, general intelligence, commercial and mechanic skill, a spirit of national enterprise, and above all a vigilance for the interest of posterity manifested in the provision made for public education. No state of society can be found more happy and attractive than yours. Many of those who are in its first ranks rose from humble beginnings, and hold out encouragement to others to follow their steps. There is, so far as I can judge, more real equality, and a more general acquaintance and intercourse among the different vocations, than is elsewhere to be found in a populous city. Those of the middling class as respects wealth, the mechanics and the workingmen, are not only eligible, but constantly elected to all offices in state and city, in such proportion as they (constituting the great majority) see fit to assign. We enjoy the blessings of a healthy climate, delightful position, and ample resources for prosperity in commerce, manufactures, and the mechanic arts, all of which, I am persuaded, are at this moment gradually reviving, after some vicissitude from time and chance, which happen to all things. May we, and those who will succeed us, appreciate the responsibleness attached to our places by the merit of our predecessors; and, though we cannot serve our country to the same advantage, may we love it with equal fidelity. And may the Guardian Genius of our beloved city forever delight to dwell in these renovated walls!

CHAPTER XXII.

CITY GOVERNMENT. 1830.

HARRISON GRAY OTIS, *Mayor*.

Address to the Citizens of Boston, on the 17th of September, 1830, the Close of the Second Century from the First Settlement of the City. By Josiah Quincy, President of Harvard University.

OF all the affections of man, those which connect him with ancestry are among the most natural and generous. They enlarge the sphere of his interests; multiply his motives to virtue; and give intensity to his sense of duty to generations to come, by the perception of obligation to those which are past. In whatever mode of existence man finds himself, be it savage or civilized, he perceives that he is indebted for the far greater part of his possessions and enjoyments, to events over which he had no control; to individuals, whose names, perhaps, never reached his ear; to sacrifices, in which he never shared; and to sufferings, awakening in his bosom few and very transient sympathies.

Cities and empires, not less than individuals, are chiefly indebted for their fortunes to circumstances and influences independent of the labors and wisdom of the passing generation. Is our lot cast in a happy soil, beneath a favored sky, and under the shelter of free institutions? How few of all these blessings do we owe to our own power, or our own prudence! How few, on which we cannot discern the impress of long past generations!

It is natural, that reflections of this kind should awaken curiosity concerning the men of past ages. It is suitable, and characteristic of noble natures, to love to trace in venerated institutions the evidences of ancestral worth and wisdom; and to cherish that mingled sentiment of awe and admiration, which takes possession of the soul, in the presence of ancient, deep-laid, and massy monuments of intellectual and moral power.

Under impulses thus natural and generous, at the invitation of your municipal authorities, you have assembled, Citizens of Boston, on this day, in commemoration of the era of the foundation of your city, bearing in fond recollection the virtues of your fathers, to pass in review the circumstances which formed their character, and the institutions which bear its stamp; to take a rapid survey of that broad horizon, which is resplendent with their glories; to compress, within the narrow circle of an hour, the results of memory, perception, and hope; combining honor to the past, gratitude for the present, and fidelity to the future.

Standing, after the lapse of two centuries, on the very spot selected for us by our fathers, and surrounded by social, moral, and religious blessings greater than paternal love, in its fondest visions, ever dared to fancy, we naturally turn our eyes backward, on the descending current of years; seeking the causes of that prosperity, which has given this city so distinguished a name and rank among similar associations of men.

Happily its foundations were not laid in dark ages, nor is its origin to be sought among loose and obscure traditions. The age of our early ancestors was, in many respects, eminent for learning and civilization. Our ancestors themselves were deeply versed in the knowledge and attainments of their period. Not only their motives and acts appear in the general histories of their time, but they are unfolded in their own writings, with a simplicity and boldness, at once commanding admiration and not permitting mistake. If this condition of things restrict the imagination in its natural tendency to exaggerate, it assists the judgment rightly to analyze, and justly to appreciate. If it deny the power, enjoyed by ancient cities and states, to elevate our ancestors above the condition of humanity, it confers a much more precious privilege, that of estimating by unequivocal standards the intellectual and moral greatness of the early, intervening, and passing periods; and thus of judging concerning comparative attainment and progress in those qualities which constitute the dignity of our species. Instead of looking back, as antiquity was accustomed to do, on fabling legends of giants and heroes, — of men exceeding in size, in strength, and in labor, all experience and history, and consequently, being obliged to contemplate the races of men, dwindling with time, and growing less amid increasing stimulants and advantages; we are thus enabled to view things in lights more conformed to the natural suggestions of reason, and the actual results of observation; — to witness improvement in its slow but sure progress; in a general advance, constant and unquestionable; — to pay due honors to the greatness and virtues of our early ancestors, and be, at the same time, just to the not inferior greatness and virtues of succeeding generations of men, their descendants and our progenitors. Thus we substantiate the cheering conviction, that the virtues of ancient times have not been lost, or debased, in the course of their descent, but, in many respects, have been refined and elevated; and so, standing faithful to the generations which are past, and fearless in the presence of the generations to come, we accumulate on our own times the responsibility, that an inheritance, which has descended to us enlarged and improved, shall not be transmitted by us diminished or deteriorated.

As our thoughts course along the events of past times, from the hour of the first settlement of Boston to that in which we are now assembled, they trace the strong features of its character, indelibly impressed upon its acts and in its history, — clear conceptions of duty; bold vindications of right; readiness to incur dangers and meet sacrifices, in the maintenance of liberty, civil and religious. Early selected as the place of the chief settlement of New England, it has, through every subsequent period, maintained its relative ascendency. In the arts of peace and in the energies of war, in the virtues of prosperity and adversity, in wisdom to plan and vigor to execute, in extensiveness of enterprise, success in accumulating wealth, and liberality in its distribution, its inhabitants, if not unrivalled, have not been surpassed, by any similar society of men. Through good report and evil report, its influence has at all times been so distinctly seen and acknowledged in events, and been so decisive on the destinies of the region of which it was the head, that the inhabitants of the adjoining colonies of a foreign nation early gave the name of this place to the whole country; and at this day, among their descendants, the people of the whole United States[1] are distinguished by the name of "Bostonians."

[1] *Bostonais.* The name is thus applied, at this day, by the Canadian French. During our Revolutionary War, Americans from the United States were thus designated in France. Nor was the custom wholly discontinued even as late as

Amidst perils and obstructions, on the bleak side of the mountain on which it was first cast, the seedling oak, self-rooted, shot upward with a determined vigor. Now slighted and now assailed; amidst alternating sunshine and storm; with the axe of a native foe at its root, and the lightning of a foreign power, at times, scathing its top, or withering its branches, it grew, it flourished, it stands — may it forever stand! — the honor of the field.

On this occasion, it is proper to speak of the founders of our city, and of their glory. Now in its true acceptation, the term *glory* expresses the splendor, which emanates from virtue in the act of producing general and permanent good. Right conceptions, then, of the glory of our ancestors, are alone to be attained by analyzing their virtues. These virtues, indeed, are not seen charactered in breathing bronze, or in living marble. Our ancestors have left no Corinthian temples on our hills, no Gothic cathedrals on our plains, no proud pyramid, no storied obelisk, in our cities. But mind is there. Sagacious enterprise is there. An active, vigorous, intelligent, moral population throng our cities, and predominate in our fields; men, patient of labor, submissive to law, respectful to authority, regardful of right, faithful to liberty. These are the monuments of our ancestors. They stand immutable and immortal, in the social, moral, and intellectual condition of their descendants. They exist in the spirit which their precepts instilled, and their example implanted. Let no man think, that, to analyze and place in a just light the virtues of the first settlers of New England, is a departure from the purpose of this celebration; or deem so meanly of our duties, as to conceive that merely local relations, the circumstances which have given celebrity and character to this single city, are the only, or the most appropriate topics for the occasion. It was to this spot, during twelve successive years, that the great body of those first settlers emigrated. In this place, they either fixed permanently their abode, or took their departure from it for the coast, or the interior. Whatever honor devolves on this metropolis from the events connected with its

the year 1795. "We may remark," says a writer in the *Collections of the Massachusetts Historical Society*, (Vol. vi., First Series, p. 69,) "that Boston was not only the capital of Massachusetts, but the town most celebrated of any in North America. Its trade was extensive; *and the name often stands for the country in old authors.*"

first settlement, is not solitary or exclusive; it is shared with Massachusetts; with New England; in some sense, with the whole United States. For what part of this wide empire, be it sea or shore, lake or river, mountain or valley, have the descendants of the first settlers of New England not traversed? what depth of forest, not penetrated? what danger of nature or man, not defied? Where is the cultivated field, in redeeming which from the wilderness, their vigor has not been displayed? Where, amid unsubdued nature, by the side of the first log hut of the settler, does the school-house stand and the church spire rise, unless the sons of New England are there? Where does improvement advance, under the active energy of willing hearts and ready hands, prostrating the moss-covered monarchs of the wood, and from their ashes, amid their charred roots, bidding the greensward and the waving harvest to upspring, and the spirit of the fathers of New England is not seen, hovering, and shedding around the benign influences of sound, social, moral, and religious institutions, stronger and more enduring than knotted oak, or tempered steel? The swelling tide of their descendants has spread upon our coasts; ascended our rivers; taken possession of our plains. Already it encircles our lakes. At this hour the rushing noise of the advancing wave startles the wild beast in his lair among the prairies of the West. Soon it shall be seen climbing the Rocky Mountains; and, as it dashes over their cliffs, shall be hailed by the dwellers on the Pacific, as the harbinger of the coming blessings of safety, liberty, and truth.

The glory, which belongs to the virtues of our ancestors, is seen radiating from the nature of their design; from the spirit in which it was executed; and from the character of their institutions.

That emigration of Englishmen, which, two centuries ago, resulted in the settlement, on this day, of this metropolis, was distinguished by the comparative greatness of the means employed, and the number, rank, fortune, and intellectual endowments of those engaged in it, as leaders, or associates. Twelve ships, transporting somewhat less than nine hundred souls, constituted the physical strength of the first enterprise. In the course of the twelve succeeding years, twenty-two thousand souls emigrated in one hundred and ninety-two ships, at a cost, including the private expenses of the adventurers, which cannot be estimated in our currency, at less than one million of dollars. At that time the tide of emigration was stayed. Intelligent writers of the last century assert, that more persons had subsequently gone from New England to Europe, than had come to it during the same period from that quarter of the globe. A cotemporary historian[1] represents the leaders of the first emigration, as "gentlemen of good estate and reputation, descended from, or connected by marriage with, noble families; having large means, and great yearly revenue sufficient in all reason to content; their tables abundant in food, their coffers in coin; possessing beautiful houses, filled with rich furniture; gainful in their business, and growing rich daily; well provided for themselves, and having a sure competence for their children; wanting nothing of a worldly nature to complete the prospects of ease and enjoyment, or which could contribute to the pleasures, the prospects, or the splendors of life."

The question forces itself on the mind, Why did such men emigrate? Why did men of their condition exchange a pleasant and prosperous home for a repulsive and cheerless wilderness; a civilized for a barbarous vicinity? Why, quitting peaceful and happy dwellings, dare the dangers of tempestuous and unexplored seas, the rigors of untried and severe climates, the difficulties of a hard soil, and the inhuman warfare of a savage foe? An answer must be sought in the character of the times; and in the spirit, which the condition of their native country and age had a direct tendency to excite and cherish.

The general civil and religious aspect of the English nation, in the age of our ancestors, and in that immediately preceding their emigration, was singularly hateful and repulsive. A foreign hierarchy, contending with a domestic despotism for infallibility and supremacy, in matters of faith. Confiscation, imprisonment, the axe and the stake, approved and customary means of making proselytes and promoting uniformity. The fires of Smithfield, now lighted by the corrupt and selfish zeal of Roman pontiffs; and now rekindled, by the no less corrupt and selfish zeal of English sovereigns. All men clamorous for the rights of conscience, when in subjection; all actively persecuting, when in authority. Everywhere religion considered as a state

[1] Johnson's "*Wonder-Working Providence of Sion's Saviour in New England*," ch. 12.

entity, and having apparently no real existence, except in associations in support of established power, or in opposition to it.

The moral aspect of the age was not less odious than its civil. Every benign and characteristic virtue of Christianity was publicly conjoined, in close alliance with its most offensive opposite. Humility wearing the tiara, and brandishing the keys, in the excess of the pride of temporal and spiritual power. The Roman pontiff, under the title of "the servant of servants," with his foot on the neck of every monarch in Christendom; and under the seal of the fisherman of Galilee, dethroning kings and giving away kingdoms. Purity, content, and self-denial preached by men, who held the wealth of Europe tributary to their luxury, sensuality, and spiritual pride. Brotherly love in the mouth, while the hand applied the instrument of torture. Charity, mutual forbearance, and forgiveness chanted in unison with clanking chains and crackling fagots.

Nor was the intellectual aspect of the age less repulsive than its civil and moral. The native charm of the religious feeling lost, or disfigured amidst forms, and ceremonies, and disciplines. By one class, piety was identified with copes, and crosiers, and tippets, and genuflexions. By another class, all these were abhorred as the tricks and conjuring garments of popery, or at best, in the language of Calvin, as "tolerable fooleries;" while they, on their part, identified piety with looks, and language, and gestures, extracted or typified from Scripture, and fashioned according to the newest "pattern of the mount." By none were the rights of private judgment acknowledged. By all, creeds, and dogmas, and confessions, and catechisms, collected from Scripture with metaphysical skill, arranged with reference to temporal power and influence, and erected into standards of faith, were made the flags and rallying points of the spiritual swordsmen of the church militant.

The first emotion, which this view of that period excites, at the present day, is contempt or disgust. But the men of that age are no more responsible for the mistakes into which they fell, under the circumstances in which the intellectual eye was then placed, than we, at this day, for those optical illusions to which the natural eye is subject, before time and experience have corrected the judgment, and instructed it in the true laws of nature and vision. It was their fate to live in the crepuscular state of the intellectual day, and by the law of their nature they were compelled to see things darkly, through false and shifting mediums, and in lights at once dubious and deceptive. For centuries, a night of Egyptian darkness had overspread Europe, in the "palpable obscure" of which, priests and monarchs and nobles had not only found means to inthral the minds of the multitude, but absolutely to lose and bewilder their own. When the light of learning began to dawn, the first rays of the rising splendor dazzled and confused, rather than directed the mind. As the coming light penetrated the thick darkness, the ancient cumulative cloud severed into new forms. Its broken masses became tinged with an uncertain and shifting radiance. Shadows assumed the aspect of substances; the evanescent suggestions of fancy, the look of fixed realities. The wise were at a loss what to believe, or what to discredit; how to quit, and where to hold. On all sides sprang up sects and parties, infinite in number, incomprehensible in doctrine; often imperceptible in difference; yet each claiming for itself infallibility, and, in the sphere it affected to influence, supremacy; each violent and hostile to the others, haughty and hating its non-adhering brother, in a spirit wholly repugnant to the humility and love inculcated by that religion, by which each pretended to be actuated; and ready to resort, when it had power, to corporal penalties, even to death itself, as allowed modes of self-defence and proselytism.

It was the fate of the ancestors of New England to have their lot cast in a state of society thus unprecedented. They were of that class of the English nation, in whom the systematic persecutions of a concentrated, civil, and ecclesiastical despotism had enkindled an intense interest concerning man's social and religious rights. Their sufferings had created in their minds a vivid and inextinguishable love of civil and religious liberty; a fixed resolve, at every peril, to assert and maintain their natural rights. Among the boldest and most intelligent of this class of men, chiefly known by the name of Puritans, were the founders of this metropolis. To a superficial view, their zeal seems directed to forms and ceremonies and disciplines which have become at this day obsolete or modified, and so seems mistaken or misplaced. But the wisdom of zeal for any object is not to be measured by the particular nature of that object, but by the nature of the principle, which the circumstances of the times or of society have identified with such object. Liberty, whether civil or religious, is among the noblest objects of human regard. Yet, to a being constituted like man, abstract liberty has no existence, and over him no practical influence. To be for him an efficient principle of action, it must be embodied in some sensible object. Thus, the form of a cap, the color of a surplice, ship-money, a tax on tea or on stamped paper, objects in themselves indifferent, have been so inseparably identified with the principle temporarily connected with them, that martyrs have died at the stake, and patriots have fallen in the field, and this wisely and nobly for the sake of the principle, made by the circumstances of the time to inhere in them.

Now, in the age of our fathers, the principle of civil and religious liberty became identified with forms, disciplines, and modes of worship. The zeal of our fathers was graduated by the importance of the inhering principle. This gave elevation to that zeal. This creates interest in their sufferings. This entitles them to rank among patriots and martyrs who have voluntarily sacrificed themselves to the cause of conscience and their country. Indignant at being denied the enjoyment of the rights of conscience, which were in that age identified with those sensible objects, and resolute to vindicate them, they quitted country and home, crossed the Atlantic, and, without other auspices than their own strength and their confidence in heaven, they proceeded to lay the foundation of a commonwealth, under the principles, and by the stamina of which, their posterity have established an actual and uncontroverted independence, not less happy than glorious. To their enthusiastic vision all the comforts of life and all the pleasures of society were light and worthless in comparison with the liberty they sought. The tempestuous sea was less dreadful than the troubled waves of civil discord; the quicksands, the unknown shoals, and unexplored shores of a savage coast, less fearful than the metaphysical abysses and perpetually shifting whirlpools of despotic ambition and ecclesiastical policy and intrigue; the bow and the tomahawk of the transatlantic barbarian, less terrible than the flame and fagot of the civilized European. In the calm of our present peace and prosperity, it is difficult for us to realize or appreciate their sorrows and sacrifices. They sought a new world, lying far off in space, destitute of all the attractions which make home and native land dear and venerable. Instead of cultivated fields and a civilized neighborhood, the prospect before them presented nothing but dreary wastes, cheerless climates, and repulsive wildernesses possessed by wild beasts and savages; the intervening ocean unexplored and intersected by the fleets of a hostile nation; its usual dangers multiplied to the fancy, and, in fact, by ignorance of real hazards and natural fears of such as the event proved to be imaginary.

"Pass on," exclaims one of these adventurers,[1] "and attend, while these soldiers of faith ship for this western world; while they and their wives and their little ones take an eternal leave of their country and kindred. With what heart-breaking affection did they press loved friends to their bosoms whom they were never to see again! their voices broken by grief, till tears streaming eased their hearts to recovered speech again; natural affections clamorous, as they take a perpetual banishment from their native soil; their enterprise scorned; their motives derided; and they counted but madmen and fools. But time shall discover the wisdom with which they were endued, and the sequel shall show how their policy overtopped all the human policy of this world."

Winthrop, their leader and historian, in his simple narrative of the voyage, exhibits them, when in severe sufferings, resigned; in instant expectation of battle, fearless; amid storm, sickness, and death, calm, confident, and undismayed. "Our trust," says he, "was in the Lord of hosts." For years, Winthrop, the leader of the first great enterprise, was the Chief Magistrate of the infant metropolis. His prudence guided its councils. His valor directed its strength. His life and fortune were spent in fixing its character, or in improving its destinies. A bolder spirit never dwelt, a truer heart never beat in any bosom. Had Boston, like Rome, a consecrated calendar, there is no name better entitled than that of Winthrop to be registered as its "patron saint."

From Salem and Charlestown, the places of their first landing, they ranged the Bay of Massachusetts to fix the head of the settlement. After much deliberation, and not without opposi-

[1] Johnson, in his *Wonder-Working Providences of Sion's Saviour in New England*, ch. xii.

tion, they selected this spot, known to the natives by the name of *Shawmut*, and to the adjoining settlers by that of *Trimount-ain;* the former indicating the abundance and sweetness of its waters; the latter, the peculiar character of its hills.

Accustomed as we are to the beauties of the place and its vicinity, and in the daily perception of the charms of its almost unrivalled scenery, — in the centre of a natural amphitheatre, whose sloping descents the riches of a laborious and intellectual cultivation adorn, — where hill and vale, river and ocean, island and continent, simple nature and unobtrusive art, with contrasted and interchanging harmonies, form a rich and gorgeous landscape, we are little able to realize the almost repulsive aspect of its original state. We wonder at the blindness of those who, at one time, constituted the majority, and had well-nigh fixed elsewhere the chief seat of the settlement. Nor are we easily just to Winthrop, Johnson, and their associates, whose skill and judgment selected this spot, and whose firmness settled the wavering minds of the multitude upon it, as the place for their metropolis; a decision which the experience of two centuries has irrevocably justified, and which there is no reason to apprehend that the events or opinions of any century to come will reverse.

To the eyes of the first emigrants, however, where now exists a dense and aggregated mass of living beings and material things, amid all the accommodations of life, the splendors of wealth, the delights of taste, and whatever can gratify the cultivated intellect, there were then only a few hills, which, when the ocean receded, were intersected by wide marshes, and when its tide returned, appeared a group of lofty islands, abruptly rising from the surrounding waters. Thick forests concealed the neighboring hills, and the deep silence of nature was broken only by the voice of the wild beast or bird and the warwhoop of the savage.

The advantages of the place were, however, clearly marked by the hand of nature; combining at once present convenience, future security, and an ample basis for permanent growth and prosperity. Towards the continent it possessed but a single avenue, and that easily fortified. Its hills then commanded, not only its own waters, but the hills of the vicinity. At the bottom of a deep bay, its harbor was capable of containing the proudest navy of Europe; yet, locked by islands, and guarded by winding channels, it presented great difficulty of access to strangers, and to the inhabitants great facility of protection against maritime invasion; while to those acquainted with its waters, it was both easy and accessible. To these advantages were added goodness and plenteousness of water, and the security afforded by that once commanding height, now, alas! obliterated and almost forgotten, since art and industry have levelled the predominating mountain of the place; from whose lofty and imposing top the beacon fire was accustomed to rally the neighboring population on any threatened danger to the metropolis. A single cottage, from which ascended the smoke of the hospitable hearth of Blackstone, who had occupied the peninsula several years, was the sole civilized mansion in the solitude; the kind master of which, at first, welcomed the coming emigrants; but soon, disliking the sternness of their manners and the severity of their discipline, abandoned the settlement. His rights, as first occupant, were recognized by our ancestors; and, in November, 1634, Edmund Quincy, Samuel Wildbore, and others, were authorized to assess a rate of thirty pounds for Mr. Blackstone,[1] on the payment of which all local rights in the peninsula became vested in its inhabitants.

The same bold spirit which thus led our ancestors across the Atlantic, and made them prefer a wilderness where liberty might be enjoyed, to civilized Europe where it was denied, will be found characterizing all their institutions. Of these, the limits of the time permit me to speak only in general terms. The scope of their policy has been usually regarded as though it were restricted to the acquisition of religious liberty in the relation of colonial dependence. No man, however, can truly understand their institutions and the policy on which they were founded, without taking as the basis of all reasonings concerning them, that *civil independence was as truly their object as religious liberty;*[2] in other words, that the possession of the former was,

[1] *Winthrop*, vol. i. p. 45; note by J. Savage.

[2] The testimony of Chalmers, in his *Political Annals of the United Colonies*, to the early and undeviating spirit of independence which actuated the first emigrants to Massachusetts, is constant, unequivocal, and conclusive. Those annals were written during the American Revolution, and published in the year 1780, in the heat of that controversy, and under the auspices of the British government. A few extracts from that work, tending to show the pertinacious

in their opinion, the essential means, indispensable to the secure enjoyment of the latter, which was their great end.

The master-passion of our early ancestors was dread of the

spirit of independence which characterized our ancestors, and corroborative of the position maintained in the text, cannot fail to be interesting.

"The charter of Charles I., obtained in March, 1628 – 9, was the only one which Massachusetts possessed prior to the Revolution of 1688, and contained its most ancient privileges. *On this was most dexterously engrafted, not only the original government of that colony, but even independence itself.*" Book I. c. vi. p. 136.

"The nature of their government was now (1634) changed by a variety of regulations, the legality of which cannot easily be supported by any other than those *principles of independence which sprang up among them, and have at all times governed their actions.*" Book I. p. 158.

Concerning the confederation entered into by the United Colonies of New England in 1643, Chalmers thus expresses himself.

"The most inattentive must perceive the exact resemblance that confederation bears to a similar junction of the Colonies, more recent, [that of 1775] extensive, and powerful. *Both originated from Massachusetts, always fruitful in projects of independence. Wise men at the era of both remarked, that those memorable associations established a complete system of absolute sovereignty, because the principles upon which it was erected* NECESSARILY LED TO WHAT IT WAS NOT THE POLICY OF THE PRINCIPAL AGENTS AT EITHER PERIOD TO AVOW!

"The principles upon which this famous association [that of 1643] was formed, were altogether those of independency, and it cannot easily be supported on any other. The consent of the governing powers in England was never applied for, and was never given." Book I. c. viii. pp. 177, 178.

"Principles of aggrandisement seem constantly to have been had in view by Massachusetts, as the only rule of its conduct." Book I. p. 180.

"Massachusetts, in conformity to its accustomed principles, acted, during the civil wars, almost altogether as an independent state. It formed leagues, not only with the neighboring colonies, but with foreign nations, without the consent or knowledge of the government of England. It permitted no appeals from its courts to the judicatories of the sovereign State, without which a dependence cannot be preserved or enforced; and it refused to exercise its jurisdiction in the name of the Commonwealth of England. It assumed the government of that part of New England which is now called New Hampshire, and even extended its power farther eastward over the Province of Maine; and, by force of arms, it compelled those who had fled from its persecutions beyond its boundaries into the wilderness to submit to its authority. It erected a mint at Boston, impressing the year 1652 on the coin, *as the era of independence.* Though, as we are assured, the coining of money is the prerogative of the sovereign, and not the privilege of a colony.

"The practice was continued till the dissolutien of its government; *thus evincing to all what had been foreseen by the wise, that a people of such principles, religious and political, settling at so great a distance from control, would necessarily form an independent State.*" Book I. c. viii. p. 181.

"The Committee of State of the Long Parliament having resolved to oblige Massachusetts to acknowledge their authority, by taking a new patent from them, and by keeping its courts in their name, that Colony, according to its wonted policy, by petition and remonstrance, declaring the love they bore the Parliament, the sufferings they had endured in their cause, and their readiness to stand or fall with them, and by flattering Cromwell, prevailed so far as that the

English hierarchy. To place themselves locally beyond the reach of its power, they resolved to emigrate. To secure themselves, after their emigration, from the arm of this their ancient

requisitions above-mentioned were never complied with, and the General Court consequently gained the point in the controversy." Book I. c. viii. pp. 184, 185.

"But Massachusetts did not only thus artfully foil the Parliament, but it outfawned and outwitted Cromwell. They declined his invitation to assist his fleet and army, destined to attack the Dutch at Manhattan, in 1653, and acknowledging the continued series of his favors to the Colonies, told him, that, "*having been exercised with serious thoughts of its duty at that juncture, which were, that it was most agreeable to the gospel of peace, and safest for the plantations to forbear the use of the sword*, if it had been misled, it humbly craved his pardon." Book I. c. viii. p. 185.

"The address of Massachusetts above-mentioned, it should seem, gave perfect satisfaction to Cromwell. Its winning courtship seems to have captivated his rugged heart, and, notwithstanding a variety of complaints were made to him against that Colony, so strong were his attachments, that all attempts, either to obtain redress, or to prejudice it in his esteem, were to no purpose. Thus did Massachusetts, by the prudence or vigor of its councils, triumph over its opponents abroad." Book I. c. viii. p. 188.

"After the death of Cromwell, Massachusetts acted with a cautious neutrality. *She refused to acknowledge the authority of Richard any more than that of the Parliament or Protector*, BECAUSE ALL SUBMISSION WOULD HAVE BEEN INCONSISTENT WITH HER INDEPENDENCE."

"She heard the tidings of the restoration with that scrupulous incredulity, with which men listen to news which they wish not to be true." Book I. c. x. p. 249.

"Prince Charles II. had received so many proofs of the attachment of the Colonies, during the season of trial, *New England only excepted*, that he judged rightly, when he presumed they would listen to the news of his restoration with pleasure, and submit to his just authority with alacrity. Nor was he in the least deceived. They proclaimed his accession with a joy in proportion to their recollection of their late sufferings, and to their hope of future blessings. Of the recent conduct of Massachusetts, he was well instructed; he foresaw what really happened, that it would receive the tidings of his good fortune with extreme coldness; he was informed of the proceedings of a society which assembled at Cooper's Hall in order to promote its interests, and with them, *the good old cause of enmity to regal power*. And in May, 1661, he appointed the great officers of state a committee, 'touching the affairs of New England.' That Prince and Colony mutually hated and contemned and feared each other, during his reign, because the one suspected its principles of attachment, and the other dreaded an invasion of its privileges." Book I. p. 243.

"The same vessel which brought King Charles's proclamation to Boston, in 1660, brought also Whalley and Goffe, two of the regicides. Far from concealing themselves, they were received very courteously by Governor Endicott and with universal regard by the people of New England. Of this conduct Charles II. was perfectly informed, and with it he afterwards reproached Massachusetts." Book I. c. x. pp. 249, 250.

"The General Court soon turned its attention to a subject of higher concernment, — the present condition of affairs. In order rightly to understand that duty which the people owed to themselves, and that obedience which was due to the authority of England, a committee at length reported a declaration of rights and duties, which at once shows the extent of their claims, and their dexterity at involving what they wished to conceal. The General Court resolved 'That the patent (under God) was the first and main foundation of the civil polity of that Colony; that the Governor and Company are, by the patent, a oppressor, they devised a plan, which, as they thought, would enable them to establish, under a nominal subjection, an actual independence. The bold and original conception which they had the spirit to form and successfully to execute, was the attainment and perpetuation of religious liberty, under the auspices of a free commonwealth.[1] This is the master key to all their policy; this the glorious spirit which breathes in all their institutions. Whatever in them is stern, exclusive, or at this day seems questionable, may be accounted for, if not justified, by its connection with this great purpose.

body politic, which is vested with power to make freemen; that they have authority to choose a governor, deputy-governor, assistants, and select representatives; that this government hath ability to set up all kinds of offices; that the governor, deputy-governor, assistants, and select deputies, have full jurisdiction, both legislative and executive, for the government of the people here, without appeals, 'excepting law or laws repugnant to the laws of England;' that this Company is privileged to defend itself against all who shall attempt its annoyance; that any imposition, prejudicial to the country, contrary to any of its just ordinances (not repugnant to the laws of England) is an infringement of its rights.' Having thus, with a genuine air of sovereignty, by its own act, established its own privileges, it decided 'concerning its duties and allegiance;' and these were declared to consist in upholding that Colony as of right belonging to his Majesty, and not subject to any foreign potentate; in preserving his person and dominions; in settling the peace and prosperity of the king and nation, by punishing crimes and by propagating the gospel. It was at the same time determined, that the royal warrant for apprehending Whalley and Goffe ought to be faithfully executed; that if any legally obnoxious, and fleeing from the civil justice of the state of England, shall come over to these parts, they may not expect shelter.' What a picture do these resolutions display of the embarrassments of the General Court, between its principles of independence on the one hand, and its apprehension of giving offence to the state of England on the other." Book I. p. 252.

"During the whole reign of Charles II. Massachusetts continued *to act as she always had done, as an independent state.*

"Disregarding equally her charter and the laws of England, *Massachusetts established for herself an independent government, similar to those of the Grecian republics.*" Book I. c. xvi. p. 400; also c. xxii. p. 682.

It is not easy to perceive on what ground Chalmers supports the charge against our ancestors of "concealment" of their real intentions by the General Court, in their declaration of rights above quoted, from page 252 of his *Annals*. On the contrary, it seems to have been conceived in a spirit of boldness, which, considering the weakness of the Colony, might be much better denominated imprudently explicit than evasive. It is difficult to conceive what the General Court could have added to that declaration of their right to independent self-government, unless they had been prepared to draw the sword against the King, and throw away the scabbard.

[1] This is apparent from the fact, that they did form and maintain such a commonwealth, and from the further fact, that in no other way could they, in that age, have had any hope successfully to maintain and transmit to their posterity religious liberty, according to their conception of that blessing. Those who reason practically concerning the motives of mankind, must take their data from their master-passions and the necessities of their situation. Acts best develop

The question has often been raised, when and by whom the idea of independence of the parent state was first conceived, and by whose act a settled purpose to effect it was first indicated. History does not permit the people of Massachusetts to make a question of this kind. The honor of that thought, and of as efficient a declaration of it as in their circumstances was possible, belongs to Winthrop, and Dudley, and Saltonstall, and their associates, and was included in the declaration, that "*the only condition on which they with their families would remove to this country, was, that the patent and charter should remove with them.*"[1]

intentions. Official language takes its modification from circumstances, and is often necessarily a very equivocal indication of motives.

To escape from the dominion of the English hierarchy, was our ancestors leading design and firm purpose. They took refuge in the forms and principles of a commonwealth; trusting to their own intellectual skill and physical power for its support. They were well apprised of the fixed determination of the English hierarchy, from the earliest times of their emigration, to subject them to its supremacy, if possible; and this design is distinctly avowed by Chalmers.

"The enjoyment of liberty of conscience, the free worship of the Supreme Being in the manner most agreeable to themselves, were the great objects of the colonists, which they often declared was the principal end of their emigration. Nevertheless, though their historians assert the contrary, the *charter did not grant spontaneously to them a freedom*, which had been denied to the solicitations of the Brownists; and it is extremely probable that *so essential an omission arose, not from accident, but design.*

"In conformity to his intentions of establishing the Church of England in the plantations, James had refused to grant to that sect the privilege of exercising its own peculiar modes, though solicited by the powerful interest of the Virginia Company. *His successor adopted and pursued the same policy, under the direction of Laud, 'who, we are assured, kept a jealous eye over New England.' And this reasoning is confirmed by the present patent, which required, with peculiar caution, that '*THE OATH OF SUPREMACY *shall be administered to every one, who shall pass to the Colony and inhabit there.'*" Book I. c. vi. p. 141.

1 The consentaneousness of the views entertained by Chalmers, with those presented in the text, respecting the motives of our ancestors in making the removal of the charter the condition of their emigration, is remarkable.

"Several persons of considerable consequence in the nation, who had adopted the principles of the Puritans, and who wished to enjoy their own mode of worship, formed the resolution of emigrating to Massachusetts. But they felt themselves inferior, neither to the governor nor assistants of the company. *They saw and dreaded the inconvenience of being governed by laws made for them without their consent; and it appeared more rational to them, that the colony should be ruled by those who made it the place of their residence, than by men dwelling at the distance of three thousand miles, over whom they had no control.* At the same time, therefore, that they proposed to transport themselves, their families, and their estates, to that country, they insisted that the charter should be transmitted with them, and that the corporate powers, which were conferred by it, should be executed, in future, in New England."

"A transaction, similar to this, in all its circumstances, is not to be easily met with in story." — Book I. c. vi. pp. 150, 151.

It is very plain, from the above extract, that Chalmers understood the transfer

This simple declaration and resolve included, as they had the sagacity to perceive, all the consequences of an effectual independence, under a nominal subjection. For protection against foreign powers, a charter from the parent state was necessary. Its transfer to New England vested, effectually, independence. Those wise leaders foresaw,[1] that, among the troubles in Europe,

of the charter to this country in the light in which it is represented in the text; — that the object was *self-government;* an intention "not to be governed by laws made for them, without their consent;" — a determination that those "should rule in New England, who made it the place of their residence;" and "*not those who dwelt at the distance of three thousand miles, over whom they had no control.*"

Two causes have concurred to keep the motives of our ancestors in that measure, from the direct development which its nature deserves. The first was, that their motives could not be avowed consistently with that *nominal dependence*, which, in the weakness of the early emigrants, was unavoidable. The other was, that almost all the impressions left concerning our early history, have been derived through the medium of the clergy, who naturally gave an exclusive attention to the predominating motive, which was, unquestionably, religious liberty, and paid less regard to what the colonial statesmen of that day as unquestionably considered to be the essential means to that end. The men who said "they would not go to New England unless the patent went with them," were not clergymen, but high-minded statesmen, who knew what was included in that transfer. Their conduct and that of their immediate descendants, speak a language of determined civil independence, not, at this day, to be gainsaid.

Winthrop gives, incidentally, a remarkable evidence of his own sensibility, on the subject of the right of self-government, in the very earliest period after their emigration.

"Mr. Winslow, the late Governor of Plymouth," Winthrop relates, "being this year (1635) in England, petitioned the council for a commission to withstand the intrusions of the Dutch and French. *Now this,*" Winthrop remarks, "*was undertaken with ill advice; for such precedents endanger our liberty,* THAT WE SHOULD DO NOTHING HEREAFTER BUT BY COMMISSION OUT OF ENGLAND." — *Winthrop*, vol. i. p. 172.

[1] That the early emigrants foresaw that the transfer of the charter would effectually vest independence, may be deduced, not only from the whole tenor of their conduct after their emigration, which was an effectual exercise of independence, but from the fact *of the secrecy, with which this intention to transfer the charter was maintained, until it was actually on this side of the Atlantic.*

Our ancestors readily anticipated with what jealousy this transfer would be viewed by the English government; and were accordingly solicitous to keep it from being known until they and the original charter were beyond their power. The original records of the General Court, in which the topic of this transfer of the charter was first agitated, speak a language on this subject, not to be mistaken.

The terms of this record are as follows: —

"At a General Court holden at London, for the Company of the Massachusetts Bay in New England, in Mr. Deputy's house, on Tuesday, the 28th of July, 1629. Present, Mr. MATHEW CRADOCK, *Governor*,
Mr. GOFF, *Deputy Governor.*"

Here follow the names of the "assistants" and "generality," who were present.

"Mr. Governor read certain propositions conceived by himself, namely, that incident to the age, and then obviously impending over their parent state, their settlement, from its distance and early insignificance, would probably escape notice. They trusted to events, and doubtless anticipated, that, with its increasing strength, even nominal subjection would be abrogated. They knew that weakness was the law of nature, in the relation between parent states and their distant and detached colonies. Nothing else can be inferred, not only from their making the transfer of the charter the essential condition of their emigration, thereby severing themselves from all responsibility to persons abroad, but also from their instant and undeviating course of policy after their emigration; in boldly assuming whatever powers were necessary to their condition, or suitable to their ends, whether attributes of sovereignty or not, without regard to the nature of the consequences resulting from the exercise of those powers. Nor was this assumption limited to powers which might be deduced from the charter, but was extended to such as no act of incorporation, like that which they possessed, could, by any possibility of legal construction, be deemed to include. By the magic of

for the advancement of the plantation, the inducing and encouraging persons of worth and quality to transplant themselves and families thither, and for other weighty reasons therein contained, *to transfer the government of the plantation to those that shall inhabit there*, and not to continue the same in subordination to the company here, as now it is. This business occasioned some debate; but *by reason of the many great and considerable consequences thereupon depending*, it was not now resolved upon, but those present are *privately* and seriously to consider hereof, and to set down their particular reasons in writing, pro and contra, and to produce the same at the next General Court, where they being reduced to heads and maturely considered of, the company may then proceed to a final resolution therein, and in the mean time THEY ARE DESIRED TO CARRY THIS BUSINESS SECRETLY, THAT THE SAME BE NOT DIVULGED." — See original *Records of Massachusetts*, p. 19.

What our ancestors thought they had gained, or what practical consequences they intended to deduce from this transfer of the patent, and from their possession of it in this country, is apparent from the reasons, given by Winthrop, for not obeying the court mandate, to send the patent to England.

Winthrop's account is as follows: —

"The General Court was assembled, [1638,] in which it was agreed, that whereas a very strict order was sent from the Lords Commissioners for Plantations, for sending home our patent, upon pretence that judgment had passed against it upon a *quo warranto*, a letter should be written by the Governor in the name of the Court, to excuse our not sending it; for it was resolved to be best, not to send it, because then such of our friends and others in England would conceive it to be surrendered, *and that thereupon, we should be bound to receive such a Governor and such orders, as should be sent to us, and many bad minds, yea, and some weak ones, among ourselves,* WOULD THINK IT LAWFUL, IF NOT NECESSARY, TO ACCEPT A GENERAL GOVERNOR." — *Winthrop*, vol. i. p. 269.

their daring, a private act of incorporation was transmuted into a civil constitution of state; under the authority of which they made peace and declared war; erected judicatures; coined money; raised armies; built fleets; laid taxes and imposts; inflicted fines, penalties, and death; and, in imitation of the British constitution, by the consent of all its own branches, without asking leave of any other, their legislature modified its own powers and relations, prescribed the qualifications of those who should conduct its authority, and enjoy, or be excluded from its privileges. The administration of the civil affairs of Massachusetts, for the sixty years next succeeding the settlement of this metropolis, was a phenomenon in the history of civil government. Under a theoretic colonial relation, an efficient and independent Commonwealth was erected, claiming and exercising attributes of sovereignty, higher and far more extensive than, at the present day, in consequence of its connection with the general government, Massachusetts pretends either to exercise or possess. Well might Chalmers assert, as in his Political Annals of the Colonies he does, that "Massachusetts, with a peculiar dexterity, abolished her charter;"[1] that she was always "fruitful in projects of independence, the principles of which, at all times, governed her actions."[2] In this point of view, it is glory enough for our early ancestors, that, under manifold disadvantages, in the midst of internal discontent and external violence and intrigue, of wars with the savages and with the neighboring colonies of France, they effected their purpose, and for two generations of men, from 1630 to 1692, enjoyed liberty of conscience, according to their view of that subject, under the auspices of a free commonwealth.

The three objects, which our ancestors proposed to attain and perpetuate by all their institutions, were the noblest within the grasp of the human mind, and those on which, more than on any other, depend human happiness and hope; — *religious liberty*, — *civil liberty*, — and, as essential to the attainment and maintenance of both, — *intellectual power*.

On the subject of religious liberty, their intolerance of other sects has been reprobated as an inconsistency, and as violating the very rights of conscience for which they emigrated. The

[1] Vol. i. p. 200. [2] Vol. i. pp. 158, 177.

inconsistency, if it exist, is altogether constructive, and the charge proceeds on a false assumption. The *necessity* of the policy,[1] considered in connection with their great design of independence, is apparent. They had abandoned house and home, had sacrificed the comforts of kindred and cultivated life, had dared the dangers of the sea, and were then braving the still more appalling terrors of the wilderness; for what?—to acquire liberty for all sorts of consciences? Not so; but to vindicate and maintain the liberty of their own consciences. They did not cross the Atlantic, on a crusade, in behalf of the rights of

[1] The object of this policy was perceived by Chalmers. Thus he reprobates the law, that "none should be admitted to the freedom of the company but such as were church members, and that none but freemen should vote at elections or act as magistrates and jurymen," because it excluded *from all participation in the government*, those who could not comply with the necessary requisites. He understood well, that it was a means of defence against the English hierarchy, and intended to exclude from influence all who were of the English church; and complains of it as being "*made in the true spirit of retaliation*," (Book I. p. 153,) and adds, that "this severe law, notwithstanding the vigorous exertions of Charles II., continued in force till the *quo warranto* laid in ruins the structure of the government that had established it."

To prove *the necessity* of this exclusive policy of our ancestors, and that it was strictly a measure of "self-defence," it is proper to remark, that as early as April, 1635, a commission was issued for the government of the Plantations, *granting absolute power to the Archbishop of Canterbury and to others*, "TO MAKE LAWS AND CONSTITUTIONS, CONCERNING EITHER THEIR STATE PUBLIC OR THE UTILITY OF INDIVIDUALS, AND FOR THE RELIEF OF THE CLERGY TO CONSIGN CONVENIENT MAINTENANCE UNTO THEM BY TITHES AND OBLATIONS AND OTHER PROFITS ACCORDING TO THEIR DISCRETION," AND THEY WERE EMPOWERED TO INFLICT PUNISHMENTS, EITHER BY IMPRISONMENT OR BY LOSS OF LIFE AND MEMBERS.

A broader charter of hierarchical despotism was never conceived. The only means of protection against it, to which our ancestors could resort, was that which they adopted. By the principle of making church-membership a qualification for the enjoyment of the rights of a freeman, they excluded from all political influence the friends of the hierarchy. To the same motive may be referred that other principle, that "no churches should be gathered but such as were approved by the magistrate." Notwithstanding that the direct tendency of these principles was to destroy the influence of the crown and the hierarchy in the colony, the obviousness of the motive is unnoticed by Chalmers, for the sake of repeating the gross charge of bigotry; and this too at the very time when he is urging their design of independence against our ancestors as their great crime. Our ancestors could not avow their ruling motive; and they seem at all times to be actuated by the noble principle of being content to submit in their own characters to the obloquy of bigotry, as a less evil than that their children should become subject to the hierarchy of the Stuarts.

It is difficult to perceive how the principles of this commission could have been otherwise resisted by our ancestors, than by putting at once out of influence all those disposed to yield submission to it. Nor was it possible for them to apply their disqualification directly to the adherents of the English hierarchy. They were compelled, if it were adopted at all, to make it general, and to acquiesce in the charge of bigotry in order to give efficacy to their policy.

mankind in general, but in support of their own rights and liberties. Tolerate! Tolerate whom? The legate of the Roman Pontiff, or the emissary of Charles I. and Archbishop Laud? How consummate would have been their folly and madness, to have fled into the wilderness to escape the horrible persecutions of those hierarchies, and at once have admitted into the bosom of their society, men brandishing, and ready to apply, the very flames and fetters from which they had fled! Those who are disposed to condemn them on this account, neither realize the necessities of their condition, nor the prevailing character of the times. Under the stern discipline of Elizabeth and James, the stupid bigotry of the First Charles, and the spiritual pride of Archbishop Laud, the spirit of the English hierarchy was very different from that which it assumed, when, after having been tamed and humanized under the wholesome discipline of Cromwell and his Commonwealth, it yielded itself to the mild influence of the principles of 1688, and to the liberal spirit of Tillotson.

But it is said, if they did not tolerate their ancient persecutors, they might, at least, have tolerated rival sects. That is, they ought to have tolerated sects, imbued with the same principles of intolerance as the transatlantic hierarchies; sects, whose first use of power would have been to endeavor to uproot the liberty of our fathers, and persecute them, according to the known principles of sectarian action, with a virulence in the inverse ratio of their reciprocal likeness and proximity. Those, who thus reason and thus condemn, have considered but very superficially the nature of the human mind and its actual condition in the time of our ancestors.

The great doctrine, now so universally recognized, that liberty of conscience is the right of the individual, — a concern between every man and his Maker, with which the civil magistrate is not authorized to interfere, — was scarcely, in their day, known, except in private theory and solitary speculation; as a practical truth, to be acted upon by the civil power, it was absolutely and universally rejected by all men, all parties, and all sects, as totally subversive, not only of the peace of the church, but of the peace of society.[1] That great truth, now deemed so simple

[1] Hume's *History of England*, vol. vi. p. 168.

and plain, was so far from being an easy discovery of the human intellect, that it may be doubted whether it would ever have been discovered by human reason at all, had it not been for the miseries in which man was involved in consequence of his ignorance of it. That truth was not evolved by the calm exertion of the human faculties, but was stricken out by the collision of the human passions. It was not the result of philosophic research, but was a hard lesson, taught under the lash of a severe discipline, provided for the gradual instruction of a being like man, not easily brought into subjection to virtue, and with natural propensities to pride, ambition, avarice, and selfishness. Previously to that time, in all modifications of society, ancient or modern, religion had been seen only in close connection with the state. It was the universal instrument by which worldly ambition shaped and moulded the multitude to its ends. To have attempted the establishment of a state on the basis of a perfect freedom of religious opinion, and the perfect right of every man to express his opinion, would then have been considered as much a solecism, and an experiment quite as wild and visionary, as it would be, at this day, to attempt the establishment of a state on the principle of a perfect liberty of individual action, and the perfect right of every man to conduct himself according to his private will. Had our early ancestors adopted the course we, at this day, are apt to deem so easy and obvious, and placed their government on the basis of liberty for all sorts of consciences, it would have been, in that age, a certain introduction of anarchy. It cannot be questioned, that all the fond hopes they had cherished from emigration would have been lost. The agents of Charles and James would have planted here the standard of the transatlantic monarchy and hierarchy. Divided and broken, without practical energy, subject to court influences and court favorites, New England at this day would have been a colony of the parent state,[1] her character yet to be formed and her independence yet to be vindicated.

[1] Lest the consequences of an opposite policy, had it been adopted by our ancestors, may seem to be exaggerated, as here represented, it is proper to state, that upon the strength and united spirit of New England mainly depended (under Heaven) the success of our revolutionary struggle. Had New England been divided, or even less unanimous, independence would have scarcely been attempted, or, if attempted, acquired. It will give additional strength to this

The non-toleration, which characterized our early ancestors, from whatever source it may have originated, had undoubtedly the effect they *intended and wished.* It excluded from influence in their infant settlement all the friends and adherents of the ancient monarchy and hierarchy; all who, from any motive, ecclesiastical or civil, were disposed to disturb their peace or their churches. They considered it a measure of "*self-defence.*" And it is unquestionable, that it was chiefly instrumental in forming the homogeneous and exclusively republican character for which the people of New England have, in all times, been distinguished; and, above all, that it fixed irrevocably in the country that noble security for religious liberty, the *independent* system of church government.

The principle of the independence of the churches, including the right of every individual to unite with what church he pleases, under whatever sectarian auspices it may have been fostered, has, through the influence of time and experience, lost altogether its exclusive character. It has become the universal guaranty of religious liberty to all sects without discrimination, and is as much the protector of the Roman Catholic, the Episcopalian, and the Presbyterian, as of the Independent form of worship. The security, which results from this principle, does not depend upon charters and constitutions, but on what is stronger than either, the nature of the principle in connection with the nature of man. So long as this intellectual, moral, and religious being, man, is constituted as he is, the unrestricted liberty of associating for public worship, and the independence of those associations of external control, will necessarily lead to a most happy number and variety of them. In the principle of the independence of each, the liberty of individual conscience is safe under the panoply of the common interest of all. No other perfect security for liberty of conscience was ever devised by man, except this independence of the churches. This possessed, liberty of conscience has no danger. This denied, it has

argument to observe, that the number of troops, regular and militia, furnished by all the States during the war of the Revolution, was . . . 288,134

Of these, New England furnished more than half, namely, . 147,674

And Massachusetts alone furnished nearly one third, namely, . 83,162

See the *Collections of the New Hampshire Historical Society*, vol. i. p. 236.

no safety. There can be no greater human security than common right, placed under the protection of common interest.

It is the excellence and beauty of this simple principle, that, while it secures all, it restricts none. They, who delight in lofty and splendid monuments of ecclesiastical architecture, may raise the pyramid of church power, with its aspiring steps and gradations, until it terminate in the despotism of one, or a few; the humble dwellers at the base of the proud edifice may wonder, and admire the ingenuity of the contrivance and the splendor of its massive dimensions, but it is without envy and without fear. Safe in the principle of independence, they worship, be it in tent, or tabernacle, or in the open air, as securely as though standing on the topmost pinnacle of the loftiest fabric ambition ever devised.

The glory of discovering and putting this principle to the test, on a scale capable of trying its efficacy, belongs to the fathers of Massachusetts,[1] who are entitled to a full share of that acknowledgment made by Hume, when he asserts, "that for *all the liberty* of the English constitution that nation is indebted to the Puritans."

The glory of our ancestors radiates from no point more strongly than from their institutions of learning. The people of New England are the first known to history, who provided, in the original constitution of their society, for the education of the whole population out of the general fund. In other countries, provisions have been made of this character in favor of certain particular classes, or for the poor by way of charity. But here first were the children of the whole community invested with the right of being educated at the expense of the whole society; and not only this, the obligation to take advantage of that right was enforced by severe supervision and penalties. By simple laws they founded their commonwealth on the only basis on which a republic has any hope of happiness or continuance, the general information of the people. They denominated it "barbarism" not to be able "perfectly to read the English tongue and to know the general laws."[2] In soliciting a general contribution for the support of the neighboring University, they declare that "skill in the tongues and liberal arts, is not

1. Neal's *History of the Puritans*, vol. i. p. 438 and 490.
2 *Old Colony Laws*, p. 26.

only laudable, but *necessary for the well-being* of the common-wealth."[1] And in requiring every town, having one hundred householders, to set up a grammar school, provided with a master able to fit youth for the University, the object avowed is, "to enable men to obtain a knowledge of the Scriptures, and by acquaintance with the ancient tongues to qualify them to discern the true sense and meaning of the original, however corrupted by false glosses." Thus liberal and thus elevated, in respect of learning, were the views of our ancestors."

To the same master-passion, dread of the English hierarchy, and the same main purpose, civil independence, may be attributed, in a great degree, the nature of the government which the principal civil and spiritual influences of the time established, and, notwithstanding its many objectionable features, the willing submission to it of the people.

It cannot be questioned, that the constitution of the state, as sketched in the first laws of our ancestors, was a skilful combination of both civil and ecclesiastical powers. Church and state were very curiously and efficiently interwoven with each other. It is usual to attribute to religious bigotry the submission of the mass of the people to a system thus stern and exclusive. It may, however, with quite as much justice, be resolved into love of independence and political sagacity.

The great body of the first emigrants doubtless coincided in general religious views with those whose influence predominated in their church and state. They had, consequently, no personal objection to the stern discipline their political system established. They had also the sagacity to foresee that a system, which by its rigor should exclude from power all who did not concur with their religious views, would have a direct tendency to deter those in other countries from emigrating to their settlement, who did not agree with the general plan of policy they had adopted, and of consequence to increase the probability of their escape from the interference of their ancient oppressors, and the chance of success in laying the foundation of the free commonwealth they contemplated. They also doubtless perceived, that, with the unqualified possession of the *elective franchise*, they had little reason to apprehend that they could not easily control

[1] *Records of the Colony*, p. 117; 19th Oct. 1652.

or annihilate any ill effect upon their political system, arising from the union of church and state, should it become insupportable.

There is abundant evidence, that the submission of the people to this new form of church and state combination was not owing to ignorance, or to indifference to the true principles of civil and religious liberty. Notwithstanding the strong attachment of the early emigrants to their civil, and their almost blind devotion to their ecclesiastical leaders, when, presuming on their influence, either attempted any thing inconsistent with general liberty, a corrective is seen almost immediately applied by the spirit and intelligence of the people.

In this respect, the character of the people of Boston has been at all times distinguished. In every period of our history, they have been second to none in quickness to discern or in readiness to meet every exigency, fearlessly hazarding life and fortune in support of the liberties of the commonwealth. It would be easy to maintain these positions by a recurrence to the annals of each successive age, and particularly to facts connected with our revolutionary struggle. A few instances only will be noticed, and those selected from the earliest times.

A natural jealousy soon sprung up in the metropolis as to the intentions of their civil and ecclesiastical leaders.[1] In 1634 the people began to fear, lest, by reëlecting Winthrop, they "should make way for a Governor for life." They accordingly gave some indications of a design to elect another person. Upon which John Cotton, their great ecclesiastical head, then at the height of his popularity, preached a discourse to the General Court, and delivered this doctrine, — "that a magistrate ought not to be turned out, without just cause, no more than a magistrate might turn out a private man from his freehold, without trial."[2] To show their dislike of the doctrine by the most practical of evidences, our ancestors gave the political divine and his adherents a succession of lessons, for which they were probably the wiser all the rest of their lives. They turned out Winthrop at the very same election, and put in Dudley. The year after, they turned out Dudley and put in Haynes. The year after, they turned out Haynes, and put in Vane. So much for the

[1] *Winthrop*, vol. i. p. 299. [2] *Ibid.* vol. i. p. 132.

first broaching, in Boston, of the doctrine, that public office is of the nature of freehold.

In 1635, an attempt was made by the General Court, to elect a certain number of magistrates as counsellors *for life*.[1] Although Cotton was the author also of this project, and notwithstanding his influence, yet such was the spirit displayed by our ancestors on the occasion, that within three years the General Court[2] was compelled to pass a vote, denying any such intent, and declaring that the persons so chosen should not be accounted magistrates, or have any authority in consequence of such election.

In 1636, the great Antinomian controversy divided the country. Boston was for the covenant of grace; the General Court, for the covenant of works. Under pretence of the apprehension of a riot, the General Court adjourned to Newtown, and expelled the Boston deputies for daring to remonstrate. Boston, indignant at this infringement of its liberties, was about electing the same deputies a second time. At the earnest solicitation of Cotton, however, they chose others. One of these was also expelled by the Court; and a writ having been issued to the town ordering a new election, they refused making any return to the warrant, — a contempt which the General Court did not think it wise to resent.

In 1639, there being vacancies in the Board of Assistants, the Governor and magistrates met and nominated three persons, "not with intent," as they said, "to lead the people's choice of these, nor to divert them from any other, but only to propound for consideration (which any freeman may do) and so leave the people to use their liberties according to their consciences." The result was, that the people did use their liberties according to their consciences. They chose not a man of them.[3] So much for the first legislative *caucus* in our history. It probably would have been happy for their posterity, if the people had always treated like nominations with as little ceremony.

About this time, also, the General Court took exception at the length of the "*lectures*," then the great delight of the people, and at the ill effects resulting from their frequency; whereby poor people were led greatly to neglect their affairs, to the great

[1] *Ibid.* p. 186. [2] *Ibid.* p. 302. [3] *Ibid.* vol. ii. p. 343.

hazard also of their health, owing to their long continuance in the night. Boston expressed strong dislike[1] at this interference, "fearing that the precedent might inthral them to the civil power, and, besides, be a blemish upon them with their posterity, as though they needed to be regulated by the civil magistrate, and raise an ill-savor of their coldness, as if it were possible for the people of Boston to complain of too much preaching."

The magistrates, fearful lest the people should break their bonds, were content to apologize, to abandon the scheme of shortening lectures or diminishing their number, and to rest satisfied with a general understanding, that assemblies should break up in such season, as that people, dwelling a mile or two off, might get home by daylight. Winthrop, on this occasion, passes the following eulogium on the people of Boston, which every period of their history amply confirms: "They were generally of that understanding and moderation, as that they would be easily guided in their way by any rule from Scripture or sound reason."

It is curious and instructive to trace the principles of our constitution as they were successively suggested by circumstances, and gradually gained by the intelligence and daring spirit of the people. For the first four years after their emigration, the freemen, like other corporations, met and transacted business in a body. At this time the people attained a representation under the name of deputies, who sat in the same room with the magistrates, to whose negative all their proceedings were subjected. Next arose the struggle about the negative, which lasted for ten years, and eventuated in the separation of the General Court into two branches, with each a negative on the other.[2] Then came the jealousy of the deputies concerning the magistrates,[3] as proceeding too much by their discretion for want of positive laws, and the demand by the deputies, that persons should be appointed to frame a body of fundamental laws in resemblance of the English Magna Charta.

After this occurred the controversy[4] relative to the powers of the magistrates, during the recess of the General Court; concerning which, when the deputies found that no compromise could be made, and the magistrates declared that, "if occasion

1 *Winthrop*, vol. i. p. 325.
2 *Ibid.* vol. i. p. 160.
3 *Ibid.* p. 322.
4 *Ibid.* vol. ii. p. 169.

required, they should act according to the power and trust committed to them," the Speaker of the House in his place replied, — "THEN, GENTLEMEN, YOU WILL NOT BE OBEYED."

In every period of our early history, the friends of the ancient hierarchy and monarchy were assiduous in their endeavors to introduce a form of government on the principle of an efficient colonial relation. Our ancestors were no less vigilant to avail themselves of their local situation and of the difficulties of the parent state to defeat those attempts; or, in their language, "to avoid and protract." They lived, however, under a perpetual apprehension, that a royal governor would be imposed upon them by the law of force. Their resolution never faltered on the point of resistance to the extent of their power. Notwithstanding Boston would have been the scene of the struggle and the first victim to it, yet its inhabitants never shrunk from their duty through fear of danger, and were always among the foremost to prepare for every exigency. Castle Island was fortified chiefly, and the battery at the north end of the town, and that called the "Sconce," wholly by the voluntary contributions of its inhabitants. After the restoration of Charles II., their instructions to their representatives in the General Court breathe one uniform spirit, — "not to recede from their just rights and privileges as secured by the patent." When, in 1662, the King's Commissioners came to Boston, the inhabitants, to show their spirit in support of their own laws, took measures to have them all arrested for a breach of the Saturday evening law, and actually brought them before the magistrate for riotous and abusive carriage. When Randolph, in 1684, came with his *quo warranto* against their charter, on the question being taken in town meeting, "whether the freemen were minded that the General Court should make full submission and entire resignation of their charter, and of the privileges therein granted, to his Majesty's pleasure," *Boston resolved in the negative, without a dissentient.*

In 1689, the tyranny of Andros, the Governor appointed by James II., having become insupportable to the whole country, Boston rose, like one man; took the battery on Fort Hill by assault in open day; made prisoners of the King's Governor and the Captain of the King's frigate, then lying in the harbor; and restored, with the concurrence of the country, the authority of the old charter leaders.

By accepting the charter of William and Mary, in 1692, the people of Massachusetts first yielded their claims of independence to the Crown. It is only requisite to read the official account of the agents of the colony, to perceive both the resistance they made to that charter, and the necessity which compelled their acceptance of it.[1] Those agents were told by the King's ministers, that they "must take that or none;" that "their consent to it was not asked;" that if "they would not submit to the King's pleasure they must take what would follow." "The opinion of our lawyers," say the agents, "was, that a passive submission to the new was not a surrender of the old charter; and that their taking up with this did not make the people of Massachusetts, in law, uncapable of *obtaining all their old privileges, whenever a favorable opportunity should present itself.*" In the year 1776, nearly a century afterwards, that "favorable opportunity did present itself," and the people of Massachusetts, in conformity with the opinion of their learned counsel and faithful agents, did vindicate and obtain all their "old privileges" of self-government.

Under the new colonial government, thus authoritatively imposed upon them, arose new parties and new struggles,—prerogative men, earnest for a permanent salary for the King's Governor; patriots resisting such an establishment, and indignant at the negative exercised by that officer.

At the end of the first century after the settlement, three generations of men had passed away. For vigor, boldness, enterprise, and a self-sacrificing spirit, Massachusetts stood unrivalled.[2] She had added wealth and extensive dominion to the English Crown. She had turned a barren wilderness into a cultivated field, and instead of barbarous tribes had planted civilized communities. She had prevented France from taking possession of the whole of North America; conquered Port Royal and Acadia; and attempted the conquest of Canada with a fleet of thirty-two sail and two thousand men. At one time, a fifth of her whole effective male population was in arms. When Nevis was plundered by Iberville, she voluntarily transmitted

[1] See *A Brief Account concerning the Agents of New England and their Negotiation with the Court of England.* By Increase Mather. London, 1691.

[2] See *A Defence of the New England Charters,* by Jeremiah Dummer, printed in 1721.

two thousand pounds sterling for the relief of the inhabitants of that island. By these exertions her resources were exhausted, her treasury was impoverished, and she stood bereft and "alone with her glory."

Boston shared in the embarrassments of the Commonwealth. Her commerce was crippled by severe revenue laws and by a depreciated currency. Her population did not exceed fifteen thousand. In September, 1730, she was prevented from all notice of this anniversary by the desolations of the smallpox.

Notwithstanding the darkness of these clouds which overhung Massachusetts and its metropolis at the close of the first century, in other aspects the dawn of a brighter day may be discerned. The exclusive policy in matters of religion, to which the State had been subjected, began gradually to give place to a more perfect liberty. Literature was exchanging subtle metaphysics, quaint conceits, and unwieldy lore for inartificial reasoning, simple taste, and natural thought. Dummer defended the colony in language polished in the society of Pope and of Bolingbroke. Coleman, Cooper, Chauncy, Bowdoin, and others of that constellation, were on the horizon. By their side shone the star of Franklin; its early brightness giving promise of its meridian splendors. Even now began to appear signs of revolution. Voices of complaint and murmur were heard in the air. "Spirits finely touched and to fine issues," — willing and fearless, — breathing unutterable things, flashed along the darkness. In the sky were seen streaming lights, indicating the approach of luminaries yet below the horizon, — Adams, Hancock, Otis, Warren, — leaders of a glorious host, precursors of eventful times, "with fear of change perplexing monarchs."

It would be appropriate, did time permit, to speak of these luminaries, in connection with our Revolution; to trace the principles, which dictated the first emigration of the founders of this metropolis, through the several stages of their development; and to show that the declaration of independence, in 1776, itself, and all the struggles which preceded it, and all the voluntary sacrifices, the self-devotion, and the sufferings, to which the people of that day submitted, for the attainment of independence, were, so far as respects Massachusetts, but the natural and inevitable consequences of the terms of that noble engagement, made by our ancestors, *in August*, 1629, *the year before their emigration;*

which may well be denominated, from its early and later results, the first and original declaration of independence by Massachusetts.

"*By God's assistance, we will be ready in our persons, and with such of our families as are to go with us, to embark for the said plantation by the first of March next, to pass the seas (under God's protection) to inhabit and continue in New England. Provided always, that before the last of September next,* THE WHOLE GOVERNMENT, TOGETHER WITH THE PATENT, BE FIRST LEGALLY TRANSFERRED AND ESTABLISHED, TO REMAIN WITH US AND OTHERS, WHICH SHALL INHABIT THE SAID PLANTATION."[1] Generous resolution! Noble foresight! Sublime self-devotion; chastened and directed by a wisdom, faithful and prospective of distant consequences! Well may we exclaim, — "This policy overtopped all the policy of this world."

For the advancement of the three great objects which were the scope of the policy of our ancestors, — intellectual power, religious liberty, and civil liberty, — Boston has in no period been surpassed, either in readiness to incur, or in energy to make useful, personal or pecuniary sacrifices. She provided for the education of her citizens out of the general fund, antecedently to the law of the Commonwealth making such provision imperative. Nor can it be questioned, that her example and influence had a decisive effect in producing that law. An intelligent generosity has been conspicuous among her inhabitants on this subject, from the day when, in 1635, they "entreated our brother Philemon Pormont to become schoolmaster, for the teaching and nurturing children with us," to this hour, when what is equivalent to a capital of two hundred and fifty thousand dollars is invested in school-houses, eighty schools are maintained, and seven thousand and five hundred children educated at an expense exceeding annually sixty-five thousand dollars. No city in the world, in proportion to its means and population, ever gave more uniform and unequivocal evidences

[1] See "A true coppie of the agreement at Cambridge, 1629," in Hutchinson's *Collection of Original Papers relative to the History of the Colony of Massachusetts Bay*, p. 25, signed by

Richard Saltonstall,	John Winthrop,	Thomas Sharp,
Thomas Dudley,	Kellam Browne,	Increase Nowell,
William Vassal,	Isaac Johnson,	William Pynchon,
Nicko: West,	John Humfrey,	William Colbron.

of its desire to diffuse intellectual power and moral culture through the whole mass of the community. The result is every day witnessed, at home and abroad, in private intercourse and in the public assembly; in a quiet and orderly demeanor, in the self-respect and mutual harmony prevalent among its citizens; in the general comfort which characterizes their condition; in their submission to the laws; and in that wonderful capacity for self-government, which postponed for almost two centuries a city organization; — and this, even then, was adopted more with reference to anticipated, than from experience of existing evils. During the whole of that period, and even after its population exceeded fifty thousand, its financial, economical, and municipal interests were managed, either by general vote, or by men appointed by the whole multitude; and with a regularity, wisdom, and success, which it will be happy if future administrations shall equal, and which certainly they will find it difficult to exceed.

The influence of the institutions of our fathers is also apparent in that munificence towards objects of public interest or charity, for which, in every period of its history, the citizens of Boston have been distinguished, and which, by universal consent, is recognized to be a prominent feature in their character. To no city has Boston ever been second in its spirit of liberality. From the first settlement of the country to this day, it has been a point to which have tended applications for assistance or relief, on account of suffering or misfortune; for the patronage of colleges, the endowment of schools, the erection of churches, and the spreading of learning and religion, from almost every section of the United States. Seldom have the hopes of any worthy applicant been disappointed. The benevolent and public spirit of its inhabitants is also evidenced by its hospitals, its asylums, public libraries, almshouses, charitable associations — in its patronage of the neighboring University, and in its subscriptions for general charities.

It is obviously impracticable to give any just idea of the amount of these charities. They flow from virtues which seek the shade and shun record. They are silent and secret outwellings of grateful hearts, desirous unostentatiously to acknowledge the bounty of Heaven in their prosperity and abundance. The result of inquiries, necessarily imperfect, however, authorize the statement, that, in the records of societies having for their objects either learning or some public charity, or in documents in the hands of individuals relative to contributions for the relief of suffering, or the patronage of distinguished merit or talent, there exists evidence of the liberality of the citizens of this metropolis, and that chiefly within the last thirty years, of an amount, by voluntary donation or bequest, exceeding one million and eight hundred thousand dollars. Far short as this sum falls of the real amount obtained within that period from the liberality of our citizens, it is yet enough to make evident, that the best spirit of the institutions of our ancestors survives in the hearts, and is exhibited in the lives, of the citizens of Boston; inspiring love of country and duty; stimulating to the active virtues of benevolence and charity; exciting wealth and power to their best exercises; counteracting what is selfish in our nature; and elevating the moral and social virtues to wise sacrifices and noble energies.

With respect to religious liberty, where does it exist in a more perfect state, than in this metropolis? Or where has it ever been enjoyed in a purer spirit, or with happier consequences? In what city of equal population are all classes of society more distinguished for obedience to the institutions of religion, for regular attendance on its worship, for more happy intercourse with its ministers, or more uniformly honorable support of them? In all struggles connected with religious liberty, and these are inseparable from its possession, it may be said of the inhabitants of this city, as truly as of any similar association of men, that they have ever maintained the freedom of the Gospel in the spirit of Christianity. Divided into various sects, their mutual intercourse has, almost without exception, been harmonious and respectful. The labors of intemperate zealots, with which, occasionally, every age has been troubled, have seldom, in this metropolis, been attended with their natural and usual consequences. Its sects have never been made to fear or hate one another. The genius of its inhabitants, through the influence of the intellectual power which pervades their mass, has ever been quick to detect "close ambition varnished o'er with zeal." The modes, the forms, the discipline, the opinions, which our ancestors held to be essential, have, in many respects, been changed or obliterated with the progress of time, or been countervailed or superseded by rival forms and opinions. But veneration for the Sacred Scriptures and attachment to the right of free inquiry, which were the substantial motives of their emigration and of all their institutions, remain, and are maintained in a Christian spirit, (judging by life and language,) certainly not exceeded in the times of any of our ancestors. The right to read those Scriptures is universally recognized. The means to acquire the possession and to attain the knowledge of them are multiplied by the intelligence and liberality of the age, and extended to every class of society. All men are invited to search for themselves concerning the grounds of their hopes of future happiness and acceptance. All are permitted to hear from the lips of our Saviour himself, that "the meek," "the merciful," "the pure in heart," "the persecuted for righteousness' sake," are those who shall receive the blessing, and be admitted to the presence, of the Eternal Father; and to be assured from those sacred records, that, "in every nation, he who feareth God and worketh righteousness, is accepted of him." Elevated by the power of these sublime assurances, as conformable to reason as to Revelation, man's intellectual principle rises "above the smoke and stir of this dim spot," and, like an eagle soaring above the Andes, looks down on the cloudy cliffs, the narrow, separating points, and flaming craters, which divide and terrify men below.

It is scarcely necessary, on this occasion, to speak of civil liberty, or to tell of our constitutions of government; of the freedom they maintain and are calculated to preserve; of the equality they establish; the self-respect they encourage; the private and domestic virtues they cherish; the love of country they inspire; the self-devotion and self-sacrifice they enjoin;— all these are but the filling up of the great outline sketched by our fathers, the parts in which, through the darkness and perversity of their times, they were defective, being corrected; all are but endeavors, conformed to their great, original conception, to group together the strength of society and the religious and civil rights of the individual, in a living and breathing spirit of efficient power, by forms of civil government, adapted to our condition, and adjusted to social relations of unexampled greatness and extent, unparalleled in their results, and connected by principles elevated as the nature of man, and immortal as his destinies.

It is not, however, from local position, nor from general circumstances of life and fortune, that the peculiar felicity of this metropolis is to be deduced. Her enviable distinction is, that she is among the chiefest of that happy New England family, which claims descent from the early emigrants. If we take a survey of that family, and, excluding from our view the unnumbered multitudes of its members who have occupied the vacant wildernesses of other States, we restrict our thoughts to the local sphere of New England, what scenes open upon our sight! How wild and visionary would seem our prospects, did we indulge only natural anticipations of the future! Already, on an area of seventy thousand square miles, a population of two millions; all, but comparatively a few, descendants of the early emigrants! Six independent Commonwealths, with constitutions varying in the relations and proportions of power, yet uniform in all their general principles; diverse in their political arrangements, yet each sufficient for its own necessities; all harmonious with those without, and peaceful within; embracing, under the denomination of *towns*, upwards of twelve hundred effective republics, with qualified powers, indeed, but possessing potent influences; — subject themselves to the respective State sovereignties, yet directing all their operations, and shaping their policy by constitutional agencies; swayed, no less than the greater republics, by passions, interests, and affections; like them, exciting competitions which rouse into action the latent energies of mind, and infuse into the mass of each society a knowledge of the nature of its interests, and a capacity to understand and share in the defence of those of the Commonwealth. The effect of these minor republics is daily seen in the existence of practical talents, and in the readiness with which those talents can be called into the public service of the State.

If, after this general survey of the surface of New England, we cast our eyes on its cities and great towns, with what wonder should we behold, did not familiarity render the phenomenon almost unnoticed, men, combined in great multitudes, possessing freedom and the consciousness of strength, — the comparative physical power of the ruler less than that of a cobweb across a lion's path, — yet orderly, obedient, and respectful to authority; a people, but no populace; every class in reality existing, which the general law of society acknowledges, except one, — and this exception characterizing the whole country. The soil of New England is trodden by no slave. In our streets, in our assemblies, in the halls of election and legislation, men of every rank and condition meet, and unite or divide on other principles, and are actuated by other motives, than those growing out of such distinctions. The fears and jealousies, which in other countries separate classes of men and make them hostile to each other, have here no influence, or a very limited one. Each individual, of whatever condition, has the consciousness of living under known laws, which secure equal rights, and guarantee to each whatever portion of the goods of life, be it great or small, chance, or talent, or industry may have bestowed. All perceive, that the honors and rewards of society are open equally to the fair competition of all; that the distinctions of wealth, or of power, are not fixed in families; that whatever of this nature exists to-day, may be changed to-morrow, or, in a coming generation, be absolutely reversed. Common principles, interests, hopes, and affections, are the result of universal education. Such are the consequences of the equality of rights, and of the provisions for the general diffusion of knowledge and the distribution of intestate estates, established by the laws framed by the earliest emigrants to New England.

If from our cities we turn to survey the wide expanse of the interior, how do the effects of the institutions and example of our early ancestors appear, in all the local comfort and accommodation which mark the general condition of the whole country; — unobtrusive indeed, but substantial; in nothing splendid, but in every thing sufficient and satisfactory. Indications of active talent and practical energy exist everywhere. With a soil comparatively little luxuriant, and in great proportion either rock, or hill, or sand, the skill and industry of man are seen triumphing over the obstacles of nature; making the rock the guardian of the field; moulding the granite, as though it were clay; leading cultivation to the hill-top, and spreading over the arid plain, hitherto unknown and unanticipated harvests. The lofty mansion of the prosperous adjoins the lowly dwelling of the husbandman; their respective inmates are in the daily interchange of civility, sympathy, and respect. Enterprise and skill, which once held chief affinity with the ocean or the sea-board, now begin to delight the interior, haunting our rivers, where the music of the waterfall, with powers more attractive than those of the fabled harp of Orpheus, collects around it intellectual man and material nature. Towns and cities, civilized and happy communities, rise, like exhalations, on rocks and in forests, till the deep and far-resounding voice of the neighboring torrent is itself lost and unheard, amid the predominating noise of successful and rejoicing labor.

What lessons has New England, in every period of her history, given to the world! What lessons do her condition and example still give! How unprecedented; yet how practical! How simple; yet how powerful! She has proved, that all the variety of Christian sects may live together in harmony, under a government, which allows equal privileges to all, — exclusive preëminence to none. She has proved, that ignorance among the multitude is not necessary to order, but that the surest basis of perfect order is the information of the people. She has proved the old maxim, that "no government, except a despotism with a standing army, can subsist where the people have arms," is false. Ever since the first settlement of the country, arms have been required to be in the hands of the whole multitude of New England; yet the use of them in a private quarrel, if it have ever happened, is so rare, that a late writer, of great intelligence, who had passed his whole life in New England, and possessed extensive means of information, declares, "I know not a single instance of it."[1] She has proved, that a people, of a character essentially military, may subsist without duelling. New England has, at all times, been distinguished, both on the land and on the ocean, for a daring, fearless, and enterprising spirit; yet the same writer[2] asserts, that during the whole period of her existence, her soil has been disgraced but by *five* duels, and that only *two* of these were fought by her native inhabitants! Perhaps this assertion is not minutely correct. There can, however, be no question, that it is sufficiently near the truth to justify the position for which it is here adduced, and which the history of New England, as well as the experience of her inhabitants, abundantly confirms; that, in the present and in every past age, the spirit of our institutions has, to every important practical purpose, annihilated the spirit of duelling.

[1] See *Travels in New England and New York*, by Timothy Dwight, S. T. D., LL. D., late President of Yale College, vol. iv. p. 334.

[2] *Ibid.* p. 336.

Such are the true glories of the institutions of our fathers! Such the natural fruits of that patience in toil, that frugality of disposition, that temperance of habit, that general diffusion of knowledge, and that sense of religious responsibility, inculcated by the precepts, and exhibited in the example of every generation of our ancestors!

And now, standing at this hour on the dividing line which separates the ages that are past from those which are to come, how solemn is the thought, that not one of this vast assembly, not one of that great multitude who now throng our streets, rejoice in our fields, and make our hills echo with their gratulations, shall live to witness the next return of the era we this day celebrate! The dark veil of futurity conceals from human sight the fate of cities and nations as well as of individuals. Man passes away; generations are but shadows; there is nothing stable but truth; principles only are immortal.

What then, in conclusion of this great topic, are the elements of the liberty, prosperity, and safety which the inhabitants of New England at this day enjoy? In what language, and concerning what comprehensive truths does the wisdom of former times address the inexperience of the future?

Those elements are simple, obvious, and familiar.

Every civil and religious blessing of New England, all that here gives happiness to human life or security to human virtue is alone to be perpetuated in the forms and under the auspices of a free commonwealth.

The Commonwealth itself has no other strength or hope than the intelligence and virtue of the individuals that compose it.

For the intelligence and virtue of individuals, there is no other human assurance than laws, providing for the education of the whole people.

These laws themselves have no strength or efficient sanction, except in the moral and accountable nature of man, disclosed in the records of the Christian's faith; the right to read, to construe, and to judge concerning which, belongs to no class or caste of men, but exclusively to the individual, who must stand or fall by his own acts and his own faith, and not by those of another.

The great comprehensive truths, written in letters of living light on every page of our history, the language addressed by every past age of New England to all future ages is this, —

Human happiness has no perfect security but freedom; freedom none but virtue; virtue none but knowledge; and neither freedom, nor virtue, nor knowledge has any vigor or immortal hope, except in the principles of the Christian faith and in the sanctions of the Christian religion.

Men of Massachusetts! Citizens of Boston! Descendants of the early emigrants! consider your blessings; consider your duties. You have an inheritance acquired by the labors and sufferings of six successive generations of ancestors. They founded the fabric of your prosperity in a severe and masculine morality; having intelligence for its cement and religion for its groundwork. Continue to build on the same foundation and by the same principles; let the extending temple of your country's freedom rise in the spirit of ancient times, in proportions of intellectual and moral architecture, — just, simple, and sublime. As from the first to this day, let New England continue to be an example to the world of the blessings of a free government, and of the means and capacity of man to maintain it. And, in all times to come as in all times past, may Boston be among the foremost and the boldest to exemplify and uphold whatever constitutes the prosperity, the happiness, and the glory of New England.

CHAPTER XXIII.

CITY GOVERNMENT. 1830.

HARRISON GRAY OTIS, *Mayor.*

An Ode, pronounced before the Inhabitants of Boston, on the 17th of September, 1830, at the Centennial Celebration of the Settlement of the City. By Charles Sprague.

I.

NOT to the Pagan's mount I turn,
For inspiration now;
Olympus and its gods I spurn —
Pure One, be with me, Thou!
Thou, in whose awful name,
From suffering and from shame,
Our Fathers fled, and braved a pathless sea;
Thou, in whose holy fear,
They fixed an empire here,
And gave it to their Children and to Thee.

II.

And You! ye bright ascended Dead,
Who scorned the bigot's yoke,
Come, round this place your influence shed;
Your spirits I invoke.
Come, as ye came of yore,
When on an unknown shore,
Your daring hands the flag of faith unfurled,
To float sublime,
Through future time,
The beacon-banner of another world.

III.

Behold! they come — those sainted forms,
Unshaken through the strife of storms;
Heaven's winter cloud hangs coldly down,
And earth puts on its rudest frown;

But colder, ruder was the hand,
That drove them from their own fair land;
Their own fair land — refinement's chosen seat,
Art's trophied dwelling, learning's green retreat;
By valor guarded, and by victory crowned,
For all, but gentle charity, renowned.
With streaming eye, yet steadfast heart,
Even from that land they dared to part,
And burst each tender tie;
Haunts, where their sunny youth was passed,
Homes, where they fondly hoped at last
In peaceful age to die;
Friends, kindred, comfort, all they spurned —
Their fathers' hallowed graves;
And to a world of darkness turned,
Beyond a world of waves.

IV.

When Israel's race from bondage fled,
Signs from on high the wanderers led;
But here — Heaven hung no symbol here,
Their steps to guide, *their* souls to cheer;
They saw, thro' sorrow's lengthening night,
Nought but the fagot's guilty light;
The cloud they gazed at was the smoke,
That round their murdered brethren broke.
Nor power above, nor power below,
Sustained them in their hour of woe;
A fearful path they trod,
And dared a fearful doom;
To build an altar to their God,
And find a quiet tomb.

V.

But not alone, not all unblessed,
The exile sought a place of rest;
One dared with him to burst the knot,
That bound her to her native spot;
Her low sweet voice in comfort spoke,
As round their bark the billows broke;

She through the midnight watch was there,
With him to bend her knees in prayer;
She trod the shore with girded heart,
Through good and ill to claim her part;
In life, in death, with him to seal
Her kindred love, her kindred zeal.

VI.

They come — that coming who shall tell?
The eye may weep, the heart may swell,
But the poor tongue in vain essays
A fitting note for them to raise.
We hear the after-shout that rings
For them who smote the power of kings;
The swelling triumph all would share,
But who the dark defeat would dare,
And boldly meet the wrath and woe,
That wait the unsuccessful blow?
It were an envied fate, we deem,
To live a land's recorded theme,
When we are in the tomb;
We, too, might yield the joys of home,
And waves of winter darkness roam,
And tread a shore of gloom —
Knew we those waves, through coming time,
Should roll our names to every clime;
Felt we that millions on that shore
Should stand, our memory to adore —
But no glad vision burst in light,
Upon the Pilgrims' aching sight
Their hearts no proud hereafter swelled;
Deep shadows veiled the way they held;
The yell of vengeance was their trump of fame,
Their monument, a grave without a name.

VII.

Yet, strong in weakness, there they stand,
On yonder ice-bound rock,
Stern and resolved, that faithful band,
To meet fate's rudest shock.

Though anguish rends the father's breast,
For them, his dearest and his best,
With him the waste who trod—
Though tears that freeze, the mother sheds
Upon her children's houseless heads—
The Christian turns to God!

VIII.

In grateful adoration now,
Upon the barren sands they bow.
What tongue of joy e'er woke such prayer,
As bursts in desolation there?
What arm of strength e'er wrought such power,
As waits to crown that feeble hour?
There into life an infant empire springs!
There falls the iron from the soul;
There liberty's young accents roll,
Up to the King of kings!
To fair creation's farthest bound,
That thrilling summons yet shall sound;
The dreaming nations shall awake,
And to their centre earth's old kingdoms shake.
Pontiff and prince, your sway
Must crumble from that day;
Before the loftier throne of Heaven,
The hand is raised, the pledge is given—
One monarch to obey, one creed to own,
That monarch, God, that creed, His word alone.

IX.

Spread out earth's holiest records here,
Of days and deeds to reverence dear;
A zeal like this what pious legends tell?
On kingdoms built
In blood and guilt,
The worshippers of vulgar triumph dwell—
But what exploit with theirs shall page,
Who rose to bless their kind;
Who left their nation and their age,
Man's spirit to unbind?

Who boundless seas passed o'er,
And boldly met, in every path,
Famine and frost and heathen wrath,
To dedicate a shore,
Where piety's meek train might breathe their vow,
And seek their Maker with an unshamed brow;
Where liberty's glad race might proudly come,
And set up there an everlasting home?

X.

O many a time it hath been told,
The story of those men of old:
For this fair poetry hath wreathed
Her sweetest, purest flower;
For this proud eloquence hath breathed
His strain of loftiest power;
Devotion, too, hath lingered round
Each spot of consecrated ground,
And hill and valley blessed;
There, where our banished Fathers strayed,
There, where they loved and wept and prayed,
There, where their ashes rest.

XI.

And never may they rest unsung,
While liberty can find a tongue.
Twine, Gratitude, a wreath for them,
More deathless than the diadem,
Who to life's noblest end,
Gave up life's noblest powers,
And bade the legacy descend,
Down, down to us and ours.

XII.

By centuries now the glorious hour we mark,
When to these shores they steered their shattered bark;
And still, as other centuries melt away,
Shall other ages come to keep the day.
When we are dust, who gather round this spot,
Our joys, our griefs, our very names forgot,

Here shall the dwellers of the land be seen,
To keep the memory of the Pilgrims green.
Nor here alone their praises shall go round,
Nor here alone their virtues shall abound —
Broad as the empire of the free shall spread,
Far as the foot of man shall dare to tread,
Where oar hath never dipped, where human tongue
Hath never through the woods of ages rung,
There, where the eagle's scream and wild wolf's cry
Keep ceaseless day and night through earth and sky,
Even there, in after time, as toil and taste
Go forth in gladness to redeem the waste,
Even there shall rise, as grateful myriads throng,
Faith's holy prayer and freedom's joyful song;
There shall the flame that flashed from yonder Rock,
Light up the land till nature's final shock.

XIII.

Yet while by life's endearments crowned,
To mark this day we gather round,
And to our nation's founders raise
The voice of gratitude and praise,
Shall not one line lament that lion race,
For us struck out from sweet creation's face?
Alas! alas! for them — those fated bands,
Whose monarch tread was on these broad, green lands;
Our fathers called them savage — them, whose bread,
In the dark hour, those famished fathers fed:
We call them savage, we,
Who hail the struggling free,
Of every clime and hue;
We, who would save
The branded slave,
And give him liberty he never knew:
We, who but now have caught the tale,
That turns each listening tyrant pale,
And blessed the winds and waves that bore
The tidings to our kindred shore;
The triumph-tidings pealing from that land,
Where up in arms insulted legions stand;

There, gathering round his bold compeers,
Where He, our own, our welcomed One,
Riper in glory than in years,
Down from his forfeit throne,
A craven monarch hurled,
And spurned him forth, a proverb to the world!

XIV.

We call them savage — O be just!
Their outraged feelings scan;
A voice comes forth, 'tis from the dust —
The savage was a man!
Think ye he loved not? who stood by,
And in his toils took part?
Woman was there to bless his eye —
The savage had a heart!
Think ye he prayed not? when on high
He heard the thunders roll,
What bade him look beyond the sky?
The savage had a soul!

XV.

I venerate the Pilgrim's cause,
Yet for the red man dare to plead —
We bow to Heaven's recorded laws,
He turned to nature for a creed;
Beneath the pillared dome,
We seek our God in prayer;
Through boundless woods he loved to roam,
And the Great Spirit worshipped there:
But one, one fellow-throb with us he felt;
To one divinity with us he knelt;
Freedom, the self-same freedom we adore,
Bade him defend his violated shore;
He saw the cloud, ordained to grow,
And burst upon his hills in woe;
He saw his people withering by,
Beneath the invader's evil eye;

Strange feet were trampling on his fathers' bones;
At midnight hour he woke to gaze
Upon his happy cabin's blaze,
And listen to his children's dying groans:
He saw — and maddening at the sight,
Gave his bold bosom to the fight;
To tiger rage his soul was driven,
Mercy was not — nor sought nor given;
The pale man from his lands must fly;
He would be free — or he would die.

XVI.

And was this savage? say,
Ye ancient few,
Who struggled through
Young freedom's trial-day —
What first your sleeping wrath awoke?
On your own shores war's larum broke:
What turned to gall even kindred blood?
Round your own homes the oppressor stood:
This every warm affection chilled,
This every heart with vengeance thrilled,
And strengthened every hand;
From mound to mound,
The word went round —
"Death for our native land!"

XVII.

Ye mothers, too, breathe ye no sigh,
For them who thus could dare to die?
Are all your own dark hours forgot,
Of soul-sick suffering here?
Your pangs, as from yon mountain spot,
Death spoke in every booming shot,
That knelled upon your ear?
How oft that gloomy, glorious tale ye tell,
As round your knees your children's children hang,
Of them, the gallant Ones, ye loved so well,
Who to the conflict for their country sprang.

In pride, in all the pride of woe,
Ye tell of them, the brave laid low,
Who for their birthplace bled;
In pride, the pride of triumph then,
Ye tell of them, the matchless men,
From whom the invaders fled!

XVIII.

And ye, this holy place who throng,
The annual theme to hear,
And bid the exulting song
Sound their great names from year to year;
Ye, who invoke the chisel's breathing grace,
In marble majesty their forms to trace;
Ye, who the sleeping rocks would raise,
To guard their dust and speak their praise;
Ye, who, should some other band
With hostile foot defile the land,
Feel that ye like them would wake,
Like them the yoke of bondage break,
Nor leave a battle-blade undrawn,
Though every hill a sepulchre should yawn —
Say, have not ye one line for those,
One brother-line to spare,
Who rose but as your Fathers rose,
And dared as ye would dare?

XIX.

Alas! for them — their day is o'er,
Their fires are out from hill and shore;
No more for them the wild deer bounds,
The plough is on their hunting grounds;
The pale man's axe rings through their woods,
The pale man's sail skims o'er their floods,
Their pleasant springs are dry;
Their children — look, by power oppressed,
Beyond the mountains of the west,
Their children go — to die.

XX.

O doubly lost! oblivion's shadows close
Around their triumphs and their woes.
On other realms, whose suns have set,
Reflected radiance lingers yet;
There sage and bard have shed a light
That never shall go down in night;
There time-crowned columns stand on high,
To tell of them who cannot die;
Even we, who then were nothing, kneel
In homage there, and join earth's general peal.
But the doomed Indian leaves behind no trace,
To save his own, or serve another race;
With his frail breath his power has passed away,
His deeds, his thoughts are buried with his clay;
Nor lofty pile, nor glowing page
Shall link him to a future age,
Or give him with the past a rank:
His heraldry is but a broken bow,
His history but a tale of wrong and woe,
His very name must be a blank.

XXI.

Cold, with the beast he slew, he sleeps;
O'er him no filial spirit weeps;
No crowds throng round, no anthem-notes ascend,
To bless his coming and embalm his end;
Even that he lived, is for his conqueror's tongue,
By foes alone his death-song must be sung;
No chronicles but theirs shall tell
His mournful doom to future times;
May these upon his virtues dwell,
And in his fate forget his crimes.

XXII.

Peace to the mingling dead!
Beneath the turf we tread,

Chief, Pilgrim, Patriot sleep —
All gone! how changed! and yet the same,
As when faith's herald bark first came
In sorrow o'er the deep.
Still from his noonday height,
The sun looks down in light;
Along the trackless realms of space,
The stars still run their midnight race;
The same green valleys smile, the same rough shore
Still echoes to the same wild ocean's roar: —
But where the bristling night-wolf sprang
Upon his startled prey,
Where the fierce Indian's war-cry rang
Through many a bloody fray;
And where the stern old Pilgrim prayed
In solitude and gloom,
Where the bold Patriot drew his blade,
And dared a patriot's doom —
Behold! in liberty's unclouded blaze,
We lift our heads, a race of other days.

XXIII.

All gone! the wild beast's lair is trodden out;
Proud temples stand in beauty there;
Our children raise their merry shout,
Where once the death-whoop vexed the air:
The Pilgrim — seek yon ancient place of graves,
Beneath that chapel's holy shade;
Ask, where the breeze the long grass waves,
Who, who within that spot are laid:
The Patriot — go, to fame's proud mount repair,
The tardy pile, slow rising there,
With tongueless eloquence shall tell
Of them who for their country fell.

XXIV.

All gone! 't is ours, the goodly land —
Look round — the heritage behold;
Go forth — upon the mountains stand,
Then, if ye can, be cold.

See living vales by living waters blessed,
Their wealth see earth's dark caverns yield,
See ocean roll, in glory dressed,
For all a treasure, and round all a shield:
Hark to the shouts of praise
Rejoicing millions raise;
Gaze on the spires that rise,
To point them to the skies,
Unfearing and unfeared;
Then, if ye can, O then forget
To whom ye owe the sacred debt —
The Pilgrim race revered!
The men who set faith's burning lights
Upon these everlasting heights,
To guide their children through the years of time
The men that glorious law who taught,
Unshrinking liberty of thought,
And roused the nations with the truth sublime.

XXV.

Forget? no, never — ne'er shall die,
Those names to memory dear;
I read the promise in each eye
That beams upon me here.
Descendants of a twice-recorded race,
Long may ye here your lofty lineage grace;
'T is not for you home's tender tie
To rend, and brave the waste of waves;
'T is not for you to rouse and die,
Or yield and live a line of slaves;
The deeds of danger and of death are done:
Upheld by inward power alone,
Unhonored by the world's loud tongue,
'T is yours to do unknown,
And then to die unsung.
To other days, to other men belong
The penman's plaudit and the poet's song;
Enough for glory has been wrought,
By you be humbler praises sought;
In peace and truth life's journey run,
And keep unsullied what your Fathers won.

XXVI.

Take then my prayer, Ye dwellers of this spot —
Be yours a noiseless and a guiltless lot.
I plead not that ye bask
In the rank beams of vulgar fame;
To light your steps I ask
A purer and a holier flame.
No bloated growth I supplicate for you,
No pining multitude, no pampered few;
'T is not alone to coffer gold,
Nor spreading borders to behold;
'T is not fast-swelling crowds to win,
The refuse-ranks of want and sin —
This be the kind decree:
Be ye by goodness crowned,
Revered, though not renowned;
Poor, if Heaven will, but Free!
Free from the tyrants of the hour,
The clans of wealth, the clans of power,
The coarse, cold scorners of their God;
Free from the taint of sin,
The leprosy that feeds within,
And free, in mercy, from the bigot's rod.

XXVII.

The sceptre's might, the crosier's pride,
Ye do not fear;
No conquest blade, in life-blood dyed,
Drops terror here —
Let there not lurk a subtler snare,
For wisdom's footsteps to beware;
The shackle and the stake,
Our Fathers fled;
Ne'er may their children wake
A fouler wrath, a deeper dread;
Ne'er may the craft that fears the flesh to bind,
Lock its hard fetters on the mind;
Quenched be the fiercer flame
That kindles with a name:

The pilgrim's faith, the pilgrim's zeal,
Let more than pilgrim kindness seal;
Be purity of life the test,
Leave to the heart, to Heaven, the rest.

XXVIII.

So, when our children turn the page,
To ask what triumphs marked our age,
What we achieved to challenge praise,
Through the long line of future days,
This let them read, and hence instruction draw:
" Here were the Many blessed,
" Here found the virtues rest,
" Faith linked with love and liberty with law;
" Here industry to comfort led,
" Her book of light here learning spread;
" Here the warm heart of youth
" Was wooed to temperance and to truth;
" Here hoary age was found,
" By wisdom and by reverence crowned.
" No great, but guilty fame
" Here kindled pride, that should have kindled shame;
" THESE chose the better, happier part,
" That poured its sunlight o'er the heart;
" That crowned their homes with peace and health,
" And weighed Heaven's smile beyond earth's wealth;
" Far from the thorny paths of strife
" They stood, a living lesson to their race,
" Rich in the charities of life,
" Man in his strength, and Woman in her grace;
" In purity and love THEIR pilgrim road they trod,
" And when they served their neighbor felt they served their God."

XXIX.

This may not wake the poet's verse,
This souls of fire may ne'er rehearse
In crowd delighting voice;
Yet o'er the record shall the patriot bend,
His quiet praise the moralist shall lend,
And all the good rejoice.

XXX.

This be our story then, in that far day,
When others come their kindred debt to pay:
    In that far day? — O what shall be,
    In this dominion of the free,
When we and ours have rendered up our trust,
And men unborn shall tread above our dust?
    O what shall be? — He, He alone,
        The dread response can make,
    Who sitteth on the only throne,
        That time shall never shake;
    Before whose all-beholding eyes
Ages sweep on, and empires sink and rise.
    Then let the song to Him begun,
        To Him in reverence end:
    Look down in love, Eternal One,
        And Thy good cause defend;
    Here, late and long, put forth thy hand,
    To guard and guide the Pilgrim's land.

APPENDIX.

(A. Page 43.)

THE MAYOR'S INAUGURAL ADDRESS, MAY, 1822.

Gentlemen of the City Council: —

THE experience of nearly two centuries has borne ample testimony to the wisdom of those institutions which our ancestors established for the management of their municipal concerns. Most of the towns in this Commonwealth may, probably, continue to enjoy the benefit of those salutary regulations for an unlimited series of years. But the great increase of population in the town of Boston has made it necessary for the Legislature frequently to enact statutes of local application, to enable the inhabitants successfully to conduct their affairs; and at the last session, with a promptness which claims our gratitude, on the application of the town, they granted the charter which invests it with the powers and immunities of a city. Those who have attended to the inconveniences under which we have labored, will not attribute this innovation to an eager thirst for novelty, or restless desire of innovation. The most intelligent and experienced of our citizens have for a long period meditated a change, and exerted their influence to effect it. Difference of opinion must be expected, and mutual concessions made, in all cases where the interests of a large community is to be accommodated. The precise form in which the charter is to be presented, may not be acceptable to all; but its provisions have met with the approbation of a large majority, and it will receive the support of every good citizen.

Mr. Chairman, and Gentlemen of the Board of Selectmen: —

The members of the City Council acknowledge their obligations to you, for the attention and care which you have bestowed in all the arrangements for their accommodation. They tender their thanks for the friendly and respectful sentiments expressed in the address which accompanied the delivery of the ancient act of incorporation of the town, and the recent charter of the city.

During the short period which has elapsed since I was elected to the office, the duties of which I have now solemnly undertaken to discharge to the best of my ability, I have devoted such portion of my time as I could command to examine the records of your proceedings, with the able assistance which your Chairman most readily afforded me; and they furnish full evidence of the ability, diligence, and integrity of those who have been justly denominated the Fathers of the town.

Gentlemen, you will now be relieved from labors, the weight of which can only be duly estimated by those excellent citizens who have preceded you in office. You retire with the consciousness of important duties faithfully and honorably discharged. Our best wishes attend you, whether engaged in public employments or in private pursuits. May you be useful and prosperous, and long continue your exertions to advance the interest and honor of our city.

Those who encourage hopes that can never be realized, and those who indulge unreasonable apprehensions because this instrument is not framed agreeably to their wishes, will be benefited by reflecting, how much more our social happiness depends upon other causes than the provisions of a charter. Purity of manners, general diffusion of knowledge, and strict attention to the education of the young, above all a firm, practical belief of that Divine revelation which has affixed the penalty of unceasing anguish to vice, and promised to virtue rewards of interminable duration, will counteract the evils of any form of government. While the love of order, benevolent affections, and Christian piety distinguish, as they have done, the inhabitants of this city, they may enjoy the highest blessings under a charter with so few imperfections as that which the wisdom of our Legislature has sanctioned.

To enter upon the administration of this government by the invitation of our fellow-citizens, we are this day assembled. When I look around and observe gentlemen of the highest standing and most active employments, devoting their talents and experience to assist in the commencement of this arduous business, in common with my fellow-citizens, I appreciate most highly their elevated and patriotic motives. I well know, Gentlemen, the great sacrifice of time, of care, and of emolument, which you make in assuming this burden. It shall be my constant study to lighten it by every means in my power. In my official intercourse, I shall not encumber you with unnecessary forms, or encroach on your time with prolix dissertations. In all the communications which the charter requires me to make, conciseness and brevity will be carefully studied. I will detain you no longer from the discharge of the important duties which now devolve upon you, than to invite you to unite in beseeching the Father of Light, without whose blessing all exertion is fruitless, and whose grace alone can give efficacy to the councils of human wisdom, to enlighten and guide our deliberations with the influence of his Holy Spirit, and then we cannot fail to promote the best interests of our fellow-citizens.

(B. Page 59.)

THE MAYOR'S INAUGURAL ADDRESS, MAY, 1823.

Gentlemen of the Board of Aldermen, and Gentlemen of the Common Council:—

In accepting the office, to which the suffrages of my fellow-citizens have called me, I have not concealed from myself the labors and responsibilities of the station. Comparing my own powers with the nature and exigencies of the present relations of the city, I should have shrunk instinctively from the task, did I not derive, from the intelligence and virtues of my fellow-citizens, a confidence which no qualifications of my own are capable of inspiring.

In entering upon the duties of this office, and after examining and considering the records of the proceedings of the city authorities the past year, it is impossible for me to refrain from expressing the sense I entertain of the services of that high and honorable individual who filled the Chair of this city, as well as of the wise, prudent, and faithful citizens, who composed, during that period, the City Council. Their labors have been, indeed, in a measure, unobtrusive; but they have been various, useful, and well considered. They have laid the foundations of the prosperity of our city deep, and on right principles; and, whatever success may attend those who come after them, they will be largely indebted for it to the wisdom and fidelity of their predecessors. A task was committed to the first administration to perform, in no common degree arduous and delicate. The change from a town to a city had not been effected without a considerable opposition. On that subject many fears existed, which it was difficult to allay; many jealousies, hard to overcome. In the outset of a new form of government, among variously affected passions and interests, and among indistinct expectations impossible to realize, it was apparently wise to shape the course of the first administration, rather by the spirit of the long-experienced constitution of the town, than by that of the unsettled charter of the city. It was natural for prudent men, first intrusted with city authorities, to apprehend that measures partaking of the mild, domestic character of our ancient institutions, might be as useful, and would be likely to be more acceptable, than those which should develop the entire powers of the new government. It is yet to be proved, whether, in these measures, our predecessors were not right. In all times the inhabitants of this metropolis have been distinguished, preëminently, for a free, elastic republican spirit. Heaven grant, that they forever may be thus distinguished! It is yet to be decided, whether such a spirit can, for the sake of the peace, order, health, and convenience of a great and rapidly-increasing population, endure without distrust and discontent, the application of necessary city powers to all the exigencies which arise in such a community.

In executing the trust which my fellow-citizens have confided to me, I shall yield entirely to the influences, and be guided exclusively by the principles of the city charter; striving to give prudent efficiency to all its powers; endeavoring to perform all its duties, in forms and modes at once the most useful and most acceptable to my fellow-citizens. If at any time, however, through any intrinsic incompatibility, it is impracticable to unite both these objects, I shall, in such case, follow duty; and leave the event to the decision of a just, and wise, and generous people. In every exigency, it will be my endeavor to imbibe and to exhibit, in purpose and act, the spirit of the city charter.

What that spirit is, so far as relates to the office of Mayor; what duties it enjoins; and by what principles those duties will, in the course of the ensuing administration, be attempted to be performed, it is suitable to the occasion, and I shall now, very briefly, explain.

The spirit of the city charter, so far as relates to the office of Mayor, is characterized by the powers and duties it devolves upon that officer.

By him, "the laws of the city are to be executed; the conduct of all subordinate officers inspected; all negligence, carelessness, and positive violations of duty prosecuted and punished." In addition to this, he is enjoined to "collect and communicate all information, and recommend all such measures as may tend to improve the city finances, police, health, security, cleanliness, comfort, and ornament."

The spirit of the city charter in this relation may also be collected, by considering these powers and duties in connection with the preceding form of government. One great defect in the ancient organization of town government was, the division of the executive power among many; the consequent little responsibility, and the facility with which that little was shifted from one department, board, or individual, to another; so as to leave the inhabitants, in a great measure, at a loss whom to blame for the deficiency in the nature or execution of the provisions for their safety and police. The duty, also, of general superintendence over all the boards and public institutions, being specifically vested nowhere, no individual member of either of them could take upon himself that office, without being obnoxious to the charge of a busy, meddlesome disposition. The consequence was, that the great duty of considering all the public institutions, in their relations to one another and to the public service, was either necessarily neglected, or, if performed at all, could only be executed occasionally, and in a very general manner.

The remedy attempted by the city charter is, to provide for the fulfilment of all these duties, by specifically investing the chief officer of the city with the necessary powers; and thus to render him responsible, both in character and by station, for their efficient exercise. By placing this officer under the constant control of both branches of the City Council, all errors, in judgment and purpose, were intended to be checked or corrected; and, by his annual election, security is attained against insufficiency or abuse, in the exercise of his authority.

The duties, enjoined by the charter on the executive authority, are concurrent with its powers and coincident with its spirit. If, in making a sketch of them, I shall be thought to present an outline, difficult for any man completely to fill, and absolutely impracticable for the individual who now occupies the station, let it be remembered, that it is always wise in man to work after models more perfect than his capacity can execute. Perfect duty, it is not in the power of man to perform. But it is the right of the people, that every man in public office should know and attempt it. Let it also be considered, that it will be advantageous, both for the individual who may hold, and for the people who judge and select, that both should form elevated conceptions of the nature of the station. The one will be thus more likely to aim at something higher than mediocrity, in execution; and the other, forming just notions of its difficulty, delicacy, and importance, will select with discrimination, and receive more readily faithful and laborious endeavor in lieu of perfect performance.

The great duty of the Mayor of such a city as this, is to identify himself, absolutely and exclusively, with its character and interests. All its important relations he should diligently study, and strive thoroughly to understand. All its rights, whether affecting property, or liberty, or power, it is his duty, as occasions occur, to analyze and maintain. If possible, he should leave no foundations of either unsettled or dubious. Towards them, he should teach himself to feel, not merely the zeal of official station, but the pertinacious spirit of private interest.

Of local, sectional, party, or personal divisions, he should know nothing, except for the purpose of healing the wounds they inflict; softening the animosities they engender; and exciting, by his example and influence, bands, hostile to one another in every other respect, to march one way, when the interests of the city are in danger. Its honor, happiness, dignity, safety, and prosperity, the development of its resources, its expenditures and police, should be the perpetual object of his purpose and labor of his thought. All its public institutions, its edifices, hospitals, almshouses, jails, should be made the subject of his frequent inspection, to the end that wants may be supplied, errors corrected, abuses exposed.

Above all, its schools, those choice depositaries of the hope of a free people, should engage his utmost solicitude and unremitting superintendence. Justly are these institutions the pride and the boast of the inhabitants of this city. For these, Boston has, at all times, stood preëminent. Let there exist, elsewhere, a greater population, a richer commerce, wider streets, more splendid avenues, statelier palaces. Be it the endeavor of this metropolis to educate better men, happier citizens, more enlightened statesmen; to elevate a people, thoroughly instructed in their social rights, deeply imbued with a sense of their moral duties; mild, flexible to every breath of legitimate authority; unyielding as fate to unconstitutional impositions.

In administering the police, in executing the laws, in protecting the rights, and promoting the prosperity of the city, its first officer will be necessarily beset and assailed by individual interests, by rival projects, by personal influences, by party passions. The more firm and inflexible he is, in maintaining the rights, and in pursuing the interests of the city, the greater is the probability of his becoming obnoxious to all, whom he causes to be prosecuted, or punished; to all, whose passions he thwarts; to all, whose interests he opposes. It will remain for the citizens to decide, whether he who shall attempt to fulfil these duties, and thus to uphold their interests, in a firm, honest, and impartial spirit, shall find countenance and support, in the intelligence and virtue of the community.

Touching the principles, by which the ensuing administration will endeavor to regulate and conduct the affairs of the city, nothing is promised, except a laborious fulfilment of every known duty; a prudent exercise of every invested power; and a disposition, shrinking from no official responsibility. The outline of the duties, just sketched, will be placed before the executive officer, without any expectation of approximating towards its extent, much less of filling it up, according to that enlarged conception. By making, in the constitution of our

32 *

nature, the power to purpose greater than the power to perform, Providence has indicated to man, that true duty and wisdom consists in combining high efforts with humble expectations.

If the powers vested seem too great for any individual, let it be remembered, that they are necessary to attain the great objects of health, comfort, and safety to the city. To those whose fortunes are restricted, these powers, in their just exercise, ought to be peculiarly precious. The rich can fly from the generated pestilence. In the season of danger, the sons of fortune can seek refuge in purer atmospheres. But necessity condemns the poor to remain and inhale the noxious effluvia. To all classes who reside permanently in a city, these powers are a privilege and a blessing. In relation to city police, it is not sufficient that the law, in its due process, will ultimately remedy every injury, and remove every nuisance. While the law delays, the injury is done. While judges are doubting, and lawyers debating, the nuisance is exhaling and the atmosphere corrupting. In these cases, prevention should be the object of solicitude, not remedy. It is not enough, that the obstacle which impedes the citizen's way, or the nuisance which offends his sense should be removed on complaint, or by complaint. The true criterion of an efficient city government is, that it should be removed before complaint and without complaint.

The true glory of a city consists, not in palaces, temples, columns, the vain boast of art, or the proud magnificence of luxury, but in a happy, secure, and contented people; feeling the advantage of a vigorous and faithful administration, not merely in the wide street and splendid avenue, but in every lane, in every court, and in every alley. The poorest and humblest citizen should be made instinctively to bless that paternal government, which he daily perceives watching over his comfort and convenience, and securing for him that surest pledge of health, a pure atmosphere.

The individual, now intrusted with the executive power by his fellow-citizens, repeats, that he promises nothing, except an absolute self-devotion to their interests. To understand, maintain, and improve them, he dedicates whatever humble intellectual or physical power he may possess.

Gentlemen of the City Council: —

In all the relations which the constitution has established between the departments, it will be his endeavor, by punctuality and despatch in public business, by executing every duty and taking every responsibility which belongs to his office, to shorten and lighten your disinterested and patriotic labors. Should his and your faithful, though necessarily imperfect exertions, give satisfaction to our fellow-citizens, we shall have reason to rejoice, — not with a private and personal, but with a public and patriotic joy; for next to the consciousness of fulfilled duty, is the grateful conviction, that our lot is cast in a community, ready justly to appreciate, and willing actively to support, faithful and laborious efforts in their service.

Should, however, the contrary happen, and, in conformity with the experience of other republics, faithful exertions be followed by loss of favor and confidence, still he will have reason to rejoice, — not, indeed, with a public and patriotic, but with a private and individual joy, — for he will retire with a consciousness, weighed against which, all human suffrages are but as the light dust of the balance.

(C. Page 121.)

THE MAYOR'S INAUGURAL ADDRESS, MAY, 1824.

Gentlemen of the City Council: —

THE first impulse of my heart, on thus entering a second time upon the duties of chief magistrate of this city, is to express my deep sense of gratitude for the distinguished support I have received from the suffrages of my fellow-citizens. It has been, I am conscious, as much beyond my deserts, as beyond my hopes. May these marks of public confidence produce their genuine fruits, truer zeal, greater activity, and more entire self-devotion to the interests of the city!

To you, gentlemen of the Board of Aldermen, who have received such gratifying proofs of the approbation of your fellow-citizens, permit me thus publicly to express the greatness of my own obligations. You have shunned no labor. You have evaded no responsibility. You have sought, with a single eye, and a firm, undeviating purpose, the best interests of the city. It is my honor and happiness to have been associated with such men. Whatsoever success has attended the administration of the past year, may justly be attributed to the spirit and intelligence which characterized your labors and councils.

The gentlemen of the last Common Council are also entitled to a public expression of my gratitude, for their undeviating personal support, as well as the zeal and fidelity which distinguished their public services.

It is proper, on the present occasion, to speak of the administration of the past year, with reference to the principles by which it was actuated. If, in doing this, I enter more into detail than may seem suitable in a general discourse, it is because I deem such an elucidation conformable to the nature of the city government, and connected with its success. Whatever there is peculiar in the character of the inhabitants of Boston, is chiefly owing to the freedom of its ancient form of government, which had planted and fostered among its people a keen, active, inquisitive spirit; taking an interest in all public affairs, and exacting a strict and frequent account from all who have the charge of their concerns. This is a healthy condition of a community, be it a city, state, or nation. It indicates the existence of the only true foundation of public prosperity, the intelligence and virtue of the people, and their consequent capacity to govern themselves. Such a people have a right to expect a particular elucidation of conduct from public functionaries; whose incumbent duty it is to foster, on all occasions, among their fellow-citizens, a faithful and inquisitive spirit touching public concerns.

The acts of the administration of the past year had reference to morals, to comfort, and convenience and ornament. A very brief statement of the chief of these, which had any thing novel in their character, will be made with reference to principle and to expense. If more prominence be given to this last than may be thought necessary, it is because in relation to this, discontent is most likely to appear. In the organizing of new systems, and in the early stages of beneficial and even economical arrangements outlays must occur. These expenditures are inseparable from the first years. The resulting benefit must be expected and averaged among many future years. No obscurity ought to be permitted, concerning conduct and views in this respect. In a republic, the strength of every administration, in public opinion, ought to be in proportion to the willingness with which it submits to a rigorous accountability. With respect to morals, there existed at the commencement of last year, in one section of the city, an audacious obtrusiveness of vice, notorious and lamentable; setting at defiance, not only the decencies of life, but the authority of the laws. Repeated attempts to subdue this combination had failed. An opinion was entertained by some that it was invincible. There were those who recommended a tampering and palliative, rather than eradicating course of measures. Those intrusted with the affairs of the city were of a different temper. The evil was met in the face. In spite of clamor, of threat, of insult, of the certificates of those who were interested to maintain, or willing to countenance vice, in this quarter, a determined course was pursued. The whole section was put under the ban of authority. All licenses in it were denied; a vigorous police was organized, which, aided by the courts of justice and the House of Correction, effected its purpose. For three months past, the daily reports of our city officers have represented that section as peaceable as any other.. Those connected with courts of justice, both as ministers and officers, assert that the effect has been plainly discernible in the registers of the jail and of prosecution.

These measures did not originate in any theories or visions of ideal purity, attainable in the existing state of human society, but in a single sense of duty and respect for the character of the city; proceeding upon the principle, that if in great cities the existence of vice is inevitable, that its course should be in secret, like other filth, in drains and in darkness; not obtrusive, not powerful, not prowling publicly in the streets for the innocent and unwary.

The expense by which this effect has been produced, has been somewhat less than one thousand dollars. An amount already perhaps saved to the community in the diminution of those prosecutions and of their costs, which the continuance of the former unobstructed course of predominating vice in that section would have occasioned.

The next object of attention of the city government was cleansing the streets. In cities, as well as among individuals, cleanliness has reference to morals as well as to comfort. Sense of dignity and self-respect are essentially connected with purity, physical and moral. And a city is as much elevated as an individual by self-respect.

To remove from our streets whatever might offend the sense or endanger the health, was the first duty. To do it as economically as was consistent with doing it well, was the second.

How it has been done, whether satisfactorily as could be expected in the first year, and by incipient operations, our fellow-citizens are the judges. As far as the knowledge of the Mayor and Aldermen has extended, the course pursued has met with unqualified approbation, and given entire content.

In respect to economy, there were but two modes, — by contract, or by teams and laborers provided and employed by the city. The latter course was adopted; and for several reasons. The value of what was annually taken from the surface of the streets of the city, as well as the quantity, was wholly unknown. There were no data on which to estimate either, and of course no measure by which the amount of contract could be regulated. The streets of the city had been almost from time immemorial the revenue of the farmers in the vicinity, who came at will, took what suited their purposes, and left the rest to accumulate.

It was thought important that the city should undertake the operation necessary to cleansing the streets itself, not because this mode was certainly the most economical, but because it would be certainly the most effectual; and because, by this means, the city government would acquaint themselves with the subject in detail, and be the better enabled to meet the farmers hereafter on the ground of contract, should this mode be found expedient.

In order, however, to leave no means of information unsought, contracts were publicly invited by the city government. Of the proposals made, one only included all the operations of scraping, sweeping, and carrying away. This person offered to do the whole for one year for *seven thousand dollars*. All the other proposals expressly declined having any thing to do with scraping and sweeping, and confined their offer to the mere carrying away. The lowest of these was *eighteen hundred dollars*. When it was found that the city was about to perform the operation on its own account, the same persons fell in their offers from *eighteen* to *eight* hundred dollars; and when this was rejected, they offered to do it for *nothing*. And since the city operations have commenced, the inquiry now is, *at what price they can enjoy the privilege*. These facts are stated, because they strikingly illustrate how important it is to the city that its administration should take subjects of this kind into their own hands, until by experience they shall have so become acquainted with them as to render their ultimate measures the result of knowledge, and not of general surmise or opinion.

The general result of the operations may be thus stated. At an expense of about four thousand dollars, between six and seven thousand tons weight of filth and dirt have been removed from the surface of the streets. All of which have been advantageously used in improving the city property, under circumstances and in situations in which these collections were much wanted, — on the Common, on the Neck lands, and at South Boston. There can be no question, that, in these improvements, the city will receive the full value of the whole expense; to say nothing of what is really the chief object of the system, that the streets have been kept in a general state of cleanliness satisfactory to the inhabitants. By sale of the collections the next year, it is expected that we shall be able to compare directly the cash receipt with the cash expenditure.

The widening of our streets, as occasions offered, was the next object to which the attention of the city administration was directed, and the one involving the greatest expense. The circumstances of the times, and the enterprise of private individuals, opened opportunities, in this respect, unexampled in point of number and importance. If lost, they might never occur again, at least not within the lifetime of the youngest of our children. The administration availed themselves of those opportunities, as a matter of duty, in the actual condition of a city so extremely irregular and inconvenient as is Boston in the original plan and projection of its streets. Important improvements have been made in Lynn, Ship, Thacher, and Mill Pond Streets; in Hanover, Elm, Brattle, Court, and Union Streets; in Temple, Lynde, Sumner, and Milk Streets; in Federal, Orange, Eliot, and Warren Streets. The expense has been somewhat less than twelve thousand dollars. A considerable cost in comparison with the extent of the land taken; but reasonable, and not more than might be expected, when considered with reference to the nature of the improvements, for the most part in thick-settled parts of the city, where the land taken was very valuable, and the improvement proportionably important.

Another object of attention during the past year has been the drains. The ancient system, by which these were placed on the footing of private right, was expensive and troublesome to individuals, involving proprietors in perpetual disputes with those making new entries, and was particularly objectionable, as it respects the city, as that in a degree it made our streets the subjects of private right, and as such placed them out of the control of the city authorities.

The principle adopted was, to take all new drains into the hands of the city; to divide the expense as equally as possible among those estates immediately benefited, upon principles applicable to the particular nature of this subject, and retain in the city the whole property, both as it respects control and assessment. In its first stages, such a system must necessarily be expensive; but the result cannot fail to be beneficial, and, in a course of years, profitable. During the past year, the city has built about five thousand feet of drain, one thousand feet of which is twenty inch barrel drain; of this the city is now sole proprietor. It has already received more than one half the whole cost from persons whose estates were particularly benefited; and the balance, amounting to about four thousand five hundred dollars, is in a course of gradual, and, as it respects the far greater part, certain, ultimate collection. Considering the effect which well-constructed drains must have upon the city expenditure, in respect of the single article of paving, there can be but one opinion upon the wisdom and economy of this system.

A new mall has been nearly completed on Charles Street, and all the missing and dead trees of the old malls, the Common, and Fort Hill, have been replaced with a care and protection which almost insure success to these ornaments of the city.

The proceedings of the Directors of the House of Industry, and the flattering hopes connected with that establishment, would require a minuteness of detail, not compatible with the present occasion. They will doubtless be made the subject of an early and distinct examination and report of the City Council.

Two objects of very great interest, to which the proceedings of last year have reference, remain to be elucidated. The purchase of the interest of the proprietors of the ropewalks west of the Common, and the projected improvements about Faneuil Hall Market.

The citizens of Boston, in a moment of sympathy and feeling for the sufferings of particular individuals, and without sufficient prospective regard for the future exigencies of the city, had voluntarily given the right of using the land occupied by the ropewalks to certain grantees for that use. In consequence of the exclusion of the water by the Mill-dam, a tract of land has been opened either for sale, as an object of profit, or for use, as an object of ornament, with which the rights of these proprietors absolutely interfered. It was thought that no moment could be more favorable than the present to secure a relinquishment of those rights. An agreement of reference has been entered into with those proprietors, and the amount to be paid by the city for such relinquishment, has been left to the decision of five of our most intelligent, independent, and confidential citizens, with whose decision it cannot be questioned that both parties will have reason to be satisfied, notwithstanding it may happen that their award on the one side may be less, or, on the other, more than their respective previous anticipations.

Touching the projected improvements in the vicinity of Faneuil Hall Market, not only the extreme necessities of the city, in relation to space for a market, have led to this project, but also the particular relations of that vicinity have indicated the wisdom and policy, even at some risk and sacrifice, of bringing together in one compact, efficient, and commodious connection, the northern and central sections of our city, so as to facilitate the intercourse of business and enterprise between them, and bring into market, and into use, and into improvement parts of the city, at present old, sightless, inconvenient, and in comparison with that competency which must result from a judicious arrangement, at present absolutely useless.

Both these measures of the city government, relative to the Ropewalks and to Faneuil Hall Market, will necessarily lead to what, to many of our citizens, is an object of great dread, — a city debt.

As this is a subject of considerable importance, and touches a nerve of great sensibility, it ought to be well considered and rightly understood by our fellow-citizens. I shall, therefore, not apologize for making, on this occasion, some observations upon it.

The right to create a debt, is a power vested by our charter in the City Council. Now this, like every other power, is to be characterized by its use. This may be wise and prudent, or the opposite, according to the objects to which it is applied, and the manner and degree of that application. Abstractedly, a debt is no more an object of terror than a sword. Both are very dangerous in the hands of fools or madmen. Both are very safe, innocent, and useful in the hands of the wise and prudent.

A debt created for a purpose, like that which probably will be necessary in the case of the ropewalks, that of relieving a great property from an accidental embarrassment, is no more a just object of dread to a city than a debt created for seed wheat is to a farmer; or than a debt for any object of certain return is to a merchant.

So in the case of Faneuil Hall Market; what possible object of rational apprehension can there be in a debt created for the purpose of purchasing a tract of territory, whose value must be increased by the purchase, which, if sold, cannot fail to excite a great competition, and if retained, the incomes of which, so far as respects the market, are wholly within the control of the city authorities? It is possible, indeed, that more may be paid for some estates than abstractedly they may be worth. It is possible that great changes may take place in the value of real estate between the time of the commencement and the time of completing such a project. But the reverse is also quite as possible. Providence does not permit man to act upon certainties. The constitution of our nature obliges him, in every condition and connection, to shape his course of conduct by probabilities. His duty is to weigh maturely, previous to decision, to consider anxiously both the wisdom of his ends and the proportion of his means. Once decided, in execution he should be as firm and rapid as in council he has been slow and deliberate; cultivating in his own breast and in the breasts of others just confidence in the continuance of the usual analogies and relations of things.

The destinies of the city of Boston are of a nature too plain to be denied or misconceived. The prognostics of its future greatness are written on the face of nature too legibly and too indelibly to be mistaken. These indications are apparent from the location of our city, from its harbor, and its relative position among rival towns and cities; above all, from the character of its inhabitants, and the singular degree of enterprise and intelligence which are diffused through every class of its citizens. Already capital and population is determined towards it from other places, by a certain and irresistible power of attraction. It remains then for the citizens of Boston to be true to their own destinies; to be willing to meet wise expenditures and temporary sacrifices, and thus to coöperate with nature and Providence in their apparent tendencies to promote their greatness and prosperity; thereby not only improving the general condition of the city, elevating its character, multiplying its accommodations, and strengthening the predilections which exist already in its favor, but also patronizing and finding employment for its laborers and mechanics.

It is true the power of credit, like every other power, is subject to abuse. But to improve the general convenience of the city, to augment its facilities for business, to add to the comfort of its inhabitants, and in this way to augment its resources, are among the most obvious and legitimate uses of that power, which, doubtless, for these purposes, was intrusted to the City Council.

Having thus explained some of the principal proceedings and sources of extraordinary expense occurring during the past year, I feel myself bound to make some general remarks on the nature of the office I have had the honor to hold, and to which the suffrages of my fellow-citizens have recalled me. It is important that a right apprehension should be formed concerning its duties, its responsibilities, the powers it ought to possess, and what the people have a right to expect, and what they ought to exact from the possessor of it. And I do this the rather, because I am sensible that very different opinions exist upon this subject. There are those who consider the office very much in the light of a pageant, destined merely to superintend and direct the general course of administration, to maintain the dignity, and to "dispense the hospitalities" of the city, and who deem the office in some measure degraded, by having any thing of a laborious or working condition connected with it; and I am well aware that the practice in other cities justifies such an opinion. I have not thought, however, gentlemen, that a young and healthy republic, for such the city of Boston is, should seek its precedents, or encourage its officers in looking for models among the corrupt and superannuated forms of ancient despotisms. On the contrary, it seemed to me incumbent on the early possessor of this office, in a state of society like that which exists in Massachusetts, and for which this city is preëminent, to look at the real character of that office, as it is indicated by the expressions of the charter, and exists in the nature of things, with little or no regard to the practice of other places, or to opinions founded on those practices.

In this view, therefore, my attempt has been to attain a deep and thorough acquaintance with the interests of the inhabitants and of the city; and this not by general surveys, but by a minute, particular, and active inspection of their public concerns, in all their details.

Although this course has been the occasion of much trouble, and perhaps made me obnoxious to some censure, as being busy, and perhaps meddling, with matters out of my sphere, yet I have thought it better to expose myself to those imputations, than to forego the opportunities such a course of conduct afforded of obtaining a deep and thorough acquaintance with the business and interests of the city, which the charter plainly presupposed, and indeed was necessary to fulfil the duties in a very humble degree which it made incumbent. And the more experience I have had in the duties of this office, the more I feel obliged, both by precept and example, to press upon my fellow-citizens the necessity of considering this as a business office, combining as indispensable requisites, — great zeal, great activity, great self-devotion, and, as far as possible, a thorough acquaintance with the relations of the people.

Nor is it only necessary that these qualities should at all times be exacted of the chief magistrate, and that he should be held to a rigid exhibition of them, in his official conduct; but, on the other hand, it is also necessary that all the departments should be so arranged as to throw upon him the full weight of all the responsibility which the charter attaches to his office. Whatever has a tendency to weaken that sense of responsibility, above all, whatever enables the executive officer to cast the blame of weak plans or inefficient execution upon others, has a direct tendency to corrupt the executive, and to deprive the citizens of a chief benefit, contemplated in the charter.

If there be any advantage in the form of a city over that of a town government, it lies in one single word, — *efficiency*. In this point of view, all the powers of the City Council may be considered as comprehending also the executive power, of which the Mayor is but a branch. For they enact the laws which enable his department to possess that efficiency the charter contemplates. Now, efficiency means nothing more than *capacity to carry into effect*. Whatever form of organization of any department tends to deprive the executive of the city of the power to carry into effect the laws, or transfers that power to others, disconnected from his responsibility, has a direct tendency to encourage the executive in ignorance, inactivity, or imbecility, which will inevitably, sooner or later, result just in proportion as the organization enables him to throw the blame of mismanagement upon others, or not to hold himself accountable for it.

Within the narrow limits and in relation to the humble objects to which the executive power extends, its responsibility should be clear, undivided, and incapable of being evaded. On the executive should ultimately devolve the accountability for the efficiency of all the departments; and every organization is defective which enables him to escape from it. Every citizen, in making complaints to this officer, should be certain of finding redress, or of being pointed to the path to obtain it. And as to those general nuisances which offend sense, endanger health, or interfere with comfort, his power should enable him to apply a remedy upon the instant, or at least as readily as the nature of the particular subject-matter permits; and to effect this, not by reference, not by writing supplicatory letters to independent boards, but personally, by application of means in his own hands, or by agents under his control, and for whom he is responsible.

The true theory of the form of government which our fellow-citizens have chosen, results in a severe responsibility of the executive power, and with it are identified the true interests of the citizens and the real advantages of a city organization. But responsibility implies a coextensive power as its basis. The one cannot, and ought not to exist without the other. The charter makes it the duty of the Mayor "to be vigilant and active at all times, in causing the laws for the government of the city to be duly executed and put in force." Now, how can vigilance and activity be expected in an officer, in relation to a great mass of laws, and those of the most critical and important character, the execution of which is formally and expressly transferred to others, with whose execution, if he directly interferes, he takes the risk of giving offence to the nice sense of honor and right of an independent board? The charter makes it his duty "to inspect the conduct of all subordinate officers in the government thereof, and as far as in his power to cause all negligence, carelessness, and positive violations of duty to be prosecuted and punished." Now, how can he do this, when those who execute your laws do not consider themselves as subordinate, and are justified in that opinion by the form and circumstances of their organization?

Again, the charter plainly implies that the Mayor of this city should make himself acquainted thoroughly and intimately with all its great interests, "with its finances, its police, its health, security, cleanliness, comfort, and ornament."

Now, what encouragement is there to endeavor to fulfil these duties, when any of its great interests are so constituted or vested, that he has no control over them, nor any power of making any inquisition into their state or conduct, except by personal solicitation and request; not denied, indeed, out of politeness and respect, but perhaps granted, not because he has a right from his official relation to claim, but because, on the present occasion, there exists a willingness to give the desired information?

The organization of the executive power, by division among independent boards, has a direct tendency to corrupt a weak executive officer, and to embarrass one of opposite character.

The study of the former will naturally be to get along easily; for this purpose he will yield whatever power another department is disposed to take, for thus *his* responsibility is diminished; and instead of a single definite, decided, official action, on every occasion giving security to the citizen, regardless of personal consequences, his course will be timid, shuffling, and compromising, beginning with the vain design of pleasing everybody, and ending with the still vainer, of expecting in this way long to maintain either influence or character.

An executive, on the contrary, who is firm and faithful to the constitution of the city, will exercise the powers it confers. He will claim the right to inspect all subordinate officers; he will consider every branch of executive power, emanating from the City Council, as subordinate by the charter to the city executive. He will claim of all such an accountability that will enable him to understand every interest of the city in detail. Such a course would, probably, sooner or later, lead to controversies concerning the rights and dignities of independent boards; to heart-burnings and jealousies; perhaps to pamphlets and newspaper attacks, which, if he does not answer, it will be said, that it is because he cannot; and which, if he does answer, will lead to a reply, and that to a rejoinder; and thus the executive of the city, instead of a simple and plain exercise of power, humble and limited in its sphere, yet important to be both efficient and unembarrassed, may be harassed with disputes about the pretensions, authorities, and dignities of rival powers, vexatious and unprofitable, terminating in nothing but divisions in the city, and inefficiency in the execution of the laws.

I have deemed it my duty to express myself thus distinctly, and in a most unqualified manner, upon this point; and the rather, thus publicly, because opinions in this respect are liable to be misrepresented or misunderstood. On such occasions, therefore, I choose to throw myself on the intelligence and virtues of the mass of my fellow-citizens, whose interests, as I understand them, it is my single desire steadily to pursue, and who, whether they coincide or differ with me, in relation to the particular mode of pursuing those interests, will, I have a perfect confidence, justly appreciate my motives.

The result of my experience, during the past year, on this subject, is this,— that the interests of the city are most deeply connected with such an organization of every branch of executive power, as that the ultimate responsibility for the execution should rest upon the Mayor; and which he should, therefore, be incapable of denying or evading;—that, at all times, the blame should rest upon him, without the power of throwing it off upon others, in case of any defect of plan, or any inefficiency in execution.

In making these remarks, I trust I shall not be understood as not appreciating as I ought, in common with my fellow-citizens, the exertions and the sacrifices of those excellent, intelligent, and faithful men, who, in present and in past times, with so much honor to themselves and advantage to the community, have administered the concerns of independent departments. I yield to none of my fellow-citizens, in my sense of gratitude and respect to them, both as officers and individuals. But the organization of a city is, in the nature of things, essentially different from that of a town. The relation to the city, in which I have been placed, has compelled me to contemplate, and prospectively to realize, the certain embarrassments which must result from an organization of the executive department, varying from that simplicity which the charter establishes, as likely deeply to affect the efficiency of the system now upon trial, and to encourage, and sooner or later to introduce both imbecility and inactivity into an office which can alone be beneficial to the city when it is possessed by directly opposite qualities.

I have no apprehension that my fellow-citizens will attribute these suggestions to a vulgar and vain wish to extend the powers of an office holden but for a year on the most precarious of all tenures. The efficiency of this new form of government is mainly dependent on its simplicity, and on the fact that its responsibility is undivided, and cannot be evaded if the departments be organized on charter principles. Much of the benefit of the new system will depend on the spirit which characterizes its commencement. On this account, the individual now possessing the executive power is anxious, on the one hand, that none of its essential advantages should be lost through any timidity on his part, in expressing opinions, the result of his experience, or through any unwillingness to incur any labor, or meet any just responsibility. On the other, he has no higher ambition than by a diligent, faithful, and laborious fulfilment of every known duty, and exercise of every charter right, to set such an example, and establish such precedents as will give to this new government a fair impulse, and a permanent and happy influence upon the destinies of the inhabitants of this city.

Gentlemen of the City Council:—

It is the felicity of all who are called to the government of this city, that they serve a people capable of appreciating, and willing actively to support faithful and laborious efforts in their service;—a people in all times distinguished for uniting love of freedom with respect for authority. May it be your happiness, as it will be your endeavor, to maintain those institutions, under which such a people have been elevated to so high a degree of prosperity! Under your auspices, may the foundations of the fabric of their greatness be strengthened, its proportions enlarged, its internal accommodations improved! May the spirit of liberty and the spirit of good government continue to walk hand in hand within these venerable walls, consecrated by so many precious recollections. And when we shall have passed away, and the places which now know us shall know us no more, may those who come after us be compelled to say, that the men of this age were as true to the past and the future as to their own times; that while they had preserved and enjoyed the noble inheritance which had descended to them from their ancestors, they had transmitted it not only unimpaired, but improved to their posterity.

(D. Page 167.)

THE MAYOR'S INAUGURAL ADDRESS, MAY, 1825.

Gentlemen of the City Council: —

I HAVE again to acknowledge my grateful sense of the confidence of my fellow-citizens, expressed by their suffrages; and to renew assurances of my endeavors to evince my gratitude, by increased zeal, activity, and devotion to their interests.

Whatever success has attended the administration of city affairs, is chiefly to be attributed to those excellent and faithful men, who for the two years past have composed the Board of Aldermen. It is impossible for me to speak too highly of their disinterested and laborious services; or to separate from them, in official relations, without expressing my personal obligations for the uniform respect, confidence, and urbanity, with which all their proceedings have been characterized, both as it respects myself and each other. Their persevering and firm pursuit of the interests of the city, often under circumstances of great delicacy and difficulty, entitle them to be ranked among its distinguished benefactors.

Nor ought I to permit the occasion to pass, without paying a similar tribute to the labors and fidelity of the last Common Council.

It will be expected, perhaps, that, on this occasion, I should speak of the measures of the last year, and of the success which has attended them; such as the establishment of an auditor's department; the new organization of that of health; the connecting the system of scavengers with that of the House of Industry; the farther extension of Faneuil Hall Market, and others of a less obtrusive character. All these have been conducted, as far as I have been informed, generally to the satisfaction of our fellow-citizens; and I know that the detail of results would still farther justify that satisfaction.

I prefer, however, to occupy the present moment with inquiries concerning future duty, rather than with illustrations of past success. The charter of the city has made it incumbent on its executive officer to inform himself on all subjects connected with its prosperity and happiness, and to recommend measures for the advancement of both to the City Council. This injunction it has sanctioned with the solemnity of an oath. In obedience to these obligations, thus sacredly enforced, I hasten to a topic, deeply interesting to the prosperity, safety, and character of this city, which events and experience press upon the mind with an intense and absorbing interest. I do this the rather because the subject is of high responsibility; touches some interests and more prejudices; and is also of a nature easily to be mistaken and misrepresented. This subject, therefore, is one on which it is the incumbent duty of him, who is intrusted with the chief office in this city, to form and to express a decided opinion, and to leave no doubt concerning his own path, in relation to it; and none concerning his opinion of the duty of others.

What though the development of this opinion may affect that evanescent splendor, which is called popularity? Of what value is any popularity, which will not bear the hazard of fulfilled duty? Precious as is the possession of the confidence of fellow-citizens, yet even this is more worthless than "the light dust of the balance," in comparison with the infinite consequence of possessing the consciousness of deserving it.

The topic to which I allude, relates to the effect, under a city organization, of the existence of independent executive boards, and the consequences of the particular form of constituting those which exist in this city.

The existence of such boards is an anomaly under a city organization; is inconsistent with the theory of, or any known practice under, such a form of government; and seems also incompatible with the attainment of the objects which the people propose to themselves in establishing it.

In every other city the representative body, chosen by the people, as their city council, has the control of every relation of a municipal character, whether it affect economy, protection, or general superintendence. If, in any case, it act through the instrumentality of boards, the members of such boards are selected by it, and responsible to it, in like manner as the members of the City Council are, in their turn, responsible for such selection, as well as for all their other acts, to the people.

In all this there is a manifest simplicity, calculated to produce harmony and energy. The people, who look only to their City Council, know who to blame, if there be fault. The City Council, on the other hand, when any good is to be effected, is not embarrassed by fears of trenching upon rival authorities, of awakening jealousies, or of being troubled with contests about jurisdictions.

The objects a people propose to themselves in forming a city government are, efficiency and responsibility. Now, can any have a more obvious tendency to obstruct, or defeat both, than an organization which severs from each other naturally allied portions of municipal power, and divides them out by very indistinct limits among independent boards? Can any thing be better calculated to create discord, jealousies, and controversies in a community?

The form of constituting these boards, under our city charter, is still more exceptionable; and, what is very extraordinary, is just as inconsistent with the practice of the ancient town government, as it is with the theory of city organization.

Under the town government all the boards, of Firewards, Overseers of the Poor, and School Committee, were chosen by the votes of *all* the inhabitants, in a general ticket. The theory and practice of the town government was, that *those officers, in whose character and adaptation to their office, all the citizens had an interest, should be chosen by the major voice of all the citizens.*

Two consequences obviously flowed from this mode of election. 1st. A concurrence of *a majority of all* the citizens being requisite for a choice, the candidates were, for the most part, selected from men of high, general character, and from no local or sectional considerations; whereby a very fair proportion of the general talent and respectability of the town was necessarily infused into those boards. 2d. The form of election being by general ticket, previous consultation was had, not only in relation to the adaptation of the candidate for the office, but also of the adaptation of candidates to one another; so that the board might be composed of men agreeable to each other, and thus capable by consentaneousness of views and feelings, to produce a similar consentaneousness of system and action.

The necessary effect of this form of election was to enlarge the sphere out of which candidates could be obtained. Men being always more willing to undertake an office of a laborious and responsible character, when they know, previously to their election, with whom they are likely to be associated.

These consequences are obvious, and were among the causes of the long and happy organization of those boards, under the town government.

These advantages are in a great measure, and some of them wholly, lost under the provisions of our city charter.

Instead of being chosen by *all* the citizens, by a general ticket, the members are divided among the wards, each choosing its proportion. The fundamental principle of the ancient town government, — that officers, in whose character and adaptation all the citizens had an interest, should be chosen by the major voice of all, — has thus been abandoned. All the inhabitants of the city have consented to barter the common right they formerly enjoyed, of having a voice in choosing the *whole*, for the sake of an exclusive right, in wards, of choosing *a twelfth part.* And the power the whole people of the city once possessed of attaining *a certain result, conformably to the general will*, has thus been exchanged for the chance of attaining *an uncertain result of twelve particular wills*, coexisting in that number of wards.

I speak of these consequences with the more freedom, because I know they are felt and acknowledged by very many of our most intelligent and patriotic citizens; and because I have been made officially acquainted with the fact, that the effect produced by the present mode of electing these officers has been, in many instances, the openly avowed reason of declining to become candidates by some, and of the resignation of these offices by others.

The nature and extent of this evil is not to be appreciated by any estimate, since every form of organization, which tends to render wise, faithful, and business men unwilling to serve a community, is productive of mischiefs altogether incalculable.

Touching the remedy for these evils, the obligations of the city charter compel me to speak distinctly and unequivocally.

Under a city organization there is no mode of selecting such boards, consistent with harmony, efficiency, and responsibility, except, their election by the City Council.

Every other mode establishes, or gives to such board a color to assume the character of independence. And wherever this quality exists, or is assumed, jealousies, rivalries, claims of jurisdiction, and contests for authority between it and the City Council, are inevitable.

The station I have had the honor for the last two years to hold, has compelled me to witness past embarrassments, and to realize those which are to come, in consequence of this unprecedented organization of city power. Between the City Council, the Overseers of the Poor, and the School Committee, very serious and difficult questions have already arisen, and are yet unsettled. Nor is it possible, in the nature of things, that such controversies should not arise and be productive of bitterness and discord, so long as in the great interests of protection against fire, of education, and of support of the poor, the right to manage and expend money is claimed by one board, and the right to regulate, appropriate, and call to account is vested in another.

As I have no question concerning the remedy, so also I have none concerning the mode in which it ought to be sought. 1st. By an arrangement of the details by the City Council relative to each board, conformably to the subject-matter of its power, predicated on the principle of election by that body. 2d. By an application to the legislature for its sanction of those details and of that principle. 3d. By an ultimate reference of the whole, for the approbation, by general ballot, of our fellow-citizens.

Let it not be objected to such an attempt, that it will be construed into "a grasp after more power," by the City Council, and be opposed from jealousy, or prejudice. Those who thus object, do but little justice to the thoughtful and prescient character of the citizens of this metropolis; at all times as distinguished for justly appreciating the necessities of legitimate power, and for a willingness to yield whatever is plainly requisite for a vigorous and responsible action of constituted authorities, as for a keen perception and quick resistance to tyrannical control.

Grant, however, the attempt should fail, what then? The City Council stand before the public and before heaven, with the proud consciousness of fulfilled duty; discharged from all accountability for the inconveniences and embarrassments, which cannot fail to flow from the present organization so long as it exists.

For myself, whatever may be the event, I shall have the satisfaction of that internal assurance, which is better than all human approbation, that none of the evils which may occur, can be attributed either to the want of anxious precaution, or to the shrinking from just responsibility, in the executive officer. Nor have I any apprehension that these remarks will be construed into any reflection upon the gentlemen who now hold, or who recently have held seats in either of those boards. Many of them are among the most intelligent and patriotic of our fellow-citizens. Some of them, I know, concur in the general opinions above expressed. The subject has reference to the necessary and obvious effects of a particular organization of our city government, of which I am bound to speak, according to the state of my convictions, with a plainness authorized by the charter and required by the oath it has imposed. These obligations fulfilled, I leave every thing else to the candor, the intelligence, and virtue of my fellow-citizens, in which I repose an entire confidence.

Gentlemen of the City Council: —

The events of the past years of our city organization are full of satisfaction and encouragement. Between the branches and between the members of the City Council there has uniformly existed a harmonious, urbane, and conciliatory intercourse. The interests of the city have been studied and pursued with an exclusive eye, and a firm, unhesitating step.

Neither the spirit of selfishness, nor the spirit of party, has ever dared to mingle its unhallowed voice in the debates of either branch of the City Council. These are proud recollections, as it respects the past; and happy auguries, as it respects the future.

May they continue and be multiplied! May the members of the present, like those of former City Councils, close their labors with the approbation and applause of the multitude of their brethren; as those, who have sought with singleness, sincerity, and success, the interest and honor of the city; the improvement of its accommodations, the enlargement of its resources, and the advancement of all the means which constitute a prosperous, happy, and virtuous community.

(E. Page 197.)

THE MAYOR'S INAUGURAL ADDRESS, JANUARY, 1826.

Gentlemen of the City Council: –

To express gratitude for this renewed instance of the confidence of my fellow-citizens, and to repeat assurances of a zeal and fidelity in their service, in some degree proportionate to that confidence, are natural and suitable on the present occasion. It cannot be expected that he, who sustains the complicated relation of chief magistrate of this city, let his endeavors be what they may, should at all times satisfy the often-conflicting passions and interests always necessarily existing in so great a community. Much less can it be expected from the individual, who, through the indulgence of his fellow-citizens, is now permitted to enjoy that distinction. In all cases, however, of doubt and difficulty, that individual will rest confidently for support, even with those who differ with him in opinion, on the consciousness, which he trusts his general course of conduct will impress, that every act of his official conduct, whether acceptable or otherwise, proceeds from a single regard to the honor of the city, and to the happiness and best interests of its inhabitants.

It is with great delight, Gentlemen, that I must here pay a tribute, justly due to the wisdom and public spirit of all our former City Councils. Their harmony, in relation to objects of public improvement, their vigilance in maintaining the checks of our city charter, and the reciprocal coöperation of the branches and members in advancing the general interests of the city, without local, party, or selfish considerations, are facts at once exemplary and encouraging; the results of which are apparent in our streets, in our public buildings, in the augmented value of our city lands, and in the increasing satisfaction of our fellow-citizens, with their new form of government.

The unquestionable evidence derived from our recent census, has fulfilled the expectations of the most sanguine; and has put beyond question, that the increase of this city, during the five years past, has been, to say the least, not inferior to that of any of our maritime cities, on the previous actual basis of its population.

This fact may be considered as conclusive on its future prospects. For if, at a time when universal peace among European nations has changed and limited the field of commercial enterprise, on which the greatness of this city was once supposed, in a manner, altogether to depend, it appears that, notwithstanding this change and limitation, its growth, instead of being diminished, is increasing with a rapidity equal to that of the most favored of our commercial cities, it follows conclusively, that our greatness is not altogether dependent upon foreign commerce; and also, that the enterprise, capital, and intelligence of our citizens, determined inwards, and active upon agriculture, manufactures, and in our coasting trade, are producing results even more auspicious than our foreign commerce, in its most prosperous state, ever effected;—than which, to the patriot's heart and hope, no facts of a mere physical character, can be more encouraging or delightful.

Similar grounds for satisfaction will be found in comparing the increasing results of the aggregates of our valuation, and the decreasing results of the ratio of our taxes. During the five years from 1821 to 1825, inclusive, it appears by the Assessors' records, that the whole aggregate of real and personal property in this city increased from twenty millions three hundred thousand dollars, to twenty-six millions two hundred thousand; making a regular annual increase of about one million two hundred thousand dollars. Of which increased capital, it will appear, by comparing the aggregate of 1821 with that of 1825, that four millions five hundred thousand have been invested in real, and one million five hundred thousand in personal estate.

During this period, it is true, as is inevitable in a progressive state of society, increasing daily, not only in numbers, but in municipal exigencies and requisitions for expenditures, on account of improvements, the amount of our taxes have increased in the aggregate. Yet, at the same time, owing to the increased aggregates of our valuation, the ratio of assessment has diminished. Thus, if the ratios of assessment of the five years immediately preceding 1820, be compared with the five years from 1820, inclusive, it will be found that the average of the annual ratios of the former was *eight dollars and twenty-five cents* on the thousand dollars, and that the average of the annual ratios of the latter was only *seven dollars and eighty cents.* The ratio of the present year will be *seven dollars.*

A farther illustration of our general prosperity is deducible from the fact, that, notwithstanding the amount of our taxes has increased, with the increasing wealth and population of the city; yet the ratio of uncollected taxes has, in every successive year, since the existence of our city government, been diminishing.

I have been thus precise and distinct upon this point, because discontent at any existing state of things is most likely to appear in the form of complaints relative to taxes. Now, it is obviously impossible, in the nature of things, that the assessment of taxes, in any great community, should exactly proportion the burden to the ability of each individual to bear it. Some will unavoidably be taxed more and others less than their precise proportion. It cannot, therefore, but happen, even under the best form and ratio of taxation, that there must be some, who can complain with reason, as there will always be many, who will complain without reason. With respect to the community itself, however, as the best criterion it can possibly have of its progressive prosperity is a regular increase of its population, accompanied by a regular increase of its wealth, so when the aggregate of its wealth increases, and at the same time the ratio of its assessments actually diminishes, it has the best evidence, the nature of things admits, that its general expenditures are not greater than the actual state of its condition and progress requires. But in such case, however, as particular expenditures may be unwise or extravagant, it is still its duty even under such circumstances, to exact from its agents a rigid accountability.

Touching the expenditures of the past year, it is not known that any of them require a particular explanation on the present occasion. In general, I apprehend, they have been satisfactory to our fellow-citizens, so far as respects their objects. And they well understand that it is, probably, in the nature of things, impossible to conduct all the details of public expenditure with that precise economy which an individual applies to his private concerns. I am not, however, aware, that there have been any such, during the past year, which cannot, under the circumstances of each case, be satisfactorily explained by the particular agents.

In connection with this subject, it is impossible for me not to notice the happy effects produced by the establishment of the office of Auditor of Accounts, which, carried into operation by the exemplary industry and ability of that officer, and by the indefatigable fidelity of the Committee of Accounts, has introduced an order, simplicity, and correctness into that department, not only highly creditable to the city, but also facilitating, in the highest possible degree, particular inquiries and general knowledge relative to the state of our financial concerns.

Among the objects to which the attention of the City Council will be drawn the ensuing year, is that of a sufficient and never-failing supply for our city of pure river or pond water, which shall be adequate for all purposes of protection against fire, and for all culinary and other domestic purposes, and capable of being introduced into every house in the city. I deem it my duty to state unequivocally, that this object ought never to be lost sight of by the City Council, until effected upon a scale proportionate to its convenience and our urgent necessities. Physicians of the first respectability have urged this topic upon me, in my official capacity, on the ground of health, in addition to all the other obvious comforts and advantages to be anticipated from an adequate supply of such water. "The spring water of Boston, they assert to be generally harsh, owing to its being impregnated with various saline substances; and that this impregnation impairs its excellence as an article of drink, and essentially diminishes its salubrity. In the course of their practice, they say they have noticed many diseases to be relieved and cured by an exchange of the common spring water for soft water of the aqueduct, or distilled water. Hence, they have been led to the opinion, that many complaints of obscure origin, owe their existence to the qualities of the common spring water of Boston." . . "The introduction of an ample supply of pure water, would, therefore, they apprehend, contribute much to the health of the place, and prove one of the greatest blessings, which could be bestowed on this city."

I am induced to bring this subject before the City Council on the present occasion, thus distinctly, from having been informed that citizens among us of the highest respectability, both in point of talents and property, seriously contemplate an association for the purpose of supplying this city with water, and of making application to the Legislature for an act of incorporation for that object. An attempt, which, if made, I trust will be met by the City Council with the most decided and strenuous opposition; and with a corresponding spirit and determination to effect this great object, solely on the account and with the resources of the city. On this topic, I deem it my duty to declare explicitly my opinion, that in such a project the city ought to consent to no copartnership.

If there be any privilege, which a city ought to reserve, exclusively, in its own hands and under its own control, it is that of supplying itself with water.

No private capitalists will engage in such an enterprise, without at least a rational expectation of profit. To this, either an exclusive right, or a privilege of the nature of, or equivalent to, an exclusive right is essential. There are so many ways, in which water may be desirable, and in such a variety of quantities, for use, comfort, and pleasure, that it is impossible to provide, by any prospective provisions, in any charter granted to individuals for all the cases, uses, and quantities, which the ever-increasing wants of the population of a great city in the course of years may require. Besides, it being an article of the first necessity, and on its free use so much of health, as well of comfort, depends, every city should reserve in its own power the means, unrestrained, of encouraging its use, by reducing as fast as possible the cost of obtaining it, not only to the poor, but to all classes of the community. This can never be the case, when the right is in the hands of individuals, with any thing like the facility and speed, as when it is under the entire control of the city.

In addition to these considerations, the right to break up the streets which that of supplying the city with water implies, ought never to be intrusted to private hands, who through cupidity, or regard to a false economy, may have an interest not to execute the works upon a sufficiently extensive scale, with permanent materials, thereby increasing the inconvenience and expense which the exercise of the power of breaking up the streets, necessarily induces.

A letter to me from the Superintendent of the Philadelphia Water Works, (Joseph S. Lewis, Esq.,) a gentleman among those chiefly employed in their original construction, dated the 21st of December last, is so full upon this point, that I cannot refrain from quoting a considerable portion of it.

"Your object should be to have enough and to spare, and the calculation should be formed on one hundred and fifty gallons for each family, which will afford a supply for washing the streets, waste by leakage, &c.; and the experience of this city (Philadelphia) fully justifies in saying, that it is not too much, although in London, a less quantity is made to answer; and owing to rivalships amongst the several companies, the inhabitants have enough for drink, and for culinary and other family purposes. Yet none is to be seen in use in cleaning the gutters, washing the pavements, and various methods of consumption, absolutely essential to existence and comfort, in our climate, in three or four hot months of the year. Scarcely a fire happens of any magnitude in London, without complaints of a deficiency of water, and I have in my possession a paper, containing an account of a meeting of the Common Council of London, convened for the express purpose of inquiring into the cause, which it does not require much consideration to discover.

"*It is from the fatal error of suffering interested individuals to have the supply of an article of the most indispensable nature, and without which health and comfort cannot be enjoyed.* Expense is not to be regarded. If a company can supply your city, they will expect to profit by it; and this profit might as well be saved by your corporation. On the other hand, if it be a losing business, individuals should not suffer by forwarding a great public object; and if they do, the citizens will feel it by a pinched and partial supply.

"This city (Philadelphia) has expended vast sums of money out of its own resources; and if more were required, more would be cheerfully accorded. There is no one thing, in which all are so much united; and I firmly believe, that, if a question was submitted to the citizens, to sell to a company who would pay back the whole cost, with interest, that not a tenth of the population would agree to it. The increased security from fire, the abundant supply for washing the streets, the copious streams afforded for baths, for cleanliness, and, in short, many other advantages are such, and so well appreciated, that no money could purchase the surrender of the works.

"The whole cost of the water-works, including the pipes for distribution, previous to the erection of the new water-works, was $1,138,857, without adding interest. Yet, such was the eagerness for a more abundant supply, that a unanimous sanction was given to the new plan, which has happily succeeded, of raising the water by water power; the cost of which may be put down, including the river rights, at $450,000

And in addition to this, iron pipes are substituted for those of wood, the cost of which, thus far, may be called 150,000

Amounting, in the whole, to $600,000

"This sum, added to that before mentioned, with the interest paid, will amount to more than two millions of dollars.

"I have said thus much to hold out an inducement to your city to persevere in obtaining a supply, and have held out our example to show, that cost is not to be regarded by us in so essential a matter. We have been pioneers for our sister cities, who may now practically obtain a supply of water, without paying for the cost of our experiments."

Other facts and documents connected with this subject will be hereafter communicated, should the City Council deem it expedient to take it seriously into consideration.

Two occasions have occurred, during the past year, which made it necessary for the Mayor to examine, with great attention, the powers conferred on him by the city charter, in relation to the suppression of riots, and similar unlawful assemblies; so as to be enabled to justify, before a legal tribunal, the extreme resort, which, in such cases, he might possibly think requisite. After consultation with the best legal advisers, it was deemed most safe for the Mayor to act in the capacity of justice of the peace throughout the Commonwealth, which he happened to hold; inasmuch as the powers of the Mayor, as expressed in the city charter, are of the most general character, and no legislative or judicial construction has ever occurred in relation to them. The duty of the Mayor, as expressed in the city charter, is, to take care that *all laws for the government of the city* are executed. Riots, routs, and unlawful assemblies, are cognizable only under the laws of the Commonwealth. By these laws, the course of proceedings, and the persons intrusted with their execution, are expressly pointed out; and among them the Mayor of the city is not included.

In general, it may be observed, that an undefined and exaggerated notion of the powers of the Mayor has led our fellow-citizens to expect a much greater exercise of authority, in many cases, than the terms of the city charter justifies. It is, however, certain, that in respect of riots, the Mayor, by the mere virtue of his office, does not possess even the power of a justice of the peace.

It was solely, therefore, and avowedly, in virtue of a commission of the peace, and not in virtue of his office of Mayor, that the first riotous assembly was met and dispersed by that officer.

Such being the relations of his power, it is obviously, in every occurring case, his duty to decide upon his responsibility, whether the particular disturbance is of a nature to justify him in compromitting the unquestionable rights and duties of his office, in a case of a doubtful character, by his personal presence; or whether, in the free exercise of his discretion, he should leave their remedy to the prescribed executive agents of the Commonwealth, who can act without any censure from an apprehended illegal assumption of power.

If a case has occurred, or should hereafter occur, in which any persons should, in defiance of the moral sense and general feeling of the public, adopt any measures, which would naturally and almost unavoidably lead to disorder and disturbances, they could not reasonably invoke the aid of the authorities of the city, so long as the invited evil was confined *to themselves only;* but it is a question of very serious moment with the inhabitants of a city so distinguished for its religious and moral character, whether further checks ought not to be provided to prevent that, which has been merely tolerated, from becoming the source of disturbances, of danger and of disgrace to the citizens, and their government.

It is my duty, only, to call your attention to the subject, and I shall cheerfully acquiesce in your decision.

If the Mayor is to be made responsible to act, in all such cases, his powers ought to be accurately defined and his duties prescribed by law. The powers of the Mayor are sufficient for all municipal purposes; and it is as much his duty to abstain from assuming to exercise powers not vested in him by his office, as it is to exercise those powers with which he is intrusted.

Gentlemen of the City Council: —

The harmony which hitherto has, without interruption, been maintained between the departments, members, and branches of our city government, is among the auspicious auguries of the future greatness and happiness of this community. It will be your, and my, endeavor to maintain and increase this happy mutual understanding and respect. But difficult questions concerning duties, made complex and uncertain by the interfering passions, interests, and prejudices existing in all great combinations of men, must necessarily occur. On occasions of this character, those will be most sure to find the correct rule of truth and duty, who seek it with a sense of strict subordination to those moral and religious sanctions, under which the wisdom of our fathers laid the foundations of the prosperity of this people.

(F. Page 210.)

THE MAYOR'S INAUGURAL ADDRESS, JANUARY, 1827.

Gentlemen of the City Council: —

It is proper, on occasions of this kind, to survey the general relations of our city, and, from the measures of preceding City Councils and their results, to gain light and strength for future duties.

The condition of every city must be estimated from general circumstances, and particular facts. Among the former are the state of its population, whether increasing, or diminishing; the state of its improvements, whether progressive, or stationary; above all, the state of public opinion concerning the conduct of its affairs. Among the latter, are the condition of its finances, with reference to debt and resources; and the condition of its police, with reference to order, harmony, and morals. The advance of our city, in population and improvements, requires no illustration. In respect of both, it has been as rapid as there was any just reason to expect; perhaps, to desire. The satisfaction of our fellow-citizens with the general conduct of their affairs, has been indicated by recent events; the language of which cannot be mistaken, and which is at once consolatory and encouraging.

The state of the finances of our city is not less a subject of congratulation. Their condition has been, of late, very fully developed by reports of Committees of both branches of the City Council. Nothing more will be necessary, therefore, on this occasion, than to present some general views on the subject.

The character of every financial condition depends upon comparison of debt with resources. The mere fact of the existence or non-existence of a city debt, is in itself neither a matter of praise or blame. The right to create such debt is a power granted by the city charter to the City Council. Powers, granted to public bodies, are like talents, bestowed on individuals. Both are respectively responsible for the neglect, or exercise, of them. To neglect to use the power to create a debt, or any other power, on proper occasions, and for the purposes for which it was granted, is as truly an abuse, as it is to use either on improper occasions, and for purposes for which it was not granted.

Has a debt been created, by public agents, having authority to that effect? Their merit, or demerit, in this respect, depends upon the fact of its being created for proper objects, or on a just necessity. If the objects be of a nature, for which it is proper to create a debt, then merit, or demerit, depends upon the importance of the objects attained, compared with the amount of the debt created. If, by creating a debt for such objects, resources adequate to its ultimate discharge be also created, there is no case, in which the power to create a debt can be more unexceptionably exercised; nor can there be any, more indicative of the wisdom and financial skill of public agents; except it be, when the resources, thus created, shall be adequate, not only to the ultimate discharge of such debt, but also to add a considerable surplus to the public treasury.

The present city debt may be stated to be, in round numbers, one million of dollars. Of which, one hundred thousand was incurred under the town government, and nine hundred thousand under the city. Of this last amount, there was incurred, for objects of general improvement, ... $234,000

For the purchase of land west of Charles Street, ...	58,000
For the extension of Faneuil Hall Market, ...	608,000
Constituting the debt stated above as incurred by the city government, of	$900,000

With respect to the above portion of the increased debt, which has been applied to purposes of general improvement, it would, perhaps, be sufficient to remark, that the circumstances of the time, and the nature of the objects, rendered the expenditures of this class peculiarly expedient; that the concurrence of our fellow-citizens in the measures adopted on this subject by the City Council, has been indicated by unequivocal tokens; and those measures have, subsequently, been sanctioned by distinct marks of general approbation. It cannot, however, but be satisfactory to know the amount of the expenditures for these objects, which has been already paid out of the funds accruing within the years in which they were authorized, and the comparative proportion which has been cast, in the form of debt, on future years.

During the four last years, from 1823 to 1826, inclusive, there has been expended

For schoolhouses and land, ...	$80,000
" engines, engine-houses, land, and all expenses of the Fire Department, ...	34,000
" common sewers, beyond what they have as yet produced, .	15,000
" ward-rooms and buildings at Deer Island, ...	5,000
" widening streets, (exclusive of the operations of the Committee for the extension of Faneuil Hall Market,)	106,698
" paving and repair of streets, ...	119,900
" buildings, and improvements connected with the House of Industry, and Correction, ...	90,451
" reservoirs, ...	9,000
Making a gross aggregate of	$460,049

In the above enumeration, no notice has been taken of expenditures, on account of general instruction of schools, health, cleanliness of streets, general police, or support of the poor, either by the Overseers, or the Directors of the House of Industry. The objects selected are those of a permanent character and prospective usefulness, and which, from their nature, have a direct influence on the convenience and hopes of future times. When, for such objects, *four hundred and sixty thousand dollars* have been expended in a course of four years, of which *two hundred and thirty thousand* have been paid out of funds accruing within those four years, it seems altogether unexceptionable, that a like amount of *two hundred and thirty thousand dollars* should be distributed, for reimbursement, on the years which are to come.

The remaining objects, for which this increased debt has been incurred, are the lands at the bottom of the Common, west of Charles Street, and the extension of Faneuil Hall Market. In the report of the Committee on the last mentioned subject, which was printed and distributed through the city by order of the last City Council, it is, I apprehend, satisfactorily shown, that the fair estimated value of the property transferred to or vested in the city by that Committee is, in point of amount, not far short of the whole debt of the city. If to this be added the fair estimated value of the lands west of Charles Street, no man can reasonably question that both descriptions of property are, of themselves, alone sufficient to discharge the whole debt of the city, and also to add no inconsiderable, probably a large, surplus to the City Treasury. Both, as available resources, have been attained by the operations of former City Councils. Both have been chief causes of the greatness of the increase of the city debt.

To this it is no answer to say, that the property, both in the Market and in the land west of Charles Street, has very intimate relations to the ornament, comfort, and health of the city, and ought never to be sold. Grant such to be the fact; it only shows, that, while the marketable value of this property is demonstrably more than the whole city debt, its value to the city is still greater than its marketable value. Whereby the wisdom and fidelity of former City Councils is still more apparent; being evidenced, not only by the excess of the marketable value of this property beyond the city debt, but also by the great excess of its value to the city, considered as a property to be retained, over its value, considered as a property to be sold. It seems scarcely possible, that any public debt can be justified on stronger grounds, than can the whole which the city government has incurred. It has been for proper objects. It has been faithfully applied. It has created resources sufficient, if the City Council choose so to use them, to discharge forthwith not only the whole debt of which they have been the cause, but also the whole antecedently existing debt of the city. If the City Council do not choose so to use them, it is because, in their sound discretion, they believe them to be more valuable as a possession than as a resource. No better evidence can be given of financial skill and representative fidelity.

In relation to our police, it is not to be expected, that a city with a population equal to ours can exist, with fewer interruptions of its peace, or violations of its municipal rules. Complaints, under every branch of police, have diminished in a very extraordinary degree during the past year. Those parts of the city most characterized by tendency to vice and disorder, have, by the vigilance of the public officers, been kept in a state of comparative order, satisfactory to the good citizens in their vicinity.

Looking forward to the duties of the coming year, it is a subject of congratulation, that the foresight and enterprise of past years have limited to comparatively a narrow sphere the necessity of future expenditures. Those great, obvious, and expensive improvements, paving the Neck, reducing Pemberton's Hill, widening Court Street, the Roebuck Passage, and Merchants' Row; above all those, relieving the embarrassments resulting from the narrowness of the great central Market of the city, are finished. The City Councils of former years have taken the responsibility of exercising the powers intrusted to them, with a fearless and independent spirit; exhibiting a confidence in the virtue and intelligence of their fellow-citizens, which events have shown not to have been misplaced.

I do not perceive that the City Council of the present year will be called, by the public interest, to take the lead in any new and expensive project. Particular local improvements will be suggested, from time to time, by those interested in their success, and will receive from the City Council that attention they may respectively merit. Circumstances indicate, that our chief duty will be to finish what we have begun; to make productive the property we have acquired; to improve and correct existing establishments, rather than to devise new ones; above all, to arrange our resources on the principle of a distinct and permanent provision for the gradual extinction of the existing city debt. Circumstances seem favorable to such a system. At present, the proceeds of the city lands, when sold, with the addition of fifteen thousand dollars to be applied annually to the redemption of the capital, and another sum of fifteen thousand dollars to be applied annually to the payment of the interest of the city debt, constitute the general appropriations for those objects. The specific appropriation for the same objects, of the whole property and incomes transferred to the city by the Committee for the extension of Faneuil Hall Market is, in my judgment, a measure of great propriety and expediency; and I recommend it. Upon general principles, it is proper, not to consider property obtained by debt *as property;* that is, as a subject of complete ownership, and applicable to general objects of expenditure, until the debt for which it was incurred is paid. It is expedient, because such a measure would, I know, give great satisfaction to many of our very judicious fellow-citizens.

Should a measure such as I suggest be adopted, it would be right, perhaps, to withdraw one of the sums of fifteen thousand dollars at present appropriated for the debt, by way of offset for the old market revenues. The remaining fifteen thousand dollars, with the present Faneuil Hall Market and wharf revenues, will constitute an annual amount of fifty-eight thousand dollars, applicable to the discharge of the principal and interest of the debt; and, with the proceeds of the Neck lands and of the lands now to be sold, transferred to the city by the Faneuil Hall Market Committee, will make a sufficient provision for the city debt, and relieve the annual resources of the city from future burden on that account.

Should these funds be placed under the supervision of commissioners, composed of public officers, *ex officio*, appointed by the City Council, it would give a more permanent and efficient character to the system, without creating any new office or expense. Where funds are vested in a board, exclusively charged with these duties, it is found, by experience, to introduce order and distinctness into financial relations. Their general state is more easily comprehended by the community, and the productive efficiency of the funds is less likely to be disturbed or diverted, by general and extraneous financial exigencies.

Among the objects to which I allude, under the heads of finishing what we have begun, and of making productive the property we have acquired, are the making sale of the lands above-mentioned, invested in the city by the Committee for the extension of Faneuil Hall Market, and which, to whatever objects the proceeds are appropriated, ought not long to be delayed; and the putting to use parts of Faneuil Hall, formerly occupied as a market.

In this connection, I am irresistibly impelled to express opinions, which I would willingly avoid, inasmuch as I have reason to fear they may be at variance with those of men, whose judgments I respect, and cross interests or views, with which I have certainly no wish to interfere. But the city charter, by making it the duty of the Mayor, from time to time, to recommend "all such measures as may tend to improve the finances, the police, health, security, cleanliness, comfort, and ornament of the city," intended that, in fulfilling this duty, he should follow the deliberate convictions of his own judgment. To him who holds this office, and who acts in relation to it upon right principles, it ought to be of no consequence whatever, so far as respects himself, whether any particular measure he recommends be or be not adopted. But, it will always be of infinite moment to his sense of well-performed duty, that his deliberate views of the interests of the city should be known; and, fearlessly of all personal consequences, made manifest.

Under these sanctions, I recommend that the subject of the uses, to which the vacated portions of Faneuil Hall and of the space on its western end shall be applied, should be considered in connection with the sale and uses, proposed to be made of the land, lying in the rear of this (the county) court-house, and between it and Court Street.

This last-mentioned tract of land is a most valuable property. It cannot, however, be made to produce its market worth, without previously providing for the accommodation of the courts, which occupy the building at present in front of that land.

This subject has hitherto been considered as a distinct concern; and, as such, it has been proposed to erect another court-house on that part of the land which lies most distant from Court Street, at an estimated expense of certainly not less than thirty thousand dollars, exclusive of the value of the land to be occupied by the building, which, at the least fair estimate, cannot also be worth less than ten thousand dollars.

The vacated parts of Faneuil Hall have also been considered as a distinct subject; and as such it has been proposed, that they should be fitted up for shops and stores also, at a very considerable expense.

Should these plans be carried into effect, the consequence will be, that the city will possess two expensive court-houses, in the vicinity of each other; and the city authorities will be left as occupants of an inconvenient and insufficient portion of one of them, under circumstances, with which it is impossible they can be for many years content. If the present opportunity be lost, of making a simple and economical arrangement, both of the public offices and of the courts, such as the nature and relations of this property seem unequivocally to indicate, I cannot question, that, before a very few years elapse, the City Council will find themselves compelled to erect, at a great expense, a City Hall; which expense, by taking advantage of the present occasion, may be saved.

Nothing can be more inconvenient, for facilitating business, than the location of our public offices. The Mayor and Aldermen, City Clerk, Auditor, and Officer of Police, are in one building. The Assistant City Clerk in another. The Treasurer, in a third. The Assessors, Overseers of the Poor, and Directors of the House of Industry, in a fourth. Neither building convenient as it respects the other. Now the interest of the city plainly dictates, that the intercourse between these different departments of public service should be made easy by every possible local accommodation. By concentrating them under one roof, they would always be in a position mutually to derive and communicate information; and occasionally to aid each other, in case of pressure of public business in either department; thereby greatly increasing power, knowledge, and facility in conducting it.

Besides, not one of our public city offices is possessed of a fire-proof place of deposit. All the records of the city are exposed without any except the most common security, against the most destructive of all elements.

These circumstances strongly impress my mind with the duty of recommending that all these important subjects should be considered in one general, connected view.

With respect to the location of the City Council and city offices, I conceive there can be no place more suitable than Faneuil Hall. Since the removal of the Market and the widening of Merchants' Row and the Roebuck Passage, the objection on account of noise in the vicinity of that building is greatly obviated; and will be more, if not wholly, as soon as by carrying into effect the proposed Marginal Street, the heavy city and country travel from Long Wharf and State Street to the northern parts of the city, shall be determined through that avenue. Besides, the meetings of the Board of Aldermen being chiefly, and those of the Common Council, with few exceptions, wholly in the evening, they would be but little exposed to interruption from that cause.

I say nothing, concerning the natural and proud associations inseparable from that ancient and far-famed temple of American liberty, because, should other considerations justify, it is impossible there can be, on this subject, more than one sentiment and feeling among citizens of Boston, and that deeply favorable to the connecting, by an intimate and perpetual union, all future municipal labors and character, with a place, consecrated by the patriotic services of our chiefest statesmen, and endeared by recollections of talents and virtues, which have identified the name of this city with the earliest, the purest, and the most imperishable honors of our revolution.

In regard to economy, this consideration will favor the course I suggest. A building, capable of accommodating all the city offices, with suitable and separate rooms and fire-proofs, the Mayor, Aldermen, and Common Council, with their respective halls and committee-rooms, may, I have reason to believe, be erected, on the western end of Faneuil Hall, at probably a less expense, but certainly for a sum not materially greater, than the proposed new Court House; and, at a comparatively small expense, probably not more than the value of the land necessary to be occupied by the proposed new Court House, a room, as extensive in point of size as that at present occupied by the Supreme Judicial Court, might be prepared in this building, (the county Court House,) for the courts of the United States; and the present room, occupied by the Common Council, might be reserved for the Common Pleas. At any rate, when it is considered, that this is the only mode in which the public offices can be concentrated under one roof, except at the expense of a new City Hall, the evidence in favor of its economy is decisive. By a plan of this kind, the higher courts of the State, and those of the United States, will be located in one building; the city authorities, with the public offices, in another; and the whole land in the rear of this (the county) Court House, and between it and Court Street will be left, without incumbrance or diminution, at the disposal of the City Council.

I have been thus particular in detailing my views on this subject, because I deem the result of the deliberations of the City Council upon it, to be very important, in its character and consequences. Having conscientiously discharged my own duty, I cheerfully leave the subject to the City Council, with a certainty that they will do theirs; and give as much weight to these suggestions as their nature deserves, and no more. Whether they coincide or differ with me in opinion, I shall equally respect and support their decision.

It is known to the City Council, that great complaints have lately existed, concerning the state of the voting lists. In relation to the duty of preparing those lists, and of responsibility for their correctness, the general opinion was understood to be, that the provisions of the city charter had made no change, but that, as under the town government, that duty and responsibility rested on the Assessors. The Mayor and Aldermen have, accordingly, heretofore acted under that impression; and considered their duty to be only that of revising and amending errors which might occur in the voting lists furnished by the Assessors.

Antecedent to the last election, in consequence of a communication from the Assessors, the tenor and precise bearing of the terms of the city charter on this subject, were brought under the distinct consideration of the Mayor and Aldermen. By that communication it appeared that, in the opinion of the Assessors, "*the duty of making out the voting lists*," was devolved by the city charter on the Mayor and Aldermen; and that the duty of the "*Assessors, Assistant Assessors, and other officers of the city*," was to aid the Mayor and Aldermen in the performance of their duty, as they might direct.

Although this construction did not coincide with former practice, or preconceptions, the Board of Aldermen immediately adjourned to the Assessors' room, and proceeded, by a committee, to execute the duty, according to the literal construction given to the charter by the Assessors; and, calling in aid some of the Assistant Assessors and other officers of the city, in addition to the aid given by the Assessors themselves, they caused lists, additional to the printed lists, to be made out and transmitted to the wards; a course of proceeding which has, as far as has come to my knowledge, given general satisfaction, and obviated every difficulty which had been the source of complaint at former elections.

The view taken by the Assessors, of the city charter, is, as I understand, as follows. The responsibility, that correct lists are made out, rests upon the Mayor and Aldermen. As incident to this responsibility, it is incumbent on them to direct the time, manner, and form of making out the voting lists. By the provisions of the city charter, they have a right to require the aid of the Assessors, which aid it is their duty to give. By this construction, it is not understood that the Assessors claim to be exempted from the actual labor of making out the voting lists, nor yet from the duty of comparing them with their books, and certifying their correctness; but only that, so far as respects their fellow-citizens, the Mayor and Aldermen are responsible that it shall be done, and in proper time, form, and manner; and that the Assessors are responsible to them and to the City Council, that whatever aid they shall, on this subject, be required to give, shall be faithfully yielded.

Although I know, that there is not an universal assent to this construction of the city charter, yet, as above expressed and explained, I deem it my duty not to conceal my own concurrence with it. It seems to me not only just, as a matter of construction, but that such ought to be the provisions of the city charter, is wise and expedient, as a matter of principle. It is vital to the rights of election, that the voting lists should be correct. The duty of seeing, that so essential an interest is secured, should be intrusted only with the highest executive authorities of the city; and those who are responsible directly to their fellow-citizens, through the process of election.

In conformity to the obligation resulting from this opinion, the Board of Aldermen have constituted the Mayor a committee to superintend the making out the voting lists, antecedent to the ensuing spring elections. Under that authority, voting lists are now making out, by the Assessors, in a new, and, it is hoped, a more convenient form.

By this construction of the city charter it is not apprehended, that the labors of the Board of Aldermen will be, in any material degree, increased. The gratuitous labors of that important body of men, who have hitherto fulfilled their duties in a manner so exemplary, ought by every possible precautionary measure to be diminished, in order to remove objections to the acceptance of that laborious and responsible office. But the duty of general superintendence and direction, the exercise of a sound judgment concerning all the great municipal relations of the city, and particularly concerning those which most immediately affect the elective franchise, naturally belongs to that board; and, in this case, seems to result from the express terms of the city charter.

Considering the importance of the subject, and knowing that misapprehensions existed in relation to it in the community, I have deemed the preceding development due to all concerned; to the Assessors, as well as to our fellow-citizens.

I cannot close this address, without expressing my gratitude for the support yielded to me, by the recent suffrages of my fellow-citizens, under circumstances, which put to a severe trial their justice and their confidence. The right to canvass the character and conduct of all tenants of public office and candidates for it, is essential to the existence of a republic, and inseparable from its nature. So long as such animadversions are conducted in a spirit of candor and decorum, so long as care is taken to assert nothing but what is true, and to insinuate nothing which circumstances do not justify; in a word, so long as they proceed in subordination to that sublime rule of Christian charity of doing to others, as, in exchange of circumstances, we would wish and think right, that others should do to us, they are not only to be justified, but to be encouraged and applauded.

If, in any respect, this just measure of animadversion has been exceeded in times past, or shall be in times future, so far as the present incumbent of this office is concerned, it will be, as it has been, left to the free decision of the virtue, intelligence, and high sense of justice of the inhabitants of this city, without interposition, by him, directly or indirectly, of reply or defence.

He, who rightly appreciates the nature of this office, will consider it neither as a place for pageantry and display, nor yet as a vantage-ground for the vaulting of unsatisfied ambition, still less as a station for seeking private ends, for advancing personal or local interests, or for the distributing party favors; but as a condition of laborious service, including the performance of very difficult, and often very dubious duties, chiefly to be valued for the opportunity it affords of usefulness, and no longer to be desired than he shall be able to deserve and attain the confidence of his fellow-citizens, by a diligent and faithful upholding of the true interests of the city, and by a fearless maintaining of every essential principle of public virtue and honor in the conduct of its affairs.

(G. Page 229.)

THE MAYOR'S INAUGURAL ADDRESS, JANUARY, 1828.

Gentlemen of the City Council: —

WE assemble under circumstances of great municipal prosperity, and with very decisive evidences of the content of our fellow-citizens with the general conduct of their affairs. A brief recurrence to a few of the principal relations of our city, will, however, be useful, and tend to strengthen public satisfaction and confidence.

During the first years of the city government, its attention was naturally directed to important local improvements, and to the enlarging of our means of protection against the dangers to which all great cities are subject, and which the form of the ancient government was not well calculated to effect. The number and greatness of these improvements and preparations, together with the short period in which they were executed, led necessarily to the creation of debt, on a scale which excited, in some minds, apprehensions; cautious men began to fear lest an increase of debt would become the habit of the city government. The experience of the past year has shown, that it is no less willing to adopt and enforce a rigid system of economy, than the practice of preceding years had shown it to be capable of using, on proper occasions, the public credit. The appropriations made at the commencement of the last year have been respected, with an exemplary strictness. None have as yet been exceeded. To one or two, additions will be required; but in every instance, it is believed, it will be found that they have been occasioned by circumstances, accidental in their nature, and not within the control of the expending authority; and that they can be supplied by the transfer of the surplus, existing in other appropriations. There can scarcely be expected, in any future year, a greater exactness in this respect than the past has exhibited.

The measures adopted by the last City Council to give a permanent and efficient character to the reduction of the city debt, have been attended with all the success which was anticipated. Before the current financial year closes, more than one hundred thousand dollars of the preëxisting city debt will be discharged. It requires only a steady perseverance in the same system, to place the resources of the city on an enviable and satisfactory foundation.

The diminution of the number of complaints in every branch of police, indicates a very general content with its administration. In no preceding year has the general order been better maintained. Nor, in a population so great, and rapidly increasing, can it be expected that vice and crime should be less obtrusive, or more restrained.

It is a subject of congratulation, that the new arrangements in our health department, whereby responsibility and efficiency have been endeavored to be obtained by the concentration of its powers in the Board of Aldermen, the health physician and police officer, should have resulted in such apparent advantage. Notwithstanding a constant and increasing intercourse with Halifax, a city suffering under the most malign form of the smallpox, — notwithstanding the same disorder has been brought to this city in repeated instances, from that and from other cities, — and notwithstanding it has appeared with some activity in towns in our immediate vicinity, yet by the vigilance of the health department every occurring case has been detected, insulated, or removed. Until the last week, no instance of its having been communicated within this city, is known or suspected. The circumstances of that week have been the subject of a public official statement. Since that publication, only one case has occurred, and that has been promptly removed to the island. Nor is any case now known, or believed to exist within the city.

Although great credit is due to the health physician and police officer, for their vigilance and activity, yet it cannot be questioned that their labors have been diminished and their success facilitated by the general vaccination, which took place under the authority of former City Councils.

The state of the hospital at Rainsford's Island, and its general police, so far as depends on the health physician and island keeper, is very satisfactory. Applications from the local authority of several towns in this vicinity, to transfer their infected citizens to that establishment, have been promptly granted. The willingness with which those citizens have permitted themselves to be thus transferred, and even the desire, exhibited by some of them, who were individuals of great respectability in their respective towns, to avail of this privilege, in preference to remaining insulated in their own vicinity, strongly indicates the satisfaction of the public with that establishment, and their confidence in the professional ability with which it is conducted.

The general state of the health of the city is not only a subject of devout thankfulness, but is also a circumstance not to be omitted, in estimating the effects of the general arrangements of its police. Tables, founded on the bills of mortality of this city, and constructed on the usual principles, show that for the four years past, from 1824 to 1827 inclusive, the annual average proportion of deaths to population has not only been less than that in any antecedent year, but it is believed less than that of any other city of equal population on record.

The bills of mortality of this place, and calculations made on them for the eleven years, from 1813 to 1823, inclusive, show, that the annual average proportion of deaths to population was about *one* in *forty-two*.

Similar estimates on the bills of mortality of this city since 1823, show, that this annual average proportion was for the four years, from 1824 to 1827 inclusive, less than *one* in *forty-eight;* for the three years from 1825 to 1827 inclusive, less than *one* in *fifty;* for the two years from 1826 to 1827 inclusive, less than *one* in *fifty-five;* and for the last year, 1827, scarcely *one* in *sixty-three.*

Upon the usual estimates of this nature, a city of equal population, in which this annual average should not exceed *one* in *forty-seven* would be considered as enjoying an extraördinary degree of health.

Calculations of this kind are necessarily general, and exactness in precise results, owing to the uncertainty in the annual increase of population, cannot be expected. Enough appears, however, from unquestionable data, to justify the position, that, since the year 1823, this city has enjoyed an uncommon and gradually increasing state of general health, and that for the last two years it has been unexampled.

It will be recollected by the City Council, that, in the year 1823, a systematic cleansing of the city, and removal of noxious animal and vegetable substances was adopted under their auspices, and have been persevered in to this period, with no inconsiderable trouble and expense. Now, although it would be too much to attribute the whole of this important improvement in the general health of this city to these measures, yet when a new system was at that period adopted, having for its express object this very effect, — the prevention of disease, by an efficient and timely removal of nuisances, it is just and reasonable to claim for those preventive measures, and credit to them, a portion of that freedom from disease, which has, subsequently to their adoption, resulted, in a degree, so very extraordinary. It is proper to adduce this state of things, by way of encouragement to persevere in a system, which has its foundation in the plainest principles of nature and reason, and which is so apparently justified by effects.

I am thus distinct in alluding to this subject, because the removal of the nuisances of a city is a laborious, difficult, and repulsive service, requiring much previous arrangement, and constant vigilance, and is attended with frequent disappointment of endeavors; whence it happens, that there is a perpetual natural tendency, in those intrusted with municipal affairs, to throw the trouble and responsibility of it upon subordinate agents and contractors, and very plausible arguments of economy may be adduced in favor of such a system. But, if experience and reflection have given certainty to my mind upon any subject, it is upon this: that upon the right conduct of this branch of police, the executive powers of a city should be made directly responsible, more than for any other; and that it can never, for any great length of time, be executed well, except by agents under its immediate control, and whose labors it may command, at all times, in any way, which the necessities continually varying, and often impossible to be anticipated, of a city, in this respect, require.

In the whole sphere of municipal duties, there are none more important than those which relate to the removal of those substances, whose exhalations injuriously affect the air. A pure atmosphere is to a city, what a good conscience is to an individual; a perpetual source of comfort, tranquillity, and self-respect.

The general confidence resulting from our Fire Department is an ample justification of the great expenditures which have been made, in bringing it to that state of preparation and efficiency, in which it now exists. Besides the sense of security it has induced, the direct pecuniary gain to the community is capable of being very satisfactorily estimated. Since the renovation of that department, and its establishment on its present footing, the rates of insurance on real property within this city have been reduced *twenty per cent.* I am authorized by several presidents of our principal insurance offices to state, that this reduction has been *solely owing* to confidence in the present efficiency of that department. The saving in this reduction of premium alone is stated by them not to be less on the insurable real estate of this city than ten thousand dollars annually; in other words, it is equal to a remuneration, in three years, for the whole cost of the department. It is now distinguished not only for the efficiency of its engines and apparatus, but by its exemplary spirit of discipline. The utmost harmony also exists among its members, officers, and companies.

The expediency and mode of still farther extending our present system of public schools, so as to embrace higher branches than those at present taught in them will, probably, in some form, be brought before the City Council.

In a city, which already expends *sixty thousand dollars* annually on its public schools, which has a capital of certainly not less than two hundred thousand dollars invested in schoolhouses alone, and whose expenses under this head must, from the increasing nature of its population, unavoidably increase every year, attempts to extend the existing system of instruction must necessarily give occasion to much solicitude and reflection. The great interest and duty of society, and its great object in establishing public schools, is, to elevate as highly as possible the intellectual and moral condition of the mass of the community. To this end, our institutions are so constituted as to put every necessary branch of elementary instruction within the reach of every citizen, and to infuse, by the books read and branches taught in them, similar general views of duty and morals; and similar general principles, relative to social order, happiness, and obligation, throughout the whole society. Such is the present general character of our common schools; so called, because they are the common right and common property of every citizen. If other and higher branches of instruction are to be added to those embraced by our present system of public education, it deserves serious consideration, whether the duty and interest of society does not require, that they should be added to our common schools, and enjoyed on the same equal principles of common right and common property. In other words, whether the new branches shall not be for the benefit of the children of the whole community, and not for the benefit of the children of comparatively a few.

Every school, the admission to which is predicated upon the principles of requiring higher attainments, at a specified age or period of life, than the mass of children in the ordinary course of school instruction at that age or period can attain, is in fact a school for the benefit of the few, and not for the benefit of the many. Parents, who, having been highly educated themselves are, therefore, capable of forcing the education of their own children; parents, whose pecuniary ability enables them to educate their children at private schools, or who by domestic instruction are able to aid their advancement in the public schools, will for the most part enjoy the whole privilege. In form it may be general, but it will be in fact exclusive. The sound principle upon this subject seems to be, that the standard of public education should be raised to the greatest desirable and practicable height; but that it should be effected by raising the standard of our common schools.

Among the general principles of public policy, by which the prosperity of cities is effected, there is one, which, by many of our citizens, and those of great wealth and respectability, is considered to be onerous and oppressive, and which, it is thought, has a material and injurious influence on the advancement of a city like ours, engaged in an active mercantile competition with intelligent and enterprising rival cities, in which no such principle of public policy exists. Although the subject properly belongs to the sphere of State legislation, yet as the mischief is thought chiefly to affect this city, it seems desirable, and would give satisfaction to a very great class of our fellow-citizens, to have the practicability of a change in this principle submitted to the test of a public examination.

I allude to the system of *assessing taxes on the principle of an arbitrary valuation, without relief.*

Although the formal provisions of the law are so framed as to conceal the character of the principle, yet it is practically that which I have stated. It is a valuation arbitrary in its nature, and, in point of fact, without relief.

The character of the principle is concealed by the opportunity which is formally given to every individual, if he pleases, to exhibit previous to assessment, perfect lists of his estate. On his neglect of this opportunity the right to *doom*, that is, arbitrarily to value and assess, is assumed and justified.

Now, it is notorious, that, in every great mercantile city, such an exhibit would, if made truly, as it respects many, be ruinous; that, as it respects very many, it is absolutely impracticable, and that a public annual development of the exact relation of his resources, would disastrously affect almost every man of property in society, either by embarrassing his operations, or by needlessly exposing his condition to the curious, the envious, or the inimical. When, therefore, the law offers an opportunity to exhibit true lists of their property, as a privilege of which multitudes cannot avail themselves, and which it is the interest of every man in society to reject, it offers a shadow and not a substance; it is only a formal and not a real privilege. And, when it founds the right arbitrarily to assess, on the neglect of an opportunity of such a character, it exercises in effect a despotic power, not the less objectionable on account of its being veiled under the pretence of being justified by failure to perform an impracticable or ruinous condition. To show that such is the practical character of this principle, it will be sufficient simply to state, that the last year an uncommon number of persons and a greater amount of property was exhibited in previous lists than in any antecedent year in this city, yet that out of more than twelve thousand taxable persons only *twenty-six* gave in such lists, and in a city the valuation of which exceeded sixty-five thousand of dollars, the amount exhibited in these lists was only *four hundred and three thousand.* A more direct proof, how nominal and fallacious this privilege to exhibit is universally deemed, could not be adduced. It is, in effect, an arbitrary valuation, and it is without relief. For if this fallacious privilege be neglected, the Courts are by statute provision prohibited from making abatements; and in our convention of Assessors, in all cases above sixteen dollars, it is practically a settled principle, that such neglect precludes the applicant from the privilege of abatement.

Did the effect of these principles terminate with the individual, it would be of less importance; but it reacts upon society, and especially on a mercantile community, whose prosperity must necessarily be affected by it, in a greater or less degree.

It should be the settled policy of mercantile cities to allure and detain capitalists. Of all classes of men, these are the quickest to discern, and are in a situation the most favorable to take advantage of, the relative principles which the laws and policy of different cities apply to their condition. Their activity, enterprise, and capital, give life and support to the industry of the laboring and mechanic classes. Whatever drives capitalists from a city, or makes them discontented with it, has a direct tendency to deprive those classes of their best hopes. Now, what can have a more direct and natural tendency to such an effect than the certainty that there is no escape from an arbitrary valuation and assessment, except compliance with a condition which is ruinous to some, impracticable to others, and repulsive to all? Unless indeed it be a further certainty, which in this case also exists, that from such an assessment, once made, there is absolutely no hope of relief!

That this city has lost important and valuable citizens and great capitalists, in consequence of the operation of this principle, is a known fact. How many more have been deterred from uniting their destinies with ours, and have been led by it to place their capital in employ in other cities, it is not possible to estimate; but that there have been such is also positively known.

Other great cities, our neighbors and honorable rivals, have no such arbitrary principle connected with their system of assessment. Having opened a correspondence with the respective Mayors of New York, Philadelphia, and Baltimore on the subject, they have each of them, with great promptitude and politeness, transmitted a transcript of the principles and course of proceedings of their respective cities in relation to assessments.

In all of these cities there seems to exist a general content with the principle on which assessment is made, whatever discontent may individually exist in the application of it. In neither of them is any exhibit of personal property required antecedent to assessment. In all of them, previously to finally closing the assessment, an opportunity is given to those who deem themselves aggrieved, to be heard, and to have the assessment modified, according to the truth of their case.

The subject has great relations. I refer to it out of respect to an opinion, very general in this city, that our principles of taxation are injurious to its prosperity. It is a subject worthy of deliberate consideration, and an examination into it would give to many good citizens great satisfaction, even should the result be, that a change was impracticable or inexpedient.

For the renewed evidences I have recently received of the confidence of my fellow-citizens, I can only renew the assurance of a life and thoughts exclusively devoted to understand and pursue their best interests.

(H. Page 132.)

MESSAGE OF THE MAYOR TO THE CITY COUNCIL, RECOMMENDING THE EXTENSION OF THE PLAN OF IMPROVEMENT TO BUTLER'S ROW, AND EXPLAINING THE MOTIVES OF THE COMMITTEE FOR THIS RECOMMENDATION.

Gentlemen of the City Council: —

AT a meeting of the Joint Committee on the subject of the extension of Faneuil Hall Market, on the 22d instant, the following vote was passed; and the Mayor was requested to call a special meeting of the City Council, for the purpose of communicating to them the subject and proposition contained in that vote. In obedience to that request, the present meeting has been called.

The vote above alluded to is expressed in the following terms: — "Whereas counter propositions have been made to this Committee, relative to the purchase of lands adjoining the present improvements, now progressing in the vicinity of Faneuil Hall Market; and whereas this Committee are unanimously of opinion, that it will be for the interest of the city that this Committee should be enabled to meet and close on behalf of the city with one or other of those propositions, thereupon voted, unanimously, —

"That the Chairman communicate the above fact to the City Council, and state to them, that by the power to make further purchases of land to an amount not exceeding two hundred and twenty thousand dollars, great and permanently useful improvements and additions may be made to the proposed market accommodations, without any *ultimate cost, and with certain ultimate gain to the city.*"

In communicating this vote to the City Council, I deem it my duty to make such a development of the objects of that vote as the nature of the subject permits, and as the nature also of the power suggested requires.

A suspension of the sales of the sites for the south block of store lots now remaining to be sold by the city, according to the former plan exhibited to the City Council, has taken place, partly by reason of the unsettled state of that part of the city property which is contracted for with the Long Wharf proprietary, and partly on account of the opportunity which the general state of the property lying immediately south of the site of the proposed block of stores presented for most advantageous improvements in the plan, and increase of the accommodations of the New Market-House and streets, as well as for a most convenient and useful general arrangement of the land, included between Butler's Row, and the land leading to Bray's Wharf.

In contemplating the plan of the New Market and streets adjacent, as formerly presented, and on considering it in connection with its other relations, your Committee were of opinion, that, although the improvements effected by that plan were of a great and very satisfactory character, yet, that when considered in connection with the concentration of business which must result to this part of the city in consequence of the location of the New Market there, and of the creation of a new wharf on the city flats to the eastward, which at no distant period could not fail to take place, as well as from the opening of that great sixty-five feet avenue from Long Wharf eastward to the New Market, about to form the principal route of the business between the north part of the city and State, India, and Broad Streets. They were also of opinion, that the street to the southward of the New Market, called on the plan " South Market Street," was much too narrow for that great influx of city trucks and carts, and of country teams and wagons, which the union of commerce and the market would occasion in that street and vicinity.

Upon the plan above-mentioned, " South Market Street " was only " sixty feet " wide. It was obvious to your Committee, that if this street could be widened to the extent of at least one hundred feet, the contemplated accommodation of our country brethren in their attendance on the market, as well as of our citizens, would be greatly increased; and that whenever the new wharf at the eastward on the city flats should be built, the space thus obtained in streets would be highly desirable, if not absolutely necessary, for the great concentration of business above stated, which would be effected in that street and vicinity. In addition to these considerations, others of a prospective and more general character presented themselves.

It was found by calculation, made on the present demand of meat and vegetable stalls, that those contained in the New Market House were no more than sufficient for the actual existing state of the city, with its present population; and that, if any extension of the market accommodation should by the progress of society become necessary, the city authorities would have no other means to effect it than by trenching in upon the width of a " sixty feet street," which, it was agreed on all sides, was sufficiently narrow for the business for which it was about to be the scene, and to form the sphere. By effecting an augmentation of that street to at least *one hundred feet*, this inconvenience would be obviated. Those, who should come after us, might at any time add to the Market House now building,[1] should the growth of the city require, a width of thirty or forty feet through its whole length, and a street sixty or seventy feet wide would remain entire for the accommodation of the public.

Other considerations of a more general character presented themselves to the Committee. It was obvious to their reflection and observation, that there were reasons and opportunities in the progress of societies, and cities, as well as of individuals, by which, according as they were seized and improved, or suffered to escape and be neglected, their character and destinies were shaped and established. It also could not but be perceived by them, that among the circumstances which had a tendency to incommode and restrict the apparent tendencies to the growth of the city of Boston, was the narrowness and crookedness of its streets, and its want of great squares and wide public spaces for the accommodation of the business of citizens. It was plain to your Committee, that no opportunity should be suffered to pass, without being availed of, for the purpose of relieving the city from this discredit and these disadvantages. And they could not but be struck with the singular coincidence of season, places, and opportunity, which the new improvements and the general state of the real property about Faneuil Hall Market offered for these purposes.

1 This street, having been subsequently laid out by the Surveyors of Highways, the use of it here suggested is probably precluded.

At the moment when a new organization of the government has given to the authorities of Boston a greater efficiency, the state of the capital and enterprise, as well as the prevailing harmony and union in relation to public improvements among the citizens, has given a willingness to coöperate in them, altogether unexampled. The present, therefore, it is very apparent, is one of those seasons and opportunities in the progress of this city, on the neglect or improvement of which materially depends its character and destiny.

The place, also, on which the proposed improvements were carrying on, was, in the opinion of the Committee, peculiarly favorable to excite interest and union of sentiment among the citizens, as well as to stimulate to a further extension of similar improvements, on a scale highly honorable to the character of the city, and beneficial as it respects its future prospects.

Faneuil Hall Market is so located with respect to the general interests of Boston, that it may well be considered, as it were, the heart of the city. The new improvements have been planned, and are executing on a scale, calculated to connect the northern and southern sections with this great centre by a noble avenue, and to bring into a sphere of profitable use, lands or flats hitherto comparatively of little use or value. It must be apparent to every one who considers the subject, that, if the present opportunity be suffered to pass unimproved, that it will for that vicinity *be lost forever*. After the final location of the southern block of stores now about to be sold, all hope of a more extensive and accommodating plan must be abandoned. Posterity cannot without great sacrifices, if at all, effect an arrangement of streets and spaces for the business of the city, which now can be obtained with little sacrifice; and in fact with none, when compared with the greatness of the increased improvements and resulting advantages.

With these general views, the Chairman, by direction of the Committee, opened a negotiation with the different proprietors of the land and stores in the vicinity of Butler's Row, and Bray's Wharf and dock. It is very apparent, that this negotiation must be carried on under many disadvantages, not only on account of the number of proprietors, whose good-will was to be conciliated, but also from the high price at which the city sales in that vicinity had countenanced those proprietors in claiming for their lands. A conditional arrangement has, however, at length been made with all the proprietors, whose lands are necessary to be included in this plan, dependent on the will of the Faneuil Hall Market Committee. They are, therefore, now enabled to state with precision the particular plan which they deem it most for the interest of the city to adopt, considering all the relations of the property in that vicinity, and also to state the extreme possible cost and pecuniary results of that plan, should it be deemed advisable to adopt it.[1]

Upon the whole, the interest of the city is, in my opinion, so great, so obvious, and so certain, that I deem it my duty earnestly to recommend it to the City Council.

The result of this improvement, when carried into effect, according to all the greatness and utility which the relations of the property in that vicinity permits,

[1] As the plan here detailed was adopted and carried into effect by the City Council, and its advantages are at this day (1851) understood and acknowledged, the statements here made relative to the cost and anticipated result are omitted.

cannot fail to reflect great honor on the citizens of this metropolis, not only with foreigners, but with our posterity, inasmuch as it will evidence the existence of a spirit in the citizens of the present time, capable of devising and willing to meet the expenditures necessary to effect improvements on a scale calculated not merely to provide for the exigencies of a passing day, but to extend to all future generations of the inhabitants of this city by present wise prospective arrangements, the blessings of that exceeding great prosperity, which Providence in its bounty permits us to enjoy.

(I. Page 137.)

PROCEEDINGS ON LAYING THE CORNER STONE OF FANEUIL HALL MARKET.

On Wednesday, the twenty-seventh of April, 1825, the Corner Stone of the New Faneuil Hall Market was laid by the Mayor of the city, in the presence of the members of the City Council, the Superintendent and workmen of the building, and a large number of citizens. The City Government assembled in Faneuil Hall at eleven o'clock, and moved to the site of the new edifice, in the following order, preceded and flanked by peace officers:—

The Mayor.

The City Marshal, bearing the chest containing the deposits.

The other Members of the Building Committee.

Aldermen.

Members of the Common Council.

Clerks of the two Boards.

Principal Architect, &c.

The Corner Stone, (a large block of Chelmsford granite,) was suspended by a pulley over the foundation stone, in a cavity of which a leaden box, or chest, was deposited, and which contained,—

1. A colored Map of the City, recently executed.
2. Plan of the Lands, Stores, Dock, &c., on which the new Improvement is located, as they existed before the Improvement was contemplated. The sites of the New Market, Streets, Ranges of Stores, &c., being designated by dotted lines.
3. A Book, containing the Charter of the City, with the Amendments thereto; the Constitutions of the United States and of Massachusetts; and sundry Laws, passed in relation to the City.
4. Copies of the Rules and Regulations of the City Council, with a list of the Officers of the City, and the Wards, for 1824–'25.

5. Twenty-two Newspapers published during the preceding week, including all the weekly, semi-weekly, and daily papers, the Price Current, and Masonic Magazine.

6. Eight numbers of Bowen's "History of Boston," in course of publication, containing a number of views of edifices, &c. in the city.

7. A case, containing the following Coins, &c.: — An Eagle, Half Eagle, and Quarter Eagle, of gold; a Dollar, Half Dollar, Quarter Dollar, Dime, and Half Dime, of silver; and a Cent and Half Cent of the most recent coinage of the United States; a Silver (Pine-Tree) Shilling, of Massachusetts, coined in 1652, presented by Nathaniel G. Snelling, Esq.; and a Cent and Half Cent of the coinage of Massachusetts, of 1787. The latter presented by Mr. Jeremiah Kehler. Together with the following Old Continental Bills (of paper money) issued during the Revolution, to wit, — One of Eight Dollars, issued in 1776, and one of Forty Dollars, issued in 1779, presented by Mr. John Fuller; one of Four Dollars, and two of Six Dollars, (one guaranteed by Rhode Island,) presented by Isaac Winslow, Esq.; one of Two Dollars, issued in 1776; one of Five, one of Twenty, and one of Thirty Dollars, issued in 1778; one of Five Dollars, (guaranteed by New Hampshire,) and one New Hampshire Colony Bill, for Ten Pounds, issued in 1775, presented by Ebenezer Farley, Esq.; and a Rhode Island New Emission Bill, issued in 1780, for Three Dollars, presented by Stephen Codman, Esq.

It has been a subject of regret,[1] that the emblems, mottoes, and devices of the old continental paper money, have not, in our recollection, been permanently recorded. We remember to have read a glowing description of them given by a celebrated Whig Peer of England, in the British Parliament, during the Revolution, in answer to a remark of a Ministerialist, that the Americans were destitute of sound learning and science; and which was adduced by him in proof of the existence in America of classical learning, taste, and genius, not excelled by any thing of the kind of which the literati of England could boast. He then attributed the mottoes and designs to FRANKLIN, ADAMS, RITTENHOUSE, LIVINGSTON, and others, which, he said, bore equal evidence of scholarship and patriotism. The bills were extremely well engraved, and printed by HALL and SELLERS, the then BASKERVILLES and DIDOTS of America. Every denomination of bills bore distinct devices, with significant and appropriate Latin mottoes. We shall only notice those on the denominations deposited.

The Two Dollar Bills bore the emblem of a hand making a circle with compasses. Motto, *Tribulatio Ditat.* Translation, "Trouble enriches," or, "The sufferings of the present time are not worthy to be compared with the glory which shall be." — Rom. viii. 18.

The device of the Three Dollar Bills was "an eagle pouncing on a crane, whose beak annoyed the eagle's throat." Motto, *Exitus in dubio est.* Translation, "The issue is doubtful," or, "The race is not to the swift, nor the battle to the strong." — Eccl. ix. 11.

On the Five Dollar Bills was a hand grasping at a thorn-bush. Motto, *Sustine vel abstine.* Translation, "Hold fast or touch not," or, "Be not overcome of evil, but overcome evil with good." — Rom. xii. 21.

The Six Dollar Bills represented a beaver felling a tree. Motto, *Perseverando.* Translation, "By perseverance we prosper," or, "Let us run with patience the race set before us." — Heb. xii. 1. Another emission bore an anchor. Motto,

[1] The whole of this note is taken from the Columbian Centinel of the thirtieth of April, 1825, edited by Benjamin Russell, an active and efficient member of the Faneuil Hall Committee.

In te Domine speramus. Translation, "In God have I put my trust." — Psalm lxvi. 11.

The Eight Dollar Bills bore the Irish harp. Motto, *Majora Minoribus consonant.* Translation, "United we stand," or, "Let there be no divisions among you; but be perfectly joined together in the same mind and in the same judgment." — 1 Cor. i. 10.

The Thirty Dollar Bills bore a wreath on an altar. Motto, *Si recte facies.* Translation, "If you do right you will succeed," or, "Do that which is good, and thou shalt have praise of the same." — Heb. xiii. 3.

8. A Plate of silver, weighing fifteen ounces, eleven inches by seven, with the following

INSCRIPTION.

FANEUIL HALL MARKET,

Established by the City of Boston. This Stone was laid April 27, Anno Domini MDCCCXXV., in the forty-ninth year of American Independence, and in the third of the Incorporation of the city.

JOSIAH QUINCY, *Mayor*.

ALDERMEN. — Daniel Baxter, George Odiorne, David W. Child, Joseph Hawley Dorr, Asher Benjamin, Enoch Patterson, Caleb Eddy, Stephen Hooper.

MEMBERS OF THE COMMON COUNCIL.

Francis J. Oliver, President.

Ward No. 1. — William Barre, John Elliot, Michael Tombs, Joseph Wheeler. — 2. William Little, Jr., Thaddeus Page, Oliver Reed, Joseph Stone. — 3. John R. Adan, John D. Dyer, Edward Page, William Sprague. — 4. Joseph Coolidge, Jeremiah Fitch, Robert G. Shaw, William R. P. Washburn. — 5. Eliphalet P. Hartshorn, Elias Haskell, George W. Otis, Winslow Wright. — 6. Joseph S. Hastings, Joel Prouty, Thomas Wiley, William Wright. — 7. Charles P. Curtis, William Goddard, Elijah Morse, Isaac Parker. — 8. John Ballard, Jonathan Davis, John C. Gray, Hawkes Lincoln. — 9. Benjamin Russell, Eliphalet Williams, Samuel K. Williams, Benjamin Willis. — 10. Francis J. Oliver, James Savage, Phineas Upham, Thomas B. Wales. — 11. Samuel Frothingham, Giles Lodge, Charles Sprague, Josiah Stedman. — 12. Charles Bemis, Samuel Bradlee, Francis Jackson, Isaac Thom.

BUILDING COMMITTEE.

Josiah Quincy, Chairman.

David W. Child, Asher Benjamin, Enoch Patterson, Francis J. Oliver, Benjamin Russell, Charles P. Curtis, Thaddeus Page, Eliphalet Williams, Joseph Coolidge, William Wright.

Alexander Parris, Principal Architect.

JOHN QUINCY ADAMS, President of the United States.

MARCUS MORTON, Lieutenant-Governor, and Commander-in-Chief of the Commonwealth of Massachusetts.

Memoranda. — The population of the City, estimated at fifty thousand. That of the United States, eleven millions.

[*Engraved by Hazen Morse.*]

The Stone having been placed in its proper position and cemented, the Mayor announced that the Corner Stone was now erected of an edifice, which would be a proud memorial of the public spirit and unanimity of the City Council, and of the liberality of their fellow-citizens; an edifice which, he anticipated, would be an ornament to the city, a convenience for its inhabitants, a blessing to the poor, an accommodation to the rich, and an object of pleasure to the whole community. Three cheers followed the annunciation, and the ceremony closed.

The execution of the Inscription on the Plate deposited has been admired by all who have viewed it, as an excellent sample of the progress made in the graphic art, and the ornamental and scrip chirography of the day.

(K. Page 145.)

STATEMENTS RELATIVE TO THE IRRESPONSIBILITY CLAIMED BY THE OVERSEERS OF THE POOR FOR PUBLIC MONEYS.

THE Report here referred to, embodied all the facts relative to the irresponsibility of the Board of Overseers of the Poor for the great sums they annually receive from the City Treasury, and also for the great amount of eleemosynary funds in their hands. It was signed by every member of the Committee, (see p. 144,) men most faithful to the interests of the city, and solicitous to promote those of the poor. It was accepted unanimously by both branches of the City Council, and its recommendations were, in a general meeting of more than *eight hundred* inhabitants, rejected by a majority of only *thirty-one ;* a result showing, that the views presented in that report were approved by nearly half of those present, and those among the most intelligent, and possessing as great a stake as any in the city.

After the result of the struggle made in 1824 to effect a change in this claim of the Overseers for irresponsibility, a perfect silence was maintained on the nature and consequences of these pretensions, until March, 1837, when Samuel A. Eliot, Mayor of the city, in a communication to the City Council relative to the eleemosynary fund, "exclusively under the control of the Overseers of the Poor," and the expenditures, concerning which they disavowed all accountability, took occasion to make the following remarks: —

"Whether this is a state of things which should exist, or whether it would be better that all the modes of charity should be under one general supervision, and under the usual responsibility to the City Council, is for the Council and the citizens to determine. I cannot perceive, that any advantage, arising from the present system, is a counterbalance to the evil which ensues from the complication of the business in so many hands, the danger of collision between independent boards, and the tendency natural to all irresponsible bodies, to conceal their transactions. Publicity is generally and justly regarded as the best security against abuse, and the convenience of having a system of charity adopted by the city, and pursued under the direction of one board, is too manifest to require urging. In what manner this can be effected, I must leave to the deliberations of the City Council, with the conviction, that their proceedings will be marked by regard to the public good, and a just deference to enlightened public opinion."

Notwithstanding the directness and wisdom of these suggestions, no attempt was then made, or has been subsequently, to effect a change in a state of things so undeniably incorrect in point of principle, and so unquestionably liable to secret abuse. A board of twelve men, chosen not by the citizens at large, but individually, in wards, continue to be permitted to expend *from twenty-eight to thirty thousand dollars* annually of money received out of the City Treasury, and to manage a capital of upwards of *one hundred thousand dollars* of eleemosynary funds, distributing its incomes at their discretion, without accountability to any one, except to one another, which, in effect, is no accountability at all.

The cause of this apparent apathy is obvious. There is no body now existing in the city, authorized to call the Overseers of the Poor to account for their expenditures; and, should the City Council make any movement to exercise or obtain that power, a clamor would be raised, as it was in 1824, in the different wards, by those interested in maintaining the present system, and they would be denounced as attempting to interfere with an independent board, and with a desire to get under their control funds placed in other hands by the donors themselves, — a reproach and odium which few administrations are willing to meet, and perhaps fewer would be able to sustain. In the mean time, by the increase of our population and the infusion of foreigners, the necessity of public expenditures for the poor continually augments, and with it, unavoidably, the temptation and danger of secret abuse of great funds, when intrusted to irresponsible agents. It seems important, therefore, that some historical facts should be stated and preserved, especially such as relate to the eleemosynary funds, now holden and distributed by the present Board of Overseers, claiming to be successors of the former Board of Overseers, which existed under the town.

First, then, the Board of Overseers of the Poor of the town of Boston were very differently constituted than are the Board of Overseers of the Poor of the city of Boston, and consequently possessed far more elements of general confidence. Had the Board of Overseers of the Poor been then constituted as it is now, it would never have been selected as the trustees of those eleemosynary funds.

Under the town government the members of the Board of Overseers of the Poor were elected by the votes of the whole body of the inhabitants. They were consequently always men of a high general character, known to a majority of the inhabitants, and chosen by them for their integrity, capacity, and adaptation to the service. Among them were always men distinguished for their wealth, their business talents, and charities. The uniformity of this result for many years, created that general confidence, which caused them to be chosen as trustees of these eleemosynary funds. Now the Board of Overseers of the Poor, under the city government, are chosen in wards, and consequently are seldom known to the inhabitants generally, and are also often not selected for any special qualification for this great trust, but because they are popular and available candidates, or willing to accept an office which is deemed irksome, and to which no emolument is thought to be attached. A board thus constituted could never have acquired that general confidence, which the donations of those eleemosynary funds indicate. What capitalist, at this day, would select that board as trustees of such donations?

There was another element of confidence in the Board of Overseers, under the town, which is wholly wanting in that board under the city, — *every vacancy in the board was always in fact filled by the nomination of the members of the board themselves.* Hence, the new members were always well qualified for the office, and acceptable to the old members remaining as associates. When a vacancy was about to occur, it was the practice of the board to consult together, and to select the individual whose name was to be inserted in the general ticket with those of the members of the board about to remain. This course was known, and acceptable to the inhabitants. The individual thus selected, being always one whose qualities and adaptation were by them well known and approved, he was accordingly uniformly chosen, it is believed, without objection or opposition, during the whole period of the town government. This course of proceeding gave that board, under the town, a fixed and staid character, inviting confidence and sustaining it.

Concerning these eleemosynary funds, the Board of Overseers wrap themselves up in the dignity of irresponsible trustees, and deny to every one, even to the Mayor of the city, the right of raising any question concerning the management and distribution of them. Yet, they have no other ground of claim to the control of those funds than a general declaration in the city charter, that they shall have "all the powers and be subject to all the duties which appertain to the Board of Overseers of the Poor of the town of Boston." Whether such general expressions as these, which contain no words purporting a transfer of property, or implying a grant of any succession to trusts, are sufficient in law to pass funds of a great amount previously vested in a corporation "by the name of the Overseers of the Poor of the town of Boston, and their successors," is a question of law, which, if the heirs or representatives of the original donors of those funds should seriously raise in a court of justice, the result, perhaps, might be dubious. Fortunately, however, the Legislature has reserved to itself, in the very charter of the city, the right "to alter and qualify" the powers of that board. And it is believed, that the time cannot be far distant, when the Legislature, either self-moved, or on the application either of individual citizens or of the City Council, will recognize it as their duty to do justice to the charitable donors of those eleemosynary funds, and bring the Board of Overseers of the Poor under the city to as near an approximation to the character of that under the town as is now possible, by enacting a law, by which the members of that board shall be chosen by that body, which now in every thing else acts for the whole body of the citizens, that is, by the City Council; and thereby restore that board more nearly to the same elements of general confidence it possessed under the town.

An act of this kind would also relieve the city of Boston from the effect of that monstrous financial anomaly, whereby twelve men, chosen individually in wards, with little consideration by the voters of the great amounts of money placed at their disposal, and of their adaptation to distribute it, are invested annually with power to expend from twenty-eight to thirty thousand dollars out of the public treasury, at their discretion, with no other accountability than to one another. The annual publication of their receipts and expenditures, which they call accounting to their fellow-citizens, has, in fact, no one element of effective accountability.

Under the town government, it was otherwise. There every inhabitant had the right and the power, in public town-meeting, to demand explanations and specifications, concerning the modes and principles of expenditure. Under the city, no human being has such right or power, it being denied even to the City Council; and, although it naturally belongs to them, they have hitherto been deterred from attempting to obtain it, from causes well known and already intimated.

(L. Page 206.)

AN ADDRESS [1] DELIVERED AT THE UNANIMOUS REQUEST OF BOTH BRANCHES OF THE CITY COUNCIL ON THE FOURTH OF JULY, 1826, IT BEING THE FIFTIETH ANNIVERSARY OF AMERICAN INDEPENDENCE, BY JOSIAH QUINCY, MAYOR OF THE CITY.

ON the fiftieth anniversary of the independence of our country, — on the great day of our fathers' glory, — we assemble to speak concerning their virtues, and to tell of labors and sacrifices by which they gave existence to our nation.

More than half the term allotted in the ordinary course of Providence to the longest human life has elapsed since that event. Those whose age or experience guide the affairs of the present time were then children or youths; witnesses, without being partakers of that struggle. How natural and suitable is it, on such an anniversary, for the fathers of the present day to speak concerning the fathers of former days to one another and to their children, who are destined to be the fathers of the age which is to come!

We are, then, fellow-citizens, assembled, not to take part in a light and vain show, but to perform a solemn and somewhat a religious duty. Parents and children, we have come to the altar of our common faith, not like the Carthaginian, to swear enmity to another nation, but, in the spirit of obedience and under a sense of moral and religious obligation, to inquire what it is to fulfil well our duty to ourselves and our posterity. And while we pass before our eyes in long array the outspread images of our fathers' virtues, let us strive to excite in our own bosoms and enkindle in each other's that intense and sacred zeal by which their patriotism was animated and refined. Fifty years after the occurrence of the greatest of our national events, we gather with our children around the tombs of our fathers, as we trust, — and may Heaven so grant! — fifty years hence, those children will gather around ours, in the spirit of gratitude and honor, to contemplate their glory; to seek the lessons suggested by their example; and to examine the principles on which they laid the foundations of their country's prosperity and greatness.

[1] This work having been substituted, under circumstances the text explains, for one of the *orations* annually delivered by the appointment of the Mayor and Aldermen on the fourth of July, has been naturally published with that name, and usually regarded in that light.

It was, however, solicited as an *address* to the City Council and inhabitants of the city, accepted as an official duty, and executed in a style adapted to the relation in which the writer stood, and in conformity with the vote of the City Council.

But if, as Americans, it be natural and suitable to consecrate this day in our affections, how much more as citizens of Boston, — inhabitants of that city known through the world as the cradle of American liberty, — standing as we do under the canopy of that sacred temple,[1] which was honored, in the most trying times of our Revolution, by the boldest breathings of our chiefest patriots; which was polluted in the most disastrous times by the war horse, which neighed and stabled in this sanctuary; surrounded as we are by the direct descendants of those who were first and most fearless in the day of severest trial!

Where shall the memory of the great men of our Revolution be honored, if it be not in this city, in this temple, and in this assembly?

What future age, what distant region, hearing of the American Revolution, shall not also hear of "Faneuil Hall" and of the "Old South," where the early spirit of American liberty stood in dignity, fidelity, and fearlessness, while sentries, with fixed bayonets, were at our State House doors; while Boston was but a garrison — its islands and harbors possessed by a vindictive and indignant foe; its trade suspended by British cruisers; famine threatened by British edicts; and the blood of its slaughtered citizens flowed in its streets!

In what land, where the American name is known, are not, and shall not forever be, known, the names of those citizens of Boston, who were the strength and lights of their own time, and the eternal glory of their country, — Adams and Hancock, and Otis, and Warren, and others of scarcely less celebrity?

Especially shall he not be forgotten, now or ever, that ancient citizen of Boston, that patriarch of American independence, of all New England's worthies, on this great day the sole survivor.[2] He, indeed, oppressed by years, sinking under the burdens of decaying nature, hears not our public song or voice of praise or ascending prayer. But the sounds of a nation's joy, rushing from our cities, ringing from our valleys, echoing from our hills, shall break the silence of his aged ear; the rising blessings of grateful millions shall visit, with a glad light, his fading vision, and flush the last shades of his evening sky with the reflected splendors of his meridian brightness.

How peculiarly and imperiously incumbent, then, is it on us on this day, in this place and in this assembly, to speak together concerning the glory of our ancestors; to analyze that glory; and to inquire what it is to deserve, and what it is to disgrace those ancestors!

When we speak of the glory of our fathers, we mean not that vulgar renown to be attained by physical strength, nor yet that higher fame to be acquired by intellectual power. Both often exist without lofty thought or pure intent or

[1] The Old South Church.

[2] John Adams, the patriot here alluded to, expired at about five o'clock on this day; and Thomas Jefferson, another patriot of the same period, also expired at about one o'clock on the same afternoon.

Thus two of the most distinguished statesmen of the United States, both members of the Committee of Congress who drafted the Declaration of American Independence, and who both signed that instrument; both of whom had been for many years Ministers of the United States at several European courts; both of whom had held successively the offices of Vice-President and President of the United States, finished their mortal career on the fourth of July, 1826; it being the fiftieth anniversary of that most glorious and happy event for themselves and their country, — the Declaration of American Independence.

generous purpose. The glory which we celebrate was strictly of a moral and religious character, — righteous as to its ends, just as to its means. The American revolution had its origin, neither in ambition, nor avarice, nor envy, nor in any gross passion; but in the nature and relation of things, and in the thence resulting necessity of separation from the parent State. Its progress was limited by that necessity. During the struggle, our fathers displayed great strength and great moderation of purpose. In difficult times they conducted with wisdom. In doubtful times, with firmness. In perilous, with courage. Under oppressive trials, erect. Amidst great temptations, unseduced. In the dark hour of danger, fearless. In the bright hour of prosperity, faithful. It was not the instant feeling and pressure of the arm of despotism that roused them to resist, but the principle on which that arm was extended. They could have paid the stamp-tax and the tea-tax, and the other impositions of the British government, had they been increased a thousand-fold. But payment acknowledged the right; and they spurned the consequences of that acknowledgment. In spite of those acts they could have lived and happily, and bought and sold, and got gain, and been at ease. But they would have held those blessings on the tenure of dependence on a foreign and distant power, at the mercy of a king or his minions, or of councils in which they had no voice, and where their interests could not be represented, and were little likely to be heard. They saw that their prosperity in such case would be precarious; their possessions uncertain; their ease inglorious. But above all they realized that those burdens, though light to them, would, to the coming age, — to us, their posterity, — be heavy, and, probably, insupportable. Reasoning on the inevitable increase of interested imposition upon those who are without power and have none to help, they foresaw that, sooner or later, desperate struggles must come. They preferred to meet the trial in their own times, and to make the sacrifices in their own persons. They were willing themselves to endure the toil and to incur the hazard, that we and our descendants, — their posterity, — might reap the harvest, and enjoy the increase.

Generous men! exalted patriots! immortal statesmen! For this deep, moral, and social affection, for this elevated self-devotion, this noble purpose, this bold daring, the multiplying myriads of your posterity, as they thicken along the Atlantic coast, from the St. Croix to the Mississippi, as they spread backwards to the lakes, and from the lakes to the mountains, and from the mountains to the western waters, shall, on this day, annually, in all future time, as we at this hour, come up to the temple of the Most High, with song and anthem and thanksgiving and choral symphony and hallelujah, to repeat your names, to look steadfastly on the brightness of your glory; to trace its spreading rays to the points from which they emanate; and to seek, in your character and conduct, a practical illustration of public duty, in every occurring, social exigence.

In the rapid view I am compelled to take of the genius and character of our revolution, I shall chiefly fix my eye on this State, town, and vicinity. Let other States and cities celebrate with due honors the great men whose lights cluster in their peculiar sky. Massachusetts has a constellation of her own, exceeded by none in brightness, yielding to none in power, surpassed by none in influence, during the first stages of the Revolutionary struggle. In this State and in this metropolis were exhibited, among the earliest, those generous virtues and that noble daring which electrified the Continent.

If it be asked in what the peculiar glory of our fathers in that day consisted, this is my answer. It consisted in perfectly-performed duty, according to the measure of that perfection which is attributable to things human. Now, real glory, when strictly analyzed and reduced to its constituent principle, with all its tinsel and dross separated, will be found to consist, and to consist only in truth. The glory of contemplation is truth to nature. The glory of action is truth to the relations in which man is placed, — perfect fulfilment of all the obligations which result from the condition of things allotted to him by Providence.

In this point of view, the glory of our fathers at the revolution may be stated in detail to consist in being true to their ancestors, true to themselves, true to their posterity, and, above all, in being true to virtue and liberty.

Our fathers, at the Revolution, were true to their ancestors; maintaining their principles, obeying their precepts, copying their example.

The Revolution of 1776 is called, and justly, a mighty struggle for independence. But it was neither greater, bolder, nor more arduous, than the emigration of the first settlers to New England; nor was there incurred in it more hazard, nor displayed in any of its events, a more determined spirit of independence, than were incurred and displayed by the immediate descendants of those settlers, — the direct progenitors of the authors of our revolution.

Time would fail me, were I to attempt to maintain this position by historical references. One or two striking evidences of fact and opinion must suffice.

The emigration itself of our ancestors was, in truth, only a mighty struggle for independence. According to the genius of the age, and the particular bias of our ancestors' minds, their motive took the aspect of a strong desire for a higher religious freedom and a purer form of religious worship. It is impossible, however, not to perceive that even this desire was only a mode, under which existed an intense and all-absorbing spirit of civil freedom. In the nature of things, it could not possibly have been otherwise. They fled from the persecutions of the British hierarchy. Now the strength of the hierarchy was in the nerve of the secular arm. It was that odious centaur, not fabulous, church and state, which drove them for refuge into the wilderness. This monster, with a political head and an ecclesiastical body, they hated and feared; representing their emigration and sufferings under the familiar type of the woman of the Apocalypse, who fled "into the wilderness, to a place prepared of God, from the face of the beast."

We are apt to view our ancestors of the first and second generations in the light of enthusiasts. Now, if by this term is meant, according to its usual import, "men, who through a vain confidence in heaven, neglect the use of human means," there never existed a class of men less entitled to that appellation than our fathers. Of all men, they were the most practical. Their whole history, the colleges, schools, churches, all the institutions they founded, constitute one unbroken series of examples of the wise and happy use of human means. As to their opinions, take, instead of a multitude which might be adduced, a single example. In that famous work entitled "Faithful Advice to the Churches of New England," sent out into the world under the auspices of our fathers, having the signatures of both the Mathers, Davenport, Colman, and others, there is the following remarkable vindication of the use of human learning in religion, urged with their characteristic acuteness.

"No man ever decried learning without being an enemy to religion, whether he knew it or no. When our Lord chose fishermen to be ministers, he would not send them forth until they had been several years under his tuition; (a bet ter than the best in any college under heaven) and then, also, he *miraculously* furnished them with more learning than any of us, by seven years hard study, can attain unto."

It would be easy also to adduce abundant evidence of the free opinions entertained by the first settlers, relative to the right of resistance to kings and to personal and colonial freedom, by quotations from approved authors of that period. A single extract from the writings of Nathaniel Ward, the first clergyman of the town of Ipswich, in this vicinity, will sufficiently manifest the temper and spirit of our ancestors in that age on those points. This writer was so highly esteemed by our ancestors, that he was employed in 1639 by the General Court of Massachusetts to draft that code, consisting of one hundred laws, called "the body of liberties" of the Colony. In an eccentric, but highly popular work in that day, published by him in 1647, entitled "The Simple Cobbler of Agawam in America," the contest, then carrying on between the King and Parliament, is represented under the similitude of a controversy between royal prerogative (majestas imperii) and popular liberty (salus populi) and is thus stated in the quaint language of that day:—

We hear that *Majestas Imperii* hath challenged *Salus Populi* into the field; the one fighting for prerogatives, the other defending liberties. If *Salus Populi* began, surely it was not that *Salus Populi* I left in England. That *Salus Populi* was as mannerly a *Salus Populi* as need be. If I be not much deceived, that *Salus Populi* suffered its nose to be held to the grindstone till it was ground to the gristle; and yet grew never the sharper, for aught I could discern. I think that since the world began, it was never storied that *Salus Populi* began with *Majestas Imperii*, unless *Majestas Imperii* first unharbored it and hunted it to a stand, and then it must turn head and live, or turn tail and die. Commonwealths cost as much in the making as crowns; and if they be well made, would yet outsel an ill-fashioned crown in any market *overt*, if they be well-vouched.

"But *preces* and *lachrymæ* are the people's weapons; so are swords and pistols, when God and Parliament bid them arm. Prayers and tears are good weapons for them that have nothing but knees and eyes; but most men have teeth and nails. If subjects must fight for their kings against other kingdoms when their kings will, I know no reason but they may fight against their kings for their own kingdoms when Parliament say they may and must. But Parliament must not say they must until God says they may."

The bold spirit of liberty which characterized the first settlers of New England cannot be too highly appreciated by their posterity. Neither are their wisdom and prudence in maintaining their liberties, less subjects of admiration and applause. What state paper exists more solemn or comprehensive than that memorable order, by which the General Court of Massachusetts, in 1660, caused a committee to be raised to consider the consequences to their liberties to be anticipated from the restoration of Charles II.?

"Forasmuch as the present condition of our affairs, in matters of the highest concernment, calls for diligent and speedy use of the best means, seriously to discuss and rightly to understand our liberty and duty; thereby to beget unity among ourselves in the due observance of obedience to the authority of England

and our own just privileges, for the effecting whereof it is ordered that Simon Bradstreet, &c. be a committee to consider and debate such matter or thing of public concernment, touching our patent, laws, privileges, and duty to his Majesty, as they may judge expedient, that so (if the will of God be) we may speak and act the same thing, becoming prudent, honest, conscientious, and faithful men."

Now what their notion of these "just privileges" was, may be gathered from "their refusing to make the oath of allegiance necessary;" "refusing to cause proceedings at law to be in the name of the King." "Maintaining that liberty of conscience justified their removal to this quarter of the world; that with removal their subjection to England ceased; and that the sovereignty of the soil was in them, because purchased by them of the native princes."[1]

That these were doctrines holden and avowed by "persons of influence," among the early emigrants to New England we know from history. Their patent, or old charter itself, was in fact only an incorporation for trade, turned by the dexterity of the first settlers into a civil sovereignty. And the real cause of their extreme attachment to it was, that, under color of that instrument, they chose their own rulers and judges, made laws, and in effect were an independent state.

How this theory of the ancient leaders of Massachusetts was seconded by the spirit of the people, will be apparent from a single transaction of a somewhat later period. During the reign of King James II., our fathers had been insulted by the dissolution of their charter, and oppressed by the proceedings of the King's Commissioners. The leaders of the Colony were indignant. The people were stung to madness.

On the eighteenth of April, 1689,—the eighteenth and nineteenth of April are red-letter days in the calendar of American liberty,—on the eighteenth of April, 1689, say our historians, there came up from North Boston,—that northern hive has been famous in all times for a hardy, industrious, and intrepid race of men,—there came up from North Boston a multitude of men and boys running. The drums beat. The people ran to their arms. They rushed to Fort Hill, where was then a formidable fortification, "standing so thick that one gun from the fort would have killed a hundred of them; but God prevented!"[2] They scaled the sconce, and, seizing the lower battery, they turned the guns "on the red coats in the fort," who surrendering at discretion, they took the King's Council prisoners, and put the King's Governor under guard; they sent the captain of the King's frigate to jail; and turned the batteries on the King's frigate herself; and the country people coming in, the elders and fathers took possession of the King's government; and thus was effected a glorious revolution here in Massachusetts thirty days before it was known that King William of glorious memory had just effected a similar glorious revolution on the other side of the Atlantic.

It is very obvious that the fate of New England was suspended on the fate of the Prince of Orange. Had he failed, our ancestors of that day would have had to expiate the guilt of treason in exile, or confiscation, or on the scaffold. How

[1] Hutchinson's *Hist. of Mass.* vol. i. ch. 2.
[2] Hutchinson's *Hist.* v. i. ch. 3.

truly then may it be said that the spirit of our ancestors of the first age was emulated by the immediate authors of our independence, and that these descendants were true to the example and glory of their predecessors!

If we descend from the era of the English Revolution to the middle of the last century, we find the same daring spirit of liberty promulgated, not by irresponsible scribblers, in anonymous pamphlets, but by the highest colonial lawyers on the floor of state, and by the most learned colonial clergy from their pulpits. Take, for example, an extract from a sermon, entitled "*A Discourse concerning Unlimited Submission to the Higher Powers, with some Reflections on the Resistance to King Charles I., and on the Anniversary of his Death, in which the Mysterious Doctrine of that Prince's Saintship and Martyrdom is unriddled.* Preached by Jonathan Mayhew, Pastor of the West Church in Boston. Among other doctrines, not less bold and decisive, he lays down the following:—

"A people really oppressed to a great degree by their sovereign, cannot well be insensible when they are so oppressed. And such a people, if I may allude to an ancient fable, have, like the Hesperian fruit, a dragon for their protector and guardian. Nor would they have any reason to mourn, if some Hercules should appear to despatch him. For a nation thus abused, to arise unanimously and to resist their prince, even to the dethroning him, is not criminal; but a reasonable way of vindicating their liberties and just rights."

Now it must be remembered that this discourse was preached six-and-twenty years before the era of our Revolution, by the most learned and popular preacher of his day; that it was published "at the request of his hearers;" that the thing was not done in a corner, nor circulated in a whisper, but as the title-page has it, Anno, 1750. Boston: New England. "Printed and sold by D. Fowle, in Queen Street, and by D. Gookin, over against the Old South Meeting House."

There is no need of further proof that the fathers of our Revolution were true to their ancestors, both distant and immediate; obeying their precepts, copying their examples, and acting up to their characters.

It remains for us to observe, that the fathers of our Revolution were also true to themselves and true to posterity; and in this, above all, that they were true to virtue and liberty.

There were three great principles, which, in the opinion of our ancestors, in every age, constituted the essence of colonial liberty; and with which, in their minds, it was identified.

1. That their rulers and judges should be chosen by, and responsible to themselves.

2. That the right of laying taxes on the inhabitants of the Colonies should belong exclusively to their own representatives.

3. That their religious rights should depend wholly on their colonial laws and constitutions.

The first of these principles was the object of the struggles of the first settlers of New England and their immediate descendants. They exercised this liberty between fifty and sixty years. They lost it by the dissolution of their old charter. That of William and Mary did not restore it. Among other obnoxious provisions in this last charter, the appointment of the Governor, Lieutenant-Governor, and Secretary, with a qualified, appellate, judicial jurisdiction, was reserved to the Crown.

The loss of this branch of liberty was submitted to with reluctance, and endured with great impatience. The deep yearning of our fathers' hearts after their ancient liberty is to be seen in every subsequent page of their political history, and was one of the active, though hidden causes of our Revolution.

On the second great principle of colonial liberty, that taxation and representation are inseparable, the American Revolution turned.

Now, the just estimate made by our fathers of the importance of that principle, — the self-devotion with which they maintained it, the boldness with which they put in jeopardy life, liberty, property, reputation, whatever man holds dear in hope or in possession to vindicate it, — are the great central points from which radiates their glory at the Revolution.

At a superficial view, we are inclined to wonder at the inflexible firmness of our fathers, in opposition to the stamp and tea taxes, and the other British impositions at that period. The amount small; comparatively little burdensome; for the most part affecting articles of luxury or of occasional use. We are tempted to exclaim, what grievous oppression in all this? A single year of war would exceed in expense the loss in fifty years from such taxes. And when we look at the subject in point of principle, their condition would not have been a whit worse than immense classes of British subjects who pay taxes without having any voice in the choice of their rulers. Arguments and facts of this kind were urged on our fathers in every form of reason and eloquence; enforced by appeals to their hopes from the smiles of royal favor; by appeals to their fears from the terrors of royal power. But they stood as the mountain rock, which alike mocks the melting heat of the summer's sun, and the uprooting blasts of the winter's storm. By such considerations, the flame of their enkindled zeal was neither quenched nor allayed. Their unyielding fixedness of principle in this respect does infinite credit to their sagacity and virtue.

For when we consider more carefully this principle, so earnestly asserted by Great Britain, and so resolutely resisted by our fathers, we shall find that, to human view, it contained the whole hope of American independence for the then present and all future times. The possibility of American independence at any time depended upon the union of the Colonies in some common principle of opposition to the pretensions of Great Britain. Now, this right being conceded, it was scarce possible that any such common principle should exist; much less become a bond of union among the Colonies. This right admitted, every thing else was but mode and measure, — an affair of discretion. What hope that they, who could not unite in resistance to the whole right, could be ever brought to combine in resistance to a particularly oppressive degree in the exercise of it? Besides, how easy would it have been for Great Britain, by settling any obnoxious degree, in mode or measure, differently in different colonies, to take from some all motive to coöperate in the resistance of others! This principle, therefore, being yielded, there was to human view no subsequent hope of independence for the Colonies. That principle was worthy, therefore, of all the importance attached to it by our fathers; worthy of all the sacrifices they made in its defence. Their foresight, their energy and inflexible spirit on this point, are among the brightest beams in the glory of that day.

Of a similar type is the self-denial to which they submitted, and the hazards which they voluntarily incurred for the sake of that principle. By submission, they would, in their own time, have enjoyed peace, secured plenty, attained external protection under the shield of Great Britain, and in the gradual advance of society, they had reason to expect to arrive, even in the colonial state, at a very elevated and enviable condition of prosperity. On the other hand, what were the hazards of resistance? — The untried, and not to be estimated perils of civil war; — "a people in the gristle, and not yet hardened into the bone of manhood," to rush on the thick bosses of the buckler of the most powerful State in Europe, the one most capable of annoying them, — without arms or resources, to enter the lists with the best appointed nation on the globe; — destitute of a sloop of war, to wage hostilities with a country whose navies commanded every sea and even their own harbors. In case of success, — the chance of anarchy and the unknown casualties attending a new organization of society. In case of failure, — exile, confiscation, the scaffold, the fate of some; to bear the opprobrious names of rebel and traitor, and to transmit them to a disgraced posterity, the fate of all.

What appeals to selfishness! what to cupidity! what to love of ease, to fear, and to pusillanimity! But our fathers took counsel of a different spirit, — of the pure ethereal spirit which glowed and burned in their own bosoms. In spite of the greatness of the temptation and the certainty of the hazard, they resisted; and the front ranks of opposition were filled, not by a needy, promiscuous, unknown, and irresponsible crowd, but by the heart and mind and strength of the Colony; by the calm and calculating merchant; by the cautious capitalist; by the sedate and pious divine; by the far-looking, deep-read lawyer; by the laborious and intelligent mechanic. We have no need to repeat names. The entire soul and sense and sinew of society were in action.

The spirit of our Revolution is not to be sought in this or that individual, nor in this or that order of men. It was the mighty energy of the whole mass. It was the momentous heaving of the troubled ocean, roused indeed by the coming tempest, but propelled onward by the lashing of its own waters, and by the awful, irresistible impulse of deep-seated passion and power.

In this movement, those who were foremost were not always those of most influence; nor were the exciting causes always the most obtrusive to the eye. All were pressed forward by the spirit inherent in the community; by force of public opinion and sense of duty, which never fell behind, but was often in advance of those who were called leaders.

The event has shown that our fathers judged rightly in this movement; that their conception was just concerning their means and their duties; that they were equal to the crisis in which Providence had placed them; that, daring to be free, their power was equal to their daring. They vindicated liberty for themselves; they transmitted it to us, their posterity. There is no truer glory, no higher fame known or to be acquired among men.

How different would have been our lot at this day, both as men and citizens, had the Revolution failed of success, or had the great principle of liberty on which it turned been yielded. Instead of a people free, enlightened, rejoicing in their strength, possessing a just consciousness of being the authors and arbiters of their own and their country's destinies, we should have been a multitude without pride of independence, without sense of state or national sovereignty, looking across the ocean for our rulers; watching the Atlantic sky, as the cloud of court locusts, tempted by our greenness, came warping on the eastern breeze; waiting on the strand to catch the first glimpse of our descending master, — some trans-atlantic chieftain, some royal favorite, some court sycophant, — sent to govern a country, without knowing its interests, without sympathy in its prospects; resting in another hemisphere the hopes of his fame and fortune. Our judges coming from afar; our merchants denied all commerce except with the parent state; our clergy sent us, like our clothes, ready made, and cut in the newest court fashion. None but conformists allowed to vote; none but churchmen eligible. Our civil rights subject to crown officers; our religious, to a foreign hierarchy, cold, selfish, vindictive, distant, solicitous about glebes and tithes, but reckless among us of the spread of the light of learning or the influence of the gospel.

How different also would have been the fate and aspect of the present age, had the American Revolution never commenced, or had it failed! Under Providence, this Revolution has been the chief, if not the sole cause of that impulse to the human mind, which, during the last half century, has changed the face of Europe, and elevated the hope of man. The light of truth and reason reflected across the Atlantic from the mighty mirror of American liberty, penetrated the cottages of peasants and the cabinets of kings. The multitude were propelled upon thrones. Kings have consequently been induced to soften the rigors of ancient servitude. In every part of Europe the chains of subjects are lightened. Sovereigns daily realize, more and more, the necessity of admitting the people to a voice in their councils, and to a qualified weight in state affairs. Under the influence of this condition of things, knowledge has been increased and diffused; the rights of man vindicated; a free intercourse of commerce, science, and arts introduced on both sides of the Atlantic, unparalleled in human history, and giving promise of an advancement in freedom, morals, and refinement, exceeding the hope or conception of former times. Under these auspices, the patriotic theories and visions of Milton, Harrington, Algernon Sidney, and Locke, are beginning to be realized; the capacity of man to govern himself to be demonstrated; the great truth promulgated and carried home to the bosoms of all sovereigns, even the most arbitrary, that they who would govern man long must govern him justly, and treat him as a rational, accountable, and moral being; that they must respect his essential rights, and even towards servitude itself, recognize the principles of a substantial freedom.

Such was the genius and character, and such the proud results of the American Revolution; such the glory of our fathers; such the glowing points from which that glory radiates.

It is suitable, and it is our duty on this occasion to inquire, what it is to maintain that genius and character? what it is to deserve, and what to disgrace those ancestors?

In listening to the preceding development, fellow-citizens, it is impossible that each of you should not have realized, individually, your interest in the character and conduct of our fathers. It is a law of nature. The virtue and glory of fathers is the most precious inheritance of their posterity. By this law, an indissoluble, moral union, connects times past and future with times present. Without that law, man would be a creature of the day, grovelling in selfishness, wallowing in the mire of sense, with eye and taste and thought all downward, with no backward regard, with no forward hope, with no upward aim. But this eternal, moral connection, which is established by Providence in his nature, gives him, as it were, existence in the days of old, and existence in the times which are to come; and instead of a being destined, as the term of his natural life seems to indicate, to exist only a few short years, bestows upon him, even in this world, a glorious immortality.

By this law it is made the duty of man in every age, in gratitude for the inheritance he receives, to transmit it faithfully to those who succeed; not diminished, not corrupted, not soiled, but if possible enlarged, strengthened, purified, increased both in splendor and usefulness.

The occurring circumstances of every age make indeed the duties of each succeeding generation different. But in consulting concerning those duties, it will not be difficult for this or any future age to determine in what they consist, provided, according to the example, and in the language of our fathers, we endeavor "so to understand our liberty and duty as to beget unity among ourselves, and to act and speak as becomes prudent, honest, conscientious, and faithful men."

It is true, that we in this age are not called as our fathers were, to take our lives in our hands, and bare our breasts to the tempest and shock of war. But such dangers and sacrifices are not essential to the existence of true glory. This, as I have endeavored to illustrate, consists not in the particular part we are called to act, but in the manner in which we perform the part to which we are called. The essence of true glory is principle. Our fathers endured the hardships and despised the dangers of the field of battle, not for the sake of the species of glory there to be acquired, but because battle was the mode appointed by Providence for them to vindicate their truth to the relations of things in which it had placed them. They could, in no other mode, have fulfilled their duty to those relations.

Now this glory is just as applicable to us as to them. The labors and sacrifices of our fathers have indeed left us a noble inheritance. But our tenure of that inheritance is not absolute, but conditional. If we would maintain it and transmit it unimpaired to our posterity, we must, like our fathers, be true to the relation of things in which we stand; and particularly to those in which we stand to that very inheritance. Now, truth to those relations, as it respects us, consists in our fulfilling the conditions on which the continuance of that inheritance depends. These conditions are, — that we understand our liberties; that we value them as we ought; that we are willing to make the sacrifices of time, labor, and attention necessary for the preserving them, and are vigilant in defending them, not against external foes, to which, in all probability, we shall never be called, but against a much more insidious foe, — the passion, corruption, and weakness of our own hearts.

The great principle for which our fathers contended, and the maintaining of which constituted their glory was, in fact, the right of self-government, — the right of choosing their own rulers; in other words, the right of possessing themselves, and of transmitting to posterity the elective franchise in its most pure and perfect state. Now, this great privilege it belongs to us to maintain by a right and wise use of it; and to transmit it to posterity the purer by our example, the safer by our use, and the more precious from the obvious blessings resulting from this our fidelity. This is our duty. In this consists our glory.

Let every man, therefore, who inquires what it is to deserve, and what it is to disgrace our ancestors, consider his conduct in this respect. Let him ask himself, whether he truly appreciates the nature and greatness of that privilege; whether he is faithful to liberty, to morals, and religion, in the exercise of it; whether he is indifferent about it, or neglects it, or sports with it. And so let every man answer for himself; his own conscience being his judge. And let all remember that, in the ways of Providence to nations, as well as to individuals, there is retribution as well as favor. No people ever did, or ever can, long enjoy any privilege, and, least of all, the elective franchise, who systematically undervalue it, or abuse it, or are even indifferent about it.

Again, truth to liberty, to virtue, to our ancestors, and to the relation of things in which we stand, has respect also to the manner in which we conduct towards those on whom the elective lot has fallen, and in whose favor it has been declared.

It is the nature of man, under a free constitution, to divide into parties, according to that diversity of views, interest, opinions, passions, and even fancies, which are inseparable from his constitution. This condition of things is not to be deprecated or condemned. It is to be understood and acted upon.

Now, the duty which each individual in a free republic owes to rulers is just the same, whether they do or do not belong to the particular sect or party he happens to prefer. Truth to the relations of things in which we stand, requires that our rulers should be judged, not by any previous prejudice or theory, but by their conduct while in power; by the measures they recommend and countenance. These measures are to be received in a candid, generous spirit, and with fair and manly construction. Those, therefore, will be false to the genius and character of our Revolution, who, regardless of the measures of rulers, shall wage war upon them, merely because they do not belong to their own particular sect or party, or who shall decry wise measures or misrepresent the motives of just ones, with the sole view of pulling down one individual or of building up another; or who, making the liberty of debate or of the press a cloak for licentiousness, shall pervert both or either to purposes of malevolence or slander.

Above all, those will be false to the genius and character of our Revolution who shall associate themselves with political leaders without reference to principles; who shall deny rulers the chance to show their real projects by the course of their administration, but shall wage war upon them from the very beginning, on the principle of political extermination.

There can be no surer sign that the liberties of a people are hastening to a dissolution than their countenancing those who form parties on men and not upon principles. Whenever the only question is, whether Cæsar or Pompey, Lepidus or Mark Anthony shall rule, and the people are corrupt or debased enough, from mere personal affection or preference to flock to either standard, such a people are not far distant from a revolution which will not leave them even the poor privilege of choosing their own masters.

Thus you perceive, fellow-citizens, that the glory of our fathers which we this day celebrate, was not of a temporary or individual character; that there is nothing exclusive in its nature; that it may be shared and emulated by the truly noble of our race in every age; that it essentially consists in possessing and exhibiting in all our public relations a pure, just, elevated, and manly spirit.

And now, fellow-citizens, consider your privileges; consider your duties. By the virtues of your fathers, you have been preserved from colonial bondage. Beware lest you become subjected to a more grievous bondage of base, ignoble passions. As they subdued their enemies in the field, do you subdue those enemies which have their strongholds in the human heart, and which have laid low in the dust the proud hopes of all former republics, — "ambition, avarice, love of riches, and the corruptions of prosperity." [1] Be as just, as temperate, as moderate in preserving your liberty, as your fathers were bold and daring in repelling the chains of servitude. Be penetrated with "a love of liberty, of religion, of justice and virtue, and inflamed with a sacred zeal and affection for your country." [1] Thus it may be hoped, that through the combined and strenuous endeavors of true and faithful men in all times, there shall be gradually infused into the mass of mankind loftier thoughts, higher aims, more generous motives, whereby the human character being elevated and refined, shall become more worthy, and thus more capable of perfect freedom. And so this temple of liberty, the foundations of which were laid on the fourth of July, 1776, in blood and peril by our fathers, shall, by the labors, councils, and virtues of all the good and great of present and future times, be enlarged and extended in true proportions of moral architecture, till its pillars embrace the universe, and its dome vault upwards with a more than human skill, — with glorious archings of celestial wisdom, resplendent with purest faith, radiant with immortal truth, crowned with revealed hope, — to the joy and rest of man on the promise and in the presence of the Eternal.

[1] Milton's *Defensio pro Populo Anglicano, contra Claudii Salmasii Defensionem Regiam.*

(M. Page 57.)

THE MEMBERS OF THE CITY GOVERNMENT, FROM 1822 TO 1830, INCLUSIVE.

1822.

MAYOR,

JOHN PHILLIPS.

ALDERMEN.

Samuel Billings,
Ephraim Eliot,
Jacob Hall,
Joseph Head,
Joseph Jenkins,
Joseph Lovering,
Nathaniel Pope Russell,
Bryant Parrott Tilden.

COMMON COUNCIL.

WILLIAM PRESCOTT, *President.*

Ward 1.

William Barry,
Thaddeus Page,
Charles Wells,
Simon Wilkinson.

Ward 2.

Martin Bates,
Benjamin Lamson,
Henry Orne,
Joseph Stodder.

Ward 3.

Theodore Dexter,
Joshua Emmons,
Samuel Jones.

Ward 4.

Joseph Cooledge,
Samuel Perkins,
Robert Gould Shaw,
Joel Thayer.

Ward 5.

George Washington Coffin,
Thomas Kendall,
Horatio Gates Ware,
Isaac Winslow.

Ward 6.

Samuel Appleton,
Thomas Motley,
Jesse Shaw,
William Sullivan.

Ward 7.

Jonathan Amory,
Patrick Tracy Jackson,
Augustus Peabody,
Enoch Silsby.

Ward 8.

David Watts Bradlee,
Peter Chardon Brooks,
James Perkins,
Benjamin Russell,

Ward 9.

Jonathan Davis,
Hawkes Lincoln,
William Prescott,
John Welles.

Ward 10.

Andrew Drake,
Daniel Lewis Gibbens,
David Collson Moseley,
Isaac Stevens.

Ward 11.

Geo. Watson Brimmer,
Asa Bullard,
Barzillai Holmes,
Winslow Lewis.

Ward 12.

Cyrus Alger,
John French,
John Howe,
Moses Williams.

1823.

MAYOR,

JOSIAH QUINCY.

ALDERMEN.

Daniel Baxter,
George Odiorne,
David Weld Child,
Joseph Hawley Dorr,
Ashur Benjamin,
Enoch Patterson,
Caleb Eddy,
Stephen Hooper.

COMMON COUNCIL.

JOHN WELLES, *President.*

Ward 1.

Thaddeus Page,
Simon Wilkinson,
John Elliot,
Joseph Wheeler.

Ward 2.

Martin Bates,
Benjamin Lamson,
Joseph Stodder,
John Parker Boyd.

Ward 3.

Theodore Dexter,
Samuel Jones,
John Richardson Adan,
John Damarisque Dyer.

Ward 4.

Joseph Cooledge,
Samuel Perkins,
Robert Gould Shaw,
Henry Farnam.

Ward 5.

Thomas Kendall,
Isaac Winslow,
Elias Haskell,
John Sullivan Perkins.

Ward 6.

Joseph Stacy Hastings,
Joel Prouty,
John Stevens,
William Wright.

Ward 7.

Jonathan Amory,
Enoch Silsby,
Samuel Swett,
Charles Pelham Curtis

Ward 8.

Benjamin Russell,
James Savage,
Eliphalet Williams,
Samuel King Williams.

Ward 9.

Jonathan Davis,
Hawkes Lincoln,
John Welles,
Lewis Tappan.

Ward 10.

Aaron Baldwin,
David Francis,
Francis Johonnot Oliver,
Thomas Beale Wales.

Ward 11.

Asa Bullard,
Charles Howard,
Josiah Stedman,
Joseph Willett.

Ward 12.

Samuel Bradlee,
Noah Brooks,
Francis Jackson,
Charles Sprague.

1824.

MAYOR,

JOSIAH QUINCY.

ALDERMEN,

Daniel Baxter,
George Odiorne,
David Weld Child,
Joseph Hawley Dorr,
Ashur Benjamin,
Enoch Patterson,
Caleb Eddy,
Stephen Hooper, (died September,)
Cyrus Alger, (November.)

COMMON COUNCIL.

FRANCIS JOHONNOT OLIVER, *President.*

Ward 1.

William Barry,
John Elliot,
Joseph Wheeler,
Michael Tombs.

Ward 2.

William Little, Jr.,
Oliver Reed,
Joseph Stone,
Thaddeus Page.

Ward 3.

John Richardson Adan,
John Damarisque Dyer,
Edward Page,
William Sprague.

Ward 4.

Joseph Cooledge,
Robert Gould Shaw,
Jeremiah Fitch,
Wm. Rounsville Pierce Washburn.

Ward 5.

Elias Haskell,
Eliphalet Porter Hartshorn,
George Washington Otis,
Winslow Wright.

Ward 6.

Joseph Stacy Hastings,
Joel Prouty,
William Wright,
Thomas Wiley.

Ward 7.

Charles Pelham Curtis,
William Goddard,
Elijah Morse,
Isaac Parker.

Ward 8.

Benjamin Russell,
Eliphalet Williams,
Samuel King Williams,
Benjamin Willis.

Ward 9.

Jonathan Davis,
Hawkes Lincoln,
John Ballard,
John Chipman Gray.

Ward 10.

Thomas Beale Wales,
James Savage,
Phineas Upham,
Francis Johonnot Oliver,

Ward 11.

Josiah Stedman,
Samuel Frothingham,
Giles Lodge,
Charles Sprague.

Ward 12.

Samuel Bradlee,
Francis Jackson,
Isaac Thom,
Charles Bemis.

1825.

MAYOR,

JOSIAH QUINCY.

ALDERMEN.

Daniel Carney,
John Bellows,
Josiah Marshall,
John Damarisque Dyer,
Thomas Welsh, Jr.,
George Blake,
Henry Jackson Oliver,
John Bryant,

COMMON COUNCIL.

FRANCIS JOHONNOT OLIVER, *President.*

Ward 1.

William Barry,
John Elliot,
Robert Fennelly,
Lewis Lerow.

Ward 2.

Oliver Reed,
Scammel Penniman,
Benjamin Clark,
John Fenno.

Ward 3.

John Richardson Adan,
Thomas Wells,
Abraham Williams Fuller,
Amos Farnsworth.

Ward 4.

Joseph Cooledge,
Wm. Rounsville Pierce Washburn,
George Hallett,
Theodore Dexter.

Ward 5.

John Sullivan Perkins,
Ezra Dyer,
Charles Tracy,
William Simonds.

Ward 6.

Joseph Stacy Hastings,
Thomas Wiley,
Isaac Waters,
Samuel Thaxter.

Ward 7.

Charles Pelham Curtis,
William Goddard,
Elijah Morse,
Isaac Parker.

Ward 8.

Eliphalet Williams,
Benjamin Willis,
Jeffrey Richardson,
Josiah Bradlee.

Ward 9.

John Chipman Gray,
Franklin Dexter,
Jeremiah Smith Boies,
Levi Meriam.

Ward 10.

Francis Johonnot Oliver,
James Savage,
Jonathan Simonds,
John Parker Rice.

Ward 11.

Samuel Frothingham,
Giles Lodge,
George Morey, Jr.,
Joshua Vose.

Ward 12.

John Stevens,
Adam Bent,
Oliver Fisher,
Ephraim Groves Ware.

1826.

MAYOR,

JOSIAH QUINCY.

ALDERMEN.

Daniel Carney,
John Bellows,
Josiah Marshall,
Thomas Welsh, Jr.,
Henry Jackson Oliver,
John Foster Loring,
Francis Jackson,
Edw. Hutchinson Robbins.

COMMON COUNCIL.

JOHN RICHARDSON ADAN, *President.*

Ward 1.

William Barry,
Lewis Lerow,
Lemuel P. Grosvenor,
Samuel Aspinwall.

Ward 2.

Scammel Penniman,
Benjamin Clark,
John Fenno,
Nathaniel Faxon.

Ward 3.

John Richardson Adan,
William Sprague,
Amos Farnsworth,
Asa Adams.

Ward 4.

George Hallett,
William Howe,
John Warren James,
Joseph Eveleth.

Ward 5.

Ezra Dyer,
Charles Tracy,
Jonathan Thaxter,
William Parker.

Ward 6.

Joseph Stacy Hastings,
Thomas Wiley,
Isaac Waters,
Samuel Thaxter.

Ward 7.

Augustus Peabody,
Charles Pelham Curtis.
Isaac Parker,
Edward Brooks.

Ward 8.

Francis Bassett,
Joseph Helger Thayer,
Joseph Hawley Dorr,
John Baker.

Ward 9.

John Chipman Gray,
Jeremiah Smith Boies,
Levi Meriam,
Charles Torrey.

Ward 10.

Aaron Baldwin,
John Parker Rice,
Solomon Piper,
Charles Barnard.

Ward 11.

Giles Lodge,
George Morey, Jr.,
Joshua Vose,
Thomas Brewer.

Ward 12.

John Stevens,
Adam Bent,
Oliver Fisher,
Henry Hatch.

1827.

MAYOR,

JOSIAH QUINCY.

ALDERMEN.

Cyrus Alger,
John Bellows,
Thomas Welsh, Jr.,
John Foster Loring,
Jeremiah Smith Boies,
Robert Fennelly,
Thomas Beale Wales,
James Savage.

COMMON COUNCIL.

JOHN RICHARDSON ADAN, *President.*

Ward 1.

William Barry,
Simon Wilkinson.
John Elliot,
Samuel Aspinwall.

Ward 2.

Benjamin Clark,
Scammel Penniman,
John Warren James,
John Floyd Truman.

Ward 3.

John Richardson Adan,
John Damarisque Dyer,
Asa Adams,
Thomas Gould.

Ward 4.

Wm. Rounsville Pierce Washburn,
George Hallett,
William Howe,
Joseph Eveleth.

Ward 5.

Jonathan Thaxter,
William Parker,
Lewis Glover Pray,
George Lane.

Ward 6.

Isaac Waters,
Samuel Thaxter,
Jonathan Loring,
Joseph Warren Lewis.

Ward 7.

Samuel Dorr,
Samuel Dexter Ward,
John Arno Bacon,
Thomas Walley Phillips.

Ward 8.

David Watts Bradlee,
Benjamin Russell,
Eliphalet Williams,
Joshua Sears.

Ward 9.

John Chipman Gray,
Levi Meriam,
Gamaliel Bradford,
John Prescott Bigelow.

Ward 10.

Jonathan Simonds,
George Brinley,
William Parker,
Charles Sprague.

Ward 11.

Giles Lodge,
George Morey, Jr.,
Joshua Vose,
Josiah Vose.

Ward 12.

Adam Bent,
William Wright,
William Little, Jr.,
George Gay.

1828.

MAYOR,

JOSIAH QUINCY.

ALDERMEN.

John Foster Loring,
Robert Fennelly,
James Savage,
Thomas Kendall,
James Hall,
Phineas Upham,
John Pickering,
Samuel Turell Armstrong.

COMMON COUNCIL.

JOHN RICHARDSON ADAN, *President*.

Ward 1.

Samuel Aspinwall,
Ninian Clark Betton,
Horace Fox,
Eleazer Pratt.

Ward 2.

John Warren James,
Frederick Gould,
Henry Fowle, Jr.,
George Washington Johnson.

Ward 3.

John Richardson Adan,
John D. Dyer, (res. April.)
Thomas Gould,
Levi Roberts Lincoln,
James L. P. Orrok, (from May.)

Ward 4.

Joseph Eveleth.
Quincy Tufts,
Andrew Cunningham, Jr.,
James Means.

Ward 5.

George Washington Otis,
William Parker,
Lewis Glover Pray,
George Lane.

Ward 6.

Isaac Waters,
Francis Johonnot Oliver,
Ebenezer Appleton,
David Moody.

Ward 7.

John Arno Bacon,
John Belknap,
George W. Adams, (from May.)
Thomas Wren Ward, (res. July.)
Waldo Flint, (res. February.)
Benj. T. Pickman, (from August.)

Ward 8.

Benjamin Russell,
Eliphalet Williams,
Samuel King Williams,
Thomas Lamb.

Ward 9.

John Chipman Gray,
John Prescott Bigelow,
Norman Seaver,
Daniel Lewis Gibbens.

Ward 10.

Jonathan Simonds,
William Parker,
Robert Treat Paine, (from May.)
John Lowell, Jr.,
Geo. Bethune, (res. April.)

Ward 11.

Otis Everett,
Otis Turner,
Perez Gill,
Payson Perrin.

Ward 12.

Alpheus Cary,
Walter Cornell,
Joseph Neale Howe,
Benjamin Stevens.

1829.

MAYOR,

HARRISON GRAY OTIS.

ALDERMEN.

Henry Jackson Oliver,
John Foster Loring,
Thomas Kendall,
James Hall,
Samuel Turell Armstrong,
Benjamin Russell,
Winslow Lewis,
Charles Wells,

COMMON COUNCIL.

ELIPHALET WILLIAMS, *President.*

Ward 1.

Ninian Clark Betton,
Eleazer Pratt,
John Wells,
Christopher Gore.

Ward 2.

John Warren James,
Henry Sewall Kent,
Samuel Ellis,
Thomas Reed, (died February.)
Daniel Ballard, (from March.)

Ward 3.

Thomas Gould,
Levi Roberts Lincoln,
Joseph Bradley,
Amos Bradley Parker.

Ward 4.

Quincy Tufts,
Andrew Cunningham,
John Rayner,
Samuel Davenport Torrey.

Ward 5.

Jonathan Thaxter,
William Parker,
George Lane,
Joseph Eveleth.

Ward 6.

Isaac Waters,
Samuel Austin, Jr.,
Jared Lincoln,
Samuel Goodhue.

Ward 7.

Geo. W. Adams, (died May.)
Benjamin Toppan Pickman,
Thomas Wetmore,
Walter Frost,
Isaac Danforth, (from May.)

Ward 8.

John Prescott Bigelow,
Jacob Amee,
Levi Brigham,
Daniel Lewis Gibbens.

Ward 9.

Eliphalet Williams,
Samuel King Williams,
Thomas Minns,
James Brackett Richardson.

Ward 10.

Jonathan Simonds,
John Lowell, Jr.,
Samuel Leonard Abbott,
Charles Casey Starbuck.

Ward 11.

Otis Everett,
Otis Turner,
Perez Gill,
Payson Perrin.

Ward 12.

Oliver Fisher,
Walter Cornell,
Aaron Willard, Jr.,
Isaac Parker Townsend.

1830.

MAYOR,

HARRISON GRAY OTIS.

ALDERMEN,

Henry Jackson Oliver,
John Foster Loring,
Samuel Turell Armstrong,
Benjamin Russell,
Winslow Lewis,
Charles Wells,
John Burbeck McCleary,
Moses Williams.

COMMON COUNCIL.

BENJAMIN TOPPAN PICKMAN, *President.*

Ward 1.

Ninian Clark Betton,
Eleazer Pratt,
Christopher Gore,
Simon Wiggin Robinson.

Ward 2.

John Warren James,
Samuel Ellis,
Daniel Ballard,
John B. Wells.

Ward 3.

Thomas Gould,
Levi Roberts Lincoln,
Larra Crane,
Michael Lovell.

Ward 4.

Quincy Tufts,
John Rayner,
Samuel Davenport Torrey,
Washington Parker Gregg.

Ward

Winslow Wright,
Joseph Eveleth,
Levi Boynton Haskell,
Charles Leighton.

Ward 6.

Isaac Waters,
Samuel Austin, Jr.,
Jared Lincoln,
Joshua Seaver,
Benj. Parker, (seat vacated in Feb.)

Ward 7.

Benjamin Toppan Pickman,
Thomas Wetmore,
Isaac Danforth,
Elias Hasket Derby.

Ward 8.

Thomas Minns,
James Brackett Richardson,
Joseph Reynolds Newell,
Leach Harris.

Ward 9.

John Prescott Bigelow,
Jacob Amee,
Levi Brigham,
Edw. Goldsborough Prescott.

Ward 10.

John Parker Rice,
John Lowell, Jr.,
Samuel Leonard Abbott,
Levi Bliss.

Ward 11.

Otis Everett,
Perez Gill,
Jabez Ellis,
Joseph Hay.

Ward 12.

Henry Hatch,
Aaron Willard, Jr.,
Thomas Melville Vinson,
James Wright.

INDEX.

www.ingramcontent.com/pod-product-compliance
Lightning Source LLC
LaVergne TN
LVHW020935110826
845150LV00004B/874

* 9 7 8 1 4 2 5 5 5 2 0 1 5 *